★   ★

FOR THE UNION
Ohio Leaders in the Civil War

EDITED BY KENNETH W. WHEELER

FOR THE
UNION

Ohio Leaders in the
Civil War

OHIO STATE UNIVERSITY PRESS

★ ★

PREFACE

Ohio commemorated the hundredth anniversary of the Civil War by supporting a research and publication program on the subject of its participation in the conflict and the impact of the war upon the state. The Ohio Civil War Centennial Commission through its Advisory Committee of Professional Historians produced a series of scholarly essays in co-operation with the Ohio Historical Society and the Ohio State University Press on relevant subjects that had been generally neglected by scholars. Out of this effort evolved fourteen booklets ranging over such wartime Ohio topics as agriculture, colleges, Negroes, newspapers, the governors, the bounty system, the formation of an army, and portraits of three major cities.

Implicit in the work of the committee and its authors was the conviction that most major areas of inquiry about the conflict had been exhausted on the national scene and that if new revelations about the character and consequences of the war were to come, they would have to originate on the local level. The production of those booklets and the concepts behind their assignment were the genesis of this book. Additionally, as an encouragement, the Commission graciously granted permission to include in this book three manuscripts to which it held rights. Those essays, "Clement L. Vallandigham," by Frank L. Klement, "Ben Wade," by Mary Land, and "James A. Garfield," by Allan Peskin, remained unpublished at the time of the premature termination of the Commission's activities.

On the eve of the Civil War Ohio was a focal state in the Union. Third in population and wealth among the thirty-four states, the number of its people, joined with those of New York and Pennsylvania, surpassed the total that would compose the Confederacy. According to the federal census of 1860, the economy was becoming mature and balanced. Long a major agricultural producer, Ohio could now boast that the value of its farms and farm machinery was greater than any state except New York. Manufacturing developed with urbanization; at times at an even more rapid pace. Cincinnati ranked only eighth among American cities in population, but was third in importance in manufacturing, whether measured by capital invested, value of products, or number of employees. Ohio's commerce, of course, had long been important in the interstate economy, but it now was not only involved in the traditional north-south routes but also in the growing east-west trade, which would flourish after the war. Canals crossed the state and Buckeye railroad mileage included more than the combined total of Alabama, Arkansas, Florida, Louisiana, Mississippi, and Texas.

The era of the frontier had passed in the most mature of the states of the Old West, but much raw vigor remained. Added now, after more than a half-century of statehood, were occasional manifestations of cultural achievement. Cincinnati, for example, produced over fifty regular publications, including six English and four German newspapers. Ohio probably led the nation in number of colleges, and though they were often of poor quality, several, such as Oberlin, attracted national attention for excellence of teaching or uniqueness of character. Few artists, musicians, or writers of major significance were to be found in the state, but in the decade of the fifties such developing figures as William Dean Howells lived there. Cultural life paused for the duration of the war.

The contribution of manpower to the conflict was impressive. Ohio probably led the major northern states in the percentage of its eligible men serving in the military forces and was outranked in total numbers enrolled by only two states. Two hundred and thirty military organizations—which included roughly two out of every five males in the state between the ages of eighteen and forty-five—went to the field. Buckeye volunteers participated in nearly every battle of the war; indeed, they comprised over 10 per cent of the Union men killed in action. Military leadership proved substantial in numbers and often excellent in quality. Over two hundred Ohioans reached the rank of general; among them were Ulysses S. Grant, Philip H. Sheridan, and William T. Sherman.

But this book deliberately excludes the professional generals such as Grant, Sherman, and Sheridan; and it does not involve Lincoln's cabinet officials from Ohio, Secretary of War Edwin M. Stanton and Secretary of the Treasury Salmon P. Chase. These men generally had little direct involvement with Ohio wartime affairs; moreover, historians have exhaustively examined their careers. The leaders comprised in this book were known beyond Ohio's borders; yet each of them also provided leadership in, and were closely identified with, the Buckeye state.

In selecting topics, effort was made to represent various activities. Thus, a manufacturer, a minister, a military correspondent, humorists, an editor, and a civilian general have been chosen. Political figures are emphasized, since Ohio was politically the most important state in the Middle West for the last half of the nineteenth century. Carl Wittke, in the *History of the State of Ohio,* noted the significance and complexity of Ohio's political role on the eve of, and during, the war when he wrote:

The Republican triumphs of the years 1854–1860 in Ohio greatly affected the other states, and it is conceivable that a defeat here, when the Republican party was still without an adequate national organization, might have crushed the movement in its infancy. Lincoln was repudiated by Ohio in 1862, and endorsed in 1864, and the Peace Democrats and the Copperheads of the State were led by perhaps the most brilliant political triumvirate Ohio has ever seen.

Each of these Ohio leaders, even the recalcitrant Vallandigham, worked diligently for the nation. Each had a decisive influence on the course of events during those important years. May their stories bring better understanding to the Civil War and the era that followed.

K. W. W.

★ ★

TABLE OF CONTENTS

★ ★

FOR THE UNION
Ohio Leaders in the Civil War

ONE ★

Clement L. Vallandigham

FRANK L. KLEMENT

Clement L. Vallandigham threw himself with zest into the election contests of 1860. He was driven by the desire to attain re-election to Congress and to dispel the cloud still surrounding the contested election that first put him in the House of Representatives. He was also driven by the fear that Lincoln's election to the presidency could create a crisis and bring a dissolution of the Union. His southern friends boldly and baldly predicted disunion if Lincoln and "Black Republicanism" emerged triumphant. Vallandigham, consequently, feared for the future; he saw dark and threatening clouds upon the horizon. Conservatism and Stephen A. Douglas *must triumph!* Radicalism and abolition *must be checked!* Vallandigham, therefore, campaigned energetically in all parts of the Third Congressional District of Ohio, denouncing the fire-eaters of the South and "Republican disunionists" with equal vehemence and pleading for his re-election and for the cause of Douglas and conservatism.[1]

Although Vallandigham was but forty years old, he could look back upon nearly twenty years of political activity. As a young man of twenty-one in the Whig-dominated community of New Lisbon, Ohio, he had joined the Democratic party and begun to cloak himself with political dogmatism. At the age of twenty-four he won a seat in the state legislature and rapidly gained stature as a good speaker and a bold champion of Jacksonian Democracy. After serving two terms in the lower house of the legislature, he moved to Dayton in August, 1847, to edit the *Western Empire,* preach Democratic politics, and practice law. In his first editorial he spelled out his political creed, espousing the twin doctrines of states' rights and strict construction of the Constitution, glorifying "individual freedom" and sound and limited government. "We will," he wrote in his salutatory address, "war against despotism in all its forms. . . . "[2]

Vallandigham's devotion to states' rights dated back to his college days. He withdrew from college several months before he was scheduled to graduate because he disagreed with his teacher (also the college president) upon the question of states' rights. In time he blended his states'-rights views with western sectionalism. "I am as good a Western fire-eater," he brazenly announced in Congress, "as the hottest salamander in this House." He warned New Englanders and southerners that he would champion western interests. He stated his sectional creed succinctly: ". . . I am a *WESTERN MAN,* by birth, in habit, by education; and although still a United States man with United States principles, yet within and subordinate to the Constitution, am wholly devoted to Western interests. . . . "[3]

Vallandigham's advocacy of western interests made him critical of New England and Puritanism. Transplanted Yankees in Ohio invariably became his political opponents, first espousing Whig, then Republican, doctrine. The sons and scions of New England seemed determined to refashion the western man in the Yankee image. They wished to foist their temperance and antislavery views on others. They acted as if they possessed a religious and cultural superiority, holding western man to be "a sort of outside barbarian." They seemed to have naught but contempt for the "Butternut Democracy" that they found in the West. As a western sectionalist, Vallandigham bluntly stated that he was "inexorably hostile to Puritan domination in religion or morals or literature or politics." [4]

The Dayton curmudgeon supplemented his advocacy of western interests and states'-rights views with a hatred of abolition. He believed that abolition destroyed the comity of sections and engendered the secession movement. He viewed it as a crusade based upon emotion, not law. One of Vallandigham's best known speeches was a severe indictment of the abolition crusade.[5] He believed slavery to be wrong—"a moral, social, and political evil," but he regarded it as an institution to which the federal Constitution gave its tacit approval.[6] He was also a racist, regarding Negroes as inferior people who should forever be denied social, political, or educational equality.[7]

Vallandigham happened to be passing through Harpers Ferry, on his way home from Washington, when he heard the account of the "John Brown Raid." Vallandigham stopped over in Harpers Ferry to interrogate Brown and to try to link him to Ohio abolitionists. His questions and Brown's answers, copied down by an alert newspaperman, appeared in the *New York Herald* and gave the Dayton Democrat national publicity. "The [Brown] conspiracy" Vallandigham concluded, "was the natural and necessary consequence of the doctrines proclaimed every day, year in and year out, by the apostles of Abolition." [8]

Vallandigham's antiabolition and anti-New England views received the applause of three elements of Ohio's diverse population. Most Irish-Americans and many German-Americans voted the Democratic ticket, and feared that emancipation would release a flood of cheap and competitive labor upon their communities. German and Irish Catholics had another reason to seek the security of the Democratic party, for the Republican party bore the scarlet mark of Know-Nothingism, a nativist and anti-Catholic movement of the 1850's.[9]

Southern "uplanders" who crossed "the River" to pre-empt the poorer soils of Ohio formed the third element of the Democratic party. They brought their anti-Negro prejudices with them and supported those state laws that restricted the influx of free Negroes and denied them citizenship rights. They relished antiabolition and anti-Puritan arguments, and they became the "Barefeet" or "Butternut Democracy." Ridiculed by Republicans as the "Unwashed and Unterrified Democracy," these yeomen farmers lived in the areas characterized by smaller homesteads, poorer soils, and more widespread illiteracy.[10] They supported leveling movements, spoke reverently of Andrew Jackson, and voted the straight Democratic ticket. Vallandigham had learned how to appeal to the prejudices of the "Butternuts"—he claimed to be the champion of the lowly, and vehemently attacked abolition, New England, and "Black Republicanism."

Vallandigham's religious convictions were as fixed as his political creed. He had disciplined himself in the Calvinist tradition—his father was a Presbyterian divine—and the traits of sternness and self-righteousness brought him few close friends. He neither smoked nor cursed, and he seldom touched intoxicants. He abhorred idleness and drove himself to work and study. He viewed individualism and independence as virtues, yet he cloaked himself in dogmatism, confident that he possessed the truth and that virtue and Vallandigham would triumph. He possessed the courage of his convictions; he was no reed bowing to the winds.

In June, 1849, Vallandigham sold his interest in the *Empire*, stepped down as editor, and devoted himself to law. He held his head high, even in the lean months that followed,[11] but finally his income caught up with his high living standards. Then politics, like a siren, lured him back. He ran for Congress on the Democratic ticket in a district composed of Montgomery, Preble, and Butler counties. He lost by 147 votes in 1852, 2,565 in 1854, and 19 in 1856. He contested the 1856 returns, however, contending that Negro votes, cast in violation of the Ohio constitution (which limited citizenship to "male whites"), had deprived him of his just desserts. After a long and wearisome

contest, and due mainly to the support of southern congressmen, Vallandigham was finally seated on May 25, 1858, twelve
days before the Thirty-fourth Congress adjourned. Re-election
in 1858 seemed to be a vindication of his action.

Vallandigham, of course, hoped for re-election in 1860, and
he hitched himself to Stephen A. Douglas' star. Vallandigham
noted that ninety Democratic papers, including twelve Ger-
man-language ones, waved the Douglas banner in Ohio.[12] He
was pleased when Douglas' campaign train brought the "Little
Giant" to Dayton, and a crowd of about "20,000 people" paid
homage to their hero, rending the afternoon air with shouts of
joy and thunderous applause.[13] As election day, October 9,
approached, Vallandigham's speaking engagements increased
in number, and the excitement and bitterness reached a cre-
scendo. He won the election, beating Samuel Craighead, Republican candidate in the Third District, by 134 votes. The next
day, partisans and friends called to pay their respects and congratulations. There was little cause for optimism, for the Ohio
returns of October indicated that Douglas would go down to
defeat in November.

Vallandigham, nevertheless, journeyed to New York and
New Jersey to speak in behalf of Douglas and conservatism. He
raised the disunion scarecrow, envisioning a country disrupted
and business prostrate. At a Democratic rally, held in Cooper
Institute on November 2, he made a statement that would
haunt him throughout the war: ". . . If any one or more of
the States of this Union should at any time secede . . . *I never
would as a Representative in the Congress of the United States
vote one dollar of money whereby one drop of American blood
should be shed in a civil war.*" [14] Vallandigham erred in failing
to denounce secession, and he gave his political opponents ammunition they could effectively use against him.

From New York the Daytonian returned home to cast his
ballot for Douglas. He arrived in Dayton late on the afternoon

of election day and hurried to the polls. Republican optimism saddened him and he remarked to a friend that he feared the vote might be "the last which any one would give for a President of a *United States.*" [15] Lincoln's election saddened him, and he expressed his displeasure openly and boldly.

Congress convened on December 3, 1860, and Vallandigham expressed "gloomy apprehensions." "When secession has taken place," he wrote to his wife, "I shall do all in my power first to *restore* the Union, if it is possible; and failing in that, then to mitigate the evils of disruption." [16]

Congress considered compromise measures in the weeks that followed. Vallandigham, of course, repeatedly spoke in behalf of compromise. He was willing to make concessions to the South and evidently felt that southern states had just cause for secession.[17] He publicly announced his opposition to "coercion" of the seceded states.[18] Any armed forces marching southward to coerce the seceded states would do so over his dead body.[19] Vallandigham favored the Crittenden Compromise and its proposal to extend the 36° 30' line through the western territories.[20] As compromise hopes evaporated and peace hopes faded, Vallandigham stepped forward with a "four-sections scheme" to save the Union—a proposal grossly misrepresented by his political enemies. The proposal provided for a constitutional amendment that divided the states into four sections for the purpose of voting in the Senate and in the electoral college; no bill could become law without a majority vote of the United States senators in each of the four sections, and no man could become President unless he received a majority of the electoral votes of each section.[21] Republicans either ignored or ridiculed Vallandigham's bizarre scheme and misrepresented it as a plan to establish four separate confederacies. The impudent editor of the Republican newspaper published in Vallandigham's home town suggested that the Dayton congressman give Irish names to each of the "four sections" and supposed that Vallandigham had gotten his "quarteroon" idea from the ancient

constitution of the Irish nation.[22] Vallandigham refused to view
his proposal as impractical and absurd, and he continued to
insist that the scheme was intended "to maintain the Union
and not destroy it." [23]

Congress adjourned on March 3, 1861, and the next day,
Lincoln took the oath of office as President of the United States.
Vallandigham returned to Dayton soon afterward, still opposed
to coercion of the "seceded" states and still hoping that compromise might somehow be realized. He found much antiwar and
pro-compromise sentiment in Ohio. The *Dayton Empire* advocated peace, and its editor seemed to believe that time might
bring about compromise and reunion.[24] The *Cincinnati Enquirer* pleaded for peace, emphasizing the economic ties of the
South and the upper Midwest.[25] Samuel Medary, the "Old
Wheelhorse of the Ohio Democracy" and editor of the (Columbus) *Crisis,* feared that a civil war between North and South
would lead to the West becoming slave and servant of New
England.[26] Ties of blood and friendship linked many Ohioans
and residents of the slave states—Vallandigham's in-laws lived
in Cumberland, Maryland. Furthermore, there was a fear that
coercion and civil war would bring an end to representative
government in America—Napoleon was the end product of the
French Revolution, and Oliver Cromwell set up an army dicta-
torship at the close of the "Great Civil War" in England. "We
are embarking on a course," wrote editor James J. Faran in the
Cincinnati Enquirer, "that will produce some Cromwell or
Napoleon who will crush beneath his iron heel the Democratic
legacy we have so long enjoyed." [27]

The Confederate attack upon Fort Sumter broke the uneasy
peace. President Lincoln called for 75,000 troops to quell the
insurrection. A tidal wave of patriotism engulfed the countryside, "till the whole Northern heavens seemed a perfect aurora
borealis of stars and stripes." [28] Four Dayton companies of militia volunteered for service and marched off to war, but Brigadier General Clement L. Vallandigham [29] stayed at home and

expressed his opposition to the war.[30] President Lincoln, meanwhile, took some extraordinary measures to prosecute the war more effectively; he ordered a blockade of the rebellious states, increased the size of the army and navy by presidential proclamation, and suspended the writ of habeas corpus.

The flood tide of patriotism prompted most Ohioans to accept Lincoln's war measures and to intensify the war spirit. It encouraged Republicans to label as traitors those who refused to bow to the war spirit. Nevertheless, a handful of Ohio Democrats continued to speak out for compromise and peace. Vallandigham insisted that he would adhere to his antiwar views "until the end," [31] and that he would continue to watch for "the first favorable chance to move publicly for peace." [32] Medary of the *Crisis* opposed the war and feared that a despotism might envelop the country.[33] Dr. Edson B. Olds of Lancaster, John W. Kees of the *Circleville Watchman,* and Thomas H. Hodder of the *Marion Democratic Mirror* swam against the current and faced the rancor of Republican patriots. It was but a handful against the multitude.

Vallandigham tried to get Ohio Democrats to make a "cooperative protest" against Lincoln's war measures. He prepared a circular proposing a conference at Chillicothe on May 15 and sent it to twenty-five leaders of the Ohio Democratic organization. Only four responded to Vallandigham's antiwar invitation—three favored such a Democratic parlay, and the fourth advised against it. He consequently dropped the conference idea, and his effort to lead his fellow Democrats down an antiwar sideroad ended in failure.

Vallandigham, however, found other avenues to get his antiwar sentiments before the public. Some of his friends formulated a letter, requesting his opinions "on certain points concerning the war." Vallandigham's reply, an "open letter" dated May 13, 1861, appeared in several Democratic newspapers. It was a letter saturated with impudence: he would never vote to approve President Lincoln's "executive proclamations!"; not "a

dollar or a man" for an "aggressive and offensive civil war!";
the rising national debt would weigh down generations yet
unborn; Lincoln deserved impeachment. Then he stated the
peace creed that he would advocate during the war: "I am for
the *CONSTITUTION* first, and at all hazards; for whatever
can be saved of the *UNION* next; and for *PEACE* always as
essential to the preservation of either." He added that the
Lincoln administration must respect the Constitution always—even during a civil war. He ended his letter by quoting
from Stephen A. Douglas' plea for compromise: "War is final,
eternal separation." [34]

On July 4 Congress met in special session, with Vallandigham in attendance. The following Sunday, July 7, the Dayton
congressman visited one of the army camps outside Washington. Vallandigham and several friends passed by the quarters of
some Cleveland volunteers while heading for the sector where
Dayton soldiers had pitched their tents. Some of the Cleveland
soldiers taunted Vallandigham about his antiwar views, even
threatening to ride him out of the camp on a rail. Vallandigham
defended himself defiantly, and the verbal exchange led to
fisticuffs. His friends rushed in to rescue him from soldiers' fists
and insults. Undaunted, Vallandigham then visited the headquarters of the Second Ohio Volunteer Regiment, and he received courteous treatment there. Then he returned to Washington, insisting that he was a good Union man. Republican
newspapers seized upon the camp incident to put Vallandigham
in a bad light, magnifying it in order to use it against him in
the 1862 election.[35]

During the special session of Congress, Vallandigham was a
gadfly, stinging the Lincoln administration at every opportunity. He harassed the President for trespassing upon unconstitutional ground and "violating" civil liberties. He introduced a
resolution stating that Congress, not the President, had the
right to suspend the writ of habeas corpus, to raise an army and
navy, to declare war, and to establish a blockade. He found

fault with the section of the Military Academy bill that spelled out the oath required of cadets, and he wanted the volunteer army bill amended so rabbis could also serve as chaplains. He insisted upon repeal of the Morrill Tariff of February 20, 1861, recognizing it as a barrier to compromise and reunion. He also introduced a proposal to have "seven commissioners" accompany the army and be ready to consider "propositions" that might be proffered by "the so-called Confederate States." He stated his goal tersely: "I am for peace—speedy, immediate, honorable *peace,* with all its blessings." Vallandigham, however, did vote for several war measures. He voted for the bill that authorized the enlistment of 500,000 volunteers for a period of not more than three years, and he supported several bills providing for the financing of the war.[36]

After the special session of Congress came to an end on August 6, Vallandigham hurried home to be with his family and to take to the hustings. Most Ohio Democrats, swept by the tide of patriotism, favored a vigorous prosecution of the war and believed Vallandigham's antiwar views unwise and impolitic. Colonel Alexander McCook, a longtime Democrat who returned to Dayton after a harrowing experience at First Bull Run, called his congressman "a d——d traitor . . . worse than a Judas."[37] McCook and War Democrats generally favored shelving partisanship during the war—it did not seem right to place partisanship above patriotism when the country's future hung in the balance.

Republican strategists took advantage of the patriotic surge to organize a Union party and to call a Union state convention, for the gubernatorial contest lay in the offing. Some former Democrats played prominent roles in the Union state convention, and one of them, David Tod, received the "fusion" convention's nomination for governor. Tod had earlier opposed coercion and favored compromise, but, after the events at Fort Sumter and Bull Run, he beat the drums of war vigorously and drew the praise of Republican politicians. Republicans of Whig extraction also liked Tod's views on economic matters. He was engaged in railroading, iron-manufacturing, and coal-mining; more than a year before the war, he had drafted a "conspiracy bill" to smash labor unions and outlaw strikes.[38]

Vallandigham opposed the "fusion" movement. He insisted upon the maintenance of "the organization & integrity of the Democratic party," believing it to be the medium through which "public & private liberty" could be saved and the "Federal Union as it was forty odd years ago" restored.[39] Consequently, he advised Democrats to shun the Union party movement, and other party regulars did likewise. Medary of the *Crisis,* who bore a personal animosity toward Tod dating back to Polk's Presidency,[40] viewed the Union party movement as little more than a Republican strategem. George W. Manypenny, who edited the *Ohio Statesman,* shared Medary's view. "It is only the mask to cover the deformities of Abolition," he wrote. "It is the lion's skin thrown over the same old animal, the ears will stick out." [41] The Democratic party, consequently, held its own state convention and named Hugh J. Jewett as its candidate for governor.

The gubernatorial campaign of 1861 intensified party spirit. Several Democratic newspaper offices, accused of harboring "pro-Southern" or "traitorous" editors, were destroyed by mob action. Anonymous letter writers threatened to suppress the *Dayton Empire* (formerly the *Western Empire*), edited by Vallandigham's friend and fellow Democrat, J. F. Bollmeyer. Republicans rained abusive epithets upon Vallandigham's head, claiming he was disloyal and pro-southern. On one occasion Vallandigham and a Dayton grocer argued and scuffled; when the grocer got his pistol, the congressman beat a hasty retreat and sought temporary refuge in the millinery store next door.[42] It was not even safe for a man to speak a word in Vallandigham's defense upon the streets of Dayton. "There is no denying the fact now," wrote a young apostle, "that he is the most unpopular man in the north, and that here in his own district, he has but a minority of the people with him. . . ." [43]

The arrest of the Reverend Sabin Hough of Cincinnati helped to give Vallandigham more notoriety. A federal marshal arrested Mr. Hough, who had earlier served the Second Street (Protestant Episcopal) Church of Dayton. At that time he had admired Vallandigham, and had adopted extreme antiwar views. Authorities confiscated several issues of the *Banner of Union* (a paper published by Reverend Hough for several weeks) and a sheaf of personal correspondence, and offered all as evidence that he was disloyal. One issue of the *Banner of Union* blamed abolitionists for the war, predicted that "armed coercion" would not succeed, and advocated the adoption of a constitutional amendment fastening slavery in perpetuity upon the country. The sheaf of letters included three that Vallandigham had written—two in late April and the third in early September. The third letter, written shortly before Reverend Hough's arrest, expressed Vallandigham's disgust with national affairs and re-expressed Vallandigham's faith that compromise and peace would yet triumph: "Truly we have fallen upon evil times. But I believe, as God rules, that all will come out right in due season." [44] It seemed incredible to Vallandigham that his letters could be used to levy charges of treason against a friend.

Ohio Democrats built up false hopes that they might win the October, 1861, elections. Their contempt for Tod, whom they termed "a renegade," encouraged them to believe that he could not win. The depression of 1861 cast a cloud over the countryside, reacting against the party in power. Democrats railed against "corruption in high places" and tried to capitalize on Midwestern opposition to the "howls of Republican Abolitionists." Democrats blamed Republicans for bringing about the war, and some Democratic editors bid for votes by writing vaguely about compromise and peace. "The popular demand," noted the editor of the *Ohio Statesman*, "is becoming loud and urgent that the sword shall be wreathed with the olive branch." [45]

Republicans countered with a strong appeal to patriotism, equating criticism of the administration with treason. Some Republican newspaper editors charged that a pro-southern secret order, the Knights of the Golden Circle, had several thousand members exerting influence to defeat Tod in Ohio.[46] They also claimed that the Union party ticket deserved the support of all who wanted partisanship shelved in the hour of crisis. One Republican editor insisted that fusion was wrapped in the American flag, whereas voting the straight Democratic ticket was "tantamount to giving most effective aid and comfort to the enemy in arms against us." [47]

Vallandigham stayed around the polls of his ward most of the time on election day, badgering his constituents to vote the straight Democratic ticket.[48] Many Democrats, nevertheless, cast their votes for Tod and fusion, some mistakenly believing that the Union party movement heralded the death of the Republican party.[49] Tod carried Dayton and Montgomery County by handsome margins, winning the governor's chair. In neighboring states where Republicans avoided fusion, the Democrats made notable comebacks.

Republicans gloried in the Ohio election returns. The partisan editor of the *Dayton Journal* thanked God that Tod and patriotism had triumphed. The post-election headlines were gall to Vallandigham. One headline read: "TREASON DEAD AND BURIED"; the subheadline added a final, specific thrust: "Vallandigham And His Traitorous Crew Squelched." [50]

Disappointed but not despairing, Clement L. Vallandigham journeyed to Washington to be present when Congress met on December 2, 1861. In the days that followed, he wrote his contempt of abolition, his hatred of Republicans, his antipathy for New England, and his distrust of President Lincoln into the record. Since he argued against most of the measures sponsored by the majority party, his political opponents called him an obstructionist.

The Trent Affair [51] gave him a chance to needle the Lincoln administration. When the House of Representatives endorsed the action of Captain Charles Wilkes, who stopped a British mail steamer and seized Confederate commissioners James M. Mason and John Slidell, Vallandigham voted with the majority.[52] However, he predicted that the Lincoln administration would bow to British demands and surrender Mason and Slidell. Republican congressmen, at the time, mocked and ridiculed Vallandigham's prophecy. President Lincoln and Secretary of State William H. Seward recognized that statesmanship called for appeasing England, and released Mason and Slidell. Vallandigham, consequently, had the last word. He reminded his fellow congressmen that his prediction had been realized, and he scolded the administration for surrendering the Monroe Doctrine as well as Mason and Slidell. "For the first time," moaned Vallandigham, "the American eagle has been made to cower before the British lion." [53]

Vallandigham applauded when his fellow Democrat, the Hon. George H. Pendleton of Ohio, excoriated President Lincoln for suspending the writ of habeas corpus. Soon after, Vallandigham proposed the arrest and impeachment of the President if any more citizens were arrested arbitrarily.[54] If Vallandigham's resolution recommending the arrest of President Lincoln was introduced with tongue in cheek, he nevertheless opposed the centralizing tendency of the government. As an avowed champion of states' rights, he opposed all measures that strengthened the national government at the expense of the states.

Vallandigham voted against a long list of Republican-sponsored measures. He spoke against proposals to raise the tariff rates; he opposed measures that encouraged army officers to give aid and protection to fugitive slaves; he spoke against the bills to abolish slavery in the District of Columbia and to erase slavery in the territories. He also opposed Lincoln's proposals to push compensated emancipation in the border states, and he cast his vote against the confiscation bill. Vallandigham believed that the Republican-sponsored measures stymied compromise hopes—would prevent "the restoration of the Union of these States as it was." He wanted the Union of ante bellum days restored, with states' rights emphasized and with slavery recognized. He believed he was performing a service to his country and to posterity by opposing centralization of the government, emphasizing individual rights, and turning the calendar back to the prewar years. "The time will come," he confidently predicted, ". . . when *all* men who have stood firm and true to their principles and to the real interests of their country will be remembered with gratitude and honor." [55] Vallandigham failed to realize that the winds of change were blowing, and that he was a conservative opposing the course of events. He lived in the past, and he feared the changes that the war was bringing to America. "We are in the throes of a revolution," the dogmatic Daytonian wrote to a friend, "and I cannot see what the issue is to be yet; but I dread the worst." [56]

As Vallandigham gained a reputation as a critic and obstructionist, Republican congressmen paid less attention to his speeches and his comments. Sometimes when Vallandigham tried to get the floor of the House, the Speaker ignored him. One member of the House referred to him as "the young man standing in the aisle." [57] The Speaker, evidently, did not intend to let Vallandigham use the House floor as a forum to give publicity to his antiwar views and his criticisms of the Lincoln administration.

As the war engendered nationalism, critics of the administration were accused of pro-southern sympathies and denounced as "traitors." "There is one man in the House that I look upon as a traitor 'dyed in the wool,' " wrote a Radical Republican, "and that man is 'Vallandigham' of Ohio. I look upon him as one of the blackest traitors." [58] Occasionally, rumors that Vallandigham would be arrested circulated in Washington.[59]

Republican contempt for Vallandigham helped bring about several heated controversies. In February, 1862, for example, John Hickman of Pennsylvania and Vallandigham exchanged unpleasantries. The Pennsylvania congressman introduced a resolution instructing the Committee on the Judiciary "to inquire into the truth of certain charges of disloyalty" made against Vallandigham in the columns of the *Baltimore Clipper*. The editor of the *Clipper* had claimed that Vallandigham had harbored traitorous designs, "tainted" his oath to support the government and the Constitution, and referred to the South as "bleeding Dixie." Congressman Hickman, harboring a grudge because Vallandigham had bested him in a previous duel of words, used the article in the *Baltimore Clipper* to impugn Vallandigham's loyalty and to embarrass the Dayton Democrat by referring to him as an enemy of the Union and a friend of the rebels.[60]

Vallandigham answered Hickman's charges boldly. He contradicted every sentence of the article. He denied ever having used the term "bleeding Dixie"; he had never been South to meet with Confederate officials as the *Clipper* contended—he had not been south of the Mason-Dixon line since the inauguration of hostilities; he had never sent any article on politics to any Baltimore newspaper. Vallandigham refuted all the charges in a dignified way and put his adversary on the defensive. Hickman feebly defended himself and his earlier accusations of disloyalty, but Vallandigham countered effectively. Hickman then surrendered and withdrew his resolution.[61] Elated with his victory over Hickman, Vallandigham wrote to his wife, "I was never more gratified in my life with any result. It was a signal triumph. . . ." [62]

Vallandigham's joust with Hickman was followed by a controversy with "Bluff Ben" Wade, a feud that left scars that never healed. Wade, a Radical Republican and one of Ohio's United States senators, thought that Vallandigham's failure to support the administration merited censure. Furthermore, Wade's Ohio supporters reported that antiwar Democrats talked of putting Vallandigham into the Senate in Wade's stead. Friends, therefore, advised Wade to brand "the monster" (Vallandigham) with "the traitor's mark," stigmatizing both Vallandigham and the Democratic party.[63]

Wade, described by a political rival as a man "of rugged, fierce, and vindictive feeling," [64] heeded his friend's advice to denounce Vallandigham. On the floor of the Senate, Wade launched an attack upon Democrats generally and upon Vallandigham in particular. He accused the Democratic party of a "deliberate purpose" to overawe and intimidate "the men who boldly stand forth in defense of their country. . . ." Then he labeled Vallandigham a traitor and an obstructionist, *"a man who never had any sympathy with the Republic, but whose every breath is devoted to its destruction, just as far as his heart dare permit him to go."* [65]

Vallandigham's friends soon reported on the attack that Wade had launched. Vallandigham, however, waited until the slanderous charges were published in the *Congressional Globe* before he made his public reply. Then, holding a copy of the *Globe* in hand, he read Wade's comments to his fellow congressmen and secured their attention. Sloughing temperance and decorum, Vallandigham then called Wade "a liar, a scoundrel, and a coward." [66]

One of Wade's friends, sitting in the House of Representatives, immediately introduced a resolution to censure Vallandigham for his intemperate remarks. Vallandigham's knowledge of parliamentary law, and the reluctance of congressmen to interfere in a personal feud in which both parties had overstepped the bounds of propriety, helped the Dayton Democrat to escape censure. Republican criticism of Vallandigham, however, did not cease. Once, two Republican congressmen from

Ohio presented petitions printed and circulated in their own districts asking for Vallandigham's expulsion as "a traitor and a disgrace to the State of Ohio." The House subsequently referred the petitions to a committee where they were shelved.[67] The campaign against Vallandigham, however, paid dividends. It gave him notoriety and helped to isolate him. It also furnished Republicans with campaign propaganda that could be used to prevent his re-election to Congress.

Vallandigham, meanwhile, remained as adamant and self-righteous as ever. In his own heart he believed that he had bested both Hickman and Wade and that he had gained the respect of friends and foes. "God has been very good to me," he wrote to his mother, "and has delivered me out of the hands of my enemies and given me victory over them in every assault." [68]

Although an adamant member of the opposition, Vallandigham occasionally voted for an administration measure. He supported the Homestead Act and the Morrill Land Grant Act.[69] He supported all measures he believed to be in harmony with the interests of the West, and he opposed all he believed to be unconstitutional. He always voted for the army and appropriation bills, although he might criticize certain features of the bills and although he still believed that compromise was possible and desirable. Once, when Vallandigham complimented the administration, he startled the Speaker of the House, who wryly commented that he was glad to find something of which his colleague approved.[70]

During the closing months of the session Vallandigham made an attempt to rally the Democratic party and lead it back to its prewar principles. He believed that his party drifted aimlessly and failed to capitalize upon the issues. He noticed that several caucuses of congressional Democrats broke up without any agreement upon policy. Furthermore, the April elections were approaching, and there was need for some concerted action. Vallandigham stepped into the breach and tried to supply the leadership now notably lacking. He phrased a "call to action," getting the signatures of thirty-five Democratic congressmen, and set March 25, 1862, as a meeting date. He then formed an ad hoc committee to prepare an article of Democratic faith—an address to the people. The War Democrats who served on the committee feared that the report would reflect Vallandigham's views, not their own. They, therefore, used delaying tactics to prevent Vallandigham from imposing his will upon their Democratic colleagues. Vallandigham then brashly took the bull by the horns: he wrote an "Address" himself, tacked on the names of most Midwestern Democratic congressmen, and ordered it published.

The "Address of the Democratic Members of the Congress to the Democracy of the United States" urged compromise and conciliation as national policy, emphasized use of the ballot box as a means for voters to influence events, and argued that states had the right to control "domestic institutions" (i.e., slavery). It viewed events through the out-of-focus spectacles of states' rights. It tied the Democratic party to the past, for it would reconstruct the Union upon prewar ideas and prewar institutions. It gave form and meaning to the slogan "The Constitution as it is, the Union as it was." [71]

Vallandigham's bold action in drafting and publicizing the "Address" helped to deepen the schism in the Democratic party. Some of those whose names Vallandigham appended to the document were embarrassed, and they refused to espouse its principles openly. War Democrats, generally, repudiated the "Address," pretending it was no more than the dissenting report of a minority group. "I think no document ought to have been sent out," wrote one Democratic critic of Vallandigham, "which was not acceptable to the majority of our party." [72]

Early in July, Vallandigham left Washington to attend the state Democratic convention, meeting in Columbus and officially launching the election campaign of 1862. He arrived in Columbus on July 3 and found Democratic optimism contagious. Depressed farm prices and chaotic economic conditions undermined popular faith in the Lincoln administration. Grant's victories in the West—and Shiloh is usually not considered a Union victory—did not balance the many defeats suffered by the Army of the Potomac. A number of arbitrary arrests in Ohio, including that of John W. Kees [73] of the *Circleville Watchman,* gave Democrats a chance to claim that despotism threatened the country. The bold demands of prominent abolitionists scared the conservatives and gave Democrats an issue around which they could rally (the majority of Ohioans were not ready to accept emancipation in midyear, 1862).

Vallandigham met many delegates and Democrats from his own congressional district—it was reported that 550 were in attendance, some as delegates, many as observers. Late in the evening of July 3, Vallandigham responded to a serenade. He pitched into the administration, winning applause for his blunt blows and his oratorical ability.

The next morning, delegates and spectators crowded into the hall reserved for the convention, but it was filled to overflowing before half had pushed their way in. Democratic leaders changed the meeting place to the Statehouse grounds to accommodate the thousands who had come to cheer or shout. Samuel Medary, outspoken editor of the *Crisis* and even more antiwar than Vallandigham, presided over the formal sessions. The audience warmed up as an array of orators damned the administration. Vallandigham gave one of the principal addresses and received a thunderous ovation. His speech was later published in its entirety in the *Crisis.* [74]

Vallandigham also served on the Committee on Resolutions and expressed concern to find complete disagreement among the members—a party split lessened his chances of re-election. Some, like Medary, believed the Union "was gone" and the war "hopeless"; they wanted a firm stand taken for an armistice and peace. Medary had even criticized Vallandigham's support of army appropriations bills in Congress.[75] On the other hand,

War Democrats believed that all other questions should be subordinated to defeating the South and restoring the Union. Vallandigham occupied a middle ground, claiming that the war must be fought "along constitutional lines" and asking the committee to condemn President Lincoln's unconstitutional acts. He contended that the Union still existed, that the rebels must be put down, and that the West could never allow "a foreign power" to control the lower Mississippi.

After considerable debate, the committee forged its platform. One of the resolutions took a strong stand against arbitrary arrests, condemning as "a monstrous dogma" the "Republican contention" that the Constitution was suspended in time of war. Half a dozen resolutions condemned abolition—one listed twelve arguments against emancipation. Several resolutions portrayed Democrats as "devoted friends of the Constitution and the Union," defenders of civil rights, enemies of radicalism, and friends of law and order.[76]

After the resolutions were adopted by a voice vote, the delegates nominated candidates for the five state offices that would be vacated at the end of the year. Then the convention adjourned. Many of the delegates and spectators, however, spent the night of July 4 in Columbus, drinking toasts and denouncing the Republicans. A crowd of celebrants visited the headquarters hotel and called for Vallandigham. He answered their calls by stepping out on the balcony and orating against the administration—his third speech in twenty-four hours.[77]

The next day, Vallandigham hurried home to visit his family and to begin his campaign for re-election. Friends in Dayton planned a gigantic Democratic rally on August 2 and listed Vallandigham as the principal speaker. Rumors that Republicans would break up the rally and that federal authorities might arrest Vallandigham gave publicity to the mass meeting and brought an outpouring of Democrats. The hall could not seat but a portion of the audience, so the meeting was adjourned to the courthouse grounds. Vallandigham rose to the occasion, giving a scholarly and interesting oration. He posed as the champion of civil rights and advised his listeners to obey the laws and to vote the Democratic ticket. "Whoever should be drafted, should a draft be ordered according to the Constitution and the law," advised the self-styled champion of the masses, "is in duty bound . . . to . . . go; he has no right to resist, and none to run away." Then Vallandigham lashed out at the administration's emancipation leanings. He drove the spit into abolition, burning it to a crisp with fiery ridicule. He restated his views on war and compromise, asking that the Union be restored while maintaining the Constitution. He included an appeal to patriotic passions, wishing to see "the old flag" fly again in every state, and "honored once again in every land and upon every sea." The ebullient orator was willing to be a martyr for his views, defying arbitrary arrest and showing contempt for "the knife of the assassin." [78]

Democrats of the Third District met in Hamilton on September 4 to nominate their congressional candidate. Vallandigham won the nomination by acclamation, for he was unopposed. Realists recognized that their Democratic candidate had the cards stacked against him, for a Republican-dominated state legislature had changed the boundary lines of the Third District, dropping out Preble County and adding Warren— Republicans supposedly outnumbered Democrats three to one in Warren County.[79]

Republican strategists recognized they needed a strong candidate to run against Vallandigham, for a Democratic trend seemed to be sweeping the upper Midwest. The editor of the *Lebanon Star* suggested General Robert C. Schenck, a four-term congressman and well-known diplomat, a respected man and an excellent stump speaker. He was a strong antislavery man and the darling of the abolitionists of southwestern Ohio.[80] As a general, Schenck had gained publicity, and he did not intend to surrender a general's star for the ordeal of a political campaign. Some Republicans feared, therefore, that Vallandigham would win re-election by default.

While Ohio Republicans hunted for a strong candidate to oppose Vallandigham, a little known incident occurred at the second battle of Bull Run. While Brigadier General Robert C. Schenck rallied his troops late on the afternoon of Saturday, August 30, 1862, a fragment of grapeshot struck his right hand, tearing an ugly hole just above the wrist, breaking bones and severing tendons. Schenck's plucky aides led him to the rear and then hustled him off to Willard's Hotel in Washington. The next morning, a doctor examined and dressed the wound; it would be several months before Schenck could regain use of his right hand and return to the army. While General Schenck lay in his room cursing his luck, he had several important visitors. Edwin M. Stanton recognized that Schenck's ill luck on the battlefield might be turned into good fortune in the political arena. The Secretary of War urged Schenck to run for Congress in the Third District, saying, "You are the only man who can beat the traitor Vallandigham." [81] President Lincoln also called upon Schenck to convince him that he could do a greater service by sidetracking Vallandigham than by leading a brigade.[82] Schenck bowed to the pressure, and jubilant Republicans nominated him to oppose Vallandigham in the redrawn Third District.

Vallandigham, aware that he was opposed by a formidable rival, canvassed every township in his district, sometimes speaking four times a day. He believed that Lincoln's preliminary Emancipation Proclamation of September 22, 1862, enhanced his chance of re-election, and he bid anew for the votes of the "Raw Dutch" and the Irish.[83]

The Republicans, meanwhile, launched an all-out campaign to defeat Vallandigham. A procession of nationally known Republicans invaded the Third District to preach patriotism and to admonish the voters to defeat Vallandigham. The administration elevated Schenck to the rank of major general to prove he was a hero,[84] and Republicans tried to capitalize on his wound and his battlefield heroics to sway voters.[85] Intimidation stifled some of Vallandigham's supporters: mobsters wrecked the editorial offices of the Democratic-oriented *Lebanon Citizen,* and authorities arrested an outspoken law student who campaigned for Vallandigham.[86] The editor of the *Dayton Journal* waged a campaign of abuse against Vallandigham, taking his statements out of context, misdating and misquoting his speeches, and attributing forged letters to him.[87] The *Journal* labeled Vallandigham "a master of political chicanery," "a defender of secession," and "a trickster" who would co-operate with the Knights of the Golden Circle.[88] Republican postmasters assisted in flooding the Third District with propaganda pamphlets. One such document, entitled "The Secession Record of C. L. Vallandigham," called Vallandigham an out-and-out traitor. "Let the infamous Vallandigham whose *votes* convict him of having no sympathy with the Union—whose *speeches* convict him of being in the full confidence of the conspirators . . . retire from public life as one of the infamous trinity—*Arnold, Burr,* and *Vallandigham.*" [89]

Ohioans marched to the polls on October 14, and the incumbent congressman awaited the verdict apprehensively. Although Ohio Democrats elected their slate of state officials and won fourteen of the nineteen congressional seats, Vallandigham lost the Third District by a 100-vote majority.[90] He trailed the Democratic state slate by 400 votes in his own district. Vallandigham lost a battle while Ohio Democrats were winning a war.

Vallandigham's devoted supporters expressed disappointment in his defeat. "The loss the Democracy have sustained in the defeat of the Hon. C. L. Vallandigham of the Dayton district," wrote a Cleveland apostle, "is a national calamity." [91] Friends blamed his defeat upon "infamous gerrymandering" effected the previous March by a Republican-controlled state

legislature.[92] They pointed out that Vallandigham had received
an 800-vote margin in the "old district"—700 more than he had
received in 1860—and that Republican-dominated Warren
County had tipped the scales against him. So his friends pre-
tended that Vallandigham had won "a great personal and political triumph" in spite of his failure to win re-election.[93] They
interpreted the election returns to be a popular repudiation of
Lincoln's emancipation policy and the practice of arbitrary
arrests.[94] The editor of the *Dayton Empire* featured the headline: "ABOLITION LIES PROSTRATE!"; and he also addressed himself to the question of arbitrary arrests: "Let the
oppressed, denounced, and much abused Democracy of the
land rejoice and be merry, for the wand of the despot is broken
and the sceptre falls from his hand. The people have spoken in
thunderous tones that make the very bolts and bars of the
Bastiles, where innocent men are imprisoned, quake and trem-
ble." [95] Vallandigham's supporters thus contended that Vallandigham's views had popular endorsement although he himself
lost the election. Some friends, indulging in wishful thinking,
talked of electing Vallandigham to a seat in the Senate of the
United States or elevating him to the governor's chair.[96]

Vallandigham's friends failed to consider all of the factors
contributing to his defeat at the polls. His opponent, General
Schenck, was a well-known and highly respected gentleman as
well as a war hero. Some of Vallandigham's public statements
left him vulnerable to misrepresentation, and his imprudent
and extreme utterances made him seem to be pro-southern.
The spirit of nationalism had made its imprint upon public
opinion, and it emburdened those who swam against the current.[97]

Late in November, when the Lincoln administration was
still reeling from blows dealt by Democrats in the late elections,
Vallandigham journeyed to Washington to be present as a lame
duck congressman at the opening session of the House of Representatives. He questioned the worth of Lincoln's "Message"

to Congress, being disheartened by the "Niggerism" theme.[98] "The tenacity with which Mr. Lincoln holds on to his emancipation proclivities, not withstanding the rebuke administered in the result of the election in the North the past fall," wrote a disillusioned Democrat, "cannot fail . . . to alarm the friends of the Union and of Constitutional liberty throughout our broad land." [99]

Vallandigham lost no time in adding to his reputation as an obstructionist. He introduced a resolution criticizing the President for permitting wholesale arbitrary arrests and asked for a congressional investigation. The Republicans easily defeated the measure. Vallandigham voted for a Democratic-drawn resolution condemning the administration's turn toward emancipation, but the measure went down to a 94 to 45 defeat—a strict party vote.[100]

The lame duck congressman, meanwhile, received good news from Ohio. An acquaintance and fellow-Democrat, Dr. Edson B. Olds of Lancaster, won a seat in the state legislature in a special election. Dr. Olds had been arbitrarily arrested for his antiadministration tirades, and the Democrats nominated him when the death of the Hon. J. C. Jeffrey created a vacancy in a state senate district. The arrest of Dr. Olds transformed him into a martyr, and he received the largest Democratic vote ever cast in Fairfield County.[101] Martyrdom seemed to pay dividends, and the lesson was not lost on Clement L. Vallandigham.

After Congress had been in session but two weeks, Vallandigham and George H. Pendleton [102] made an excursion to New York City. While at their hotel, they were serenaded by Dodsworth's Band, which played "Dixie" as well as other airs. Calls for Vallandigham brought him out on a balcony, and he began a speech. A sympathetic audience encouraged him to plead that "humility, conciliation, and compromise" become national policy. He denounced Lincoln and despotism in the same breath, laying all arbitrary arrests at the President's door. Vallandigham spoke as one willing to be a martyr to the cause of free speech: "My birth-right, if I have it at all, is to speak plainly, because I was born a freeman and mean to die a freeman. I am not willing to seek my own personal safety by compliments to the President of the United States [Applause]. He deserves it not, and he has it not [Hisses]." [103]

As Vallandigham and Pendleton returned to Washington, they read the telegraphic reports about General Ambrose E. Burnside's depressing defeat at Fredericksburg. The heavy casualties shocked the North and gave force to Medary's contentions that the South could not be conquered. Rumors made the rounds that Secretary of State William H. Seward would propose peace terms recognizing the independence of the Confederacy. Vallandigham wanted peace but upon conditions that would restore "the Union as it was." [104] He, therefore, introduced a resolution labeling as a "high crime" any terms of peace that did not maintain "the integrity of the Federal Union." [105]

The Christmas recess of Congress occurred soon after, and Vallandigham hurried back to Dayton to spend the holidays at home. His Dayton friends told him that he was the symbol of peace in the minds of the populace and that his star was in the ascendancy. A Missouri newspaper editor listed Vallandigham as "first choice for President of the United States in 1864." [106] An admirer composed a "Vallandigham Polka"—"a spirited piece of music"—and it was reported that the number sold like hot cakes.[107]

The year 1862 ended amid general gloom and the tears of widows and mothers weeping for husbands or sons lost at Fredericksburg. Some Democrats wanted Lincoln impeached.[108] There was widespread fear for the future. Vallandigham read the gloomy note that Medary of the *Crisis* wrote in the waning hours of 1862: "The year 1862 has been a year of blood and plunder, of carnage and conflagration, . . . of falsehood and corruption, . . . of bastiles, persecutions and tears, . . . of despotism, desolation and death." [109] The editor of the *Dayton*

Empire wrote in a like vein: "Civil War stalks through the land. The earth is crimson with the blood of brave men. Desolation, ruin, and suffering follow the march of contending armies. . . . In almost every household there is a mourner, and in almost every heart a vacant place. The ferryman on the river Styx has done a heavy freighting business during the past twelve months." [110]

When Vallandigham returned to Washington after the Christmas recess was over, he took back with him the anguish, the worries, and the despair of his friends. He heard reports that Union troops had been bested in the West, and he read criticism of Lincoln's Emancipation Proclamation of January 1, 1863. Editors of the *Crisis,* the *Dayton Empire,* the *Cincinnati Enquirer,* and the *Hamilton True Telegraph* wrote columns condemning the President for surrendering to the abolitionists. Vallandigham believed that the Emancipation Proclamation was unconstitutional, unnecessary, and divisive. It would discourage enlistments, breed discontent in the border states, unite the South to a man, and prompt Democrats to plump for peace. Some of the more extreme Democrats said that Lincoln's proclamation absolved Democrats from further support of the war. [111]

Vallandigham thought about the future of his country and the conflicting ideas of war and peace. He heard defeatists expound their views. One ex-Ohioan was sure that the country had "gone to the Devil," that the South would "soon gain her independence," and that the Southern Confederacy would become "the garden spot of this continent." [112] War Democrats, on the other hand, were willing to close their eyes to Republican partisanship and think only of their desire to defeat the rebels. Vallandigham wanted peace and compromise; it was easy to wish for, difficult to attain.

After wrestling with the problem, Vallandigham decided to give a major speech in Congress and bid for national leadership of the peace crusade. He worked for a week, preparing with care. Then, on January 14, he dropped his "peace bomb" on the floor of the House of Representatives.

He began gradually enough, reviewing events leading to the failure of the compromise efforts of 1861. Then he heaped blame for the war upon the Republicans. He then spoke of civil rights evaporating in the heat of war and of the cost in money and men—"three hundred thousand lives lost or bodies mangled." The Lincoln administration had both erred and failed. Westerners disapproved of Lincoln's surrender to the abolitionists and his obeisance to New England; westerners might be forced to seek separation too. "The people of the West want peace," Vallandigham bluntly asserted, "and they begin to more than suspect that New England is in the way." [113]

Congressmen, immune to speech-making, began to listen, recognizing Vallandigham's speech to be an extraordinary one. Thaddeus Stevens, one of the leaders of the Radicals, and Schuyler Colfax, a respected Indiana Republican, moved closer so they could hear every word. John A. Bingham, most outspoken of Ohio's Radical Republican congressmen, started to take notes and prepare a rebuttal. A prominent Democrat, Hendrick B. Wright of Pennsylvania, occasionally wrote a comment as he developed the theme that Vallandigham's views on peace did not reflect those of the Democratic party. "Even the reporters woke up," wrote Vallandigham at a later date; "the ladies ceased their eternal chattering, and leaned forward to catch every word." [114]

Master of the situation, Vallandigham became more dramatic and dogmatic. He claimed that the South could not be conquered and proposed an armistice as a means to eventual reunion. [115] He spoke for an hour without an interruption of any kind, "and had most attentive listeners." [116] There was no applause when he finished and took his seat.

Even before Vallandigham had returned to his desk, Bingham asked the Speaker for permission to take the floor and reply to "the words of treason" uttered by his Ohio colleague.

Bingham called the speech "an apology for rebellion" and denied most of Vallandigham's assumptions. As Bingham's rapier-like thrusts cut Vallandigham, the crowd in the galleries broke out in applause, repeatedly drawing a reprimand from the Speaker. Hendrick B. Wright, a War Democrat, then added weight to Bingham's critical comments by denying that Vallandigham's views were acceptable to his party.[117]

Republican editors turned their wrath full force upon Vallandigham. The editor of the *New York Independent* warned his subscribers that they must "prepare to meet at home, an enemy more deadly and unprincipled than the armed rebels of the South." [118] The *Chillicothe Advertiser* labeled Vallandigham's speech "a treasonable production," and the *Cincinnati Gazette* stated that such sentiments should no longer be "tolerated." [119] "The people of the Northwest spurn him," wrote the angry editor of the *Ohio State Journal*, "and spit upon his detestable doctrine." [120] One irate citizen called Vallandigham a "hyena" and suggested he be hung immediately and to "apologize if necessary afterwards." [121]

Most Ohio Democrats regarded Vallandigham's speech as imprudent—he had given way to despair and had embarrassed his party. A few editors openly endorsed his sentiments and rallied to his defense. The *Newark* (Ohio) *Advocate* published the entire oration, calling it the "ablest speech he has ever made." [122] Thomas H. Hodder of the *Marion Democratic Mirror* called it "the greatest effort of the age." [123] The *Dayton Empire,* of course, contained flattering remarks and unabashedly termed Vallandigham "the greatest living American statesman." [124] The editor of the *Holmes County Farmer* named Vallandigham as his choice for the presidency.[125] James Faran of the *Cincinnati Enquirer* lauded the speech as worthy of a Webster or a Chatham, remarkable for its "force of reasoning, a richness of historical illustration, or depth of patriotism." [126] Medary of the *Crisis* also wrote paeans of praise. "This is no ordinary speech," he wrote, "—made by no ordinary man, and under circumstances the most remarkable which ever overtook any nation or people. It may be well if this nation ponders seriously and with judgment over the words of wisdom and burning eloquence which runs through every paragraph, sentence, and line." [127] " 'Peace' is on a million lips," added Dr. John McElwee of the *Hamilton True Telegraph,* "and it will thunder, ere long, in the ears of our rulers like an Alpine storm." [128]

As Peace Democrats and Radical Republicans hurled epithets at each other and discussed the merits of "the Peace Speech," Vallandigham decided to seek his party's nomination for the governorship of his state.[129] A few peace-minded Democratic editors hoisted Vallandigham-for-governor banners. The lame duck congressman hoped to get more attention and some sympathy from a speech against the conscription bill. He called the measure unwise and unconstitutional, undemocratic and unfair. He defined the provost marshal system, delineated in the conscription bill, as a means to establish a despotism. He introduced an amendment aimed at curbing the power of the President, and he closed his speech against the conscription measure with a dire prediction: "The guillotine! the guillotine! the guillotine follows next!" [130]

In the closing days of the session, Vallandigham made his farewell speech in Congress. It was brief and to the point—a refutation of the personal remarks Congressmen and others had made against him. It was wrong and unfair, he argued, for Radical Republicans to label Democrats as "traitors" or "secessionists"; patriotism would not be served by name-calling, nor unity by misrepresentation.[131]

After Congress adjourned, Vallandigham took a brief trip to Philadelphia and New York City. Peace Democrats of the two cities arranged "grand celebrations." Those who wanted peace lionized him, for he put their wishes into words. In both speeches he condemned Republicans for sponsoring a smear campaign, and he excoriated the administration for violating traditional rights. He loved liberty and intended to defend it. He closed his New York speech on a tone of defiance and in words that caught the fancy of his followers: "I will never surrender my rights . . . ; I will never consent to be a slave." [132]

The overwhelming reception he received in Philadelphia and New York convinced him that the country wanted peace, that Lincoln was out of tune with the popular melody. He headed back to Dayton with the applause of war-weary New Yorkers still ringing in his ears.

Dayton Democrats knew on what train and at what time Vallandigham was expected to arrive "back home." They planned a noteworthy and noisy homecoming. When Vallandigham arrived at the Dayton depot, "thousands of persons" surged forward, giving him a hero's welcome. A cannon boomed its thunderous tones of welcome; two bands enlivened the occasion. The crowd was so dense that it was almost impossible for Vallandigham to make his way to a decorated carriage. The parade marshals finally turned the milling mass into a procession, which headed for the courthouse. The bands and banner-bearers led the long procession, while Vallandigham doffed his hat or waved his hand to those who watched the parade.

At the courthouse, the "honored guest" had a chance to reply to the tributes heaped upon his head. Vallandigham abused the administration. Then he attacked the conscription act, saving his most caustic and critical remarks for the three hundred dollar commutation clause. He called the three hundred dollar provision "the price of blood," a clause that discriminated against the poor. He echoed the bold words the editor of the *Dayton Empire* had written a week earlier: "If we are cowards, unworthy the freedom our forefathers wrested from tyrants' hands, then we will meekly wear, and deservedly, too, the chains which Abolition despots are forging for our hands." [133]

The reverberations of the "gala homecoming" carried down

to Cincinnati, where General Ambrose E. Burnside assumed command of the Department of the Ohio on March 16, 1863. General Burnside worked hard to forget the bitter memories of Fredericksburg and made an effort to become familiar with his new assignment. He believed the cock-and-bull stories about the Golden Circle that Colonel Henry B. Carrington concocted in Indianapolis and sent to Cincinnati newspapers.[134] Carrington broadcast tales about subversive societies to cover his mistakes and justify the arbitrary acts of Governor Oliver P. Morton. Carrington seized a lot of pistols (twenty-four in number) from a Richmond, Indiana, hardware store kept by a Democrat and soon after issued General Orders, No. 19, which denied the right of people to keep or bear arms. General Burnside also expressed concern about the threats and counterthreats that followed the mobbing of the *Crisis* office on March 5, 1863. The defiant Democrat who edited the *Dayton Empire* dared Republicans to mob his quarters—they would be welcomed "with bloody hands to hospitable graves." He gave radical advice to his friends: "For every drop of Democratic blood spilled by Abolition mobites, let theirs flow in retaliation." [135]

To General Burnside it seemed as if he were sitting on the edge of a crater of a volcano. Antidraft sentiment intensified the undercurrent of discontent. Reports reached Cincinnati that armed resistance to military authority had occurred in Cambridge, Noble County.[136] It seemed that Democratic victories (in the April, 1863, elections) in Columbus, Portsmouth, Toledo, Hamilton, and Dayton encouraged Lincoln's critics to be bolder and more bellicose. Furthermore, Burnside digested the political pap produced in the editorial offices of the *Cincinnati Gazette,* and could not understand that there were two sides to most political controversies. He therefore interpreted criticism of the Lincoln administration as sympathy for the rebels, believing that it gave aid and encouragement to the enemy. Consequently, on April 13, 1863, the gullible and gritty general issued General Orders, No. 38, an edict that stated that "the habit of declaring sympathy for the enemy" would no longer be tolerated, and that individuals arrested would be subject to military procedures.[137] Burnside thus set himself up as a censor who could decide where the fine line between criticism and treason existed and when freedom of speech or the press gave aid and comfort to the enemy.

While General Burnside charted his course at his Cincinnati headquarters, Vallandigham intensified his campaign to capture his party's gubernatorial nomination. He put the final touches to a compilation of his speeches, entitled it *The Record of Hon. C. L. Vallandigham on Abolition, the Union, and the Civil War,* and waited for the volume to come off the press.[138] He hoped the book would give a nudge to his gubernatorial hopes and provide some funds to finance the campaign. He spoke at occasional political rallies, and he wrote letters to try to create a ground swell for the Vallandigham-for-governor movement. He found little support of his candidacy among the party bigwigs; they knew he did not represent the majority view of their party and that only a miracle could put him in the Statehouse. Vallandigham also gave some attention to his law practice, and he read the many military orders emanating from the pens of Colonel Carrington and General Burnside. The military orders angered Vallandigham, building up in him a mountain of resentment and indignation. In a speech at Hamilton the ex-congressman denounced Colonel Carrington for denying the people of Indiana the right to bear arms and told his audience to give the Spartan answer: "Come and get them." [139] To Vallandigham it seemed that military officials, acting as satraps, were pushing the patience of the people to the utmost limits of endurance.

A speaking engagement in Columbus gave Vallandigham a chance to pose as the champion of civil rights. He spoke intemperately against General Burnside's "General Orders, No. 38," contending that citizens had the right to speak and to criticize both civil and military officials.[140] Vallandigham believed a despotism was enveloping the country, and that only cowards could be cowed by erring and blustering generals. Men deserved freedom only if they merited it, and they merited it only if they possessed the courage and determination to have it. Vallandigham often thought of the scornful exclamation of Tiberius regarding the degraded and servile Roman senate: "O Homines ad Servitutem paratos." [141] He put Tiberius and General Burnside in the same class: both had scorn for citizens and for traditional rights.

General Burnside felt the sting of the bold and defiant words Vallandigham uttered in Columbus. He knew that the Daytonian was scheduled to speak at Mount Vernon at a Democratic rally on May 1, so he sent two agents there to take notes on the speech. The presence of one of General Burnside's agents, leaning against the speakers' platform and scribbling in a little black book, encouraged Vallandigham to blast away with both barrels. He made a bid for martyrdom, criticizing both Burnside and the Lincoln administration. He spoke for two hours, failing to show proper consideration for Samuel S. Cox and George H. Pendleton, who followed him.[142] But Vallandigham found the audience most responsive, and he was intoxicated by the adulation rendered him. He charged that the Lincoln administration had deceived the people as to its true objectives; its purpose seemed to be to free the blacks and enslave the whites. He stated that it was his right to speak and to criticize. "General Orders, No. 38" was a base usurpation of arbitrary power. He could spit upon it and stamp it under foot. His right to speak was based upon "General Order, No. 1," the Constitution of the United States. Oppression, he asserted, occurred in direct proportion to the servility of a people. "The sooner the people inform the minions of usurped power that they will not submit to such restrictions upon their liberties," shouted Vallandigham, "the better." [143]

As soon as the two agents reported to Burnside and related what Vallandigham had said, the general dispatched a train and a detail of 150 soldiers to Dayton. The soldiers arrived at Vallandigham's home at 2:40 A.M. the morning of May 5 and surrounded the house. The commanding officer rang the bell and pounded on the front door. When Vallandigham opened a second-story window and inquired who was there, the commanding officer asked Vallandigham to surrender. "If Burnside wants me," Vallandigham answered defiantly, "let him come and get me." Soldiers battered the front door with axes and heavy logs, but it did not yield. Meanwhile, a soldier gained entrance by opening a rear window, and the doors were then unlocked to permit a squad to enter. Vallandigham's wife and sister-in-law, "in 'dishabille,' " screamed and defied the soldiers. The soldiers finally cornered Vallandigham in a back bedroom and led him from the house amid the screams and yells of those left behind. Within thirty minutes of their arrival in Dayton, the soldiers were back on the train, headed for Cincinnati with their glum prisoner.[144]

In Cincinnati, the soldiers placed their political prisoner in Kemper Barracks. To prevent Vallandigham's friends from trying to rescue him, General Burnside transferred Vallandigham to Newport Barracks, Kentucky, and kept him under a strong guard while setting machinery in motion for a military trial.

The next morning, Dayton Democrats reconstructed the story of the arrest out of reports, rumors, and an interview with members of Vallandigham's family. Some friends, headed by the Democratic mayor, took an early train down to Cincinnati to consult with Vallandigham and decide what course to pursue. Everywhere, there were crowds of excited men, and prominent Republicans went into hiding lest pent-up wrath be unleashed against them. In the grogshops and on the street corners, there was strong talk—the ears of Lincoln, Burnside, and prominent Dayton Republicans must have burned.

Editor William T. Logan wrote a fiery editorial and inflam-

matory headlines, and they appeared in the afternoon edition
of the *Dayton Empire*. The headlines read:

VALLANDIGHAM KIDNAPPED

A dastardly Outrage!!

Will free men submit?

The hour for action has arrived.

The editorial cursed the "cowardly, scoundrelly abolitionists"
of Dayton, holding them responsible for "the hellish outrage."
The editorial even suggested that "blood and carnage" were
necessary to rescue "endangered liberties." [145]

Logan's editorial, liquor from the grogshops, and widespread
indignation combined to bring a mob into being. A crowd of
several hundred resentful residents gathered in front of the
Empire building, as if seeking inspiration from that edifice of
Democratic dogma. Across the street stood the building that
housed the editorial offices and printing plant of the *Dayton
Journal*. The *Journal* editor had written that Vallandigham
would get "into a scrape," and his editorials had criticized
prominent Dayton Democrats viciously. Members of the milling mob saw the *Journal* building as a symbol of arbitrary rule
and "Black Republicanism." Some members of the capricious
crowd hurled verbal insults in the direction of the building;
others tried their aim with sticks and stones; a few exhibited
their marksmanship with pistols. Egged on by the mob spirit,
several made balls of pitch, lighted a match, and threw the
burning missiles through the open or broken windows. One
such missile landed among newspapers and started a fire.
Smoke poured out of the building and "in an incredibly short
space of time flames burst from the roof." [146] Some of the mis-
guided malcontents cheered—they imagined that another Bas-
tille was being destroyed. Dayton hotheads thus gave an unfor-

tunate and devilish answer to General Burnside's arrest of Vallandigham.

Blame for the riots rested upon the shoulders of Vallandigham, General Burnside, and Editor William T. Logan. Vallandigham had repeatedly stated that people who would be free must have the courage to defy arbitrary acts. Burnside's bad judgment begot "General Orders, No. 38," and aroused an apprehensive public. Editor Logan's bad-tempered and ill-advised editorial, "a crazy article [that] did more mischief than anything else," encouraged readers to show their defiance.[147] Imprudent acts produced unfortunate results.

The fire spread as the rioters interfered with the work of the Dayton fire department. After a regiment of soldiers sent by General Burnside arrived, and after one of the mobsters was shot while trying to cut the hose, the fire was brought under control and so was the mob. Burnside's agents arrested Editor Logan of the *Empire* and suspended publication of his newspaper. General Burnside used the Dayton riot of May 5 as an excuse to institute martial law throughout Montgomery County.[148] Bluecoats carrying bayonets patrolled the streets of Dayton, and an uneasy peace existed in Vallandigham's home town.

While confined in Kemper Barracks, Vallandigham received a Bible inscribed "Prepare to meet thy God." [149] He prepared a brief "address" with the salutation "To the Democracy of Ohio" and gave it to Dayton friends to publish and publicize. "I am here in a military bastile," the opening line read, "for no other offence than my political opinions, and the defence of them and the rights of the people, and of your constitutional liberties." The "address" asked Democrats to be "firm" and "true" to their principles and the Constitution. Burnside was guilty of gross misjudgment and despotic practices. He assured his friends that time would vindicate him and that all would yet be well.[150] It was evident that Vallandigham refused to believe that his immoderate statements hampered the war effort or affected the loyalty of Ohioans.

Burnside organized a military commission to try Vallandigham. The Daytonian faced the commission and bluntly stated that a military commission had no right to try him in a region where civil courts functioned. The judge advocate ignored Vallandigham's protest and read the charges: violating "General Orders, No. 38," and publicly declaring disloyal sentiments "with the object and purpose of weakening the power of the government in its efforts to suppress an awful rebellion." [151]

Vallandigham continued to deny that the military commission had jurisdiction over him, but the presiding officer proceeded with the trial. Burnside's two agents who took notes at Mount Vernon testified; and Vallandigham, acting as his own lawyer, cross-examined them. Samuel S. Cox, who had shared the platform at Mount Vernon, appeared to testify for the prisoner and claimed the "odious epithets" credited to Vallandigham as his own. After the witnesses had testified, the prisoner read a two-paragraph protest he had prepared; again he denied the jurisdiction of the commission. The court, nevertheless, found him guilty of the charges and ordered him "to be placed in close confinement in some fortress of the United States" for the duration of the war. General Burnside approved the findings of the military commission and selected Fort Warren, in Boston harbor, as the place of confinement.[152]

Two days after the trial was over and before General Burnside announced the verdict, the Hon. George E. Pugh moved for a writ of habeas corpus on behalf of Vallandigham before Judge Humphrey H. Leavitt of the United States Court for the Southern District of Ohio. Judge Leavitt required that notice of the application for a writ of habeas corpus be given to General Burnside. The intrepid general prepared a forthright defense of his authority and his actions; Mr. Pugh countered with strong arguments in behalf of habeas corpus action. After the formal arguments, Judge Leavitt spent several days formulating his opinion. On May 16 the judge gave his opinion, stating reasons for refusing to grant a writ of habeas corpus in Vallandigham's behalf. "The sole question," wrote Judge Leavitt, "is whether the arrest was legal; and . . . its legality depends on the necessity which existed for making it, and of that necessity . . . this Court cannot judicially determine." [153]

Judge Leavitt, prudently avoiding a conflict of civil and military authority, side-stepped the question of the jurisdiction of a military commission in a state where the civil courts were functioning (a postwar case, *Ex parte Milligan,* ruled that trial of civilians by military commissions was illegal) .[154]

When General Burnside announced the decision of his military tribunal, a wave of indignation swept Democratic circles. "Would to God," wrote Medary in the *Crisis,* "that the authorities were fully sensible of the great blunder they have made; of the slumbering volcano underneath." [155] McElwee of the *Hamilton True Telegraph* described Burnside's seizure and trial of Vallandigham as "the most atrocious outrage ever perpetrated in any civilized land." [156] Lecky Harper, the Mount Vernon editor who had induced Vallandigham to give a speech in his city, claimed that the ex-congressman had been arrested because he was a Democrat, a sentinel who warned the public to protect its liberties, and an enemy of the twin brothers of Discord and Abolition. He predicted, furthermore, that Vallandigham would be honored when the "Reign of Terror" was over.[157] Many would-be critics, however, held their tongues, for they had no wish to join Vallandigham in his prison cell. "The arrest of Vallandigham," noted a Republican observer, "operated finely. For a while they played shy." [158]

President Lincoln was somewhat embarrassed by General Burnside's independence and brashness. It seemed strange to General Henry W. Halleck, the general-in-chief, that Burnside would keep his superiors in the dark as to his action.[159] Some members of Lincoln's cabinet also felt that General Burnside had acted improperly and in a manner damaging to the administration. Some wished that Vallandigham "had been sent over the lines to the Rebels." Imprisonment might make him a martyr; exile might help to develop the notion that he was a traitor. Lincoln therefore changed Vallandigham's sentence from imprisonment to banishment. The President then instructed his secretary of war to order Burnside to send Vallandigham "beyond the lines." [160]

General Burnside, subsequently, put Vallandigham aboard the gunboat "Exchange"—most appropriately named—bound for Louisville. From Louisville, he was conducted by rail to General William S. Rosecrans' headquarters at Murfreesboro, arriving there on Sunday night, May 24. General Rosecrans, in turn, assigned the task of putting Vallandigham beyond the lines to his provost marshal, Major William M. Wiles. The wily major secured a light wagon and selected a company of cavalry to help him carry out the assignment. At two o'clock on the morning of May 25, the detail left for the Confederate lines by way of the Shelbyville pike. A small squad of cavalry led the way, and nearly a company followed the wagon. Just as the sun rose, the party reached the extreme outposts and discovered the rebel vedettes one-half mile ahead on the turnpike. While Vallandigham had breakfast at the house of a Mrs. Alexander, Major Wiles started toward the rebel lines with a flag of truce, "to see if they would accept him [Vallandigham] or not," [161] and he was soon in communication with the Confederate officer in charge of the picket lines.

The Confederate colonel, unsure whether or not to accept Vallandigham, hurriedly contacted his superior; and in time, a query was dispatched to General Braxton Bragg at Shelbyville, sixteen miles away. For a time the transfer seemed to hang in mid-air, complicated by Vallandigham's insistence that he was an involuntary prisoner. Major Wiles, anxious to unload his prisoner, urged the Confederates to receive the exile, and the Confederate colonel finally assented. Vallandigham, then, addressed himself to the Confederate soldiers: "I am a citizen of Ohio and the United States. I am here in your lines by force and against my will. I, therefore, surrender myself to you as a prisoner of war." [162]

General Bragg finally sent word that Vallandigham should be brought to his headquarters. The "prisoner" rode in an ambulance, escorted by a squad of cavalry. The strange procession passed through numerous camps and reached Shelbyville after dusk. He was kindly received and directed to the house of a Mrs. Eakin, where a spacious and pleasant room was provided for him.[163] He retired early, having slept but half an hour since Saturday night. The next day, Vallandigham restated his "I am an involuntary prisoner" line to General Bragg, who put him on parole and contacted the Confederate secretary of war. After a week in Shelbyville, Vallandigham was ordered to report to General Whiting at Wilmington, North Carolina, and there the exile hoped to catch a blockade runner for Bermuda.[164]

Vallandigham took passage on the steamer "Cornubia," and on the evening of June 17 the ship ran safely through the blockade squadron and arrived at Bermuda on June 20. He spent ten days in Bermuda before securing passage on a steamer for Halifax. He arrived in Halifax on July 5, an exile in a neutral nation. From Halifax, Vallandigham traveled to Picton by way of Truro, then took a steamer up the gulf and the St. Lawrence River to Quebec, where he was "cordially and honorably received." [165] The same evening he left by special train for Niagara Falls and arrived at the Clifton House the next day, July 16, after a journey of more than four thousand miles by land and sea.

When Vallandigham arrived at the Clifton House, from which he could see the Niagara River and the shoreline of the United States, he met his wife and son.[166] He was glad to find her well, for reports had circulated that his arrest and exile had caused her to "become insane." [167]

Political reports from his home state heartened him. Democratic reaction to the summary treatment that General Burnside accorded to Vallandigham helped bring "the exile" his
party's gubernatorial nomination. Before Vallandigham's arrest, he had no chance to gain the nomination. "His nomination, in my judgment," wrote a realistic Democratic politician
of the Buckeye State, "would ruin us in Ohio next fall." [168]
Practical politicians conceded that the Hon. Hugh J. Jewett
had the nomination in hand.[169] After his arrest Vallandigham
became a martyr for civil rights in the minds of many Democrats. Medary of the *Crisis* and McElwee of the *Hamilton True
Telegraph* wanted the administration rebuked; and emotional-
ism, rooted in reaction to the arrest, caused Democrats to cut
the cord of restraint. Jewett, aware that reaction swept all before it, withdrew from the canvass for the nomination. Conservative Democrats wrung their hands, but they were incapable of
heading off the developing whirlwind.[170] When the state Democratic convention met in Columbus on June 11, 1863, Vallandigham's defenders had no trouble gaining his nomination by
acclamation. The convention also named a committee to "earnestly request" President Lincoln "to return Clement L. Vallandigham to his home in Ohio." [171]

Samuel Medary, who presided over the convention, appointed a Committee of Nineteen to meet with President Lincoln and to ask for Vallandigham's return to Ohio. Members
who made up the Committee of Nineteen met with Lincoln on
June 25, and the President tactfully suggested that they reduce
their request to writing. The committee promptly prepared a
letter stating the case for Vallandigham's "release." [172] The
President, in turn, replied with a letter that was really a state
paper. The whole burden of Vallandigham's speeches, noted
Lincoln, seemed to have been to stir up men's minds against the
prosecution of the war. He defended suspension of habeas corpus and the arrest of Vallandigham as essential to "public
safety." [173] The Committee of Nineteen countered with a sec-

ond letter that implied that the summary treatment accorded Vallandigham was an attack upon the rights of all members of the opposition. The second letter again asked the President to revoke the order banishing Vallandigham, "not as a favor, but as a right due to the people of Ohio." [174] Lincoln wisely chose to ignore the second letter of the Committee of Nineteen. He believed that erasing Vallandigham's sentence would be a show of weakness. Furthermore, President Lincoln believed that Vallandigham's utterances had injured the war effort and had given substantial aid and comfort to the enemy.[175]

After Vallandigham's arrival at Niagara Falls, Upper Canada, he hurriedly composed a statement accepting the nomination and defining the issues. His "Address to the People," dated July 15, made a bid for votes as well as for sympathy. It emphasized that civil rights were the central issue of the campaign. It argued that only the Democratic party possessed the qualifications to reunite and rebuild the nation. The Address closed with a rhetorical flourish: "And may the God of heaven and earth so rule the hearts and minds of Americans everywhere that a Constitution maintained, a Union restored, and liberty henceforth made secure, a grander and nobler destiny shall yet be ours than that which blessed our fathers the first two ages of the Republic." [176]

The nomination of Vallandigham had stirred Ohio Republicans to action. They eased General Burnside out of Ohio and made him the scapegoat for the arrest and trial episode. They reintroduced the Union party movement into Ohio politics as an instrument to defeat Vallandigham. Aware that Tod had lost his popularity and convinced that he had served their purpose, Ohio Republicans engineered the selection of "Honest Johnny" Brough, a War Democrat, as the Union party's nominee for the governorship.[177]

The 1863 election campaign was a strange one in many ways. It featured a contest between candidates who were poles apart as to personality and convictions; one was an exile willing to die for his beliefs, the other a citizen who could adjust his views to the changing times. It featured a contest between a divided party, with "war" and "peace" wings, and a party united by its hatred of Vallandigham and hiding behind the Union party label it had devised. It was a contest of ideas, with Vallandigham's followers advocating states' rights, constitutionalism, and peace, while Republicans preached centralism, reunion through war, and emancipation.

Republican strategists made an effort to simplify the complex issues by pretending the contest was simply one between patriotism and treason. Republicans claimed that their party had a monopoly on patriotism, and that Vallandigham's supporters were friends of the rebels. "To vote against this ticket [headed by Brough], as matters now stand," wrote the partisan editor of the *Ashtabula Sentinel,* "is to vote against the country. It is, in fact, TREASON at the ballot box, and a neglect to vote is *half-way treason.*" [178] The flag-waving editor of the *Cincinnati Gazette* boldly called Vallandigham a "traitor," and he saw the ghost of treason under every Democratic bed. "Vallandigham is put in nomination by the Confederates . . . and by means of a secret organization [the Knights of the Golden Circle] instituted by the Secessionists," wrote the *Gazette* editor, "he contrives to seize the machinery of the party. . . ." [179] Republican editors published a forged letter, supposedly written by Vallandigham to a Confederate officer, expressing a wish that the South might win. Vallandigham and Democratic leaders immediately labeled it a hoax and a forgery, but the damaging item continued to circulate as a campaign document. [180]

The Republican State Central Committee printed and circulated a basketful of anti-Vallandigham tracts and campaign documents. One document, "A Savory Dish for Loyal Men," called Vallandigham an out-and-out traitor. [181] Another booklet, "The Peace Democracy, Alias Copperheads," assured gullible readers that Vallandigham had told Jefferson Davis that the Northwest was willing and ready to revolt. The anonymous author compared Vallandigham to Judas Iscariot, and depicted him as a man of "morbid prejudices" and "excess vanity." [182]

Republican propagandists blamed Vallandigham for the New York draft riots of July 13–16 and implied that he helped plan the Morgan Raid into Indiana and Ohio. [183] They popularized a catchy chant:

> "Hurrah for Brough and Abraham,
> And a rope to hang Vallandigham." [184]

A parade of notables invaded Ohio to orate in behalf of Brough. Governor Oliver P. Morton of Indiana even visited Vallandigham's home town to denounce the exiled Ohioan and to tell "a huge crowd" that slavery was dead. [185] John Sherman returned from Washington to campaign for Brough and to condemn Vallandigham. He called the exile "a convicted traitor" and told Daytonians that Vallandigham's election might bring civil war to Ohio. [186] Linking Vallandigham and treason bore political fruit, and a number of Democrats of long standing publicly announced they would support Brough rather than him. [187]

Samuel Medary of the *Crisis* tried to rally the Democratic forces, which reeled under the merciless Republican attacks. His editorials spewed hatred of Republicanism and the Lincoln administration. He blamed the President for all of the nation's ills, even entitled an editorial "Abraham Lincoln More of a Traitor than Jefferson Davis." The new editor of the *Dayton Empire* [188] and the radical who edited the *Hamilton True Telegraph* tried to keep pace with Medary.

Vallandigham's friends followed divergent roads while promoting his candidacy. Some sought votes among the war-weary, depicting Vallandigham as the apostle of peace. Some contended that civil rights could be preserved only if the "military despotism" in Washington was rebuked by a flood of pro-Vallandigham votes: "Every vote that is cast for Vallandigham is a vote for Liberty," wrote one Democratic editor, "and every vote cast for Brough is a vote for Despotism." [189] Others cultivated the spirit of western sectionalism, decrying the ascendancy of New England and eastern capital. These sectionalists claimed that Brough, a railroad president, was "the tool of the monopolists, speculators, and army contractors." [190] Still other Vallandighamers railed against abolitionism, cultivating the twin heresies of racism and negrophobia. "If Abolition were dead and buried beyond the power of resurrection," wrote one Democratic dreamer, "in less than thirty days hereafter, we would have a Union which all the fanatics in Christendom could not disrupt." [191] Abolition-hating Democrats reminded Irish workmen that Brough had praised "the nager" and "damned" the Irish-Americans.[192] "The 'irrepressible conflict' between white and black laborers," warned a Dayton racist, "will be realized in all its vigor upon Ohio soil if the policy of Lincoln and Brough is carried out." [193] Samuel S. Cox, speaking in Vallandigham's behalf in Columbus, derisively denounced Brough as a "flailing Falstaff" and a "fat knight of the corps d'Afrique." [194] When Republicans called Vallandigham a "branded traitor," Democrats retorted that Brough was a "brandied patriot." [195]

While Democrats and Republicans exchanged insults and insinuations, Vallandigham busied himself as best he could. He received scores of visitors, the curious mingling with old friends.[196] He wrote letters to political acquaintances, urging them to make an all out effort to defeat " 'Shoddy' and Shoddy's wife and daughters." [197] He hoped that his friends could convince Brough to withdraw from the canvass, so the Ohio Democratic organization could be "one and indivisible." [198] He also awaited news from his brother, the Rev. James L. Vallandigham, who had been arrested at his home in Newark, New Jersey, for criticizing the Lincoln administration and praying publicly for peace.

In mid-August the Ohioan moved his base of operations

from Niagara Falls to Windsor, across the river from Detroit. "He has changed his *base*," observed editor William D. Bickham of the *Dayton Journal*, "but not his *baseness*." [199] In Windsor, Vallandigham secured quarters in the Hirons House, almost next to the ferry landing. His reception room faced the river, giving the occupant a fine view of Detroit. Through the window, he could also see the United States gunboat "Michigan," a reminder of the federal power that had made him a prisoner and an exile. [200] Federal agents in Detroit kept track of Vallandigham's every move; they had orders to arrest him as soon as he set foot upon Michigan soil and send him under strong guard to Fort Warren. [201]

In Windsor there were even more visitors than had come to Niagara Falls; he often had to lock his doors to secure quiet. [202] He wrote a number of letters to be read at Democratic rallies. He met delegations of Ohio Democrats, and he applauded the energy of George E. Pugh in campaigning extensively for the "Union Democratic" ticket. Pugh publicly promised that if Vallandigham were elected, he would lead 100,000 Democrats to Windsor to escort the exile back to Ohio and the Statehouse. [203] Vallandigham maintained an air of optimism, even though his friends knew that the tide was swinging against them.

As the weeks went by, the Republicans gained confidence. Then they became concerned with piling up a winning majority "as overwhelming as possible": [204] a decisive margin would silence the blatant Democratic critics of the administration. Republican strategists knew they had forty thousand soldier votes in the bag to pad the majority. ". . . Every Ohioan in Washington who could possibly get away," wrote a federal appointee, "held it to be his duty to go home and vote." [205] Republicans recognized that the Union victories at Gettysburg and Vicksburg would help their cause by giving the lie to Vallandigham's contentions that the South could not be con-

quered, and that the Lincoln administration had failed miserably.

Election day dawned bright and clear. The forests and the
plains were clothed in a wealth of sunshine and beauty. Multi-
colored leaves in the autumn woods were admired by the voters
as they went to the polls. But October 13 was an unlucky day
for Vallandigham and the Ohio Democratic organization.
Brough defeated the exiled Ohioan by more than 100,000 votes,
including 43,000 soldier votes.[206]

Republicans crowed lustily, and Brough received scores of
congratulatory telegrams. "Your election is a glorious victory,"
Secretary of War Edwin M. Stanton telegraphed, "worthy of
the rejoicing which will greet it." [207] "Count every ballot,"
wrote Salmon P. Chase, the secretary of the treasury, "a bullet
fairly aimed at the heart of the rebellion." [208] Lincoln, too, was
elated, although he wished Brough's majority had been even
larger. "Glory to God in the highest," the President supposedly
telegraphed to Brough, "Ohio has saved the Union." [209]

Republican editors wrote words of joy, for the election returns seemed to vindicate their views. Ohio soldiers, well indoc-
trinated by Republican propaganda, cheered lustily when they
heard of Vallandigham's defeat at the polls.[210] "Have we not
made copper suffer in Ohio," queried a Buckeye supporter of
Lincoln, "by converting it into dross?" [211] Dayton Republicans
sponsored a "Union jollification, and some of the displays and
transparencies added insult to injury. One transparency
showed a coffin bearing the legend "Copperhead Remains—
please forward to Winsor [sic], Canada"; another bore a picture of a dejected Vallandigham with a bodyguard: a cordon of
copperhead snakes; a third displayed the words "Ohio stands by
her soldiers!" [212] Republicans also interpreted the election returns in Ohio as a repudiation of the peace movement that
Vallandigham had come to symbolize.[213]

Ohio Democrats offered a variety of excuses for their defeat in the elections of October 13. Some, seeking a scapegoat, blamed Vallandigham for all of their party's ills. They sought to reorganize their party machinery, purging it of the Vallandigham element.[214] Medary of the *Crisis* closed his eyes to the facts and blamed the Democratic defeat upon "widespread fraud and stuffing of the ballot-boxes by a systematic arrangement of the *Union Leagues,* through force, fraud, and perjury." [215] Democrats realized that the soldier vote, to a degree, was a controlled vote: one Republican colonel reported that his regiment (Twenty-third Ohio) gave Brough a unanimous ballot (514 votes), and that Vallandigham did not get a single vote in the entire brigade.[216]

Some of the Democrats made wry faces as they swallowed the bitter medicine of political defeat. "He who sustains this war upon its present basis is not a Democrat," wrote the embittered editor of the *Dayton Empire,* "and if he claims to be such, he should be kicked out of the Democratic organization into the Abolitionist ranks where he belongs." [217] One of Vallandigham's best friends viewed the election returns more realistically. "The people have voted in favor of the war and the way it is at present conducted," Thomas O. Lowe wrote to his brother, "and it has to go on of course. The case went to the jury and they have rendered their verdict and I am not disposed to move for a new trial." [218]

Vallandigham, in Windsor, refused to believe that Ohio voters had cast him overboard. In a post-election letter to the "Democrats of Ohio" he thanked all for their votes, sympathy, and efforts. He asked Democrats to retain their spirit and maintain their principles and their party organization. Time and events, he added, would vindicate him.[219] "As to the future," he wrote to his lonely wife, "*posterity will vote for me,* and there will be neither chance nor motive for violence or fraud." [220]

After the excitement of the election had run its course, life became lonelier for the exile. The chance of victory in the election had given him a ray of hope, but defeat made the future seem bleak and dreary. He considered renting a residence and having his wife and son join him in exile, but he was beset by money woes. In Dayton Mrs. Vallandigham lived frugally, charging groceries at the stores and receiving provisions from local Democrats.[221] Vallandigham devoted most of his time to reading and studying—books furnished an escape from reality. He also took long hikes into the nearby woods or walked along the river banks, trying his hand with a fishing pole. The visitors, so numerous before the election, dwindled in number. Once a group of sympathetic students from the University of Michigan came to call upon the well-known exile. He avoided discussing politics, giving a speech on morality and virtue instead. He did add, however, that a statesman must be guided by principles rather than expediency, as a mariner is guided by a compass. "It is easy to be a politician or a demogogue," he told the attentive students, "it is easy to sail with the wind or float with the current." [222] In part, the speech was a justification of his own inflexibility and his conviction that he was right and that the majority of the voters of Ohio were wrong.

He spent a lonely Christmas, cheered somewhat by the news that Samuel Medary had taken the lead to raise money for a "Vallandigham Fund" [223] to help his wife buy household necessities and to enable him to pay for his board and room. He was disheartened, however, to see the split in the Democratic party widening; Medary of the *Crisis* led the "unconditional peace party," while George W. Manypenny of the *Ohio Statesman* (Columbus) headed the War Democrats.[224] The halo of the martyr, meanwhile, lost some of its glow. His faith in Providence—and in his own righteousness—however, helped to sustain him in his exile. ". . . I will with faith and patience," he wrote to his brother, "devote myself to those studies and pursuits which shall fit me for whatever Providence may yet have designed for me." [225]

Vallandigham hoped against hope that the Supreme Court of the United States might bring him freedom and vindication (earlier, in *Ex parte Merryman* [1861], the Court had reprimanded the administration). George E. Pugh applied to the Supreme Court for a writ of certiorari to review and annul the proceedings of the military commission that had tried Vallandigham. The Court, however, refused to accept Pugh's arguments, for it denied that it had appellate jurisdiction in such cases. The Court thus side-stepped the question and avoided a clash with the military while the war was in progress.[226] "The Supreme Court," noted one Ohio Democrat sarcastically, "has no jurisdiction in matters of individual liberty, unless the party claiming redress can prove that he was outraged *according to law.*" [227]

The news from Ohio was as disheartening as that from Washington. Democratic editors felt the punitive hand of "King Mob." The *Democratic Press* at Wauseon was destroyed by "a mob of soldiers" in mid-February, 1864. A couple of weeks later, some soldiers, home on furlough, invaded the building that housed the offices and printing plant of the *Dayton Empire,* destroying equipment and threatening to hang the editor.[228] Then on March 5 soldiers and civilians joined hands in mobbing the quarters of the *Greenville Democrat.*[229] Democrats threatened to enforce the "law of retaliation" vindictively, and Vallandigham wrote from Windsor endorsing the law of reprisals: ". . . instant, summary, and ample reprisals upon the persons and property of the men at home, *who by language and conduct are always inciting these outrages.*" [230]

Some Democrats felt that their safety lay in organizing a secret society, one that would serve as a mutual protection society and advance Democratic party fortunes.[231] Some Peace Democrats, like Harrison H. Dodd of Indiana, wanted a secret league created as a vehicle to insure the nomination of a "peace man" as the party's 1864 presidential candidate. Two such Democratic secret societies had been created in 1863, but both languished on the vine.[232]

Vallandigham inadvertently became enmeshed in the efforts

of Peace Democrats to establish the Sons of Liberty as a secret society to protect the rights of Democrats, win elections, and counteract the Republican-sponsored Union Leagues.[233] At the insistence of Dodd and Dr. Thomas C. Massey of Ohio he accepted the nominal headship of the Sons of Liberty, with the title "Supreme Commander." But it was never more than a paper organization, existing more in theory than in fact. As "Supreme Commander," Vallandigham never issued an order or called a meeting. Yet Vallandigham and others who claimed they belonged to the Sons of Liberty wanted Republicans to believe that a widespread Democratic secret order existed to defend civil rights, secure free elections, and advance the party's welfare.[234]

Early in 1864, political-minded grooms started preparing for the presidential sweepstakes. Lincoln's supporters worked backstage to effect his renomination and re-election. Democrats hoped that the presidential ambitions of Salmon P. Chase and John C. Frémont would create a Republican party rupture and enhance the election of a Democratic candidate.[235] Democrats like Samuel S. Cox also hoped that their party would name George B. McClellan as the presidential nominee; they believed that "Little Mac" stood the best chance of defeating Lincoln. Peace Democrats, on the other hand, opposed the nomination of McClellan and hoped that Horatio Seymour or Franklin Pierce would throw their hats into the ring.

The approach of the state Democratic convention at Columbus on March 23, 1864, brought the clash of the Peace Democrats and the War Democrats out into the open. Samuel S. Cox publicly announced he favored McClellan. Some Peace Democrats of Ohio wanted Vallandigham named as a favorite son.[236] At a meeting the Democratic organization of Montgomery County named Clement L. Vallandigham as "the first choice" for the presidency.[237]

McClellan's Ohio supporters worked actively to prevent the

selection of Vallandigham as one of the four delegates-at-large to the national convention. Democratic congressmen and members of the state slate also feared that Vallandigham's "dead weight" might affect their election or re-election.[238] Vallandigham's friends, on the other hand, marshaled their forces to secure a delegate's post for the exiled Ohioan.[239] The first ballot assured the selection of William Allen, Allen Thurman, and George H. Pendleton as delegates. Rufus P. Ranney, Vallandigham, and Medary, in that order, came next, but lacked a majority. Medary's friends threw their support to Vallandigham on the second ballot, but Ranney won the post by a narrow margin: Ranney, 216½; Vallandigham, 211½; and William M. Corry, 1.[240] McClellan's supporters applauded, for they were pleased that the Vallandighamers had been rebuked.[241]

Vallandigham nevertheless remained the symbol of the peace movement, and the months that followed seemed to give an impetus to the peace crusade. War weariness nurtured the peace movement. In Congress, Alexander Long boldly suggested that the administration turn to peace and end the "slaughter." "If the time ever was when the Union could be restored by war," he emphatically declared, "it has long since been dispelled by emancipation, confiscation, . . . and like proclamations." [242] Dr. John McElwee of the *Hamilton True Telegraph* entitled an editorial "Stop the War" and ended his plea for peace bluntly: "This murderous crusade has gone on long enough." [243]

Vallandigham, meanwhile, grew restless in his Canadian retreat. He wanted to return to Ohio to engage in the crusade for peace and compromise. He knew his friends sought to have him named as a delegate to the national Democratic convention from the Third Congressional District.[244] Furthermore, his mother was seriously ill—perhaps upon her deathbed. Then, too, Confederate agents in Canada were anxious to implicate him in their schemes, and they embarrassed him by their very presence in Windsor. Perhaps Lincoln might ignore him if he returned.

Vallandigham decided to use the Third District Democratic convention, scheduled to be held in Hamilton on June 15, as an excuse to return to Ohio. Dr. John McElwee and David Brant, two prominent Hamilton Democrats, hurried to Windsor to escort the exile back to Butler County. In disguise, Vallandigham crossed the border. The rest of the trip was uneventful, and Vallandigham reached the home of a friend two miles outside of Hamilton. There he planned a dramatic re-entry into public life.[245]

While the Montgomery County delegates were in caucus on the morning of convention day, a messenger handed a Dayton representative a note from Vallandigham. The letter stated that Vallandigham was "two miles from Hamilton and would speak at 3 o'clock." [246] The announcement created some excitement, and friends hurried over to the quarters of the *Hamilton True Telegraph* to print handbills stating that Vallandigham had returned and that he would address the crowd.

When the convention reconvened at one-thirty in the afternoon, Mr. Chris Hughes of Hamilton read from a handbill that Vallandigham was back in Butler County and would speak at three o'clock. "The whole crowd," noted a reporter, "joined in one prolonged, furious, and overwhelming yeli that lasted for several minutes." [247] The convention then proceeded to the business of naming two delegates to the national convention. The selection, by acclamation, fell upon Vallandigham and Chris Hughes.

The convention then adjourned to the courthouse yard where nearly three thousand interested spectators had congregated. Vallandigham's platform appearance electrified the crowd. "He came unheralded from his exile," a devotee later wrote, "and his sudden appearance was like an apparition from the clouds." [248] Vallandigham spoke deliberately, denying he was guilty of any crime. He was ready to answer any charges before any civil court, and he said that the 186,000 Democrats who voted for him the previous fall were his "sureties." He hoped Democrats would help him enjoy his full civil rights:

> I am here for peace, not turbulance [*sic*]; for quiet, not convulsions; for law and order, not anarchy. Let no man of the Democratic party begin an act of violence or disorder; but let none shrink from any responsibility, however urgent, if forced upon him. Careful of the rights of others, let him see to it that he fully and fearlessly exacts his own. Subject to rightful authority in all things, let him submit to excess or usurpation in nothing. Obedience to the Constitution and the law—let him demand and have the full measure of protection which law and Constitution secure to him.[249]

Federal agents in the crowd scribbled down his statements.[250] No incidents occurred. In the evening Vallandigham returned to Dayton and to his wife and son.

Governor Brough, excited at the news of Vallandigham's return to Ohio, asked for his arrest and imprisonment.[251] Most Ohio Republicans, however, advised President Lincoln to ignore Vallandigham—to "let him be." [252] The President wisely did so, hoping that the taint of treason linked to Vallandigham might rub off on the Democratic party.

Grant's failures before Richmond and a Republican party rift gave Democrats cause to hope and prompted them to postpone the date of their national convention to August 29. Peace Democrats favored the postponement. Another call for 500,000 troops by President Lincoln could hurt his chances of reelection—might make Lincoln *"deader* than dead." [253]

By the time Democrats met in Chicago on August 29, McClellan's nomination was a foregone conclusion. Bets of four to one were offered that McClellan would receive the nomination on the first ballot.[254] Vallandigham and Fernando Wood of New York, both recognized Peace Democrats, pledged themselves to support the candidate of the convention, whoever he would be.[255] The first task, however, was to write a platform, and Vallandigham secured an appointment to the twenty-three member platform committee. He sought the chairmanship of the committee, but McClellan-pledged delegates bestowed the honor upon James Guthrie of Kentucky.[256] Vallandigham, nevertheless, wrote the second or "peace" resolution of the "Chicago Platform," carrying it through the subcommittee and the general committee despite "persistent opposition" of the McClellan men. The peace plank, however, was a far cry from the peace-at-any-price position favored by such adamant "armistice men" as Alexander Long or William M. Corry. It demanded that immediate efforts be made to bring about a cessation of hostilities, "with a view to an ultimate convention of all the States." [257]

After the adoption of the platform—Alexander Long cast one of the four votes against it—the convention set about nominating McClellan. On the first ballot McClellan received but seventeen of Ohio's forty-two votes. Horatio Seymour of New York, who insisted he was not a candidate, received four, including the votes of William Allen and Allen G. Thurman; and Thomas H. Seymour, of Connecticut, received twenty-one votes, including those of Vallandigham, Alexander Long, and George H. Pendleton. But before the first ballot results were announced, various state delegations clambered aboard the McClellan bandwagon. The recast ballot of the Ohio delegation gave McClellan thirty votes and Thomas H. Seymour, choice of the peace men, but twelve votes. Vallandigham, switching to McClellan on the recount, made the motion that the nomination be unanimous. Second place on the ticket went to George H. Pendleton, regarded more as a Peace Democrat than a War Democrat (he seemed to keep a foot in each camp).

As soon as the convention adjourned, Vallandigham returned home to campaign for both McClellan and the Chicago Platform. When reports reached Vallandigham that McClellan intended to repudiate the peace plank in his letter of acceptance of the nomination, the Dayton Democrat advised him, "for Heaven's sake," not to do so, or "two hundred thousand men in the West" would "withhold their support." [258] Vallandigham evidently thought that McClellan would follow his advice, for two days later he gave a speech in his home town in which he assured his listeners that the Democratic platform meant "peace and possible reunion" and that no conditions were attached to the "peace plank." [259]

McClellan, regarding the peace plank as a millstone around his neck and at variance with his principles, ignored Vallandigham's advice and came out for war. He wrote a letter in which he accepted the nomination but rejected the peace plank. McClellan's repudiation of the peace plank embarrassed Vallandigham, and he sulked in his tent. The Daytonian, however, was a practical politician who had speaking engagements listed on his calendar, so he bowed to the entreaties of George H. Pendleton and one of McClellan's agents [260] and entered the lists.

In a speech before some of the faithful in Dayton, Vallandigham introduced George H. Pendleton, the vice-presidential nominee, to the crowd and said a few words in defense of states' rights, peace, and the Chicago Platform.[261] A week later, on September 24, he spoke in Sydney, Shelby County. He praised McClellan as an excellent general, a capable administrator, and an honorable man; but he publicly spanked "Little Mac" for repudiating the peace plank and deviating from Democratic principles. The practical choice, however, lay between McClellan and Lincoln, and Vallandigham preferred McClellan and conservatism.[262] From Sydney, Vallandigham went to Banker's Grove, then to Post Town, Chillicothe, and Hamden.

While Vallandigham was campaigning for the Democratic ticket, Judge Advocate General Joseph Holt introduced a new issue into the political canvass. At the request of the secretary of war, the judge advocate general investigated rumors that an extensive serpentine society, linked to the Democratic Party, existed in the northern states. Then the judge advocate general authored a 14,000-word report and saw to it that the account appeared as a campaign pamphlet. Holt's report claimed that a subversive secret society, entitled the Sons of Liberty, existed in the North. Vallandigham commanded the "northern half," Confederate General Sterling Price headed the southern division. The Sons of Liberty, asserted Holt, was but the successor to the traitorous Knights of the Golden Circle and the nefarious Order of American Knights. He set Ohio's membership in the Sons of Liberty at 40,000, and he even linked the "McClellan Minute-Men" to the subversive society. Treason lurked in antechambers, and Vallandigham held the scepter! The report closed with a literary flourish: "Judea produced but one Judas Iscariot, and Rome, from the sinks of her demoralization, produced but one Cataline; and yet, as events prove, there has arisen in our land an entire brood of traitors, all animated by the same parricidal spirit, and all struggling with the same ruthless malignity for the dismemberment of the Union." [263]

Holt's report became an effective campaign document. Vallandigham felt compelled to explain his link to the Sons of Liberty on his speaking tour to Chicago, Peoria, and Joliet. He insisted that the Sons of Liberty was a patriotic society, organized to defend constitutional rights, win Democratic votes, and counteract the work of the Union Leagues. In an open letter he labeled Holt's charges "absolute falsehoods and fabrications from beginning to end." "They are false in the aggregate, and false in detail," wrote Vallandigham. "More than that, they are as preposterous and ridiculous as they are without foundation. . . . " [264]

The Holt report helped to turn public sentiment against Vallandigham and McClellan. Even long-time supporters of Vallandigham were taken in by the secret society exposé. [265] Sherman's capture of Atlanta also helped, and so did war prosperity, "healing by its touch the wounds of war and desolation." [266] Vallandigham, in a way, was the Achilles' heel of

McClellan; in the public mind Vallandigham spelled treason, and some of the black brand rubbed off on the Democratic party.

The 1864 election returns assured Lincoln of a second term and proved to be a resounding Republican victory. Not only did the Ohio voters choose Lincoln over McClellan, but such prominent Ohio Democrats as S. S. Cox and Alexander Long tasted the dregs of defeat.

After the election Vallandigham turned his attention to long neglected private affairs. A public notice in the *Dayton Empire* stated that he had resumed the practice of law—that his home would double as his law office.[267] He spent much time in his huge library, reading and studying.

In March, 1865, Vallandigham voluntarily testified before a military commission meeting in Cincinnati and trying prisoners linked to a Chicago-based conspiracy to free Confederate prisoners held in nearby Camp Douglas. Before the commission Vallandigham explained why and how he became associated with the Sons of Liberty. He testified, under oath, that the objectives of the secret society were honorable: to protect the rights of Democrats, to win elections, and to nullify the activities of the Union Leagues.[268]

Lincoln's death at the hands of an assassin shocked the country and saddened Vallandigham. He continued to believe that Lincoln had grievously wronged him, but he rose above personal resentment to express his horror at the act of assassination. He complimented Lincoln for his "most liberal and conciliatory course" of "the last three months." "He who at this moment does not join in the common thrill and shudder which shocks the land," Vallandigham wrote, "is no better than the assassin." [269]

Vallandigham survived Lincoln by a little more than six years. During those six years he had trouble accepting the results of the war, and he became both a critic of Radical

Republican reconstruction policy and the stormy petrel of Ohio politics. Try as he would, he could not shake off the stigma that he was a Copperhead, a critic, and an obstructionist during the Civil War years. His Republican opponents had called him "a traitor," but he was actually a constitutionalist and a conservative who opposed the changes that the Civil War was bringing to America: centralizing the government, extending the frontiers of democracy (freedom for the slaves), and putting industrialism in the driver's seat. He always wanted to turn the calendar back to the prewar years, to the days of the federal union and of slavery. He sincerely believed in the slogan "The Constitution as it is, the Union as it was." He was always conscious of his own rectitude and prone to believe that time would vindicate him, but the storm of nationalism and the apotheosis of Lincoln helped to cast a cloud over his head. He never seemed to grasp the lesson that those who swim against the current seldom win the plaudits of posterity.

1. Some of the speeches Vallandigham gave during the campaign of 1860 are included in *The Record of Hon. C. L. Vallandigham on Abolition, the Union, and the Civil War* (Columbus, Ohio, 1863) as well as in the columns of the *Dayton Daily Empire,* edited by a close personal friend.

2. The long "Salutatory Address," which appeared in the *Empire* of September 1, 1847, is included in entirety in James L. Vallandigham, *A Life of Clement L. Vallandigham* (Baltimore, 1872), pp. 56–58.

3. *Congressional Globe,* 36th Cong., 1st Sess. Appendix, 43.

4. *Ibid.,* p. 58.

5. "History of the Abolition Movement: Speech Delivered at a Democratic Meeting Held in Dayton, Ohio, October 29, 1855," published in full in *Record of Hon. C. L. Vallandigham,* pp. 5–39.

6. Letter (typewritten copy), Vallandigham to Stanley Matthews, Jan. 31, 1850, Clement L. Vallandigham Letters, Southern History Collections, Library of the University of North Carolina.

7. *Cong. Globe,* 35th Cong., 1st Sess. Part III, 2320.

8. Letter, Vallandigham to "Editor of the *Enquirer*," Oct. 22, 1859, published in *Cincinnati Enquirer*, Oct. 26, 1859.

9. Most of the Ohio cities that returned Democratic majorities possessed a large quota of immigrant-Americans. The "raw Dutch" of Dayton and the Third Congressional District invariably voted Democratic, and Democratic politicians always placed several German-Americans on the county election tickets. The editor of the Republican-oriented *Dayton Daily Journal* of July 16, 1862, complained that Vallandigham used Negrophobia as an "electioneering weapon" with the "raw Dutch" and the Irish. "The jealousy of the Low German and Irish against the free negro," wrote the touring reporter of a European newspaper, "was sufficient to set them against the war which would have brought four million of their black rivals into competition for that hard and dirty work which American freedom bestowed on them"—(London) *The Times*, Dec. 1, 1863. A fuller analysis of the immigrant-American vote in the election of 1860 awaits someone interested in analyzing election returns and population backgrounds.

10. The conflict of southern and Yankee culture in the states north of the Ohio River is admirably treated in Richard L. Power, *Planting, Corn Belt Culture: The Impress of the Upland Southerner and Yankee in the Old Northwest* (Indianapolis, 1953). In his specialized study, "Economic and Political Aspects of Western Copperheadism" (Ph.D. dissertation, Ohio State University, 1942), John Stipp put the historical microscope upon the Democratic counties and concluded that the Copperhead (Democratic opposition to the Lincoln administration) country was the poorer and more backward area of Ohio. When Samuel P. Heintzelman watched a Democratic rally in the Ohio backwoods, he noted that many of the women wore riding skirts "so old, rusty, ragged & dirty, they might have belonged to their grandmothers."—Heintzelman "Journal," entry of Oct. 20, 1864, Samuel P. Heintzelman Papers, Library of Congress.

11. F. T. Brown, "Recollections of C. L. Vallandigham," published in the *St. Paul Pioneer*, June 21, 1871. Brown's recollections were published shortly after Vallandigham's death in 1871.

12. *Dayton Daily Empire*, July 26, 1860. Only eight Ohio Democratic newspapers—all charged with being recipients of federal patronage—supported the Breckinridge ticket.

13. Entry of Sept. 26, 1860, Daniel L. Medlar "Journal" (MS), Dayton Room, Dayton and Montgomery County Public Library; *Dayton Daily Empire*, Sept. 24, 1860.

14. *Cincinnati Enquirer*, Nov. 10, 1860; *Dayton Daily Journal*, Nov. 15, 1860.

15. Quoted in Vallandigham, *Life of Clement L. Vallandigham*, p. 141.

16. *Ibid.*, p. 144.

17. *Dayton Daily Journal*, Dec. 22, 1860.

18. *Record of Hon. C. L. Vallandigham*, pp. 239–40. The occasion was a serenade given for George E. Pugh of Ohio because of an anticoercion speech he made in the Senate on December 20. John J. Crittenden and Vallandigham also spoke, and Vallandigham took a strong anticoercion stand.

19. *Dayton Daily Journal*, Dec. 22, 1860, Jan. 11, 1861.

20. *Cong. Globe*, 36th Cong., 2d Sess. 237; *Dayton Daily Journal*, Jan. 18, 1861. The Missouri Compromise of 1820 established the 36°30′ line (the southern boundary of Missouri) to divide the rest of the Louisiana Purchase between "free" and "slave" territory. The Dred Scott Decision of 1857 negated the 36°30′ line and, in effect, opened up all of the territories to slavery.

21. *Cong. Globe*, 36th Cong., 2d Sess. Appendix, 23–42. Later, Vallandigham explained his scheme more fully in a letter to the "Editor of the *Enquirer*," dated Feb. 14, 1861, and published in the *Cincinnati Daily Enquirer*, Feb. 14, 1861. Misrepresentation caused him to explain his scheme and the two proposed amendments again in another letter (dated Dec. 18, 1862) published in the *Daily Enquirer* of Dec. 18, 1862.

22. *Dayton Daily Journal*, Feb. 9, 12, 14, 22; Mar. 4, 23, 1861.

23. Letter, Vallandigham to "Editor of the *Enquirer*," Feb. 14, 1861, published in the *Cincinnati Daily Enquirer*, Feb. 19, 1861 and in the (Columbus) *Crisis*, Feb. 28, 1861.

24. *Dayton Daily Empire*, Mar. 29, 30; Apr. 13, 1861.

25. *Cincinnati Daily Enquirer*, Feb. 12; Mar. 30, 1861. The economic ties of Cincinnati and the South are treated in Charles R. Wilson, "Cincinnati, a Southern Outpost in 1860–61?", *Mississippi Valley Historical Review*, XXIV (March, 1938), 473–82, and in Frank L. Klement, "Economic Aspects of Middle Western Copperheadism," *Historian*, XIV (Autumn, 1951), 27–44.

26. *Crisis*, Jan. 31; Apr. 2, 1861. The sectional aspects of Midwestern Copperheadism are revealed in Charles R. Wilson, "The *Cincinnati Daily Enquirer* and Civil War Politics: A Study in Copperhead Opinion" (Ph.D. dissertation, University of Chicago, 1934), and in Frank L. Klement, "Middle Western Copperheadism and the Genesis of the Granger Movement," *Mississippi Valley Historical Review*, XXXVIII (March, 1952), 679–94.

27. *Cincinnati Daily Enquirer*, Jan. 31, 1861.

28. *Prairie Farmer* (Chicago), June 6, 1861.

29. Vallandigham had been elected brigadier general in August, 1857.

His brigade (Third Brigade, Second Division, Ohio Volunteers) took part in the Sept. 28–30, 1857, military encampment at the Montgomery County Fair Grounds. Both Vallandigham and his brigade won compliments from the commanding general.

30. *Dayton Daily Journal*, Apr. 17, 1861.

31. Vallandigham, "Card to the *Enquirer*," Apr. 17, 1861, published in the *Cincinnati Daily Enquirer*, Apr. 20, 1861.

32. Letter, Vallandigham to Rev. Sabin Hough, Apr. 30, 1861, published in the *Dayton Daily Journal*, Sept. 18, 1861.

33. *Crisis*, Apr. 16, 23, 30, 1861.

34. Letter, Vallandigham to Richard H. Hendrickson, N. G. Oglesby, John McClellan, *et al.*, May 13, 1861, published in the *Crisis*, May 23, 1861.

35. The incident is treated in cursory fashion in *Record of Hon. C. L. Vallandigham*, p. 242.

36. *Cong. Globe*, 37th Cong., 1st Sess. 59, 100, 130–32, 171, 332, 348. Vallandigham's peace speech of July 10, 1861, was printed in full in the *Crisis*, July 25, 1861.

37. Entry of Aug. 12, 1861, Medlar "Journal."

38. *Cincinnati Daily Enquirer*, Mar. 11, 17, 1860; *Stark County Democrat* (Canton), Sept. 11, 1861. Tod's efforts to undermine and wreck labor unions is exposed in Ruth Wood Gold, "The Attitude of Labor in the Ohio Valley toward the Civil War" (M.A. thesis, Ohio State University, 1948).

39. Letter, Vallandigham to Alexander S. Boys, Aug. 13, 1861, Alexander S. Boys Papers, Ohio Historical Society.

40. Medary had sought a consular appointment from Polk, only to be double-crossed by Tod, who promised to deliver it. The incident is treated in Edgar A. Holt, "Party Politics in Ohio, 1840–1850," *Ohio State Archaeological and Historical Quarterly*, XXXVIII (1929), 47–182, 260–402.

41. *Ohio Statesman* (Columbus), Aug. 1, 1861.

42. Entries of Aug. 29–30, 1861, Medlar, "Journal"; *Dayton Daily Journal*, Aug. 31, 1861.

43. Letter, Thomas O. Lowe to "Dear Johnnie," Aug. 24, 1861, Thomas O. Lowe Papers, Dayton and Montgomery County Public Library.

44. *Cincinnati Daily Enquirer*, Sept. 17, 1861; *Dayton Daily Journal*, Sept. 18, 1861.

45. *Ohio Statesman*, Aug. 11, 1861.

46. *Dayton Daily Journal*, Aug. 22, Oct. 10, 1861.

47. *Ohio State Journal* (Columbus), July 24, Oct. 1, 1861; *Dayton Daily Journal*, Sept. 27, Oct. 7, 1861.

48. *Dayton Daily Journal*, Oct. 9, 1861.

49. Entry of Oct. 8, 1861, Medlar "Journal."

50. *Dayton Daily Journal*, Oct. 9, 1861.

51. On November 8, 1861. The incident produced considerable war talk on both sides of the Atlantic.

52. *Cong. Globe*, 37th Cong., 2d Sess. 5.

53. *Ibid.*, pp. 101, 208–12. The Republican-edited *Dayton Daily Journal*, Jan. 4, 1862, stated that Vallandigham was "Jeff. Davis' prophet": "He is a prophet of evil, speaking with a lying tongue. He is a prophet without honor in his own, or any other country, save in 'Secessia,' where his predictions of evil to our Government are hailed with delight, and his name is enrolled in the calendar of secession saints."

54. *Cong. Globe*, 37th Cong., 2d Sess. 67. "Vallandigham's resolution is a good joke—for him—pretty sharp," wrote John W. Kees, Democratic editor of the *Circleville Watchman* and outspoken critic of Lincoln and the war. Kees added, "His friends better admonish him that if he does not desire to be expelled, he should not get so sarcastically funny."—letter, John W. Kees to S. S. Cox, Dec. 20, 1861, Samuel Sullivan Cox Papers (microfilm copies), Hayes Memorial Library, Fremont, Ohio.

55. Letter (photostatic copy), Vallandigham to Franklin Pierce, Apr. 11, 1862, Franklin Pierce Papers. Library of Congress; "Proceedings of Congress," summarized in the *Crisis*, Jan. 29, Apr. 30, 1862.

56. Letter, Vallandigham to Hon. Alexander S. Boys, Jan. 27, 1862, Boys Papers.

57. Quoted in Vallandigham, *Vallandigham*, p. 174.

58. Letter, L. A. Pierce to Zachariah Chandler, Dec. 6, 1861, Zachariah Chandler Papers, Library of Congress.

59. Entry of Jan. 6, 1862, Charles Mason "Diary, 1862," Charles Mason Papers, State Department of History and Archives, Historical Library, Des Moines.

60. *Cong. Globe*, 37th Cong., 2d Sess. 879.

61. *Ibid.*, 879–81.

62. Quoted in Vallandigham, *Vallandigham*, p. 192.

63. Letters, J. H. Geiger to Wade, Feb. 5, 1862, and Peter Zinn to Wade, Apr. 15, 1862, Benjamin F. Wade Papers, Library of Congress.

64. Samuel S. Cox, *Three Decades of Federal Legislation, 1855–1885* (Providence, 1885), p. 88. Wade's friend-biographer (Albert G. Riddle)

called him "the first man in the Senate," and another devotee, Noah Brooks, characterized Wade as "tender-hearted" and "lovable" and at the same time, vehement, impatient, and possessed of "bulldog obduracy." See Albert G. Riddle, *Recollections of War Times: Reminiscences of Men and Events in Washington, 1860–1865* (Cleveland, 1895), p. 40, and Noah Brooks, *Washington in Lincoln's Time* (New York, 1895), p. 26.

65. *Cong. Globe,* 37th Cong., 2d Sess. 1414–16.

66. *Ibid.,* 1414. James L. Vallandigham treated the Wade-Vallandigham feud at length in his biography; see Vallandigham, *Vallandigham,* pp. 193–202.

67. *Cong. Globe,* 37th Cong., 2d Sess. 1414–16.

68. Letter, June 12, 1862, published in Vallandigham, *Vallandigham,* pp. 211–12.

69. The Homestead Act of May 20, 1862, provided that any citizen, either the head of a family or twenty-one years of age, could acquire a tract of public land, not exceeding 160 acres. In the Morrill Act of July 2, 1862, land from the public domain (30,000 acres for each representative and senator in Congress) was turned over to the states to subsidize agricultural and mechanical education at the college level.

70. *Cong. Globe,* 37th Cong., 2d Sess. 60. Vallandigham's congressional course is reviewed in Christena M. Wahl, "The Congressional Career of Clement Laird Vallandigham" (M.A. thesis, Ohio State University, 1938).

71. "Address of the Democratic Members of the Congress to the Democracy of the United States" (Washington, D.C., 1862), *passim.*

72. Letter, James A. Cravens to William H. English, June 25, 1862, William H. English Papers, Indiana Historical Society Library.

73. Letter, P. C. Smith to Secretary of War Edwin M. Stanton, June 30, 1862, Lafayette C. Baker-Levi C. Turner Papers, 1862–1865, Adjutant General's Records, National Archives. Kees receives some attention in M. O. Wertman "The Democracy of Pickaway County in the Civil War" (M.A. thesis, Ohio State University, 1932).

74. *Crisis,* July 16, 1862.

75. Letter, John D. Martin to Philip Ewing, Jan. 2, 1862, Thomas Ewing Papers, Ohio Historical Society; *Crisis,* Jan. 28, 1862.

76. "Report of the Democratic State Convention, 1862" (MS), dated July 4, 1862, in Samuel Medary Papers, Ohio Historical Society.

77. *Ohio Statesman,* July 4, 7, 8, 1862; *Crisis,* July 9, 16, 1862.

78. *Dayton Daily Empire,* Aug. 4, 1862; *Dayton Daily Journal,* Aug. 4, 1862.

79. The *Dayton Daily Journal,* Sept. 5, 1862 treated the story of the

Democratic convention in Hamilton tersely: "C. L. Vallandigham was re-nominated for Congress yesterday at Hamilton. Of course it was very enthusiastically done, for such a political trickster [Vallandigham] pulls the wires to suit himself. He has determined to ride rough shod over every principle of true Democracy, and has given ample evidence that he will stickle at no means for self-aggrandizement."

80. *Lebanon Star,* n.d., quoted in the *Dayton Daily Journal,* Aug. 6, 1862.

81. Quoted in Lloyd Ostendorf, *Mr. Lincoln Came to Dayton* (Dayton, Ohio 1959), p. 39.

82. *Ibid.*; letter, Sept. 1, 1862, written by a member of Schenck's staff to his nephew (names not given), published in *Dayton Daily Journal,* Sept. 10, 1862.

83. The Republican editor in Dayton ridiculed Vallandigham repeatedly for depending upon the votes of the "Raw Dutch" and the Irish.—*Dayton Daily Journal,* July 16, Oct. 13, 1862.

84. Although Schenck was promoted on September 18, 1862, the commission was dated August 30.

85. *Dayton Daily Journal,* Sept. 20, 1862.

86. *Dayton Daily Empire,* Nov. 25, 1862; *Dayton Daily Journal,* Aug. 21, 1862. The *Lebanon Citizen* was wrecked by "an Abolition mob" on August 12, 1862.

87. *Dayton Daily Journal,* Oct. 11, 13, 1862. One of the forged letters was published the morning of election day so that denials or repudiation could not be made until it would be too late to affect the vote.

88. *Ibid.,* Sept. 12, 23; Oct. 2–4, 6, 11, 13, 1862.

89. Pamphlet, author unknown, "The Secession Record of C. L. Vallandigham" (n.p., 1862), p. 16. Democrats suspected that the pamphlet came off the presses of the *Dayton Journal.*

90. Schenck received 10,720 votes to Vallandigham's 10,126. Warren County (substituted for Preble in the redistricting) gave Schenck 3,312 votes and Vallandigham 1,398 votes, more than cancelling out the majority that Butler County gave the incumbent.

91. Letter, A. T. Goodman to Alexander Long, Oct. 28, 1862, Alexander Long Papers, Cincinnati Historical Society.

92. Letter, William G. Beggs to S. S. Cox, March 25, 1862, Cox Papers. At the time district lines were being redrawn, Beggs wrote: "It is settled that Vallandigham shall be relieved . . . so determined is the feeling that the districts adjoining have been entirely disregarded."

93. *Cincinnati Daily Enquirer,* Oct. 16, 1862; *Crisis,* Oct. 22, 29, 1862; *Dayton Daily Empire,* Oct. 16, 17, 1862.

94. Letter, Robert G. Dun to John G. Dun, Oct. 20, 1862, published in *Ohio History*, LXXI (July, 1962), 143; *Dayton Weekly Empire*, Nov. 1, 1862. A couple of historians have developed the "repudiation" theme; see Winifred A. Harbison, "The Election of 1862 as a Vote of Want of Confidence in President Lincoln," *Papers, Michigan Academy of Science, Arts, and Letters* (1930), pp. 499–513, and Harry E. Pratt, "The Repudiation of Lincoln's War Policy in 1862—Stuart-Swett Congressional Campaign," *Journal of the Illinois State Historical Society*, XXIV (Apr., 1931), 129–140.

95. *Dayton Daily Empire*, Oct. 17, 18, 1862.

96. *Hamilton True Telegraph*, Nov. 20, 1862; (New Lisbon) *Ohio Patriot* (n.d.), quoted in *Dayton Daily Empire*, Nov. 12, 1862; *Coshocton Democrat* (n.d.), quoted in *Dayton Daily Empire*, Nov. 11, 1862.

97. The editor of the *Cincinnati Daily Commercial* (n.d.), quoted in the *Dayton Daily Empire*, Nov. 11, 1862, called Vallandigham a traitor—"servant, sympathizer, and apologist for the seceded states." The Cleveland postmaster, one of the editors of the *Cleveland Leader*, suggested the assassination of Vallandigham, and he wrote: "Brutus slew a man for treason whose lowest characteristics would ennoble Vallandigham."—*Cleveland Leader*, Nov. 2, 1862.

98. The editor of the *Dayton Daily Empire*, Dec. 5, 1862, expressed views held by Vallandigham: "The message is chiefly, and almost exclusively, devoted to the negro question. The 'poor African' seems always uppermost in Abraham's mind. He argues at length in favor of various emancipation schemes, but entirely fails to show that it is either possible, practical, or constitutional."

99. Letter, Thomas P. Dudley to John J. Crittenden, Dec. 8, 1862, John J. Crittenden Papers, Library of Congress.

100. *Cong. Globe*, 37th Cong., 3d Sess. 14–15, 76, 195–96.

101. *Dayton Daily Empire*, Dec. 3, 1862.

102. Pendleton represented the First District of Ohio in Congress. In later years, Democrats considered him a presidential possibility.

103. *New York Times*, Dec. 13, 1862, quoted in the *Dayton Daily Empire*, Dec. 18, 1862.

104. *Ibid.*

105. *Cong. Globe*, 37th Cong., 3d Sess. 104. Vallandigham's resolution was laid on the table by a 79 to 50 vote.

106. *Platte City Conservater* (n.d.), quoted in the *Dayton Daily Empire*, Dec. 12, 1862.

107. *Dayton Daily Empire*, Dec. 9, 1862; (New York) *Freeman's Journal* (n.d.), quoted in *Dayton Daily Empire*, Dec. 23, 1862.

108. George B. Smith, final entry in "Diary, 1862," George B. Smith Papers, Wisconsin State Historical Society Library.

109. *Crisis,* Dec. 31, 1862.

110. *Dayton Daily Empire,* Jan. 3, 1863.

111. *Cong. Globe,* 37th Cong., 3d Sess. 130; *Crisis,* Jan. 28, 1863; *Dayton Daily Empire,* Jan. 3, 5, 7, 10, 16, 1863; *Dubuque Democratic Herald,* Jan. 3, 8, 10, 1863.

112. Letter, Robert Graham Dun to Robert George Dun, Jan. 27, 1863, published in *Ohio History,* LXXI (July, 1962), 143.

113. *Cong. Globe,* 37th Cong., 3d Sess. Appendix, 52–58.

114. *Record of Hon. C. L. Vallandigham,* p. 169; *Dayton Daily Journal,* Jan. 16, 1863; *Boston Herald* (n.d.), quoted in *Dayton Weekly Empire,* Jan. 31, 1863.

115. *Cong. Globe,* 37th Cong., 3d Sess. Appendix, 57–58.

116. *Boston Herald* (n.d.), quoted in the *Dayton Weekly Empire,* Jan. 31, 1863.

117. *Cong. Globe,* 37th Cong., 3d Sess. 318.

118. Quoted in *Dayton Weekly Empire,* Feb. 7, 1863.

119. *Ibid.,* Feb. 7, 14, 1863.

120. (Columbus) *Ohio State Journal* (n.d.), quoted in *Dayton Weekly Empire,* Feb. 7, 1863.

121. Letter, Edwin B. Morgan to Elihu B. Washburne, Jan. 31, 1863, Elihu B. Washburne Papers, Illinois State Historical Library.

122. Quoted in *Dayton Daily Empire,* Jan. 31, 1863.

123. *Ibid.*

124. *Dayton Daily Empire,* Jan 24, 1863.

125. (Millersburg) *Holmes County Farmer* (n.d.), quoted in *Dayton Weekly Empire,* Feb. 21, 1863.

126. *Cincinnati Daily Enquirer,* Jan. 20, 1863.

127. *Crisis,* Jan. 21, 1863.

128. *Hamilton True Telegraph,* Jan. 31, 1863.

129. Letter, C. L. Vallandigham to David F. Cable, Jan. 16, 1863, published in the *Cincinnati Daily Enquirer,* Jan. 30, 1863.

130. *Cong. Globe,* 37th Cong., 3d Sess. Appendix, 174–76.

131. *Ibid.,* pp. 1415–16.

132. *Philadelphia Daily Inquirer,* Mar. 7, 1863; *New York World* (n.d.), quoted in the *Dayton Daily Empire,* Mar. 27, 1863.

133. *Dayton Daily Empire,* Mar. 6, 1863. The *Daily Empire* of March 14, 1863, contains a detailed account of the "homecoming celebration."

134. Carrington commanded the subdistrict of Indiana, a portion of the Department of the Ohio, and frequently reported to his superior, General Burnside. Legends about the Knights of the Golden Circle are partially debunked in Frank L. Klement, *The Copperheads in the Middle West* (Chicago, 1960), pp. 134–69.

135. *Dayton Weekly Empire,* Mar. 14, 1863.

136. *Dayton Daily Empire,* Mar. 19, 1863.

137. *Official Records of the Union and Confederate Armies* (4 series, 128 vols.; Washington, D.C., 1880–1901), Ser. 2, XXIII, Part 2, 237.

138. The volume, of 250 pages, contained "complete and accurate copies" of Mr. Vallandigham's principal speeches. It was published by J. Walter & Company of Cincinnati. Cloth copies sold for one dollar, paperback copies for sixty cents.

139. *Dayton Weekly Empire,* Mar. 28, 1863.

140. *Ohio Statesman,* May 2, 1863.

141. Letter (photostatic copy), Vallandigham to Franklin Pierce, Apr. 11, 1862, Pierce Papers.

142. *Mount Vernon Democratic Banner,* May 9, 1863.

143. "Report on Vallandigham's Military Trial," Citizens' File, 1861–65, War Department Collection of Confederate Records, National Archives.

144. Entry of May 5, 1863, Daniel R. Larned "Journal," Daniel R. Larned Papers, Library of Congress.

145. *Dayton Daily Empire,* May 5, 1863.

146. Letter, Thomas O. Lowe to "Brother Will," May 11, 1863, Lowe Papers.

147. *Ibid.; Dayton Daily Journal,* May 6, 1863.

148. "Special Order, No. 164," published in the *Cincinnati Daily Enquirer,* May 7, 1863, and the *Dayton Daily Journal,* May 7, 1863. The *Dayton Empire* did not resume publication until August, 1863.

149. *Cincinnati Daily Gazette,* May 6, 1863.

150. The address, "To the Democracy of Ohio," was published in the *Crisis,* June 17, 1863.

151. "Proceedings of the Military Commission Convened in Cincinnati, May 6, 1863" (MS.), in Citizens' File, 1861–1865, War Department Collection of Confederate Records, National Archives.

152. *Ibid.*

153. Ex parte Vallandigham, 68 U.S. 243.

154. Ex parte Milligan, 7, U.S. 119, 127.

155. *Crisis,* May 13, 20, 1863.

156. *Hamilton True Telegraph,* June 11, 1863.

157. *Mount Vernon Democratic Banner,* May 16, 1863.

158. Letter, Q. V. Brian to Benjamin Wade, Aug. 4, 1864, Wade Papers.

159. Letter, Halleck to Francis Lieber, May 18, 1863, Francis Lieber Papers, Huntington Library.

160. Gideon Welles, *Diary of Gideon Welles* (3 vols.; New York, 1911), I, 306; Roy P. Basler (ed.), *The Collected Works of Abraham Lincoln* (9 vols.; Brunswick, 1953), III, 506–7.

161. Letter, Merritt Miller to "Brother Clement," May 30, 1863, Merritt Miller Papers, in the possession of V. L. Rockwell, Union Grove, Wisconsin.

162. When Vallandigham spoke in Mount Vernon after the war (Oct. 24, 1867), he reviewed the details of his exile, and the speech was fully reported in the *Dayton Daily Ledger,* Oct. 30, 1867. Major Wiles' report is in the National Archives; see Report, Major William M. Wiles to Brig. Gen. James A. Garfield, May 25, 1863, Citizens' File, 1861–65, War Department Collection of Confederate Records.

163. *Dayton Daily Ledger,* Oct. 30, 1867.

164. *Ibid.*

165. *Ibid.*

166. The *Crisis,* July 15, 1863, reported, "Mrs. V. passed up last week in that direction [Niagara Falls], probably to meet him [Vallandigham] there."

167. *Cincinnati Daily Enquirer,* May 26, 1863; *Mount Vernon Democratic Banner,* May 30, 1863.

168. Letter, A. L. Perrill to S. S. Cox, Feb. 8, 1863, Cox Papers.

169. *Crisis,* May 27, 1863.

170. Letter, John Law to S. S. Cox, June 18, 1863, Cox Papers; *Crisis,* May 20, 1863; *Hamilton True Telegraph,* May 21, 1863; *Detroit Free Press,* June 11, 1863; *Mount Vernon Democratic Banner,* May 23, 1863.

171. *Crisis,* July 17, 1863.

172. Letter, Messrs. Birchard, *et al.,* to Lincoln, June 26, 1863, Robert Todd Lincoln Papers, Library of Congress.

173. Letter, Lincoln to Birchard *et al.*, June 29, 1863, in Basler, *Collected Works of Lincoln,* VI, 300–06.

174. Letter, Messrs. Birchard *et al.*, to Lincoln, July 1, 1863, Robert Todd Lincoln Papers.

175. Before Lincoln's exchange of letters with the Birchard-headed committee, the President had exchanged letters regarding Vallandigham's arrest with New York State Democrats. In Lincoln's reply to the "Albany Resolutions," the President incorporated the oft-quoted query: "Must I shoot a simple-minded soldier boy who deserts, while I must not touch a hair of a wily agitator who induces him to desert?"

176. *Crisis,* July 28, 1863.

177. Letter, R. H. Stephenson to William Henry Smith, Aug. 13, 1863, William Henry Smith Papers. See also Harold Navagon, "The Ohio Gubernatorial Campaign of 1863" (M.A. thesis, Ohio State University, 1934) and Delmer J. Trester, "The Political Career of David Tod" (Ph.D. dissertation, Ohio State University, 1951).

178. *Ashtabula Sentinel* (n.d.), quoted in the *Hamilton True Telegraph,* June 9, 1863.

179. *Cincinnati Weekly Gazette,* Sept. 30, 1863.

180. *Detroit Free Press,* Oct. 29, 1863.

181. "A Savory Dish for Loyal Men," n.p.d. (perhaps it came off the presses of the *Cincinnati Gazette*) ; *Detroit Free Press,* Sept. 14, 1863.

182. "The Peace Democracy Alias Copperheads: Their Record, Speeches, and Votes of Vallandigham and Others" (Columbus, 1863), p. 5, *passim.*

183. *Dayton Daily Journal,* July 15, 16, 1863.

184. *Ibid.,* Oct. 2, 1863.

185. *Cincinnati Daily Gazette* (n.d.), quoted in the *Indianapolis State Sentinel,* Oct. 13, 1863. "Slavery has cut its own throat," said Morton, "and there is no surgery in the reach of Providence to close the wound."

186. *Dayton Daily Journal,* Aug. 27, 1863.

187. *Ibid.,* July 11, 1863.

188. When the *Dayton Empire* resumed publication on August 19, 1863, the editor was George Baber, formerly of the *Nashville Banner,* a "Peace" paper.

189. *Mount Vernon Democratic Banner,* Sept. 5, 1863.

190. *Ibid.*

191. *Dayton Daily Empire,* Aug. 21, 1863.

192. *Ibid.,* Oct. 8, 1863.

193. *Dayton Daily Empire,* Oct. 9, 1863.

194. S. S. Cox, quoted in *Dayton Daily Empire,* Sept. 24, 1863.

195. *Hancock Courier,* Aug. 25, 1863.

196. *Crisis,* Aug. 19, 1863; *Dayton Daily Empire,* Oct. 9, 1863.

197. Letter, Vallandigham to Alexander S. Boys, Sept. 1, 1863, Boys Papers.

198. *Ibid.*

199. *Dayton Daily Journal,* Aug. 15, 1863.

200. *Cleveland Plain Dealer,* Sept. 29, 1863.

201. Telegram, W. P. Anderson to Col. J. R. Smith, Aug. 27, 1863, Citizens' File, 1861–1865, War Department Collection of Confederate Records.

202. *Cleveland Plain Dealer,* Sept. 29, 1863.

203. *Mount Vernon Democratic Banner,* Sept. 5, 1863; *Dayton Daily Empire,* Oct. 12, 1863.

204. Report, Whitelaw Reid to *Cincinnati Gazette,* Oct. 12, 1863, in William Henry Smith Papers.

205. *Ibid.*

206. Brough received 247,216 "home votes" to Vallandigham's 185,464. Montgomery County gave Brough 5,092 votes and Vallandigham 5,025 votes, while Dayton, the exile's home town cast 1,920 votes for Brough and 1,749 votes for his rival.

207. Quoted in the *Dayton Daily Journal,* Oct. 17, 1863.

208. Quoted in the *Indianapolis State Sentinel,* Oct. 16, 1863.

209. Lincoln is often credited with this statement; e.g., Irving L. Schwartz, "Dayton, Ohio, During the Civil War" (M.A. thesis, Miami University, 1949), p. 65, and Eugene H. Roseboom and Francis P. Weisenburger, *A History of Ohio* (New York, 1934), p. 284; but no such telegram or note has been found, and Lincoln scholars believe this to be just another of the mythical quotations attributed to the Civil War President.

210. Entry of Oct. 17, 1863, "Sanderson's Journal," John P. Sanderson Papers, Ohio Historical Society.

211. Letter, T. S. Bell to Joseph Holt, Oct. 16, 1863, Joseph Holt Papers, Library of Congress.

212. *Dayton Daily Journal,* Oct. 17, 1863.

213. *Indianapolis Daily Journal,* Oct. 21, 1863.

214. Letter, C. M. Gould to S. S. Cox, Oct. 15, 1863, Cox Papers.

215. *Crisis*, Oct. 22, 29; Nov. 11, 25, 1863.

216. Entry of Oct. 13, 1863, "Diary," James M. Comly Papers, Ohio Historical Society.

217. *Dayton Daily Empire,* Oct. 14, 1863.

218. Letter, Thomas O. Lowe to "Dear Brother" (Will), Oct. 26, 1863, Lowe Papers.

219. Open letter, Oct. 14, 1863, published in *Dayton Daily Journal,* Oct. 20, 1863.

220. Letter, Vallandigham to his wife, Oct. 14, 1863, published in part in Vallandigham, *Vallandigham,* pp. 335–36.

221. *Hillsboro Gazette* (n.d.), in the *Crisis,* Dec. 16, 1863; *Dayton Daily Empire,* Dec. 14, 15, 1863.

222. *Detroit Free Press,* Nov. 15, 1863; *Dayton Daily Empire,* Nov. 19, 1863.

223. *Crisis,* Dec. 16, 1863.

224. *Dayton Daily Journal,* Nov. 20, 1863.

225. Letter, Vallandigham to brother (James L.), Jan. 16, 1864, published in part in Vallandigham, *Vallandigham,* p. 346.

226. Ex parte Vallandigham, 68 U.S., pp. 243–54 (decision announced on Feb. 15, 1864.

227. *Dayton Daily Empire,* March 1, 1864.

228. Letter, Thomas O. Lowe to "My dear Brother" (Will), Mar. 6, 1864, Lowe Papers.

229. *Dayton Daily Empire,* Mar. 8, 1864.

230. *Ibid.,* Mar. 12, 1864; *Ohio Statesman,* Feb. 17, 1864.

231. Letter, S. Corning Judd to Lincoln, Mar. 3, 1865, John Nocolay–John Hay Papers, Illinois State Historical Library.

232. H. H. Dodd set up an imaginary organization that he called the Sons of Liberty, and Phineas C. Wright of St. Louis planned the Order of American Knights, giving it a strong states'-rights bent.

233. Testimony of Clement L. Vallandigham, Mar. 29, 1865, before the Cincinnati Military Commission, published in the *Cincinnati Daily Enquirer,* Mar. 30, 1865.

234. *Ibid.*; letter, S. Corning Judd to Lincoln, Mar. 3, 1865, Nicolay-Hay Papers.

235. *Dayton Daily Empire,* Feb. 17, 19, 1864.

236. Letter, A. Norton to McClellan, Feb. 28, 1864, George B. McClellan Papers, Library of Congress.

237. *Dayton Daily Empire,* Mar. 21, 1864.

238. *Ibid.,* Mar. 31, 1864.

239. Letter, John A. Trimble to David A. Houk, Apr. 4, 1865, Boys Papers.

240. *Ohio Statesman,* Mar. 24, 1864.

241. Letter, George Morgan to McClellan, Mar. 28, 1864, McClellan Papers.

242. *Cong. Globe,* 38th Cong., 1st Sess. 1499–1503.

243. *Hamilton True Telegraph,* June 16, 1864.

244. Letter, John A. Trimble to David A. Houk, Apr. 4, 1864, Boys Papers.

245. *Dayton Daily Empire,* June 16, 1864.

246. *Ibid.*

247. *Ibid.*

248. Stephen D. Cone, *Biographical and Historical Sketches: A Narrative of Hamilton and Its Residents from 1792 to 1896* (Hamilton, Ohio, 1896), p. 198.

249. *Dayton Daily Empire,* June 16, 1864.

250. Report of William Thorpe (MS), June 18, 1864, Sanderson Papers.

251. Entry of June 15, 1864, "Heintzelman Journal."

252. Letter, Murat Halstead to William Henry Smith, June 21, 1864, Smith Papers.

253. Letter, Charles Medary to "Dear Father," July 20, 1864, Samuel Medary Papers.

254. *Dayton Daily Empire,* Aug. 29, 1864.

255. *Ibid.,* Aug. 29, 30, 1864.

256. Guthrie received 12 votes (a bare majority) on the first ballot, while Vallandigham received 8 votes.

257. *Dayton Daily Empire,* Aug. 31, 1864. The 1864 campaign in Ohio is treated in several scholarly articles: William Frank Zornow, "Clement L. Vallandigham and the Democratic Party in 1864," *Bulletin of the Historical and Philosophical Society of Ohio,* XIX (July, 1961), 21–37, and Elizabeth F. Yager, "The Presidential Campaign of 1864 in Ohio," *Ohio State Archaeological and Historical Quarterly,* XXXIV (Apr., 1925), 548–89.

258. Letter, Vallandigham to McClellan, Sept. 4, 1864, McClellan Papers.

259. *Dayton Daily Empire,* Sept. 7, 1864.

260. Telegram, William McLean to Manton Marble, Sept. 13, 1864, Manton Marble Papers, Library of Congress. The McLean-to-Marble telegram read: "Difficulties all arranged. Vallandigham all right. Have no fears."

261. *Dayton Daily Empire,* Sept. 16, 1864.

262. *Ibid.,* Sept. 24, 26, 1864.

263. Report, Joseph Holt to Edwin M. Stanton, Oct. 8, 1864, in *Official Records,* Series 2, VII, 930–53.

264. Letter, Vallandigham to "Editor of the *New York News,*" Oct. 22, 1864, newspaper clipping in "Scrapbook, 1864," Sanderson Papers.

265. Letter, John McGaffey to William Henry Smith, Nov. 17, 1864, Smith Papers. "I suppose," wrote a friend of the judge advocate general, "[that] the discovery of the conspiracy will go far to accounting for the great majority with which the West voted for the Union."—Letter, William B. Lord to Joseph Holt, Nov. 13, 1864, Holt Papers.

266. *Cincinnati Daily Gazette,* Nov. 9, 1864.

267. *Dayton Daily Empire,* Nov. 14, 1864.

268. Testimony, Mar. 29, 1865, published in the *Cincinnati Daily Enquirer,* Mar. 30, 1865.

269. Quoted in the *Dayton Daily Empire,* Apr. 16, 1865.

TWO

James A. Garfield

ALLAN PESKIN

Throughout the Civil War a bitter struggle was carried on within the ranks of the Union army itself. This struggle, sometimes silent and under the surface, at other times strident and out in the open, was waged between the professional soldiers and the civilian appointees, or "political" generals. Both groups often aimed their sharpest invective at each other rather than at the rebels. To the professionals, scorned and ignored in peacetime, the volunteers (mainly politicians ignorant of the craft of war) seemed a greater menace than the enemy. "Unless something is done to rescue the army from the politicians," warned one, "patriots will hang up their swords in disgust and despair." [1]

To many volunteer generals, on the other hand, the West Pointers, with their authoritarian ways, seemed the very personification of the undemocratic system they were fighting. As James A. Garfield, one of their most articulate spokesmen, put it, "If the Republic goes down in blood and ruin, let its obituary be written thus: 'Died of West Point.' " [2]

It was scarcely surprising that this rivalry should develop. The American Civil War, like all civil wars, was, after all, essentially a political conflict. What was surprising, in view of all the furor over political generals, was how few genuine political generals there really were in the Union army. For Ohio, at least, the purely political general was quite rare.

Out of the twenty-two Ohioans who reached the rank of major general during the war, sixteen boasted a West Point education as their professional badge.[3] Two others, Robert C. Schenck and Jacob Dolson Cox, had had some acquaintance, however slight, with military affairs before entering the army. Schenck had grown up in a military family, and Cox, whose many talents included a fluent knowledge of French, had busied himself before the war by translating French military manuals into English. Only four Ohio generals were completely innocent of military knowledge when the war began: Wager Swayne, Mortimer D. Leggett, James B. Steedman, and James A. Garfield. Both Swayne, the son of a Supreme Court justice, and Leggett, a prominent educator, received the stars of a major general quite late in the war, and neither led troops in battle after they had attained that rank. Of Ohio's twenty-two, therefore, only Steedman and Garfield can properly be labeled political generals. Neither, however, owed their elevation to their political connections alone; both had begun as colonels and had been thoroughly tested on the field of battle before they won their stars.

In Ohio, therefore, the purely political general did not exist. Yet it must be admitted that neither Steedman nor Garfield found themselves hindered by their political connections. Steedman, a Douglas Democrat, owed his military opportunity to his position as spokesman for that faction. Garfield was a more interesting case. A Republican, and a radical one at that, Garfield, of all Ohio generals, came the closest to personifying that elusive specimen, the political general. In his career, therefore, can best be seen the involved process by which an Ohio politician was transformed into a soldier.

Except for a prescient phrenologist he had consulted in his youth, no one ever predicted that the young Garfield would grow up to wear a soldier's uniform. The circumstances of his early childhood were not only unmilitary but profoundly anti-military. Born in a log cabin and raised in rural poverty without the guiding hand of a father, Garfield spent much of his boyhood in the company of waterfront loafers. Very likely, he would have become one himself had he not, so he thought, been saved by "the providence of God." [4] A revival meeting conducted by the Campbellites, or Disciples of Christ, bent his life in a new direction. After his conversion he vowed to abstain from "low vulgar company and expressions," and raise his mind "to noble and sublime thoughts." [5] As an eager Disciple, Garfield renounced not only sin but the sinful world itself. Disciples regarded all politics with disdain and neatly side-stepped the growing slavery controversy, preferring to take the Bible as their sole platform. Taking the sixth commandment at its face value, they regarded war as murder and soldiers as hired killers.

Impelled by his new-found faith, Garfield immersed himself in books, finding in literature—particularly the sentimental, humanitarian variety—a congenial complement to his religious faith. As a student and teacher at the Disciple-oriented Western Reserve Eclectic Institute at Hiram, Ohio, Garfield discovered himself. He found that he excelled as an orator, and he discovered that he had a capacity for hard, disciplined intellectual activity.

His friends assumed that he would employ these talents in the pulpit, but as Garfield grew into manhood, his religious fervor slowly waned. Two years of close contact with eastern ideas at Williams College convinced him that he lacked a true vocation for the ministry. At Williams, Garfield became a Republican, converted by tales of "Bleeding Kansas." He hated slavery like sin, and resolved to fight it as he had once fought with the Devil. "I feel like throwing the whole current of my life into the work of opposing this giant Evil," he vowed. "I don't know but the religion of Christ demands some such action." [6] His former pacifism now seemed cowardly, and he had nothing but contempt for "that puling sentimentalism of modern days which, in the safe closet, will pray for freedom; but holds up its hands in pious horror when the sword is unsheathed to purchase that precious boon amid the carnage of the battlefield." [7]

When he returned to Hiram to assume the presidency of the Eclectic Institute, Garfield found himself unable to reconcile his new attitudes with his old Disciple faith. He found a fresh outlet for his evangelical impulse in politics, and in 1859 he won election as a Republican to the Ohio senate, much to the consternation of his religious associates.

At Columbus, Garfield threw himself into political life with his customary energy, winning the admiration of Governor Dennison and other seasoned observers as "a rising man." The latter half of Garfield's term was darkened by the secession crisis following the election of Lincoln. At first, Garfield discounted southern threats as pure bluster, but he was soon reconciled to the possibility of war. If he should be forced to choose between his youthful pacifism and his new-found abolition fervor, there was no question which path he would take. "I am inclined to believe that the sin of slavery is one of which it may be said that 'without the shedding of blood there is no remission,' " he martially declared. [8]

When the war came, Garfield was ready. He thundered defiance at the southern rebels. "I hope we will never stop short of complete subjugation. Better lose a million men in battle than allow the government to be overthrown." [9] Garfield was eager to take part in what he hoped would become a glorious anti-slavery crusade. Even though he had no military training or experience, he never doubted his ability to command. Like most Americans, he had a low opinion of the military mind. "Pluck," he insisted, was far more important than mere "military science." [10]

Consequently, when Garfield offered his services to Governor

Dennison, "in any capacity he may see fit to appoint me," he was confident that the governor would not undervalue his offer. Garfield felt that he was entitled to be a colonel at the very least, and even the star of a brigadier general did not seem out of the question.[11] He scorned the suggestion that he enlist as a private in the ranks as "buncombe . . . an unmanly piece of demagogism." "I looked the field over," he explained, "and thought if I went into the army I ought to have at least as high a position as a staff officer. . . . The Governor would have given me one still higher if he had one in his gift." [12]

For the time being, though, Garfield had to defer his military career. Governor Dennison needed support in the legislature more than he needed another enthusiastic amateur soldier; but as soon as the session was over, Garfield hurried home to rouse his neighbors to the war effort. He and Senator John Sherman made a whirlwind circuit of the district, addressing patriotic meetings in every corner of the Reserve. "Garfield goes forth, like an apostle of Liberty, a preacher of righteousness, proclaiming the Gospel which demands equal obedience to God and resistance to tyrants." [13]

In late April Garfield helped raise troops for the Seventh Regiment of Ohio Volunteer Infantry, and he confidently expected to be elected colonel in return for his services. Unfortunately for his cause, he was unable to campaign in person, for at that moment he was called away to Illinois on a secret mission for the governor. While he was gone, his chief rival, Erastus Tyler, was busily at work. He took advantage of Garfield's absence by campaigning in his flashy Ohio Militia uniform, which so impressed the recruits that it virtually assured his election.[14]

Garfield withdrew with as good grace as he could muster and looked around for another command. The Nineteenth Ohio beckoned, but he was again disappointed. His enemies gleefully made political capital out of his discomfiture. The opposition press gloated:

. . . When a man, without military education, experience or training refuses to join the ranks, but endeavors to leap from the walks
of a private citizen to the position of a military chieftain, it is
transparent that *self*, and not country, prompts his actions. In our
opinion, Hon. James A. Garfield is of this class. Ever since the
commencement of the present troubles, he has been hovering
around military encampments, (always cautious, however, to keep
clear of the ranks) literally begging for a commission, but failing to
get it, his patriotism has oozed out and for the last two weeks, he
appears to have subsided.[15]

In mid-June Governor Dennison offered Garfield a commission as lieutenant colonel of the Twenty-fourth Ohio Infantry.
Originally, Dennison had rashly promised to make him a full
colonel. Now he backed down and offered only a subordinate
post. William Bascom, the governor's private secretary, tried to
soothe Garfield's ruffled feelings. "Of course, you understand it
is solely on the point that you have no special military education or experience," he explained, assuring Garfield that the
governor "is fully satisfied as to your military *genius* and capacity. . . . But the trouble is, the people, the rest of mankind do
not know this. . . ." [16] Garfield struggled with his pride for a
few days; but finally, he declined the commission.

A month later, Governor Dennison again asked Garfield to
accept a lieutenant-colonelcy. This time, there was no hesita-
tion. Garfield immediately wired back his acceptance. In mid-
August he was sworn in as lieutenant colonel of the Forty-
second Ohio Volunteer Infantry, and a few weeks later, the
governor relented and appointed him full colonel of the regiment.

Garfield *was* the Forty-second Regiment. Except for him, the
regiment existed only on paper. He had no officers to instruct,
no troops to command, no horses, no uniforms—only a commission. He had to create his entire command from the ground up.
To find his soldiers, Garfield turned first to those he knew
best—his students at Hiram. Within an hour after he spoke at

the village church, sixty boys had stepped forward, and the rest of the company was filled within the week. The Hiram boys were shipped down to Camp Chase, on the outskirts of Columbus. They were soon joined by six more companies, and drill began in earnest.

The regiment did not reach its full strength until November. Until then, Garfield had to scour the countryside for recruits. His recruiting methods were modeled on the revivalist techniques he had learned in the pulpit, the only difference being that at the end of his sermon he would ask his listeners to stand up for the Union rather than for Jesus. Naturally, he used Disciple churches for his platform whenever he could. Some of the Brethren, however, still clung to their pacifist principles and refused to open their churches to a warrior. In Ashland County, for example, Garfield encountered "a style of over-pious men and churches . . . who are too godly to be human." He had to hold his meeting on the platform of the town hall, where he castigated "the Christianity of Ashland and all people who were afraid to 'do good on the Sabbath Day.'" Eight recruits, including a Methodist minister, came forward to enlist after this appeal.[17]

These recruiting trips were snatched whenever Garfield could spare a few days from his duties at camp. Camp Chase, a hastily thrown-together collection of whitewashed barracks, swarming with flies and mired in mud, was as little prepared for war as Garfield himself. His first night in camp, Garfield had only a pile of straw to sleep on. The next day, bone-stiff and weary, he began his military lessons. Before his regiment showed up at camp, Garfield had to learn how to command them. "It is a little odd for me to become a pupil again," he mused; but he quickly adjusted.[18]

He had much to learn. Before he could turn his green recruits into soldiers, he had to become a soldier himself. Applying the studious habits of a lifetime, he conned his strange new curriculum with all the persistance and ingenuity he had once devoted to Latin verbs. He used a set of wooden blocks to represent companies, battalions, officers and men, and would march his blocks across his desk in response to the proper command until he had mastered the elements of infantry tactics and drill.[19] Camp Chase had no officers' training school; Garfield had to learn his job as best he could. The daily routine of camp life could be an education in itself for an officer who kept his eyes open. His very first day in camp, Garfield was appointed officer of the day. He supervised sentry duty, issued passes, reprimanded disorderly soldiers, censored mail, guarded rebel prisoners ("a hard looking set—of the species of the great unwashed"), and in countless little ways began to learn the great truth that war is mostly drudgery.[20]

By the time his troops reached camp, Garfield was ready for them. He had only a few weeks to whip these boys into shape. No time was wasted. For six to eight hours each day, his tired, sweaty troops marched and countermarched across the sunbaked fields of Camp Chase, practicing company and squad drill, regimental evolutions, tactical maneuvers, and bayonet exercises until ready to drop with fatigue. The officers were not spared. Always a schoolmaster at heart, Garfield organized an officers' school and drilled them with his little wooden blocks. In the evening the colonel and his staff would repair to the rifle range for target practice, where Garfield, the veteran of innumerable boyhood squirrel shoots invariably came off the best shot.[21]

Garfield displayed unexpected qualities of military leadership. His civilian experience turned out to be highly appropriate for his present tasks. Managing a thousand boys was, after all, very much the same whether they were in school or in uniform.

After three months at Camp Chase, the long hours of drill and discipline began to transform the boys of the Forty-second into soldiers—ready, they hoped, for the hour of danger. That hour was near at hand. The regiment had been marking time at camp until its ranks could be filled. By the end of November, after repeated recruiting forays by Garfield and his officers, it had finally reached its full strength of ten companies. Garfield, bored and weary from filling out all the forms required to activate his regiment, looked forward to action. His only fear was that the Forty-second might be assigned the inglorious duty of guarding the "slaughter yards and pork packers" of Cincinnati.[22] He need not have worried. On the fourteenth of December he received orders to proceed at once with his regiment to Kentucky.

The next day the men packed their knapsacks with three days' rations and marched four miles down the pike to Columbus. They were in good spirits, happy to leave the now detested Camp Chase. A private of Company K vividly remembered how "when we marched out on that clear cold December morning to the step of martial music, every heart was buoyant and hopeful and fully resolved to battle manfully for the old Flag." [23]

This early in the war, troops on their way to battle were still enough of a novelty to inspire enthusiasm. In Columbus flags fluttered from every window, and curious crowds gathered at the railroad depot, where the regiment was reviewed by Governor Dennison. After "an earnest and patriotic address," he presented the regiment with a stand of battle flags, admonishing them never to let these colors trail in the dust. Colonel Garfield accepted the flags and assured the governor that they would be carried "through many a sanguine field to victory." The men gave the governor three cheers and marched smartly into the train.[24]

Their destination was eastern Kentucky, and their mission was to block a Confederate advance through the Sandy Valley. This miniature invasion, so poorly planned and equipped, actually posed no serious threat to the Union position; [25] but just to be on the safe side, Don Carlos Buell, the Union commander in Kentucky, dispatched a brigade to deal with the matter. The brigade consisted of the Fortieth and Forty-second Ohio, plus a few ragged Kentucky units. None of these troops had yet seen action, and all were as innocent of experience as their commander, Colonel Garfield.

Garfield had never seen a battle, "never heard a hostile gun." He was not a soldier, only a country schoolmaster who dabbled in politics; and now, he found himself with an independent command in a strange wild country, bearing sole responsibility for the success or failure of what could be an important campaign. The more he studied a map of the region, the more appalled he became. His command embraced six thousand square miles of wilderness untapped by railroads or telegraph lines. The land was too desolate to support an army even in the best of seasons, much less in winter.[26]

Garfield was forced to learn the soldier's trade in the hardest possible way—on his own, in actual combat. His opponent, General Humphrey Marshall was a West Point graduate with an impressive Mexican War record, yet Garfield, the novice, easily bested him. Garfield's very inexperience served him well, for it led him to take risks that more careful officers might have shunned. When he looked back on his campaign in the years after the war, Garfield shuddered at his folly. "It was a very rash and imprudent affair on my part," he admitted. "If I had been an officer of more experience, I probably should not have made the attack. As it was, having gone into the army with the notion that fighting was our business I didn't know any better." [27]

The result of the campaign was that within a month Marshall's column was streaming out of Kentucky back to Virginia. His retreat had begun even before he and Garfield had traded shots, but Garfield preferred to believe that the almost bloodless, drawn battle of Middle Creek had been instrumental in securing his victory. Marshall, however, insisted that hunger, "an enemy greater than the Lincolnites," [28] was the only reason for his withdrawal; but he missed the point. Supplies were as important to military success as victory in battle. Garfield handled his supply problem with imagination and skill; Marshall trusted to luck. A truly enterprising commander would have solved his supply shortage (as some Confederate generals were to do) by attacking the Federals and seizing their stores. Instead, Marshall was content to manufacture excuses and slink away.

This happy outcome only lent further support to Garfield's faith in the prowess of the amateur soldier. He had, after all, beaten the West Pointer at his own game, and with surprising ease. The confidence that this victory inspired in him was later to color his relations with the regular army, and helps account for his low opinion of many West Pointers.

Whatever the reason for Garfield's success in the Sandy Valley, the victory-starved North hailed it as a welcome relief from the dreary Union record of defeat and ineptitude. On the strength of this performance, Garfield was promoted to brigadier general and ordered to join Buell on the march to Pittsburg Landing.

He had barely time to be introduced to his new brigade before they were needed in action. The Confederate attack on Shiloh had caught the Union forces unaware, and Buell's army, including Garfield's brigade, had not yet reached Grant when the battle began. Garfield drove his troops at a frenzied pace for thirty hours, through a violent thunderstorm, until they reached Shiloh. Their efforts were all in vain, for at the very moment that they reached the front, the rebel line broke and the Battle of Shiloh was over.[29]

After the battle Garfield's brigade took part in the "siege" of Corinth. General Henry Halleck, commander of all Union armies in the West, personally took charge of the campaign, assembling over a hundred thousand men to dislodge Beauregard's considerably smaller force. His bulging forehead and ready supply of military maxims had earned Halleck the nickname "Old Brains," but at Corinth his caution outran his wisdom. Halleck was determined not to repeat Grant's neglect of fortifications, so for two months his vast army crept toward the enemy, throwing up earthworks each step of the way—virtually tunneling its way to Corinth.

To Garfield's brigade the prolonged move toward Corinth proved a greater disaster than battle. Sleeping for weeks on end in wet, filthy uniforms, on a campsite that was actually a burial ground for thousands of decaying corpses, many of the men under Garfield's command succumbed to "camp fever." The rest endured as best they could the endless monotony of picket duty, drill, and maneuver. To his friends Garfield bitterly unburdened his indignation at seeing this magnificent army go to waste. This indignation rose even higher with the absurd conclusion of the Corinth campaign.

For weeks Halleck's mammoth army had inched its way toward the Confederate stronghold, carefully preparing all the proper textbook parallels and investments until it was finally positioned perfectly. Garfield's men were nerving themselves for the expected battle when into their lines early on the morning of May 30 sauntered an old Negro gaily shouting, "Dey's all gone, boss, shuah! . . . You-uns can jess walk right into de town if yer wants to!" [30] Beauregard had nimbly evacuated his entire army while the fatuous Halleck was blindly perfecting his dispositions.

Garfield was disgusted with this "disgrace upon Generalship," and he fumed even more when he read in Halleck's dispatches that Corinth was claimed as a glorious Union victory.[31] Inescapably, he was brought around to "the sad truth that we have no Generals." [32] For this state of affairs he blamed West Point. His explanation was simple: West Point–trained officers did not want to win the war if victory meant the end of slavery. After all, he reasoned, "a command in the army is a sort of tyranny and in a narrow and ignoble mind engenders a despotic spirit which makes him sympathize with slavery and slave holders." The more Garfield saw of his West Point com-

manders, the more convinced he became that they were engaged in a concerted plot, "amounting almost to a conspiracy
among leading officers—especially those of the Regular
Army—to taboo the whole question of anti-slavery and throw
as much discredit upon it as upon treason." [33]

Here was the heart of Garfield's quarrel with the regular
army—the Negro question, or in the inelegant language of the
day, "What to do with Sambo." Garfield knew what to do. As
the representative of the Western Reserve, the inheritor of
decades of antislavery fervor, he naturally looked upon the war
as the culmination of that crusade. Many Union officers, however, hated rebels, Negroes, and abolitionists with equal passion. To them the war was not an antislavery crusade at all. If
this was treason, as Garfield seemed to think, it was widespread.
It was shared by a large segment—possibly a majority—of
northern opinion, and it even had official sanction. At this stage
of the struggle the official war aims of the North remained
merely the restoration of the Union, without interfering in the
"established institutions of the States," i.e., slavery.

Garfield, of course, disagreed. As he saw the war drag on, as
he felt the deep hostility of the southerners he met, as he
witnessed the bumbling efforts of seemingly half-hearted Union
commanders, he found himself "coming nearer and nearer to
downright Abolitionism." [34] The more he saw of the South, the
more Garfield was convinced that the eradication of slavery
and destruction of the planter class were necessary before the
Union could be restored. As he marched past rich plantations
heavy with grain "which the planters boast openly is intended
to feed the Southern Army," he burned to make these proud
southerners pay for the war they had started. He wanted to
carry the war to southern civilians; but his commanders, bound
by the traditional rules of warfare they had learned at West
Point, refrained. In the later years of the war, after bitter
passions had been aroused, the fine distinctions between soldiers and civilians would be forgotten, and many Union com-

manders (especially Sherman and Sheridan) would wage the total war that Garfield advocated; but in 1862 it was still possible to retain some notions of chivalry.

Garfield, however, viewed this chivalry as coddling of the enemy, and he suspected treason lay behind it. "My heart sinks down very low when I see the mode in which this war is conducted," he said. "Until the rebels are made to feel that rebellion is a crime which the Government will punish there is no hope of destroying it. I declare it as my deliberate conviction that it [is] better in this country, occupied by our troops, for a citizen to be a rebel, than to be a Union man. Everything they have is protected with the most scrupulous care, especially their property in human flesh." [35]

Negroes, sensing the jubilee, flocked to the Union camp, forming pathetic bands of stragglers. This "contraband" posed a problem for Union commanders. Legally they were still the property of their masters, and some punctilious Union generals ordered that they be returned to bondage. When Garfield was directed to surrender a fugitive slave hiding in his camp, he exploded in anger and openly defied his commander, telling him that if the general wanted to hunt down slaves, he would have to do it himself. The general backed down and the slave was left in peace, but to Garfield the incident seemed a bad omen. "It seems to me hardly possible that God will let us succeed while such enormities are practiced," he feared.[36]

Garfield's God was no longer the Prince of Peace, but the God of Battles, and he enlisted Him in his struggle against West Point. "It may be part of God's plan," he reflected, "to lengthen out this war till our whole army has been sufficiently outraged by the haughty tyranny of proslavery officers and the spirit of slavery and slaveholders with whom they come in contact that they can bring back into civil life a healthy and vigorous sentiment that shall make itself felt at the ballot box and in social life for the glory of humanity and the honor of the country." [37]

This reference to the ballot box was not haphazard. Garfield's thoughts were beginning to turn back to politics. With each mail came letters from home imploring him to run for Congress. Garfield was tempted. "I would, of course, rather be in Congress than in the army, if there is to be no more active service," he admitted, "for I have no taste for the dull monotony of Camp life." [38] Nor was he eager to continue in the army if that meant taking "any place which West Point management will be likely to assign me." If, as he believed, "the war in the west is substantially ended, and its future operations are to consist of holding garrisons here and there, and keeping down guerrillas," then he could honorably retire from a military career that would be "doing the country little good and myself but little credit." [39]

He refused to give the movement his active support, but his friends back home busied themselves in his cause. The nomination was hard-fought, but after eight ballots Garfield was chosen Republican nominee for Congress in the Nineteenth District. The unswerving Republicanism of the district made his election a certainty, and he did not bother to campaign.

His position in the army, however, was far less certain. Late in the summer of 1862, his health, never robust, broke down. Relieved of his command, he was sent home on sick leave. After he recovered, he was faced with the problem of finding a new assignment. His Congress would not convene until December of 1863, which meant that he still had more than a year of military life ahead of him, should the war last that long. Early in September, he was ordered to Washington to confer with the War Department about his next post.

He spent his first day in Washington closeted with Secretary of War Stanton. Interviews with the energetic, excitable little tyrant of the War Department could be nerve-wracking; but toward a potential political ally like Garfield, Stanton was all charm and cordiality. They spent most of the afternoon denouncing West Point and all its works, and though the Secretary grandly promised to give Garfield any position within his power to bestow, he warned that it would be difficult to find a place in the army where he could be free from West Point harassment.[40] In the meantime, he was free to shop around.

Garfield looked the field over, but the hand of West Point was everywhere. He scouted the non–West Point generals, but they all seemed out of favor and out of work. He toyed with the idea of joining General Franz Sigel's German brigade, but on second thought rejected Sigel's "Dutchmen" on political and personal grounds. He then offered his services to the Massachusetts politician-turned-soldier, Nathaniel Banks, whom he ranked, for some curious reason, as "one of our finest generals"; but Banks was not very encouraging. "In short," Garfield sadly concluded, "it is quite impossible to see any way to usefulness or distinction that does not go down before West Point first." [41]

Fortunately, Garfield found an ally in his war against the regular army in the person of Salmon Portland Chase, secretary of the treasury. Chase too was indignant that the army was so overstocked with Democratic generals while good Republicans like Garfield went unrewarded. He took up Garfield's cause, virtually adopting the younger man as his protégé. Chase and Garfield hit it off splendidly from the start. They had much in common: both admired Chase, despised Democrats, and looked down on Lincoln. They spent many pleasant hours in cozy chats, as Garfield told Chase horror stories about the pro-southern, proslavery West Point officers he had known, and Chase regaled Garfield with fresh evidence of Lincoln's incompetence. Chase was so taken with Garfield that he insisted he leave his lonely hotel room and move into the Chase household.

The Chase hospitality was pleasant, but it was not for this that Garfield had come to Washington. As the weeks dragged on without an assignment from the War Department, the restless Garfield fretted with impatience "at being kept here in suspense, like Coleridge's Ancient Mariner—'As idle as a painted ship / Upon a painted ocean.' " [42] All the while, the War

Department, with fiendish ingenuity, kept dangling assignments before his eyes, only to snatch them away. Each day of delay stretched his already taut nerves closer to the snapping point. Rather than continue to mark time waiting for a suitable assignment, he declared himself ready to take command of a brigade, a regiment, or even a company. "I am thoroughly ashamed to be seen on the streets in uniform," he said, and he seriously considered resigning his commission and issuing an angry public letter explaining his reasons. "Still," he reflected, "my work is always to be assigned 'very soon,' but I, like every other general of positive opinions, am kept in idleness. I shall wait a few days more." [43]

While his spirits were at this low ebb, news reached him that gave fresh hope: General George B. McClellan, his evil genius, had been removed from command. "God be praised . . . ," Garfield rejoiced. "The day is dawning. I cannot leave the army now." [44]

Garfield now settled down for a long war. Chase's prolonged hospitality had become embarrassing, so Garfield seized upon the arrival of his staff to move to their bachelor quarters in a Pennsylvania Avenue boarding house. There he sat as the weeks slipped by, "still doomed to drag out my days here in Washington." [45] The War Department insisted that an assignment of some sort was in the offing, and to keep Garfield busy until a suitable command could be found, they assigned him to the Fitz-John Porter court-martial.

Garfield was scarcely an unbiased judge in this case, but impartiality was not expected from this court. The Porter trial was the great show trial of the Civil War, the high-water mark of the campaign to discredit West Point. Everyone knew that the trial was really aimed at McClellan. The unhappy Porter was to be the sacrificial goat for the sins of his chief.

Garfield's hatred of McClellan amounted to an obsession. "Little Mac" was the epitome of all the Democratic, West Point, proslavery generals who had thwarted his military career

and kept him idle in Washington. Chase had once suggested
that McClellan deserved to be shot for his conduct at Antietam,
and Garfield, as usual, agreed with Chase. They regarded
McClellan as a far more sinister menace to the republic than a
mere incompetent. Both were convinced that he sat at the
center of "a very insidious and determined scheme" to overthrow the government "by a kind of French *Coup d'etat.*"
Much to their disgust, the President laughed at their fears.
"These things . . . would forbode a thunder gust if there were
any lightning in him," they complained. "But doubtless he will
respond with an anecdote and let these raskals fillip his nose or
pluck his beard at pleasure." [46]

As fresh evidence of McClellan's suspected treason mounted,
Garfield grew more and more alarmed. He was particularly
disturbed by a remark attributed to a McClellan aide, that "it
is not the plan to whip the rebels. They are to be kept in the
field till both sections of the country are exhausted, and the
armies and the Democracy will compromise the matter." "From
all I can see," Garfield concluded, "I am almost convinced that
McC[lellan] is not misrepresented in that statement." [47]

It was widely believed by Republican officers that Porter's
fatal tardiness at Second Bull Run had been inspired by similar
treason, as well as by personal pique. It was rumored that at the
critical moment of the battle Porter had advised McClellan to
withhold reinforcements, since, as he was supposed to have said,
"we have Pope where we can ruin him." [48] At Pope's instigation
official charges were brought against Porter, and in November,
1862, a court-martial was ordered. The court was composed
entirely of generals of volunteers; no West Pointers were allowed who might have sympathy with their old classmate. [49] The
first impulse of the court, a witness later recalled, was to order
Porter shot; but instead, he was merely drummed out of the
army and prohibited from ever again holding federal office. [50]

The Porter trial moved with glacier-like deliberation. It
required over two weeks merely to organize the court, and not

even the new innovation of shorthand reporting could speed the endless flow of testimony. Garfield, who was trapped in Washington at least until the trial was over, grew more and more depressed as the case dragged on. He vowed to have a showdown with the War Department as soon as the work of the court was done. "They must give me something to do," he raged, "or they must take my commission. I will not endure it." [51]

To pass the time during his enforced idleness, he began to write a study of his latest hero, Frederick the Great. A thoroughgoing pacifist only ten years before, Garfield had now swung to the opposite extreme, taking for his model the archetype of Prussian militarism. He now believed that the pacifism he had once endorsed had nearly been the cause of the nation's undoing. "In our present war," the onetime Campbellite preacher argued, "the Republic is paying a fearful price for its neglect of military organization and its failure to preserve the military spirit among its people. . . . No nation ever so recklessly neglected the art of war, nor came so near to ruin in consequence of that neglect." [52] To remedy that neglect and to reawaken the nation's slumbering martial spirit, he undertook to edit the works of Frederick for publication.

The transformation of Garfield from citizen to soldier was now complete. Indeed, in some respects he was more martial spirited than the West Pointers he despised. It was a professional soldier who insisted that war was all hell, but Garfield sometimes gave the impression that he actually enjoyed the experience. To Garfield, as to many of his comrades, this was the great adventure of their lives. It rescued them from humdrum surroundings and gave their lives purpose and excitement. Many may have felt that way, but few expressed themselves as candidly as Garfield, who told a Cleveland audience, "We have all frequently heard of the horrors of war, but we have not so often thought of the horrors of peace. Bad as war may be, greater evils sometimes emerge from a long peace.

The nation's life becomes stagnant. . . . " He conceded that war had its horrors. "But," he added, "there is one advantage of this war that is evident. . . . The young men of the present day never saw or read of a time as grand as this. They never had such opportunities of doing great and noble actions." [53]

Garfield never had a chance to finish his book on Frederick. It was almost ready for the printer when a summons came from the West: William S. Rosecrans, commander of the Army of the Cumberland, needed a general. Garfield was so impatient after marking time for four months in Washington that he snapped at the opportunity, even though Rosecrans was a West Pointer. He hopped the first train west, and within a few days he reported for duty at General Rosecrans' headquarters in Murfreesboro, Tennessee.

The general, fresh from his ambiguous but widely hailed victory at Stone's River, was then at the peak of his fame. Voluble, inventive, excitable, charming, and irritable by turns, Rosecrans was always in motion: "nervous and active in all his movements, from the dictation of a dispatch to the rearing and chewing of his inseparable companion, his cigar." [54] His restless energy and teeming mental fertility struck many as authentic evidence of genius. But others, with the advantage of hindsight, were less impressed. "His mind scattered; there was no system in the use of his busy days and restless nights," [55] declared Charles A. Dana. Another observer put it more succinctly: "It seems as if a screw was loose in him somewhere." [56]

Into the hands of this curious, contradictory personality, Garfield had placed his military future. They took to each other at once. When Garfield went to the general's quarters his second night in Murfreesboro to discuss his assignment, Rosecrans would not let him leave. He insisted that Garfield sleep in his room, and kept him up until three o'clock while they discussed religion, a subject particularly close to Rosecrans' heart. [57] These midnight sessions continued night after night, often until four o'clock in the morning. The very intimacy of their association was becoming an embarrassment to Garfield. Rosecrans enjoyed his company so much that he was reluctant to assign him to active duty. Almost a month passed in this manner without further mention of the assignment Rosecrans had hinted at on their first interview. Was it for this that Garfield had joined the army—to become the paid companion of an insomniac?

One evening in the middle of February, Rosecrans suddenly turned to Garfield and said: "I am almost alone in regard to counsel and assistance in my plans, and I want a power concentrated here that can reach out through the entire army and give it unity and strength." Would Garfield, he asked, be willing to take the post of chief of staff and become that power? If not, he added, Garfield could command a division in the field.[58] Although he had had his heart set on a field command, Garfield was, he admitted, sorely tempted by Rosecrans' offer. After much soul-searching he decided to accept, primarily because of the opportunity it presented to "exercise more influence on the army, and more fully impress my views and policy on its administration."[59]

With the painful decision safely behind him, Garfield cheerfully settled into the routine of his new post. Army headquarters occupied a spacious, if slightly down at the heels, southern mansion, hastily vacated by its secessionist owner. Inside, within rooms of shabby gentility, arose a constant hum of activity. Rosecrans drove his staff hard. He expected from others the same tireless energy that propelled him. Few could keep up with the pace. Young aides, groggy with fatigue, often slumped at their desks until their commander, suspending his dictation in mid-sentence, would pinch their ears and send them off to bed.[60] Headquarters was Garfield's domain, and he presided over all this activity from an anteroom, where he sat perched regally on a high stool in front of an unpainted pine desk.

Visitors to camp were impressed by the chief of staff. To a

passing journalist he presented a "far more commanding and attractive appearance" than Rosecrans himself.[61] This admiration, though widespread, was not universal. To Colonel (later General) John Beatty, who affected the blunt, soldierly virtues, Garfield's uniform, with its gleaming double row of buttons, seemed ostentatious; and he read in Garfield's very handshake the message, "Vote right, vote early." [62] Rosecrans ignored the criticism. In Garfield he had found, for once, an aide whose capacity for work matched his own, and he entrusted to him many duties and responsibilities beyond his official position.

The chief of staff was supposed to serve as the transmission belt between the general and his army. He handled all the routine business that kept the army running smoothly, issued orders in the general's name, collected information and summarized it for the general's attention. But because of Garfield's intimacy with his chief (he was the only one privileged to call him "Rosey" to his face), his actual influence was much greater than his official position might warrant. With Rosecrans' encouragement, Garfield had his hand in every aspect of army organization, from the creation of an intelligence corps unsurpassed in the Union army to plans for injecting some "of the old Prussian and French fire" into troop morale. Bubbling over with plans and projects, Garfield helped pull the Army of the Cumberland into shape during its long stay at Murfreesboro.

To a large extent, therefore, Garfield succeeded in his goal of elevating the authority of the chief of staff beyond that of a mere clerk. Rosecrans leaned heavily upon Garfield for advice, particularly for problems of a political nature, and Garfield used his influence with his commander to press at every moment for his Radical measures. His pet proposal was to arm Negroes and enlist them to fight for the Union. Like Chase, he wanted them employed in something more useful than "pick and shovel brigades." Rosecrans seemed to be swayed by his arguments, and when Garfield reported his success to Chase, the Secretary was jubilant. His confidence in Garfield was unbounded: "My trust in you is as complete as that of the good deacon in his minister. I can sleep if it is you who preaches." [63]

What with one thing and another, being chief of staff for a great army kept Garfield's days full. Yet, with all the varied demands that Rosecrans made on his attention, Garfield never lost sight of the reason he had taken that position rather than command of a division. More than anything else, being chief of staff meant to Garfield an opportunity to carry out his own strategic concepts unhampered by West Point opposition. Ever since he had left the Sandy Valley, he had resented his West Point commanders. During his long, bitter feud with the regular army, he had accused them of incompetence, and even treason. These were serious charges, but they seemed to Garfield the only way he could account for the otherwise incomprehensible behavior of the West Pointers.

There was, however, a simpler explanation. At West Point young officers were trained in the strategic doctrines of Baron Jomini, whose classic textbooks on the art of war had shaped the strategic concepts of a generation of plebes. To Jomini and his many translators and popularizers, including Halleck, war was a fine art that was best left in the hands of professional soldiers. Their ideal was eighteenth-century warfare, conducted with a minimum of bloodshed by well-disciplined soldiers fighting for limited, clearly defined aims, the most important of which were the occupation of the enemy's territory and the capture of his capital city. Enthralled by the prospect of turning war into a science, Jomini and his school disregarded all the untidy and unscientific factors, such as politics and ideology, which could upset their neat diagrams. Recoiling in horror from the excesses of the French Revolution, they deplored total wars, or wars waged for the subjugation of entire peoples. [64]

These principles might have been sound for European wars of the eighteenth century, but the American Civil War was a different case entirely. It was pre-eminently a political war, fought between peoples, not soldiers. Garfield, no soldier but very much a politician, was actually better equipped to understand the true nature of this war than were many professional soldiers. Convinced that no military solution was possible without the abolition of slavery and the thorough reconstruction of southern society, he rejected Jomini's principles and advocated a total war fought to the finish. "It may be a philosophical question whether 11,000,000 of people *can be subdued*," he conceded, but he insisted "this is the thing to be done before there can be union and peace." [65]

If southern submission was at all possible, Garfield contended, it would have to be reached through bloodshed: by destroying their armies and breaking their will to resist, so as to impose a political solution they would not accept otherwise. Garfield had not read Clausewitz, but he instinctively regarded war as a continuation of politics by other means. Consequently, he advocated an offensive strategy—"striking, striking and striking again, till we break them." [66] "One thing is settled in my mind," he declared,

direct blows at the rebel army—bloody fighting—is all that can end the rebellion. In European wars if you capture the chief city of a nation you have substantially captured the nation. The army that holds London, Paris, Vienna, or Berlin, holds England, France, Austria, or Prussia. Not so in this war. The rebels have no city, the capture of which will overthrow their power. If we take Richmond, the rebel government can be put on wheels and trundled away into the interior . . . in two days.

"Hence," he concluded, in flat contradiction to accepted military doctrine, "our real objective point is not any place or district, but the rebel army wherever we find it. We must crush and pulverize them, and then all places and territories fall into our hands as a consequence." [67]

With such aggressive views Garfield could not help but be unhappy over the protracted idleness of the Army of the Cumberland at Murfreesboro. As the months passed by without

Rosecrans' stirring from camp, Union gratitude for Stone's River began to sour into exasperation. "I would not push you to any rashness," Lincoln gently prodded, "but I am very anxious that you do your utmost, short of rashness." [68] Lincoln's irony passed unnoticed; no one else seemed to be worried about rashness from Rosecrans. Even the quartermaster general, not usually considered one of the more aggressive departments of the army, chimed in with some gratuitous advice: "The rebels will never be conquered by sitting in their front." [69]

To Garfield, chafing for action, impatient for the great battle that would smash the rebellion and let him go home, this long delay while Rosecrans perfected his interminable preparations was maddening. "It is very trying to the patience," he grumbled, "to stand here like a wrestler tripping and making feints at his adversary, and watching his movements, keeping the muscles strained all the while, yet never grappling and making a decisive end to the delay and struggle." [70] As he brooded over Rosecrans' reluctance to move, Garfield was filled with "a sense of disappointment and mortification almost akin to shame." [71] In his opinion, the Army of the Cumberland had reached a peak of fighting efficiency by the early weeks of May. When at the same time his spies reported that Bragg had weakened his army in order to send reinforcements to Vicksburg, Garfield was sure that the time to strike was at hand.

To prod his reluctant chief, Garfield drafted plans for an offensive, plans that by early June seemed to have won Rosecrans' approval. Orders for the march were issued, and all the preparations set in motion for a grand offensive. "I have made my personal preparations, said my goodbyes to absent friends by letter, commended the cause, and myself to God and nerved myself up for the shock," Garfield announced. But on the eve of the movement, much to Garfield's dismay, "there seemed to fall down upon the leading officers of this army, as suddenly as a bolt from the blue, a most determined and decided opinion that there ought to be no immediate or early advance." The offensive was canceled, and Garfield told his disappointed friends back home, "I have given up all hope of either fighting or dying *at present.*" [72]

Before calling off the offensive, Rosecrans had taken the precaution of polling his leading generals. Not surprisingly, they voted for delay, perhaps sensing the answer that was expected of them. Garfield chose to believe that Rosecrans was eager to advance but had been overruled by his officers.[73] But if Rosecrans really wanted to fight, why would he ask his friends to hold him back? Rosecrans, who knew all the military maxims, scarcely needed Halleck's cutting reminder: "Councils of war never fight." [74]

Garfield did not participate in the council's deliberations, but he was asked to prepare a report summarizing its arguments. On his own initiative he expanded this report from the expected bare synopsis into an examination and refutation of the council's decision. As he summarized their arguments, he found that although the members of the council started from different premises, their conclusions were virtually unanimous in favor of caution and delay.

This chorus of despair was grounded in part on the fear that Bragg's forces outnumbered those of the Army of the Cumberland. Garfield disagreed. According to his calculations, Bragg's army was weaker because of recent detachments to Vicksburg than it had ever been or was likely to be again. The Army of the Cumberland, on the other hand, was at its peak strength; and as Garfield pointedly reminded Rosecrans, in view of Washington's unsympathetic attitude, "we have no right to expect re-enforcements for several months, if at all." Garfield, therefore, was for striking at once, while they still retained their advantage.

Garfield then examined, one by one, the possible results of his proposed advance. These were three: defeat; victory in battle; and the retreat of Bragg without a battle. The possibility of defeat had to be faced. "No man can predict with cer-

tainty the result of any battle. . . . Such results," he reminded
his pious commander, "are in the hands of God." Garfield was
willing to run that risk, confident that God generally favored
the strongest battalions.

But Garfield was hopeful that if Bragg could be maneuvered
into an all out battle, the chances of victory were excellent; and
the consequences, he believed, "would be in the highest degree
disastrous to the rebellion." As Garfield had argued, over and
over again: "Our true objective point is the Rebel army, whose
last reserves are substantially in the field, and an effective blow
will crush the shell, and soon be followed by the collapse of the
Rebel government."

The advance could result in neither victory nor defeat, if
Bragg fell back without giving battle. The other officers had
argued that this situation would be most undesirable, since
Bragg could thereby lure the Army of the Cumberland deeper
into the wilds of Tennessee, where its superior numbers would
be neutralized by rugged terrain and lengthened supply lines.
From a purely tactical point of view, their fears had considerable substance; but Garfield's superior grasp of the economic
and psychological factors of warfare led him to conclude that
such a retreat would be disastrous for Bragg. "Besides the loss
of *matériel* of war and the abandonment of the rich and abundant harvest now nearly ripe in Central Kentucky," he argued,

he would lose heavily by desertion. It is well known that a widespread dissatisfaction exists among his Kentucky and Tennessee
troops. They are already deserting in great numbers. A retreat
would greatly increase both the desire and the opportunity for
desertion and would very materially reduce his physical and moral
strength.

On the other hand, what would be the consequences of not
advancing? A politician like Garfield always had one eye on the
coming elections, so he realized what the professional soldier,
who scorned "mere politics," often tended to forget—that the

ultimate decision depended as much on the steadfast will of the voter back home as it did on the soldier in the field. The administration needed a military victory to sustain public confidence, and it needed it before, not after, the elections. In this case, the much-derided "political general" displayed a broader vision than the West Point military specialists when he argued that "the turbulent aspect of politics in the loyal States renders a decisive blow against the enemy at this time of the highest importance to the success of the Government at the polls, and in the enforcement of the Conscription Act."

Garfield reminded his chief, perhaps unnecessarily, that "the Government and the War Department believe that this army ought to move upon the enemy. The army desires it, and the country is anxiously hoping for it." There was an implied threat behind these words. If Rosecrans continued to disappoint the government, Garfield not so subtly suggested, the government might very well replace him with a more aggressive commander.

Garfield immediately softened this threat with praise for Rosecrans' previous course of action. "You have, in my judgment," he said, "wisely delayed a general movement hitherto, till your army could be massed, and your cavalry could be mounted." Now, however, the time for delay was past, and the time for action had arrived. "Your mobile force can be concentrated in twenty-four hours, and your cavalry, if not equal in numerical strength to that of the enemy, is greatly superior in efficiency and morale. For these reasons," Garfield concluded, "I believe an immediate advance of all our available forces is advisable, and, under the providence of God, will be successful." [75]

With this report Garfield performed what may very well have been his greatest service to the Union cause during his entire two years in uniform. Faced with Garfield's remorseless logic, which undercut all his excuses, Rosecrans had no choice but to advance.

On the twenty-fourth of June, 1863, the Army of the Cumberland struck camp and began its long-delayed advance into Tennessee. However, instead of moving immediately, as Garfield had urged in his report of June 12, Rosecrans had lingered at Murfreesboro for twelve more days—"days which seemed months to me," Garfield said.[76] To make matters worse, the whole campaign was waged during one of the most intense, prolonged rainstorms Garfield had ever seen. Garfield found a measure of melancholy satisfaction in the reflection that the campaign might have succeeded completely had Rosecrans taken his advice and started the advance while the weather was still clear.

As it turned out, Bragg was able to evacuate Tullahoma just one step ahead of the Army of the Cumberland. From there he retreated across the Tennessee River to Chattanooga. With the capture of Tullahoma, Middle Tennessee was in the Union's hands once more, at the cost of less than a thousand casualties; but Bragg's army, the main object of Garfield's strategy, although demoralized was still intact. Garfield had foreseen this result as a possibility when he had first conceived the Tullahoma campaign. It was not the ideal result for which he had hoped—for that he needed a battle—but it was a substantial victory nonetheless and amply vindicated Garfield's judgment in arguing for the advance against the opposition of virtually the entire army.

Garfield did not join in the congratulations over the Tullahoma campaign. He looked upon it as only half a victory, and he could not rest content until the true objective—Bragg's army—had been crushed. With his customary eagerness he begged Rosecrans to follow up his success with a vigorous pursuit. Rosecrans ignored his advice. After his burst of energy in the Tullahoma campaign, he lapsed once more into his customary caution.

At length, prodded by Garfield and the War Department, Rosecrans finally set his army in motion by mid-August, almost a month later than Garfield had thought he should. This campaign was to be the climax of Garfield's military career, but he almost missed it. When the Chattanooga campaign began, Garfield was lying in sickbed with a recurrence of the fever that had laid him low the preceding year. He was almost tempted to return to Ohio on sick leave, but, after pleading so long for an advance, he could not bear to leave his post once the move had begun. "It is not vanity," he candidly asserted, "for me to say that no man in this army can fill my place during this movement. It would take him several months to learn the character and condition of affairs as I know them and to hold that influence with the commanding General that I do." [77]

The campaign went off without a hitch. Once safely across the Tennessee River, the Army of the Cumberland debouched behind the mountains, swiftly pouring through the gaps south of Chattanooga. When Bragg woke up to what was happening, it was almost too late. He pulled out of Chattanooga before he was trapped inside, allowing this nearly impregnable citadel, and with it all of East Tennessee, to fall effortlessly into the hands of the Union. It seemed to be the story of Tullahoma all over again, with Bragg outmaneuvered and retreating before Rosecrans' superior generalship. Victory was in the air, and Garfield's thoughts began to turn to Congress, now that peace seemed so near.

But to the more experienced officers, something seemed terribly wrong. General Hazen sensed that Bragg's force was not behaving the way a retreating army should. Where were the stragglers and deserters, he wondered? Where was the pillage and looting that always accompanied a demoralized army? [78] Bragg, in fact, was not demoralized, nor was he in flight. After abandoning Chattanooga, he had withdrawn behind the mountains, ready to pounce upon the unsuspecting Army of the Cumberland.

Meanwhile, at his headquarters in Chattanooga, a glimmer of suspicion was beginning to disturb Rosecrans' tranquility.

"A battle is imminent," Garfield declared on September 13.[79] Rosecrans' imprudently scattered divisions were hastily called together, and telegrams went out to clergymen all over the nation to pray for victory. While this frantic concentration was being carried out, Bragg obligingly stayed his hand. By the sixteenth of September, Garfield was beginning to breathe easy once more. The danger, however, was still acute; and by September 19, the two armies lay face to face across a creek called Chickamauga, a Cherokee word that (according to a dubious tradition) meant "River of Death." [80]

At nine o'clock on the morning of September 19, the roar of gunfire reached Garfield's headquarters at Crawfish Spring, Georgia. At one o'clock Rosecrans shifted his command post nearer to the scene of action, taking over a cabin belonging to the Widow Glenn. Garfield spread out his maps and dispatches on her kitchen table, while the widow herself, with frightened children clinging to her skirt, hovered nervously by. Every now and then, Garfield looked up from his work to chat for a moment with the old lady and give the children a reassuring pat on the head. Then he would return to his improvised desk to take up again the direction of the bloodiest battle yet fought in the West.[81]

The battle raged throughout the day: a series of blind, un-co-ordinated, bloody skirmishes. With the approach of night the firing died down, and the weary soldiers slept on their arms, ready to resume the battle with the dawn. A clammy fog hung over the battlefield on the morning of September 20. By a freak of light, the atmosphere was suffused with a dull red glow—an eerie and ominous portent which would long be remembered as "the bloody dawn" of Chickamauga.[82] The battle was resumed at about nine o'clock, concentrated, as on the day before, mostly on the left, but with increasing activity on the right. Shortly after ten thirty, a staff officer galloped up to headquarters and reported that Brannan's division seemed to be out of its proper place in line, leaving a gap between Wood and

Reynolds. Jumping to the conclusion that he had already ordered Brannan elsewhere earlier that morning, Rosecrans dashed off an order to General Thomas J. Wood to close up the gap.

The order was written down by Major Frank Bond, not by Garfield. Garfield wrote most of the orders Rosecrans issued that day, but although he was standing nearby, he did not, for some reason, write this fatal order to Wood. Garfield prided himself on the clarity and precision of his prose. As chief of staff, he had cultivated a direct, vigorous style for his dispatches. For the sake of clarity he was always careful to explain the reasons behind orders, as well as to provide a discretionary escape clause to take care of changing circumstances. The prose style of Rosecrans, on the other hand, tended to be ambiguous, running from windy oratory to laconic obscurity.[83]

The order to Wood was terse and peremptory: "The general commanding directs that you close upon Reynolds as fast as possible and support him." [84] When the messenger hesitated for a moment, not fully understanding the order's intent, Garfield called out that its purpose was to enable Wood to fill the gap left by the withdrawal of Brannan. The order, with its supplementary verbal explanation was carried to Wood, who was at that time only six hundred yards from Rosecrans' command post. When he read the order, Wood was dumbfounded. As anyone could plainly see, Brannan was right where he belonged, between Wood and Reynolds. In that case, the messenger replied, there is no order, and he rode back to Rosecrans to explain the mix-up.[85]

This was not the end of the matter, however. Wood, whom Garfield had once described as a very narrow and impetuous man, lacking both prudence and brains (the very personification, to Garfield, of the West Pointer),[86] was still smarting from a squabble he had had with Rosecrans only a few days before, when Rosecrans had humiliated him for not obeying an order to the letter. Now, as he looked more closely at the order

handed him on the battlefield, he saw that technically it left
him no discretion. Whether through spite or an untimely conversion to the virtues of blind obedience, he decided to ignore
the verbal qualifications and execute the written order to the
letter. He directed his division to "close upon Reynolds," as
commanded. Since Brannan's division was in the way, Wood
had to take his troops out of line and march them behind
Brannan. By doing this, Wood created the very thing Rosecrans' order had intended to prevent: a gap in the line.

Directly opposite Wood's position, the Confederates had
been preparing an attack for most of the morning. By unhappy
coincidence they launched it at the precise moment when
Wood was out of place. Screaming their wild rebel yell, they
poured out of the woods and swept over the token resistance
that tried to stem them. The Union line was shattered, and
astonished Federals looked up to see a horde of grey swarming
over what had been, only moments before, rear headquarters.
Garfield was in the very center of the rout. He and other officers
tried to restore order, but it was no use, "for men were as deaf
to reason in their mad panic as would be a drove of stampeded
cattle." [87] Both Garfield and Rosecrans were swept completely
off the battlefield by the human tide.

When they realized that nothing could be done to check the
collapse of the right wing, Garfield and Rosecrans turned down
the Dry Valley Road to the safety of Rossville and Chattanooga. Making their way through the debris of defeat, they
struggled past overturned wagons, abandoned artillery, terri-
fied horses, and panic-crazed stragglers swarming to the rear.
Rosecrans was oblivious to the tumult. He sat slumped in his
saddle, lost in despair. He seemed drained of both energy and
will. Never again would he be "Old Rosey," so confident and
assured. He was now a broken man.

From all that Garfield and Rosecrans could see, the disaster
had been complete. Yet, as they rode north, they could still hear
sounds of battle coming from George H. Thomas' position on

the left wing. To Garfield, the steady, disciplined volleys seemed to indicate that Thomas' men were still holding their ground. If so, the battle was not yet lost. He begged Rosecrans to go to Thomas, or at least halt for a time at Rossville until they had definite information. Rosecrans, however, insisted that the gunfire they heard was only scattered firing, such as would come from a shattered army. Convinced that the field was already lost, his only thought was to reach Chattanooga and prepare its defenses. Garfield disagreed, and he asked for permission to try to contact Thomas on his own, to determine for himself the condition of the army. Rosecrans finally gave his assent, "listlessly and mechanically," [88] and then bade Garfield an emotional farewell, as if he never expected to see him alive again.[89] The two men parted, and the dazed general took up again his mournful retreat to Chattanooga.

As Rosecrans was trudging sadly northward, Garfield was riding across Missionary Ridge into legend. Garfield himself never described his ride except in conversation with friends, but in later years it would be embroidered by imaginative biographers into a heroic epic. As they told the story of "that world-famous ride," Garfield and his small escort galloped up and down the Dry Valley Road, through the gantlet of rebel troops, trying to find a way to reach Thomas. Rebels seemed everywhere, and for all Garfield could tell, Thomas might be completely surrounded or even wiped out. "It was a race between the rebel column and the noble steed on which Garfield rode." Despairing of finding a clear road, they cut across open country: "Over ravines and fences, through an almost impenetrable undergrowth, sometimes through a marsh, and then over broken rocks, the smoking steed plunged without a quiver. . . . Crashing, tearing, plunging, rearing through the forest dashed the steed. Poets song could not be long to celebrate that daring deed." In a cottonfield they suddenly ran into a rebel ambush. With rifle balls whizzing about their ears, they scattered for safety. One by one, the escort dropped by the way,

until only Garfield was left to reach Thomas and discover that
the Union still held the field. As a final touch to the epic, "the
horse which had borne Garfield on his memorable ride,
dropped dead at his feet" when he reached safety.[90]

Whatever did happen on that famous ride, its practical results were negligible. Thomas was perfectly capable of holding
firm without Garfield's assistance. Garfield had really undertaken the ride for his own private satisfaction. By leaving Rosecrans, he had disassociated himself from the taint of defeat.
There was nothing he could do for Thomas; he just wanted to
be there. He spent the rest of the day at Thomas' side in a fever
of exaltation. Garfield fully realized that he was watching one
of the great moments of the war. Outnumbered, almost surrounded, Thomas held his ground for five hours against repeated Confederate charges, earning forever the title "Rock of
Chickamauga." The last Confederate attack was beaten off
shortly before sunset. Ammunition was so low that the charging
rebels had to be shoved back by naked bayonets, but at sunset
Thomas still held the field.

This was Garfield's farewell to arms. Two years before, when
he had joined the army to save the Republic, he had enlisted
with no experience and no qualifications except massive self-
assurance. Oddly enough, this assurance proved justified. He
learned his new craft with surprising ease, demonstrating that a
country schoolmaster and smalltime politician, whose education was mainly literary and theological, could transform himself into a soldier. In his very first campaign, in the Sandy
Valley, he had been thrown on his own and had performed
quite creditably, displaying a sound tactical sense and avoiding
pitfalls that his more experienced opponent stumbled into.
This first campaign was also his last. For the rest of his military
career Garfield served in subordinate posts, eventually as Rosecrans' right-hand man, all but managing a great army. Along
the way he developed a strategic doctrine quite similar to that
evolved by another self-taught westerner, Abraham Lincoln.

Both Lincoln and Garfield were unencumbered by military theory, and hence both were able to view their war with a fresh, common-sense practicality. Both were accused of allowing political considerations to influence their military acts. But these critics, mostly professional soldiers, missed the point. A civil war is not a military exercise. It is the result of a breakdown in the political process, and can only be cured, as Garfield realized, by a political solution. At bottom this was the source of Garfield's conflict with West Point—a fundamental disagreement over the nature of war in a democracy.

After Chickamauga, Garfield remained with the Army of the Cumberland for a few weeks longer, unable to leave while they were trapped in the siege of Chattanooga; but as soon as he could, he left for Washington to take his place in Congress. He seriously considered resigning his seat and returning to the army. He had originally stood for Congress on the assumption that the war would be over by the time it convened. But the war still dragged on, and Garfield felt that his proper place was in the field. He was a major general now, with his commission dating from the battle of Chickamauga, and he could reasonably expect a desirable command.

He took his problem to the President. Lincoln told him that although the government "had more commanding generals around loose than they knew what to do with," there was a shortage of administration congressmen, particularly those with a practical knowledge of army affairs.[91] Garfield bowed to Lincoln's suggestion and resigned his commission.

On December 5, 1863, still wearing his general's uniform, Garfield was introduced to his future colleagues in Congress. The next day, a soldier no more, he put aside the old uniform and took the congressional seat he would occupy for the next seventeen years. For the rest of the war Garfield was an active member of the House Military Affairs Committee, where he put his expert knowledge to use in the construction of an improved conscription bill.

In the army Garfield had been a political general; in Congress he became a military-minded politician. His military record would prove the foundation of his political career, and when he ran for President in 1880, his supporters would devote more attention to his ride at Chickamauga than to his less spectacular congressional service. As the years passed, Garfield gradually made his peace with West Point. He even became the regular army's champion against the attacks of economy-minded congressmen.

As the bitterness of wartime slowly faded, Garfield took up again the old pattern of his life. He was never quite the same, however. He once told William Dean Howells that something went out of him during the war, a sense of the sacredness of human life.[92] Perhaps he meant that a sort of innocence he had once known had vanished when his life had been touched with violence. Something may have been lost, but something was gained as well. In the war Garfield found himself, and the country found him. It was the great watershed of his life.

1. Mary P. Dearing, *Veterans in Politics: The Story of the G.A.R.* (Baton Rouge, La., 1952), p. 2.

2. James A. Garfield to J. H. Rhodes, May 1, 1862. This letter is part of a collection of Garfield material, mainly of a personal nature, that was, for a time, retained by the Garfield family. I wish to thank the Garfield family, and Professors Harry Brown and Frederick De Forest Williams of Michigan State University for allowing me to examine the collection before it was sent to the Library of Congress. In future citations this collection will be cited as Garfield Family Papers, to distinguish it from the main body of Garfield Papers at the Library of Congress.

3. The sixteen were: General Ulysses S. Grant; Lieutenant General William Tecumseh Sherman; Major Generals George B. McClellan, William S. Rosecrans, Philip H. Sheridan, James B. McPherson, Ormsby M. Mitchel, Quincy A. Gillmore, Irvin McDowell, Don Carlos Buell, William B. Hazen, George A. Custer, Godfrey Weitzel, David S. Stanley, George Crook, and Alexander M. McCook. Biographical information on Ohio's

generals was found in Whitelaw Reid, *Ohio in the War: Her Statesmen, Garfield* (2 vols.; New Haven, Conn., 1925), I, 98.

4. James A. Garfield Diary, Oct. 1, 1850, Garfield Papers, Library of Congress.

5. *Ibid.*, Feb. 28, 1850.

6. *Ibid.*, Nov. 2, 1855.

7. In Theodore Clarke Smith, *The Life and Letters of James Abram Garfield* (2 vols.; New Haven, Conn., 1925), I, 98.

8. Garfield to Burke Aaron Hinsdale, January 22, 1860, Western Reserve Historical Society. The Garfield letters in this collection are photostats of the originals; the Hinsdale side of the correspondence is found on typed copies.

9. Garfield to J. H. Rhodes, Apr. 14, 1861, Garfield Family Papers, LC.

10. Garfield to [F. A. Williams?], Mar. 23, 1861, *ibid.*, typed copy.

11. Garfield to J. H. Rhodes, Apr. 17, 1861, *ibid.*

12. Garfield to his wife, May 5, 1861, *ibid.*

13. *Portage County Democrat* (Ravenna, Ohio), Apr. 24, 1861.

14. G. W. Shurtleff, "A Year with the Rebels," in *Sketches of War History 1861–1865. Papers Prepared for the Ohio Commandery of the Military Order of the Loyal Legion of the United States* (Cincinnati, Ohio, 1896), IV, 389–90.

15. *Portage Sentinel* (Ravenna, Ohio), May 29, 1861.

16. William Bascom to Garfield, June [11?], 1861, LC.

17. Garfield to his wife, Nov. 4, 1861, Garfield Family Papers, LC.

18. *Ibid.*, Aug. 22, 1861.

19. James A. Garfield, "My Campaign in East Kentucky," *North American Review*, CXLIII (Dec., 1886), 525.

20. Garfield to "The Friends at Home," Aug. 19, 1861; Garfield to J. H. Rhodes, Aug. 31, 1861, Garfield Family Papers, LC.

21. Garfield, "My Campaign," pp. 526–27; Garfield to J. H. Rhodes, Aug. 31, 1861, Garfield Family Papers, LC.

22. Garfield to J. H. Rhodes, Aug. 31, 1861, *ibid.*

23. Otto F. Bond (ed.), *Under the Flag of the Nation: Diaries and Letters of a Yankee Volunteer in the Civil War* (Columbus, O., 1961), p. 12.

24. *Ibid.*, pp. 12–13; see also F. H. Mason, *The Forty-Second Ohio Infantry* (Cleveland, 1876), p. 46.

25. For a full discussion of the Sandy Valley campaign, see Allan Peskin, "The Hero of the Sandy Valley: James A. Garfield's Kentucky Campaign of 1861–1862," *Ohio History,* Part I, Jan., 1963, pp. 3–24; Part II, Apr., 1963, pp. 129–39.

26. Garfield, "My Campaign," pp. 527–28; Garfield to his wife, Dec. 16, 1861, 11:45 P.M., Garfield Family Papers, LC.

27. Reid, *Ohio in the War,* I, 747 n.

28. *The War of the Rebellion: A Compilation of the Official Records of the Union and Confederate Armies* (Washington, 1880–1901), Series I, VII, 48. Cited hereafter as *Official Records.* As all references are to Series I, the series number is omitted from subsequent citations.

29. Wilbur F. Hinman, *The Story of the Sherman Brigade* (n.p., [1897]), pp. 135–49.

30. *Ibid.,* 161.

31. See Garfield to J. H. Rhodes, June 10, 1862, Garfield Family Papers, LC.

32. Garfield to his wife, June 10, 1862, *ibid.*

33. Garfield to J. H. Rhodes, May 1, 1862, *ibid.*

34. *Ibid.*

35. Garfield to Harmon Austin, June 25, 1862, *ibid.*

36. *Ibid.* According to Garfield, he was the first Union commander to refuse to obey such an order. See Reid, *Ohio in the War,* I, 762.

37. Garfield to J. H. Rhodes, May 1, 1862, Garfield Family Papers, LC.

38. Garfield to his wife, July 5, 1862, *ibid.*

39. Garfield to J. H. Rhodes, June 10, 1862, *ibid.*

40. Garfield to his wife, Sept. 20, 1862, *ibid.*

41. Garfield to J. H. Rhodes, Sept. 22, 1862, *ibid.*

42. Garfield to his wife, Oct. 3, 1862, *ibid.*

43. Garfield to J. H. Rhodes, Oct. 26, 1862, *ibid.*

44. Garfield to J. H. Rhodes, Nov. 10, 1862, *ibid.*

45. Garfield to B. A. Hinsdale, Dec. 1, 1862, WRHS.

46. Garfield to J. H. Rhodes, Dec. 24, 1862, Garfield Family Papers, LC.

47. Garfield to his wife, Oct. 3, 1862, *ibid.*

48. Otto Eisenschiml, *The Celebrated Case of Fitz John Porter: An American Dreyfuss Affair* (Indianapolis and New York, 1950), p. 73.

49. General W. W. Morris of the regular army was originally named to the court, but he was quickly replaced by a non–West Pointer.

50. Ed. P. Brooks to Garfield, Apr. 15, 1878; see also Benjamin Prentiss to Garfield, Feb. 11, 1880; LC.

51. Garfield to J. H. Rhodes, Dec. 14, 1862, Garfield Family Papers, LC.

52. From the preface to Garfield's unpublished edition of the works of Frederick the Great, cited in Smith, *Life and Letters of Garfield*, I, 267–68.

53. Speech to the Cleveland Sanitary Fair, Feb. 22, 1862, in *Portage County Democrat*, Mar. 2, 1864.

54. Reid, *Ohio in the War*, I, 349.

55. Charles A. Dana, *Recollections of the Civil War. With the Leaders at Washington and in the Field in the Sixties* (New York and London, 1913), p. 128.

56. H. A. Alden to Garfield, Mar. 7, 1876, LC.

57. Garfield to his wife, Feb. 13, 1863, Garfield Family Papers, LC.

58. Garfield to J. H. Rhodes, Feb. 14, 1863, *ibid.*

59. Garfield to his wife, Feb. 26, 1863, *ibid.*

60. See Reid, *Ohio in the War*, I, 347 n.

61. Henry Villard, *Memoirs of Henry Villard, Journalist and Financier, 1835–1900* (2 vols.; Boston and New York, 1904), II, 66.

62. John Beatty, *Memoirs of a Volunteer, 1861–1863*, edited by Harvey S. Ford (New York, 1946), pp. 169, 239.

63. Salmon P. Chase to Garfield, May 31, 1863, LC.

64. For essays on the influence of Jomini see: T. Harry Williams, "The Military Leadership of North and South," in David Donald (ed.), *Why the North Won the Civil War* (New York, 1962); and David Donald, "Refighting the Civil War," in David Donald (ed.), *Lincoln Reconsidered. Essays on the Civil War Era* (New York, 1961).

65. Garfield to B. A. Hinsdale, Sept. 12, 1862, in Smith, *Life and Letters of Garfield*, I, 237.

66. Garfield to Salmon P. Chase, May 3, 1863, unidentified newspaper clipping, Garfield Family Papers, LC.

67. Garfield to C. E. Fuller, May 4, 1863, in Corydon E. Fuller, *Reminiscences of James A. Garfield* (Cincinnati, 1887), p. 337.

68. Kenneth P. Williams, *Lincoln Finds a General: A Military Study of the Civil War* (5 vols.; New York, 1949–59), V, 211.

69. *Ibid.*, p. 209.

70. Garfield to his wife, May 12, 1863, Garfield Family Papers, LC.

71. Garfield to J. H. Rhodes, June 11, 1863, *ibid.*

72. *Ibid.*

73. Garfield to his wife, June 14, 1863, *ibid.*

74. See Villard, *Memoirs,* II, 70.

75. Garfield's report can be found in Reid, *Ohio in the War,* I, 753–56.

76. Garfield to Salmon P. Chase, July 27, 1863, in Burke Aaron Hinsdale (ed.), *The Works of James Abram Garfield* (2 vols.; Boston, 1883), I, 773.

77. Garfield to his wife, Aug. 23, 1863, Garfield Family Papers, LC.

78. W. B. Hazen, *A Narrative of Military Service* (Boston, 1885), p. 120.

79. Garfield to J. H. Rhodes, Sept. 13, 1863, Garfield Family Papers, LC.

80. A less prophetic, more prosaic translation of Chickamauga might be "stagnant waters." See Glenn Tucker, *Chickamauga: Bloody Battle in the West* (Indianapolis, 1961), p. 122.

81. *New York Herald,* Sept. 29, 1863, in Smith, *Life and Letters of Garfield,* I, 324.

82. William S. Lamers, *The Edge of Glory: A Biography of William S. Rosecrans, U.S.A.* (New York, 1961), p. 337.

83. See Williams, *Lincoln Finds a General,* V, 202.

84. *Official Records,* XXX, Pt. 1, p. 103.

85. *Ibid.,* pp. 103, 983–84.

86. Garfield to J. H. Rhodes, May 1, 1862, Garfield Family Papers, LC.

87. Jacob Dolson Cox, *Military Reminiscences of the Civil War* (2 vols.; New York, 1900), II, 9–10.

88. *Ibid.,* p. 10.

89. Tyler Dennett (ed.), *Lincoln and Civil War in the Diaries and Letters of John Hay* (New York, 1931), p. 110.

90. This account of Garfield's ride is based on that in John Clark Ridpath, *The Life and Work of James A. Garfield* (1882), pp. 155–57.

91. Montgomery Blair to Rosecrans, September 21, 1880, in Lamers, *Edge of Glory,* p. 412; Garfield to Mark Hopkins [December, 1863], in Smith, *Life and Letters of Garfield,* I, 355.

92. William Dean Howells, *Years of My Youth* (New York, 1916), pp. 205–6.

THREE

Whitelaw Reid

ROBERT H. JONES

The *Cincinnati Daily Gazette,* April 11, 1861, in a story date-lined Columbus, announced that "[Clement L.] Vallandigham made his appearance here this morning. . . . Of course, the Dayton patriot is anxious to do all he can . . . against his own State, and in favor of the enemies of his country." The next day, under the same dateline, with reference to the same famed legislator, the *Gazette* lamented, "What heinous sin has Ohio committed that Providence should send upon her such a miserable traitor as this?" Both stories bore the byline "Agate." [1]

The fiery Agate, of course, was Whitelaw Reid, then Columbus correspondent for the *Gazette,* the Cincinnati *Times,* and the *Cleveland Herald.* A native of Xenia, Ohio, Whitelaw (born October 27, 1837) was the second of three children, the eldest being Gavin (born 1828), and the youngest, Christina (born 1844). Reid's mother wanted him named James, in honor of General James Whitelaw, but his baptismal certificate read simply "Whitelaw Reid." However, he used the "James" through school, even though his nickname was "White." Reid dropped the "James," as he said, "when becoming of age." [2]

At Xenia Academy, presided over by his uncle, the Reverend Hugh McMillan, Reid received a sound enough basic education to matriculate at Miami University as a fifteen-year-old sophomore. Reid graduated in 1856, with honors in science and the classics, and became superintendent of the "graded" schools at South Charleston, Ohio. But that job could not hold him long, and at the age of twenty he bought and edited the weekly *Xenia News*. An active Republican, this weekly reflected his partisanship. He ran the paper for ninety-nine issues, but gave it up when his health failed him. Reid traveled west to frontier Minnesota during the summer of 1860 for physical rehabilitation. There he picked up a number of agates that fascinated him enough to provide him with a pen name. While in Minnesota, the Chippewa chieftan Hole-in-the-day entertained him. This same Indian warrior two years later kept his nation from joining the Sioux in their decimation of the Minnesota frontier. In the fall of 1860 Reid threw himself into Lincoln's campaign, and after it ended, wound up in Columbus as the correspondent of three newspapers.[3]

Agate reported twenty-nine times from Columbus between April 8 and May 16 (the day the legislature adjourned). On April 10, when the possibility of war seemed very close, he wrote that Governor William Dennison would soon make recommendations for the "efficient support of the federal government," and that the legislature was ready to support Dennison "to an unlimited extent . . . provided that a vigorous policy shall be inaugurated." After the news of Sumter reached the capital, Reid recalled how "on the 15th . . . Columbus was wild with the excitement of the call to arms. On the 16th the feeling was even more intense; troops were arriving . . . the very air came laden with the clamor of war and the swift, hot haste of the people to plunge into it." Still on the next day "every pulse . . . was at fever heat." Reid missed no opportunity at this juncture to gibe at the Democrats. He broadcasted their opposition to the "war measures" (especially appropriations and militia bills), and observed that "when *words* are wanted, they are all ready, but they have a mortal aversion to *votes*."[4]

Attacks such as Agate's reflected the wave of Union feeling in Columbus and throughout the state that shook the Democratic opposition. Obviously pleased when the Democrats began to waver in their opposition to Ohio's war measures, Reid reported on April 16 that "there is a great shaking among the dry bones of Democracy this morning," and on April 19 that "the most uneasy politicians ever seen in this city were the Democrats, yesterday afternoon. *They had begun to hear from their constituents.*" Suddenly, the Democrats unanimously supported the "Million Bill" (appropriations), the passage of which they had contested only days before.[5]

Fervently in favor of the war, Reid boasted how, from all parts of Ohio, the state alone could furnish one-third "or more" of all volunteers (75,000) called for by the President. He excitedly pointed out, April 24, how "troops continue pouring in. . . . Ohio seems all in arms. . . . Nothing but military legislation receives any attention." In his history *Ohio in the War* Reid later recalled that even before the legislature adjourned, "the acting speaker had resigned to take a command in one of the regiments starting for Washington; two leading [state] Senators had been appointed Brigadier-Generals; and large numbers of the other members had . . . entered the service." Agate's relative inattention to committee reports, the temperance question, and Cincinnati sewage bills in favor of troop movements and militia affairs was also shared by the legislators. Militia bills flooded the assembly, and now and then, one would especially catch the reporter's eye. The House passed a bill, Agate smiled, "about which nobody seemed to know very much. The general idea was that it reduced the number of Generals in Hamilton County."[6]

After the war, Reid vividly remembered the temper of Columbus in those first few days following Sumter. He noted that "twenty full companies were offered to the Governor of Ohio for immediate service" even before the bombardment of Sumter had ended. He recalled that the "excitement became fervidly intense" in Columbus with the news of Sumter's surrender and the President's call for volunteers. "But a single day was required to raise the first two regiments" in support of Lincoln's call. However, "there were no arms, uniforms, equipments, [or] transportation for them." In spite of this, " 'Send them on instantly,' was the order from Washington, 'and we will equip them here.' " Trains bearing this enthusiastic mob of Ohio volunteers left the station in Columbus before dawn on April 19, "but before they started, fresh arrivals had more than filled their places." [7]

On April 23, 1861, the "Little Giant" from Illinois, Stephen A. Douglas, spoke from the statehouse steps in Columbus. The Senator contended, reported Agate, that the "great question" was the South's restriction of the Mississippi Valley trade. Douglas rated this more important than the Negro question, and insisted that this sinister practice be resisted. In addition he agreed that the endangered national capital should be defended, and that constitutional authorities should be supported. Samuel S. ("Sunset") Cox followed Douglas to the rostrum; but Agate showed more interest in the words of Edwin M. Stanton, who followed Cox. Stanton, Reid observed, disagreed with Douglas. No "mere commercial question" faced the nation, but rather a constitutional one that involved rebellion, which, Stanton emphasized, had to be suppressed! Agate agreed.[8]

Once the state legislature adjourned, there was little reason for Reid to remain in Columbus, although the pulse of the state still raced in an accelerated manner. Agate's reports after April 24 became briefer, on the average, and after May 1 perhaps this was due to an editor's appeal for brevity from his correspondents. The *Gazette* published an edition of forty columns, ten to a page, with an average of a fourth of those in advertisements, and doubtless every report filed could not be printed. In addition, by May 2 Agate sounded bored. This "tall, graceful youth" with his "enviable black moustache and imperial," who wore "his hair long in the Southern fashion" and carried himself with "native grace," champed at the bit, only to be rescued by the *Gazette* and the post of city editor.[9]

Agate's by-line appeared once more, May 20, as a "special reporter" from Morrow, Ohio, where a convention met to nominate a successor for Thomas Corwin's Seventh District seat in Congress, and then not again until June 8, 1861. In June, Agate joined an energetic group of "special correspondents" who reported to the *Gazette* from the field. "Patapiso" reported regularly from Baltimore; "Philander" first from Ohio camps and then from elsewhere in the Midwest; "X" from St. Louis, Missouri, then Wisconsin, and other points farther west; "J.G." from Washington, D.C.; "W.L.M." from various points in the field, often close to Agate; and others. These correspondents attracted a personal following, and their combat dispatches were often widely reprinted.[10]

At the age of twenty-three, Reid went into the field as an aide-de-camp on the staff of General Thomas A. Morris, to report on the operations in Western Virginia. Agate filed twenty-two reports from Virginia between June 8 and July 27, 1861, ranging from five columns in the July 22 issue of the *Gazette* to one-third or less of a column on other occasions. His dispatches reflected less his moods than they did the spirits of the Ohio soldiers he accompanied, but they always echoed his opinions on men and events.[11]

His first field report came from Grafton, Virginia. In this one Agate, whom the *Gazette* called "Our Own Correspondent," told of his uneventful ride on the B&O from Wheeling to Grafton and his survey of the troops camped there and in Philippi. Although he commented on the poor quality of the uniforms, the morale of the "boys" appeared excellent. He found them "having an uproarious time in their camps, singing 'The Star Spangled Banner' and 'The Girl I left behind me,' . . . and growling about the extraordinary capacity for running manifested by those valorous Virginians," who, Reid noted, were each supposed to be "equal to six craven Yankees in the field." This opinion as well as the soldiers' high spirits came from their recent victory at Philippi over a handful of Confederates. Also, as Agate reported in the June 10 *Gazette,* the Union success had decided the fate of Western Virginia. People had been deceived by the rebels, but were now converted into "loyal citizens." [12]

Like the soldiers in the camps, Agate soon learned the monotony of camp life. "We are in the lull which, 'wise men' say, comes before the storm. Around us, everywhere, are the preparations for a protracted struggle." And the impatience to do something: "at Philippi our troops are waiting, waiting, waiting." He read and reported on captured Confederate mail, with the themes of Yankee hatred, fear of Negro insurrection, and even love letters from their women back home. He described camp activities designed to pass the hours, including the practice of "eyeballing." This was the sport "that mysteriously spirits away everything from a pistol to a camp-stool, the moment it is left for an instant beyond the range of your own eye." So fine an art did Ohio soldiers make it, that "the old saying about the Ohio volunteers in Mexico, that if they couldn't take a town they could always steal it, applies with literal truthfulness to the camps here." But, Agate added, "to be just, the 'eyeballing' is more a matter of fun . . . than of profit." [13]

Another device for relieving the monotony of the camp has always been faultfinding. An encampment without complaint would be like a garden without flowers. About nine thousand Union troops faced Laurel Hill, Reid reported, a position that "a week ago, before the [Confederate] reinforcements arrived, it would have been an easy task [to take]. Now we are meeting the usual fate of procrastination." A couple of days later, Agate complained, "It is evident, here as elsewhere, this war is to be conducted on peace principles. . . . We are to out-maneuver the enemy, before out-fighting him." After Reid moved to Philippi with General Morris, he confided to his readers, "I have written nothing since my arrival here, till this morning, for two good and sufficient reasons: first, I had nothing to write; and, second, I was weary of predicting a fight." [14]

Eventually, the Union army in Virginia's mountains moved. General George B. McClellan led one column to Clarksburg (accompanied by the *Gazette*'s "W.L.M."), and Morris took the other to Philippi. The general idea was to catch the Confederates at Laurel Hill in a pincers movement. Morris' column would hit them from the front as McClellan's swung around to catch them from the rear. On July 8, from Bealington, opposite Laurel Hill, Reid described the night march from Philippi. The men were roused at 1:00 A.M., and in reasonable time swung out on the Beverly pike. "The night was cloudy, and in the darkness we could only faintly discern the gleam of the bayonets nearest to us, while the steady tramp alone told of the passage of an army." They approached Bealington after dawn "with great caution. There was every opportunity for ambuscades." It was after seven in the morning when the first shots were heard, as the skirmishers drove in the Confederate pickets, who ran "like quarter nags." The column dug into position on the hill above Bealington, and skirmishers continued firing until nightfall. Agate described the ebb and flow of the skirmishes very well. The hail of bullets "whistling overhead" until one "struck the saber of an artillery officer. This was getting a little too warm," so the officer "dropped a shell in the wood" from whence came the offending bullet. "For a little while the enemy seemed repulsed; then they returned." Another shell "was thrown toward the rebels. Our boys instantly sprang forward . . . and poured in a galling volley upon the enemy, picking off particularly the mounted officers. . . . For a few moments all was quiet; then the rattle of musketry began again." Reid described the skirmish as "a most spirited affair." [15]

Once in position, Morris' column was to await McClellan's arrival behind the Confederate position. " 'Where is McClel-

lan?' We have been expecting him . . . ever since our own
arrival," Agate wrote. "If the enemy is still trapped . . . it will
be attributable to our good luck, not to our good management." Two days passed, and still Morris awaited McClellan.
"Manifestly we are to have a little more warfare on the peace-
able system," Reid snorted. "we must . . . go through the old,
sad process of waiting for our enemy to get ready before attacking him." To keep the troops busy, they engaged in "deviling"
(taunting) the enemy. But the Confederates would not be
lured into a general skirmish.[16]

July 13 dawned upon Morris' column at Laurel Hill only to
reveal that the enemy had evacuated their positions. In a surprise move Brigadier General Robert S. Garnett, C.S.A., pulled
out in order to escape the obvious attempt to trap him. Morris'
troops followed the retreating rebels, and Agate, along with
many Union soldiers, surveyed the recent campsite. "Everywhere were left camp stools, tables, camp cots, camp chests,
underclothing, uniforms, overcoats, bundles of socks, drawers,
shirts, knapsacks, valises, . . . axes, . . . bowie-knives, shovels, inkstands, love-letters, spurs, boots," and many other items,
evidence of a hasty move. "The accumulation of bottles was
amazing. Evidently the rebels had been a thirsty tribe. And of
playing cards, what *shall* I say? . . . The whole camp was sown
broadcast with cards and whisky bottles," Reid remarks, "not a
single one . . . found with anything save the memory of departed spirits." Union soldiers delayed an hour or two and
worked "like beavers, to accumulate whatever they could lay
their hands on." [17]

The excitement of looting the abandoned camp delayed the
pursuit of the rebels as much as did the trees felled across the
roads. The chase continued the following day, this time in the
rain and mud. Discarded baggage convinced the soldiers that
they must be on the very heels of the enemy, whom the soldiers
now called the "F.F.V.": fleet-footed Virginians. From time to
time there was the sound of firing or other sign of combat, most

of which proved false alarms. Morris halted his column at the Cheat River, but Reid rode on ahead. He came upon a medical aid station caring for wounded of the Fourteenth Ohio, ambushed during a rear-guard action by Garnett's troops. Spurring on, Agate came upon the rebel rear guard at Carrick's Ford, directed by Garnett himself. The "battle," wrote Reid, was "very short," about half an hour, but "very brilliant." Garnett himself perished, forty wagons, much equipage, and many prisoners fell into Union hands.[18]

Reid returned to the bluff where the Confederate rear guard had fought and where Garnett had died, after the skirmish at Carrick's Ford ended. "Along the brink of that bluff lay ten bodies, stiffening in their own gore," Agate informed readers of the *Gazette*. "Others were gasping in the last agonies, and still others were writhing with horrible but not mortal wounds. . . . Never, before had I so ghastly a realization of the horrid nature of this fraternal struggle." He expressed the sad realization that "these men were all Americans." He continued with a description of the depressing aftermath of battle. "One poor fellow was shot through the bowels. The ground was soaked with his blood. I stooped and asked him if anything could be done to make him more comfortable; he only whispered, 'I'm so cold!' " Reid pictured other wounded, some with horrible head wounds but still living. "May I never see another field like that!" he exclaimed.[19]

Reid, before returning to Grafton, joined the detail chosen to accompany Garnett's body on its journey to the Rowlesburg railway station. There he telegraphed to Cincinnati the news of Garnett's death, scooping the rest of the press, since Garnett was the first general officer killed in the war. The group traveled over poor roads and through territory where they could expect to encounter Confederates. At night the passage proved even more difficult than by daylight, and in the early morning hours they were fired upon as they approached an encampment. They held up until dawn revealed they faced a Union force.

Agate later snorted that "a pack of cowards from the Fifteenth Ohio," who in his opinion appeared "never to have been properly trained," were responsible for firing on the body detail.[20]

Back at Grafton, July 18, Reid summed up the campaign in terms quite unflattering to McClellan. "The bepraised galaxy of victories leaves us today precisely where we stood the morning after the affair at Philippi," Agate opined. The plan at Laurel Hill was "to *catch* the [Confederate] army, instead of driving it. *That has failed.*" The "practical results" of McClellan's strategy (and Agate expressed his contempt by putting the word in quotation marks) proved *"that it failed, and that he didn't catch them!"* Morris' army moved easily enough into proper position, but McClellan "was stopped at Rich Mountain. The rebels were given ample time to see the trap closing. . . . Of course they escaped. . . . This," wrote Reid acidly, "is the culmination of the brilliant Generalship, which the journals of the sensational persuasion have been besmearing with such nauseous flattery." [21]

This "nauseous flattery" won McClellan the job of commanding the eastern armies. McClellan did not disappoint Reid subsequently with the Army of the Potomac. After the war, Reid wrote that "the historian who shall seek to trace in detail the steps to the strange torpor that subsequently befel the Army of the Potomac may indeed find in . . . [the West Virginia campaign] suggestive hints." He characterized McClellan as one who "delayed needlessly, lost the advantage . . . handled his force irresolutely and without nerve." Reid lamented, "it was the peculiar misfortune of the first General whom Ohio gave to the War for the Union . . . that his friends insisted upon crowning him at the very moment of his entrance. Christened 'Young Napoleon' before he had ever commanded a regiment under fire," Reid continued, ". . . it was not wonderful that when [1861–62 in the East] summer had ripened into fall around his motionless battalions, and winter snowed them in, and spring had found them motionless still, he discovered the patient people began to demand some sign of Napoleonic deeds." Even so, Reid noted that this man who "had begun by . . . holding back" possessed exceptional organizational ability.[22]

The *Gazette,* filled with bad news from Manassas, crowded Reid's other follow-ups onto interior pages. Reid soon returned to Ohio from Grafton, and next appeared at Columbus again to cover the Democratic state convention. He found the "atmosphere . . . unwholesome," and made short shrift of the whole proceedings. "The . . . party hacks, small-fry politicans, and 'local great men,' who are opposed to uniting with all loyal citizens for the support of the Union" had come to town. He deplored "the sickening air of party politics" at a time when the Union was in danger. After this slap at the Democrats, he returned to Cincinnati; in October he left for Kentucky. His reportorial roamings soon took him west to General Ulysses S. Grant's army, which he followed after the Forts Henry and Donelson campaign to Pittsburg Landing.[23]

Reid went up the Tennessee River with a couple of members of Grant's staff and spent several early April days visiting all parts of the encampment at Pittsburg Landing. For a reporter who had struggled to explain the strategy of Magenta and Solferino to readers of the *Xenia News* a couple of years earlier, Reid had no difficulty grasping the essence of the Union movement in the present instance. Break the Memphis and Charleston Railroad line at Corinth, "and the Southern Confederacy is cut in two as effectually as if a Chinese wall were built between the Gulf and the seaboard States. [Gen. P. G. T.] Beauregard . . . is engaged in defending the last connected line of defense the rebels can possibly adopt." But it was not merely defense that Beauregard and General Albert S. Johnston had in mind. Reid apparently had been reassured by Grant's belief that no attack would be made at Pittsburg Landing, because his reports prior to the battle do not reflect undue concern. Once the affair had begun, however, Reid's hindsight indicated that all the danger signs had been present.[24]

"Our great Tennessee expedition had been up the river some four weeks," Agate began. "We had occupied Pittsburg Landing for about three. . . . Beyond this we had engaged in no active operations." Reid's travels over the field and his conversations with the officers brought to him the information that the Confederates "began massing their troops" until "presently they had more in the vicinity than we had. Then we waited for [Gen. Don C.] Buell" and his army, approaching from Nashville. Johnston's troops became "restive under our slow concentrations," and an attack by them "seemed probable. Yet we had lain at Pittsburg Landing, within twenty miles of the rebels . . . without throwing up a single breastwork or preparing a single protection for a battery." The troops encamped in random fashion "as they arrived." [25]

On April 4 a skirmish with the Confederates revealed a battery they had "already in position, at no great distance from our lines." Yet federal officers "generally supposed that the affair had been an ordinary picket fight, presaging nothing more." By this time Grant admitted "there was great probability of a rebel attack," but, Agate reported, he made "no . . . preparation for such an unlooked-for event, and so the matter was dismissed." Yet skirmishing continued the following day as well. Reid noted rumors that the Confederates had been ordered to attack Grant before Buell's army could join him, since the rebels "could not possibly expect to hold their vitally important position at Corinth" against the Union combination. "Fortunately," Agate added, "they timed their movements a day too late." [26]

Reid spent April 5 ill in bed at General Lew Wallace's headquarters at Crump's Landing, northwest of Shiloh. Grant, whose horse fell on his leg the evening before, temporarily laming the General, remained at Savannah, April 5, awaiting

Buell. Buell actually arrived in Savannah that evening, but did
not call on Grant; and the rapid sequence of events the following morning precluded a meeting of the two men then. "The
sun never rose on a more beautiful morning than that of Sunday, April sixth," Reid recalled. "By sunrise I was aroused by
the cry: 'They're fighting above.' " Agate heard the "volleys of
musketry" and "the sullen boom of artillery" which meant, by
their increasing volume, that this was much more than another
skirmish. Reid breakfasted with Wallace and his staff on board
their steamboat at Crump's Landing. When Grant appeared on
board the "Tigress" at eight-thirty to give Wallace his orders,
Reid boarded the commander's vessel and in this way arrived
on the field with Grant.[27]

As the "Tigress," with Reid and Grant on board, sped
toward Pittsburg Landing, "the west bank of the river was
lined with the usual fugitives from action hurriedly pushing
onwards . . . down stream and away from the fight." When
challenged by officers on board the steamboat, "they all gave
the same response: 'We're clean cut to pieces, and every man
must save himself.' " As the party approached the landing, the
"two Cincinnati wooden gunboats, 'Taylor' [sic] and 'Lexington' were edging uneasily up and down the banks," looking for
a spot for their broadsides, "but unable to find" one. By this
time "the roar o[f] the battle was startlingly close." As the
steamer docked, Reid observed the landing and the bluff above
it "covered with cowards who had fled . . . to the rear for
safety" and who told "the most fearful stories of the rebel onset
and the sufferings of their own . . . regiments." Reid hurried
"out toward the scene of action" and soon discovered "there
was too much foundation for the tales of the runaways." Sherman's and Prentiss' divisions were falling back in disorder.
"McClernand's had already lost part of its camps." In the midst
of the disaster Agate saw "one consolation—only one— . . .
History, so the divines say, is positive on the point that no
attack ever made on the Sabbath was eventually a success to the

attacking party." Even so, Agate added, "the signs were sadly against the theologians." [28]

Reid stopped to describe the topography of the region for his readers. The narrow ravine of Pittsburg Landing through which the road to the riverbank passes; the Landing itself, where there is no town; "two log huts comprise all the improvements visible." Beyond the river bluffs was rolling country, with some ravines, some cultivation, "the greater part thickly wooded with some underbrush." The field was divided by many roads, "the most inextricable maze of cross-roads, intersecting everything and leading everywhere, in which it was ever my ill-fortune to become entangled." Agate then described the random arrangement of Grant's five divisions "on and between these roads" so that the reader would "hardly fail to observe the essential defects of such arrangements." [29]

As the Confederates attacked near dawn, "the enemy were into the camps almost as soon as the pickets" they drove before them. In the camps "many, particularly among our officers," had not yet risen. "Others were dressing, others washing, others cooking, a few eating. . . . In short, the camps were completely surprised." Shot and shell whined into the Union camps, and right behind this deadly warning "thronged the rebel regiments, firing sharp volleys . . . and springing forward upon our laggards with the bayonet. Scores were shot down as they" ran weaponless, "hatless, coatless, toward the river." Others died in their tents or struggling to leave them. In the flight "our shattered regiments" did what they could. "Falling rapidly back through the heavy woods till they gained a protecting ridge . . . Sherman's men succeeded in partially checking the rush of the enemy, long enough to form their hasty line of battle." [30]

Part of Sherman's division, on the left, composed of raw troops, "hundreds" of whom had "never heard a gun fired in anger," just ran, a fact Reid found "hardly surprising." Sherman himself, by "dashing along the lines," and "exposing his own

life with the same freedom with which he demanded their offer
of theirs . . . did much to save the division from utter destruction." McClernand threw forward troops to help bolster Sherman's left, while veterans such as McDowell "held their ground
fiercely." Prentiss, on the left of Sherman, formed a line of
battle, but in the open. His "men held their position with an
obstinacy that adds new laurels to the character of the American soldiers, but it was too late." The Confederates pushed their
front and pressed their flanks, and "more and more rapidly
they fell back, less and less frequent became their returning
volleys." By ten in the morning Prentiss' division was out of
combat, the gap in the Federal line only partially plugged by
General W. H. L. Wallace's division, which rushed to Prentiss'
assistance. As Sherman's division fell back, McClernand's came
to bear the shock of the rebel advance. Eventually, Sherman's
troops had so scattered that McDowell had no support and had
to retire, at which point Reid remarked, "the greater part of
Sherman's division passes out of view." This did not reflect on
Sherman, who had been "indefatigable in collecting and reorganizing his men" and who took himself "a musket-ball
through the hand." [31]

Agate reported how McClernand fell back in better order,
even attacking the enemy at one point, but in the end forced
into retreat. It was about this time that both Grant and Reid
arrived on the field. General S. A. Hurlbut's division, encamped behind McClernand, took the weight of the Confederate advance as McClernand's men, exhausted, faltered. From
"thick woods," with "open fields before them" they stood their
ground and held the enemy in check "from ten to half-past
three." The Confederates charged them "three times during
those long hours . . . and three times they were repulsed, with
terrible slaughter." Finally, "after six hours' magnificent fighting, it [Hurlbut's division] fell back . . . to a point within
half a mile of the Landing." W. H. L. Wallace's division had
taken up the fight about ten o'clock and "manfully bore up"

until about four in the afternoon. They took four rebel
charges, but they could not remain in line long after Hurlbut
finally fell back.[32]

"We have reached the last act in the tragedy of Sunday,"
Reid recorded. "It is half past four o'clock. Our front line of
divisions has been lost since half past ten. Our reserve line is
now gone, too. . . . Our whol[e] army is crowded in . . . to a
circuit of half to two-thirds of a mile around the Landing."
The next charge, said Agate, "puts us into the river." Lew
Wallace's division could still save the day, "but where is it?"
The Union camps, camp equipment, half the field artillery,
and many men were lost. "The hospitals are full to overflowing.
A long ridge bluff is set apart for surgical uses. It is covered
with the maimed, the dead and dying. . . . Our men are discouraged." Only the "most energetic exertion" by the officers
kept the soldiers "from becoming demoralized." [33]

"Meanwhile there is a lull in the firing. For the first time
since sunrise you fail to catch the angry rattle of musketry or
the heavy booming of the field guns." Reid feared that the
Confederates were preparing "for the grand, final rush," or else
were puzzled by the last retreat "and are moving cautiously lest
we spring some trap upon them." Looking about the Landing,
Agate beheld Grant and his staff in conversation beside one of
the log buildings. " 'We can hold them off till to-morrow,' " a
confident Grant advised, " 'then they'll be exhausted, and we'll
go at them with fresh troops.' " Reid sneered at the "great
crowd" of uniformed armed men at the Landing around Grant,
when "we are needing troops in the front so sorely!" [34]

Agate described in reproachful terms the "three thousand
skulkers lining the banks" of the river. Their excuses all
sounded alike: their regiments had been cut up; they couldn't
find their officers; and, Agate added, "that would be the very
last thing [they] would want to do." Reid portrayed the major
who made "a sort of elevated, superfine Fourth of July speech"
to all who would listen exhorting these fugitives to return to

the battlefield. None responded. Reid, who claimed to know "well enough the nature of the skulking animal" from other performances, had never witnessed them "on so large a scale, never with such an utter sickness of heart as I looked, as now." But across the Tennessee River, Agate saw a body of Buell's cavalry awaiting transportation across. Then came a glimpse of shining gun barrels and "the steady, swinging tramp of trained soldiers." A division of Buell's army marched up to join the cavalry. The skulkers around Pittsburg Landing sent up three cheers for Buell. "*They* cheering! May it parch their throats," snarled Reid, "as if they had been breathing the Simoon!" [35]

By now "that driven, defeated, but not disgraced army of Gen. Grant's" had set up the remaining artillery—twenty-two guns, Reid counted—in a semi-circle to protect the landing. The time remained half-past four o'clock "perhaps a quarter later still" when the rebel artillery opened fire again. A furious cannonade followed, and Agate wished that one or two rebel shells might drop "among the crowd of skulkers hovering under the hill at the river's edge." Not only the relocated Union artillery acquitted themselves very well at this moment but "very handsome was the response our broken infantry battalions poured in. . . . The rebel infantry gained no ground." A Confederate attack began on the Union left, along the river-bank, and now the gunboats, the "Tyler" and "Lexington" that had been "all day impatiently chafing for their time," opened up with "broadside after broadside of seven-inch shells and sixty-four-pound shot." The gunboat attack "sadly disconcerted" the Confederate battle plan. "And thus," Reid wrote, "amid a crash, and roar, and scream of shells and demon-like hiss of Minie-balls, that Sabbath evening wore away. We held the enemy at bay; it was enough." [36]

At dusk the firing tapered off. One of Buell's advance brigades, coming on the field on the double, had managed to get in a few rounds. Lew Wallace's division finally arrived from Crump's Landing, and was assigned the Union right, and

Buell's divisions as well as hastily reorganized troops of Grant's army "stealthily . . . crept to their new positions and lay down in line of battle on their arms." All night the gunboats kept up a steady, probing, cannonade. A thunderstorm swept across the battlefield about midnight. Discussing the dispositions of troops for the second day of battle, and the slight rebel withdrawals during the night, doubtless to consolidate their positions, Agate observed that "thus far I have said little or nothing of any plan of attack or defence among our commanders. It has been simply because I have failed to see any evidences of such a plan." Reid claimed that on Sunday it seemed that every soldier "imitated the good old Israelitish plan of action, by which every man did what seemed good in his own eyes." During the night there was a council of war, but if Grant developed any plans beyond the arrangement of the battle lines, Reid was "very certain that some of the division commanders didn't find it out." [37]

Monday morning "by seven o'clock Lew Wallace opened the ball by shelling, from the positions he had selected the night before, the rebel battery" that stood in the way of his advance. Wallace and the right wing began to move, while simultaneously the left wing pushed forward for nearly a mile "till it came upon [the rebels] . . . in force." The left wing advanced steadily until "half past ten o'clock . . . sweeping . . . over the ground of our sore defeat on Sunday morning, [and] forward over scores of rebel dead, resistlessly pressing back the jaded and wearied enemy." Reid observed the rebels received few reinforcements overnight, "their men were exhausted with their desperate contest of the day before, and manifestly dispirited by the evident fact that . . . they were fighting Grant and Buell combined." At one point the rebels hurled a sharp counterattack at the advancing Union left, and threatened to turn their victory into defeat, when a "regular battery came dashing up. Scarcely taking time to unlimber, [the captain] . . . was loading and sighting his pieces before the caissons had turned, and in an instant was tossing shell . . . into the compact and advancing rebel ranks." Agate pinpointed this as "the turning point of the battle on the left. The rebels were . . . checked." Two hours of hard fighting ensued, until the enemy "began to waver. Our men pressed on, pouring in deadly volleys. Just then, Buell, who assumed the general direction of his troops in the field, came up," and ordered the men forward "at double quick." Reid noted "our men leaped forward as if they had been tied," and pushed the Confederates off the field.[38]

The left center moved forward in much the same fashion. "Farther to the right, McClernand and Hurlbut were gallantly coming on with their jaded men. The soldiers *would fight,* that was the great lesson of the battle." The troops that had been forced off the field during Sunday's hard battle took much of the Confederate attention on Monday. "Four times McClernand regained and lost again the ground to the front of his division," Agate reported. "Similar were Hurlbut's fortunes." Lew Wallace and Sherman on the far right repelled a very determined rebel effort to turn the flank, but "by four o'clock . . . a general rebel retreat—then pursuit, recall, and encampment on the old grounds of Sherman's Division, in the very tents from which those regiments were driven" marked success of that flank by late afternoon. Calculating roughly the number of troops involved in the two-day battle, Agate concluded "it was *not* numbers that gained us the day, it was fighting. All honor to our Northern soldiers for it." [39]

Bearing the dateline Pittsburg Landing, Tennessee, Arpil 9, Agate followed up his famous account of the battle with a typical critique that appeared in the *Gazette* April 15. Reid, disappointed that no new federal strikes had then been made, pointed out that the Confederate "rear guard was still within eight miles of us. If cavalry is ever to be of any use to us, then was the time to let it out. But no pursuit has been made." Reid understood that "Grant is not permitted by his orders to pursue. . . . We are expecting Gen. [Henry W.] Halleck by Friday night or Saturday morning to take the command in person. He may go into things with a dash, but I should doubt it yet." Actually, Grant had a different reason for not ordering the pursuit. "I . . . had not the heart to order the men who had fought desperately for two days, lying in mud and rain whenever not fighting . . . to pursue." Grant thought perhaps he should have ordered Buell to follow, but having been Buell's senior in rank "only a few weeks," he hesitated. And then he "did not meet Buell in person until too late to get troops ready and pursue with effect." [40]

"Certainly it was not a defeat," wrote Agate, as he opened the final paragraph of his critique. "But was it a decisive victory? . . . If they were defeated so badly . . . as to turn their defeat into a rout; or if the killing of Johnston . . . should produce . . . demoralization enough . . . to prevent their making a firm stand at Corinth," then, said Reid, "the victory was—*or might be made*—the most decisive of the war. But if . . . they are able to perfect their defenses at Corinth" this "greatest battle of the war . . . will become mainly a success in regaining camps from which we had been driven by a surprise." [41]

On April 15 Agate had a few more footnotes to add to his battle notes. Of his own account, he observed it had been "certainly long enough to accomplish the double work of exhausting alike myself and the public." Of Sherman, Agate reported "that he escaped with [only] two slight wounds seems almost unaccountable." Of the Confederates, Reid returned to a theme he had also elaborated upon in Western Virginia. "It was curious to find the origin of the *elan* and dash with which the rebels came . . . against our lines," he reported, "on the bodies of their dead, in the shape of canteens filled with whisky, or with the more maddening compound of whisky and gunpowder. On our side," Reid boasted, "there were no such stimulants to courage—if for no better reason, at least for the very satisfactory one that they couldn't get it." [42]

In another report Agate addressed himself to the question *"Did* the Ohio troops run?" His answer, frank and straight to the point, came without equivocation. "They ran. Certainly,—ran, some of them without their arms, all of them in a confusion. . . . You would have done the same." The reason was not cowardice. "The men were completely surprised. Some of their officers were bayoneted in their beds; others were shot in their tents . . . all were under heavy fire." Reid asked, "The trouble is in *being* surprised, whose fault is that? . . . It is astonishing," he observed, that Grant did not have an effective network of scouts and pickets out.[43]

On Grant, Agate praised the commander's coolness, even when a bullet struck his scabbard. But Reid's real tribute to Grant came after the war. "That the son of a tanner, poor, unpretending . . . should rise—not suddenly, . . . not at all for what he had done—but slowly, grade by grade . . . till, at the end of a four years' war he stood at the head of our armies," seemed to Reid a "satisfactory answer to criticism and a sufficient vindication of greatness. Success succeeds." But Shiloh left Agate, even at war's end, with mixed feelings. "Of Grant's conduct during this battle nothing can be said but praise; of his conduct before it little but blame." It was as if the General despised his enemy. "The neglect of pickets and out-posts approached criminality," but when "the storm which he thus invited had burst . . . Grant rose to the height of a hero. More than that, he rose . . . to the height of a General." [44]

Reid's report of Shiloh, on the spot, reasonably accurate, and frank, reprinted in whole or in part in a number of papers besides the *Gazette,* particularly in the West, brought Reid a bright reputation as a correspondent. He began the account on the field, and added to it on a hospital boat and on the train as he made his way back to Cincinnati. Reid's biographer observed that "the very outspokenness which made him popular at home" made him "anything but popular at camp." When he returned to the field of Shiloh a couple of weeks later to join the army for its campaign against Corinth, Halleck, then in command, "let loose his famous war upon the press." Halleck told the correspondents that their passes from Edwin M. Stanton's War Department would not be recognized. Reid and the other correspondents bristled understandably when General John Pope pressed Halleck for an explanation, and Halleck, who had tried to dodge the question, was forced to include the correspondents in the category of "unauthorized hangers-on" who would not be permitted to accompany the army. After a fruitless protest to Halleck, the correspondents withdrew, including Reid. The Gazette's answer was to promote Reid and send him to join their Washington staff. This job did not keep him off other battlefields, however. He spent some time in Kentucky castigating Buell in his attempt to catch Braxton Bragg and Kirby Smith.[45]

In the spring of 1863 Reid returned to Columbus once more to cover the state Democratic convention that nominated Vallandigham for governor of Ohio. He wrote about "the scandalous affair" in all its "grotesque features" when news of General Richard S. Ewell's Confederate raid into Pennsylvania flashed across the wires. Reid took the first train for Philadelphia, discounted the "panic-stricken stories" he heard, and continued on to Washington. But clearly something was up; the Army of the Potomac was on the move, so Reid went to Frederick to learn what he could. The Gazette, as curious as he, ordered Reid to join the army as quickly as possible. Finding a horse, Agate rode to General George G. Meade's headquarters at Taneytown.[46]

On the way, the "whole road was lined with stragglers." Reid thought no more of them than he had of the skulkers at Pittsburg Landing, and sailed into them with editorial gusto. "Take a worthless vagabond," he wrote, "who has enlisted for thirteen dollars a month instead of patriotism, who falls out of ranks because he is a coward . . . or because he is rapacious and wants to . . . frighten or wheedle timid countrywomen . . .

make this armed coward . . . drunk on bad whisky," add in "scores and hundreds" of others like him, "and then . . . you have the condition of the country in the rear of our own army, on our own soil, today." The rebels take care of this problem better than does the Union, Agate opined. "Death on the spot is said to be their punishment . . . and in the main it is a just one." [47]

Headquarters, actually a half-mile east of Taneytown, bustled with activity as Reid arrived. "Everybody is ready to take the saddle at a moment's notice," he told his readers. Reid saw Meade in his "plain little wall tent" poring over a map. "Tall, slender, . . . thin-faced, with grizzled beard and moustache," Meade impressed Agate "rather as a thoughtful student than as a dashing soldier." Then, suddenly, a rider galloped up and dismounted. Reid recognized him as a fellow correspondent, L. L. Crounse of the *New York Times*. Crounse hurriedly told of a fight near Gettysburg and of the death of General John F. Reynolds, "and . . . rumors of more bad news." The two writers hastily mounted, and Crounse guided Reid to Gettysburg. They made slow progress along roads choked with infantry, but they managed to keep in advance of Meade and his headquarters. Unlike Shiloh, where Reid reached the field along with Grant, this time he intended to get there before the commander. The slow going and the darkness caused the correspondents to take a by-pass, which allowed them to make better time. They stopped to catch a few hours' sleep at a farmhouse about four miles from Gettysburg, and, figuring the battle to continue at dawn, were on their way again at four in the morning.[48]

Riding past "farm houses turned into hospitals," batteries moving into position, troops forming into new lines, they came up to Meade and his headquarters. "By his [Meade's] side is the calm, honest, manly face of [General O. O.] Howard. . . . They are arranging the new line of battle." The correspondents moved on, until, standing atop Cemetery Hill, "the buzzing hiss of a well-aimed minie" passed over their heads. Reid recognized this spot as "the key to the whole position," and described the Union lines correctly as horseshoe in shape. Howard made his headquarters on this hill, and shortly, he arrived. "During the lull that still lasted" Howard explained the fight of the preceding day as he had seen it. From Howard's account, and that of others, Reid wove "their statements into a connected narrative." [49]

"I am a poor hand to describe battles I do not see," Agate began. Also he had no opportunity to familiarize himself with the battleground, as he had at Shiloh, "save from the descriptions of others and the distant view one gets from Cemetery Hill." Reid proceeded to describe the encounter with the Confederate vanguard at Gettysburg and the confident movement of the Union veterans that made up their forward elements. "The fire of the rebel skirmishers rattled along the front, but, shaking it off as they had the dew from their night's bivouac, the men pushed hotly on." General John F. Reynolds sent for reinforcements, and rode forward to select a line of battle. But Reynolds "fell, almost instantly, pierced by a ball from a sharp-shooter's rifle." His veterans, the old "Iron Brigade" of Indiana, Michigan, and Wisconsin troops, and another, "well mated," of New Yorkers, had "no time to wait for orders from the new corps commander [General Abner Doubleday]; instantly, right and left, . . . [they] wheeled into line of battle on the double-quick. Well-tried troops, those; no fear of their flinching." The men held well, repulsed the Confederate advance guard, and took a large number of prisoners; but by the time Howard came on the field and assumed command at one o'clock, it was clear that "the old, old game was playing. The enemy was concentrating faster than we." Stonewall Jackson's troops, minus their leader, pushed the Union right back upon the town. Then by half-past three the left, having held their positions since morning, faltered under the weight of A. P. Hill and Ewell, and also retired.[50]

A crisis at hand, Howard, the "brave, one-armed, Christian fighting hero," rose to master it. "One cavalry charge, twenty minutes' well-directed cannonading, might wipe out nearly a third of the enemy." Howard selected Cemetery Hill for a new position, hurried batteries into line, "and when the rebel pursuit had advanced half way through the town a thunderbolt leaped out from the whole length of that line . . . and smote them where they stood. The battle was ended," the Federals retreated no farther. The iron brigade, that morning "1,820 strong . . . came out with 700 men." The Union army continued to arrive on the scene all night, just as Reid himself had, and had not yet completed concentrating by the dawn of July 4, the second day. Reid described the line of battle, with Generals Howard, Winfield Scott Hancock, the dashing Daniel E. Sickles, and George Sykes holding center to left, while Henry W. Slocum's corps stretched to the right next to Howard. John Segwick's corps waited in reserve.[51]

"All Thursday forenoon there was lively firing between our skirmishers and those of the enemy, but nothing betokening a general engagement." Agate visited Meade's headquarters about noon, and observed that Meade resisted pressure from his staff to attack the enemy's center. *"The enemy was to fight him where he stood* . . . wisely decided, as the event proved." The afternoon was quiet also, and "passed on in calm and cloudless splendor," which allowed Reid time to ride all along the line and visit various headquarters. Meade expected an attack upon the left, and ordered Sickles' corps out "to unmask" the enemy's preparations. "It did." Longstreet brought up his whole corps, and the fight "at once opened." About four o'clock, the first rebel charge was "shattered and sent whirling back on the instant" by "a storm of grape and canister" from Union artillery.[52]

"Another and a grander charge is preparing," however. Rebel artillery showered the Union positions. "Death moves visibly over the whole field, from line to line, and front to rear." After two hours Sickles fell back, reserves moved in, and the line held. "At six the cannonade grew fiercer than ever, and the storm . . . swept over the field from then till darkness ended the conflict. In the main our strengthened columns held the line. . . . Both sides lay on their arms exhausted, but insatiate, to wait for the dawning." At dusk, Ewell feinted on the right, badly weakened from its use reinforcing the left, but failed to exploit this advantage.[53]

"At daybreak crashing volleys woke the few sleepers there were." A sharp contest began on the right, as the Federals sought to dislodge Ewell from his advance of the evening before. Reid heard this action and strove to ride up toward it. As he moved amid the throng on the Baltimore pike to the field, Agate found Sickles. "On a stretcher, borne by a couple of stout privates, lay Gen. Sickles, but yesterday leading his corps . . . to-day with his right leg amputated," calmly resting, "with his cap pulled over his eyes . . . and *a cigar in his mouth!* For a man who had just lost a leg . . . it was cool indeed." An honor guard carried him to the nearest railroad that he might be sent to a city for better care. By the time Reid reached the field, he observed that the rebels had not been dislodged from the positions on the right that they occupied at dusk. Union artillery fired, but the rebels did not answer. When he reached Cemetery Hill at eight o'clock, "it was comparatively quiet again." [54]

Reid visited Hancock, and as he did so the fire grew a "little hotter on the hill." Rebel artillery began to open, but Hancock did not flinch. "I have seen many men in action," Agate reported, "but never one so imperturbably cool as this General." Reid dodged when he heard a minie whizz past, but Hancock "did not move a muscle by the fraction of a hair's-breadth." About nine-fifteen action increased in volume on the right, but subsided again within half an hour. Reid then visited Meade's headquarters. It was a scene of bustling activity, of course— even more so when the Confederates began dropping round shot at its door. Reid rode off and watched artillery play along the left, then over to the right where Ewell's men were finally forced from their positions of the evening before. It was quarter-past eleven. The fighting so far had been continuous, but except for the right, not heavy.[55]

Reid described the cavalry skirmishes in the rear, and the lull in the fighting on the main field until about one o'clock. He knew, as did the Union officers, that "some final, desperate effort must be maturing." About one o'clock came the "thunder of cannonading that rolled over our army like Doom. They had concentrated immense quantities of artillery—'two hundred and fifty pieces, at least'" according to one of Meade's staff, on the center and left. The target seemed to be Howard on Cemetery Hill, but he remained where he was and "meant to stay." When the cannonade slowed, "down came the rebel lines . . . as if for a parade. . . . They were well up to our front when that whole corps . . . sprang up and poured out their sheet of flame and smoke, and swiftly-flying Death." The batteries opened, "the solid lines broke. . . . Our men charged. . . ." The rebel attack faltered, "and the cannonade on both sides continued at its highest pitch." Reid, who had not been on the spot until this point, "saw such a sight as few men may ever hope to see twice in a lifetime."[56]

"Around our centre and left, the rebel line must have been from four to five miles long." With the noise and smoke of the massed artillery, "it was a sensation for a Century!" The battle slackened about two o'clock, and "the great, desperate, final charge" came at four. They came on as before, "the flower of their army to the front—victory staked upon the issue. In some places they literally lifted up and pushed back our lines," but whenever they entered the Union position "enfilading fires . . . swept away their columns. . . . [Confederate General George E.] Pickett's splendid division" led the attack. Under the Union artillery the Confederate "line literally melted away, but there came a second. . . . Up to the rifle-pits,

across them, over the barricades—the momentum of their charge
. . . swept them on. . . . They were upon the guns, were
bayoneting the gunners, were waving their flags above our
pieces." Then, "the enfilading fire of the guns of the western
slope of Cemetery Hill" hit them. "The line reeled
back . . . in an instant in fragments. Our men . . . leaped
forward upon the disordered mass; but there was little need for
fighting now. A [Confederate] regiment threw down its arms,
and . . . surrendered." The battle was over.[57]

"It was a fruitless sacrifice," Reid observed. "It was not a
rout, it *was* a bitter, crushing defeat. For once the Army of the
Potomac had won a clean, honest, acknowledged victory." But
it had been a narrow victory, for "there stood in the rear just
one single [Union] brigade that constituted the entire
reserve. . . . Forty thousand fresh troops to have hurled forward upon that retreating mass would have ended the campaign with the battle." But the Union had only one fresh
brigade. "The rebels were soon formed again, and ready for
defence—the opportunity was lost!" Reid's readers put down
the July 8 issue of the *Gazette*. They had to await the next day
for Agate's follow-up.[58]

On July 9 the *Gazette* printed the remainder of Agate's
Gettysburg dispatches. "The morning after the battle was as
sweet and fresh as if no storm of Death had all the day before
been sweeping over those quiet Pennsylvania hills and valleys,"
the account began. "The roads were lined with ambulances,
returning to the field for the last of the wounded." Reid rode
over the battlefield of the day before, "at the cost of some
exposure," for all along the lines on the left "a sharp popping
of skirmishers was still kept up." Agate "got a view of the
thickly strown rebel corpses that still cast up to heaven their
mute protest against the treason that had made them what
they were." But he drew no word pictures of the scene, for the
details were "too sickening, and alas! too familiar." Reid found
headquarters the usual busy spot, with the officers breakfasting

on fried pork and hard bread "in a style that a year ago would have astonished the humblest private." [59]

Meade had ordered heavy cavalry reconnaissances. "The bulk of the rebel army was believed to be in full retreat; one strong corps was known to be still strongly posted on well-chosen heights to the northward, and drawn up in line of battle, to receive any attempt on our part at direct pursuit." The headquarters had been under heavy artillery fire the day before, but casualties had been "wonderfully small." Reid quoted in full a lengthy paragraph written by "my friend" Samuel Wilkeson, of the *New York Times* that described the shelling. Reid added that Wilkeson remained at the headquarters through it all. "Mr. Frank Henry, also of the *Times,* likewise stood it out. . . . C. C. Coffin, of the Boston *Journal,* and L. L. Crounse, of the New York *Times* as well as several other journalists . . . were at different times under almost equally heavy fire." Crounse even "had his horse shot under him" during his activities on Thursday.[60]

This account, which Reid put together from his field notes, he wrote "on swaying railroad cars, and amid jostling crowds" on his way back to Cincinnati. "Out of the field once more," he concluded. "May it be forever." Agate had had enough. The Gettysburg report had been a good one, but did not surpass or equal the Shiloh columns. Reid himself agreed with this estimate. "I know that my account of Gettysburg must be inaccurate in many points," he wrote to Edmund C. Stedman nine years later. "On the Pittsburg Landing fight I think I was more accurate, having a better knowledge of the troops and the ground." Evidence in the *Official Records* and in *Battles and Leaders* bear out Reid. His accuracy even at Shiloh may be questioned on a number of points, but not his color or his feeling for excitement and his ability to impart his impressions to thousands of readers. In this he proved himself a superb war correspondent.[61]

After returning to Cincinnati, Reid hastened to New York to

cover the end of the draft riots, and found Horace Greeley's office "transformed into an arsenal." He covered the 1864 political conventions, and was among the first reporters into Richmond after the fall of that city. He wrote up Lincoln's funeral, a melancholy task, for he had sat by the fallen President's bier in the White House and witnessed the long procession up Pennsylvania Avenue from the roof of the Treasury Building. Reid, the Washington correspondent, brought to that reporting the frankness and clarity that filled his war columns. The summer of 1863 found Reid's words appearing in the *New York Times* as well as the *Gazette,* a service for which the *Times* paid him well. His friendship with Salmon P. Chase won him a position as librarian of the House, a job that opened many political avenues and was of great assistance to him as a reporter. He became fast friends with Senator Charles Sumner, and "knew and loved" Ben Wade and Henry Winter Davis. He also knew well and "profoundly admired" Thaddeus Stevens. James A. Garfield and Lincoln's secretaries, J. G. Nicolay and John Hay, also became close acquaintances. Reid numbered Walt Whitman, Orestes Brownson, Count Gurowski, and above all, Greeley, among his literary friends.

But these later events and his Washington activities belong to another, still unwritten, chapter. Agate, the war correspondent, had left the battlefield "forever," just as he had wished.[62]

1. *Cincinnati Daily Gazette,* Apr. 11, 1861; *ibid.,* Apr. 12, 1861. Hereafter referred to simply as the *Gazette.*

2. Royal Cortissoz, *The Life of Whitelaw Reid* (New York, 1921), I, chap. i. This biography is a thorough one, although it slights Reid's career as a war correspondent, devoting only two chapters out of twenty-four in the first volume to the subject. Reid as a Washington correspondent during the war also receives short shrift, only one chapter on that involved episode. Cortissoz' biography has two major defects besides his desire to gloss over Reid's early career: first, it is completely undocumented (and

occasionally, in minor ways, inaccurate, especially in quotations); and second, as Frederic Logan Paxson wrote, Cortissoz, "long an editorial associate" of Reid's believed that Reid was "always right." F. L. Paxson, review of *Life of Reid,* in *The American Historical Review,* XXVII (October, 1921), 135.

3. *Ibid.,* 12–62; on Hole-in-the-day and the Sioux uprising, see Robert H. Jones, *The Civil War in the Northwest* (Norman, Okla., 1960), especially pp. 128 ff.

4. *Gazette,* Apr. 8–May 16, 1861; Cortissoz, *Life of Reid,* I, 71 (italics are Reid's); Whitelaw Reid, *Ohio in the War* (2 vols.; Cincinnati, 1868), I, 20, 21.

5. *Gazette,* Apr. 16, Apr. 19; italics in quotes are always Reid's unless otherwise identified.

6. *Ibid.,* Apr. 10, Apr. 16, Apr. 24; Reid, *Ohio in the War,* I, 24.

7. Reid, *Ohio in the War,* I, 25–28.

8. *Gazette,* Apr. 24.

9. *Ibid.,* Apr. 25–May 15, 1861; Cortissoz, *Life of Reid,* I, 68.

10. *Gazette,* May 20, 1861. Besides those correspondents who contributed to the *Gazette,* Reid joined other great names in the field: Sydney H. Gay, of the *New York Tribune;* Joseph B. McCullagh, of the *Cincinnati Commercial;* Albert D. Richardson, of the *New York Tribune;* Edmund C. Stedman, of the *New York World;* William Swinton, of the *New York Times;* Samuel Wilkeson, of the *New York Tribune;* Lorenzo L. Crounse, of the *New York Times;* Charles C. ("Carleton") Coffin, of the Boston *Journal;* and others who risked their lives on various of the Civil War battlefields as members of the so-called Bohemian Brigade, the war correspondents of the Union. There are a number of histories of the group; two of the most recent and best are: Louis M. Starr, *Bohemian Brigade* (New York: Alfred A. Knopf, 1954), and Emmet Crozier, *Yankee Reporters, 1861–65* (New York, 1956).

11. Cortissoz, *Life of Reid,* I, 71; *Gazette,* June 8–July 27, 1861.

12. *Gazette,* June 8, 1861; *ibid.,* June 10, 1861.

13. *Gazette,* June 17, July 1, July 8, July 10, 1861.

14. *Ibid.,* July 1, July 4, July 8, 1861.

15. *Ibid.,* July 15, 1861.

16. *Ibid.,* July 15, July 16, 1861.

17. *Ibid.,* July 19, 1861.

18. *Ibid.*

19. *Ibid.,* July 22, 1861.

20. *Ibid.*, July 20; Virgil Carrington Jones, in *Gray Ghosts and Rebel Raiders* (New York, 1956), p. 30, credits Agate with the scooping of the rest of the press on the death of Garnett. A minor point, but V. C. Jones is mistaken in calling Reid "John" Whitelaw Reid.

21. *Gazette,* July 22, 1861.

22. Reid, *Ohio in the War,* I, 48, 275, 282, 284.

23. *Gazette,* Aug. 8, 1861; Cortissoz, *Life of Reid,* I, 82–84.

24. *Gazette,* Apr. 9, 1862; Cortissoz, *Life of Reid,* I, 36–37, 84–85.

25. *Gazette,* Apr. 14, 1862. The full report of Shiloh included thirteen columns on the first two pages of the paper (not 10, as Cortissoz reports, p. 84). The account is reprinted in Frank Moore (ed.), *The Rebellion Record* (New York, 1862), IV, 385–400. The account in Moore differs in minor respects from the original.

26. *Gazette,* Apr. 14, 1862.

27. *Ibid.;* Cortissoz, *Life of Reid,* I, 84–85; Ned Bradford (ed.), *Battles and Leaders of the Civil War* (New York, 1956), report of Ulysses S. Grant, p. 85.

28. *Gazette,* Apr. 14, 1862. Reid errs in the name "Taylor"; it should be "Tyler."

29. *Ibid.*

30. *Ibid.* The Confederate advance took its toll of the press corps too. A Philadelphia *Inquirer* reporter was captured in his tent. A *Chicago Tribune* reporter's head was blown off by a six-pound shot. Another *Chicago Tribune* man was badly wounded, and Frank W. Reilly of the Cincinnati *Times* was shot in the leg. Starr, *Bohemian Brigade,* 101.

31. *Gazette,* Apr. 14, 1862.

32. *Ibid.*

33. *Ibid.*

34. *Ibid.*

35. *Ibid.*

36. *Ibid.*

37. *Ibid.* Ambrose Bierce, another Ohioan, and a writer of ability himself, crossed Reid's path at Shiloh, although it is doubtful that one knew the other. Bierce had enlisted in an Indiana regiment as a private at the age of eighteen, in April, 1861. He, too, had been at Philippi, where he won a commendation for coolness under fire. At nineteen, at Shiloh, he had risen in rank to sergeant in Buell's army. In December, 1862, he won a commission as lieutenant, and fought in a string of battles: Stone River, Chickamauga, Chattanooga, Missionary Ridge, Kennesaw Mountain

(where he was wounded) , Franklin, and Nashville. He arrived on the field of Shiloh in the "black-dark" night. He described the skulkers, "a . . . demented crew," that surrounded the Landing when the steamers brought Buell's army across the river. "Whenever a steamboat would land, this abominable mob had to be kept off her with bayonets; when she pulled away, they sprang on her and were pushed by scores into the water. . . . " Buell's men, "disembarking insulted them, shoved them, struck them. In return they expressed their unholy delight in the certainty of our destruction by the enemy." So dark and wet the night, Bierce wrote, "inch by inch we crept along, treading on one another's heels," until they were "put into position by somebody." Ambrose Bierce, *Ambrose Bierce's Civil War*, ed. William McCann (Chicago, 1956) , pp. v, vi, vii, 17–18.

38. *Gazette,* Apr. 14, 1862.

39. *Ibid.*

40. *Ibid.,* Apr. 15, 1862; Bradford, *Battles and Leaders,* p. 90.

41. *Gazette,* Apr. 15, 1862; "Reid's report," wrote a recent commentator, "raised serious questions about the military leadership which had blundered to victory at such frightful cost." His words in the *Gazette* reflected his "righteous indignation" that "glowed like heat lightning." Crozier, *Yankee Reporters,* p. 218.

42. *Gazette,* Apr. 17, 1862.

43. *Ibid.,* Apr. 18, 1862.

44. *Ibid.,* Apr. 17, 1862; Reid, *Ohio in the War,* I, 351, 377.

45. Cortissoz, *Life of Reid,* I, 86, 89, 90–92; Crozier, *Yankee Reporters,* pp. 322–25; Starr, *Bohemian Brigade,* pp. 118–19.

46. Cortissoz, *Life of Reid,* I, 92–93; *Gazette,* July 8, 1863.

47. *Gazette,* July 8, 1863. Agate's Gettysburg report occupied slightly more than twelve columns on the first two pages of the *Gazette.* It is also reprinted, again with minor alterations, in Moore's *Rebellion Record,* VII, 85–100, plus additional dispatches of Agate's from the July 9, 1863, *Gazette,* on pages 100–102.

48. *Gazette,* July 8, 1863.

49. *Ibid.*

50. *Ibid.*

51. *Ibid.*

52. *Ibid.*

53. *Ibid.*

54. *Ibid.*

55. *Ibid.*

56. *Ibid.*

57. *Ibid.*

58. *Ibid.*

59. *Ibid.*, July 9, 1863.

60. *Ibid.*

61. *Ibid.;* letter to Stedman, Mar. 19, 1872, quoted in Cortissoz, *Life of Reid,* I, 96–97; Starr, *Bohemian Brigade,* p. 216, disagreed with Reid and thought his story "one of the finest battle accounts of the war." To compare Reid with official reports, see: Bradford, *Battles and Leaders,* 83–95, 349–99; *The War of the Rebellion: A Compilation of the Official Records of the Union and Conferedate Armies* (74 vols. in 132, Washington: Government Printing Office, 1885–1901), Series I, vols. 10, 27, 50, 51, 52.

62. Cortissoz, *Life of Reid,* I, 104–6, 113–17. Reid, of course, became famous as the man who followed Greeley as editor of the *New York Tribune,* and later as an American diplomat. Reid ended his days in London as Ambassador to the Court of St. James. He died in that post in 1912. His works, besides the millions of inches of newspaper copy, include *Ohio in the War* (2 vols.; Cincinnati, 1868), *After the War* (Cincinnati, 1866), and *American and English Studies* (2 vols.; New York, 1913). Passages from *After the War* have been recently reprinted in W. Thorp (ed.), *A Southern Reader* (New York, 1955), 119–26, and in W. B. Hesseltine (ed.), *The Tragic Conflict* (New York, 1962), 464–71. In addition, C. Vann Woodward recently edited the entire volume (New York, 1965).

BIBLIOGRAPHICAL NOTE

Reid's Writings

Cincinnati Daily Gazette, April, 1861–July, 1863. Agate's columns.

REID, WHITELAW. *After the War.* Cincinnati: Moore, Wilstach, & Baldwin. 1866.

REID, WHITELAW. *American and English Studies.* 2 vols. New York: Charles Scribner's Sons, 1913.

REID, WHITELAW. *Ohio in the War.* 2 vols. Cincinnati: Moore, Wilstach, & Baldwin, 1868.

Biography

CORTISSOZ, ROYAL. *The Life of Whitelaw Reid.* 2 vols. New York: Charles Scribner's Sons, 1921.

Books and Documents

BIERCE, AMBROSE. *Ambrose Bierce's Civil War,* ed. WILLIAM McCANN. Chicago: Gateway Editions, Inc., c. 1956.

BRADFORD, NED (ed.). *Battles and Leaders of the Civil War.* New York: Appleton-Century-Crofts, Inc., c. 1956.

CROZIER, EMMET. *Yankee Reporters, 1861–65.* New York: Oxford University Press, 1956.

HESSELTINE, W. B. (ed.). *The Tragic Conflict.* New York: George Braziller, 1962.

JONES, ROBERT H. *The Civil War in the Northwest.* Norman: University of Oklahoma Press, 1960.

JONES, VIRGIL C. *Gray Ghosts and Rebel Raiders.* New York: Henry Holt & Co., 1956.

MOORE, FRANK (ed.). *The Rebellion Record.* New York: G. P. Putnam, 1861–69. Vols. IV and VII.

The War of the Rebellion: A Compilation of the Official Records of the Union and Confederate Armies. Washington: U.S. Government Printing Office, 1885–1901. Series 1, Vols. X, XXVII, L, LI, LII.

STARR, LOUIS M. *Bohemian Brigade.* New York: Alfred A. Knopf, 1954.

THORP, W. (ed.). *A Southern Reader.* New York: Alfred A. Knopf, 1955.

WEISBERGER, BERNARD A. *Reporters for the Union.* Boston: Little, Brown & Co., 1953.

FOUR

Ben Wade

MARY LAND

In 1868, with conviction of Andrew Johnson seemingly assured, one vote kept "Bluff" Ben Wade of Ohio out of the White House. It is clear that naming Wade president pro tem of the Senate, and thereby heir-apparent, gave "impeachment its death blow." James Blaine, General Grant, James Garfield, Thaddeus Stevens, Hugh McCulloch, Gideon Welles, Georges Clemenceau, and a large array of editors testified that hostility to Wade rather than constitutional scruples dictated the verdict. Wade has made too many enemies; he was too extremist; the harshness of his attacks on Lincoln were too well remembered in the face of an already developing Lincoln mystique. "Sooner than Wade should be President, they would welcome the deluge," the *Washington Chronicle* summed it up, meaning by "they" his enemies in the Senate.[1] The ironic story of how Republicans, determined to remove "His Accidency," broke ranks at the last moment to support a President they had brought to trial, cannot be retold here in detail. But from Wade's relationship with Lincoln during the war years, it should become apparent why Johnson's opponents chose not to exchange one incubus for another.

In most accounts of war and reconstruction Wade cuts a poor figure, ignorant and profane, a poorly oiled cog in the Jacobin machine, without enough wit or subtlety to be as malevolent as Stevens, as arrogant as Sumner, as oleaginous as Stanton. His unremitting warfare against Lincoln has turned him into a boorish villain when he is remembered at all. Yet in 1867 Horace Greeley found he exerted "by far the most influence" of any senator. Formidable contestant for the Presidency in 1860, war hero, chairman of the powerful Committee on the Conduct of the War, Wade achieved constant headlines during the years of conflict. The testimony of William Dean Howells, who studied law with him for a while, and of the scholarly Andrew White indicates he was of "wider cultivation" than legend and the coonskin personality he adopted make him out to be. Nor was he unsupported; of all national leaders, said the *New York Times* in 1864, he was the least likely to be rebuked by his constituents.[2] His relations with Lincoln and his Republican colleagues were far more complex than is usually assumed. His chief animus against Lincoln was the historic Whig animus against "executive usurpation," a point of view Lincoln shared. The point of contention between them was over what in fact did constitute executive usurpation in the area of conducting the war and restoring the seceded states. But Wade's doctrine of restoration during Lincoln's lifetime was closer to Lincoln's than to Stevens' or Sumner's, a point that the violence of his invective against the President should not obscure.

It was his talent for profanity and invective plus his utter intransigence and an unmistakable aura of self-righteousness that won him so many enemies. From the outset he was as stony an "old-line Roundhead" as his forebears, the Reverend Seaborne Cotton, Governor Thomas Dudley, Simon and Anne Bradstreet, and Michael Wigglesworth. As lawyer, Ohio state senator, circuit judge, United States senator, and committee chairman, he lived by a statement he made during the impeachment crisis when attempts were made to persuade him that he had been mistaken in staking his senatorial seat on Ohio's acceptance of Negro suffrage: "I won't back a d——d inch. . . . I'm for it because I think it's right, and I know it's right; and, if a thing is right, the only way is to keep at it till it wins, for it's sure to win sometime or other." [3] This attitude prevailed throughout a long political career running from his conversion to the antislavery cause in 1836 to his denunciation of Hayes's withdrawal of federal troops from the South in 1876. Elected state senator in 1837, he followed his mentor, Theodore Weld, to become the idol of antislavery people with his speech against Texas annexation, his phillipic against a stricter Ohio fugitive slave law, and his attempts to have the state's infamous "Black Laws" repealed.[4] Such a stand was not unusual in Ohio's Western Reserve, a district Webster termed "a laboratory of abolitionism, libel, and treason." [5] However, Wade had a flair for causes in general; not only the slave's cause, but women's rights, public schools, prison reform—the entire cluster of crusades congenial to Whigs with a New England background. Further, he had a tendency to cross political lines to advocate antimonopoly, antispeculator, agrarian, prolabor doctrines from which Whigs and, later, Republicans shrank. In 1838 he called the wrath of the Whig party down on his head for voting with the Democrats to make stockholders personally liable for company debts. He then failed to be re-elected because he joined the opposition to push through a "Locofoco" and "Jacobinical" measure abolishing imprisonment for debt. He further outraged his colleagues by personally drawing up an "Anti-Plunder" bill designed to undercut the Whig practice of awarding state subsidies to canal and railroad builders.[6] After the Whigs purged him, he refused renomination three times, stating, "No, I am not changed. The Whigs defeated me before. I do not want the office. I will do as I please." When they took him back on his own terms and he returned to Columbus, he continued as before, introducing a measure to lower interest rates, another to relieve debtors, and again standing with the "Locofocos" against attempts to reimpose imprisonment for debt or to fine debtors.[7]

Another reason advanced for his failing to be returned to the

Ohio senate in 1839 was that he allowed his name to appear on the resolutions committee of the Ashtabula County Anti-Slavery Society. Subsequently, ardent Liberty party men and Free-Soilers like his brother Edward and his law partner, Congressman Joshua Giddings, claimed that his defeat made him overly cautious. They saw his long adherence to the Whigs and his support of Generals Taylor and Scott as small-souled opportunism.[8] But Wade had no use for third parties, which he saw as having as much influence in Washington "as they would in Timbucto." He considered that it was his task to change Whig thinking inside party councils.[9] Temporarily out of office between 1845 and 1850, he continued as circuit judge to do what he could for the antislavery cause. He had tried to have the Black Laws repealed. This failing, he developed his own stratagems. Under the existing laws a Negro could not appear as a witness. Once, a very black Negro appeared before him. The Black Laws were "a disgrace," opposed to common law, he told the prosecuting attorney. "You have offered no evidence that the witness is a Negro. Proceed with the examination." When the fugitive slave provisions of the Compromise of 1850 became known, he announced from the bench that he would grant habeas corpus to any runaway slave appearing before him. At another time he left his courtroom to address a meeting where he urged all citizens to disobey the law. Anyone accepting the office of federal marshal and enforcing the law should be branded as a traitor. Such forthrightness in a rapidly changing political atmosphere won him a new post. In 1850 the Ohio legislature named him United States senator.[10]

In Washington from 1850 to 1868 Wade continued his stubborn course. Attached to the Whigs until the crisis over Kansas, he was one of the few politicians in the capital to proclaim himself openly an abolitionist. In the "slave-cursed" atmosphere of this "rotten borough [the Senate], I glory in the name." With the issues drawn, "pride and self-respect compel a man either to be a dough-face, flunky, or an abolitionist, and I choose the latter." [11] He spent his evenings at the home of Dr. Gamaliel Bailey, editor of the antislavery *National Era,* and followed a strict abolitionist program on the Senate floor. At first he attempted to force repudiation of the Compromise and the "servile" action of "Old Black Dan" on the Whig party and its candidate, Winfield Scott. Failing this, he brought himself at last to deliver what Horace Greeley called "The Funeral Oration of the Whig Party." [12] He voted and expressed vehemently his antislavery convictions on the Nebraska Act, the Lecompton Constitution, and Cuban annexation. He was crude but effective in deflating the squat Douglas, "the dwarfish medium" for "free communication" to "Pandemonium [the slave states]." Parodying Douglas' most frequently quoted declaration, he said he supposed the senator from Illinois would claim the Territories had a perfect right to vote cannibalism in or vote it out. He tried to explain John Brown as a "sublime hero" to his colleagues and defended Hinton Helper's *The Impending Crisis* as "just, right, and proper," after John Sherman had disavowed the book in order to placate southern colleagues.[13] In a Senate used to seeing northerners quail before Bourbon bowie knives, canes, and pistols, he awed his fellow solons by offering to fight duels with two senators. His silencing of the terrifying Toombs with an ostentatious display of a brace of pistols and a deflating offer to meet on the field of honor with squirrel rifles became a Senate legend. His compact with two other lawmakers to "carry the quarrel into the coffin" was remembered as causing a notable subsiding of southern belligerence.[14]

During the prewar years his acquaintance with proslavery Presidents reinforced his opposition to "executive usurpation." Language he had once applied to Jackson, Van Buren, and Polk reappeared in his accusations against Pierce and Buchanan. Pierce had overstepped Presidential prerogative in Kansas with a policy that resulted in the "sacking of cities, the burning of towns, the murdering of inhabitants." Buchanan had invaded

congressional domain by sending troops into Kansas to enforce
the proslavery Lecompton Constitution. His adventurism in
the Caribbean and his bill for Cuban annexation were other
instances of executive usurpation. When the Cuba bill took
precedence over a homestead act Wade had been trying to push
through, he echoed Seward's pleas for "land for the landless" in
the crudest language: "The appropriation bills lie very easy
now behind this nigger operation. When you come to niggers
for the niggerless, all other questions sink into perfect insignifi-
cance." After the Dred Scott decision, Wade made it clear that
he bowed no more to the Supreme Court than to the President.
"I deny the doctrine—the most dangerous that could be admitted in a free country—that these judges, holding their office for
life . . . have any right to decide the law of the land for any
department of this government." This would be "despotism," a
talismanic word for Wade. "No, sir, each department must act
for itself. . . . I follow my own interpretation of the Constitution." [15]

Such solipsism insured that in Washington he would quarrel
with everyone, including his own party. The agrarian in him
continued to oppose speculators and monopolies, the major
villains in speeches he made on the Homestead Act, the Union
Pacific bill, the bill to establish land grant colleges, and the
wartime Red River campaign.[16] He pressed to have the Homestead Act extended to aliens, a stand at the height of Know-
Nothing furor that jeopardized his re-election in 1856.[17] With
the outbreak of the war he took a characteristically obdurate
stand on conciliation proposals, on confiscation of slaves and
rebel real estate, on emancipation, and on retaliation for Confederate atrocities. He advocated denying immunity to witnesses before congressional committees, seizing railroad and
telegraph lines, limiting congressional debate to five minutes,
operating cotton plantations in areas under army control, and,
at one time when the Union seemed near military collapse,
granting "absolute and despotic powers" to a lieutenant gen-

eral.[18] However, as the war continued, his onetime heterodoxy came close to being considered Republican orthodoxy. The Radical wing of the party was growing steadily. A majority came to share Wade's impatience with the conduct of the war and plans for restoring the seceded states. Many saw him as a savior in having rid the northern armies of their jinx, McClellan, and thus paving the way for bringing in Grant from the West. Whatever sympathy the party had with Lincoln over his plan versus Wade's for restoring the southern states was dissipated by Andrew Johnson's encouragement of the South to reject congressional methods of restoration. Repudiation of the Fourteenth Amendment following on Johnson's unequaled string of vetoes convinced the Republican majority that he must be unseated. Wade at the moment was at the peak of his influence, "one of the . . . most respected of the anti-slavery champions," according to Carl Schurz, the most influential of all senators in Greeley's version.[19] Twenty out of twenty-four senators in a Radical caucus named him president pro tem of the Senate in order to succeed Johnson. A majority of senators was pledged to convict Johnson. What, then, went wrong?

The banker Henry Cooke gives a partial clue in a letter to his brother nine months later. Wade was wrecking the Republican party with his "wild agrarianism . . . clamoring for the unsexing of women . . . and mad project [for] . . . the enfranchisement of negroes." Cooke referred to an unfortunately worded speech Wade made out in Kansas on June 10, 1867, calling for no more than the eight-hour day and woman suffrage, but turned by the malicious reporting of the *New York World* and *New York Times* into a Proudhonist cry for redistribution of property. For a month after the speech, comments, mostly critical, filled the press.[20] When the furor over it had begun to subside a bit, he piled Pelion on Ossa, in Henry Cooke's eyes, by heading a list of senators supporting equal rights for women. Then he lost his own seat in the Senate when Ohio voters would not accept Negro suffrage. In an editorial entitled

"Honor to Ohio," Greeley held that Ohio Republicans "deliberately chose to be right rather than safe." Wade's refusal to
"back a d———d inch" on this question was the same trait that
caused him to comment when overruled by the Ohio Supreme
Court: "I will give them a chance to get right." It was the same
obduracy he displayed when accused of not following Republican policy: "I am very apt to consult my own view of
propriety." [21]

By the time the impeachment crisis had reached its peak,
Wade's fitness rather than Johnson's unfitness for office had
become crucial. His wartime relations with Lincoln and his
senatorial colleagues were mulled over; his speeches and actions
in committee reviewed. His unshakeable conviction that he and
few others obeyed the "higher law" was recalled, particularly
his habit of remarking "I have ever had one polar star to guide
my action. . . . I fix my eye upon the great principles of eternal justice, and it has borne me triumphantly. . . ." [22] In his
own way he was as lacking in any will or ability to mediate as
was Johnson. His character had been particularly well revealed
in his duel with Lincoln. With the growing Lincoln mythology,
his rejection became inevitable.

II

Wade's characteristic animus against "executive usurpation"
plus his own devotion to the "higher law" determined his relationship with Lincoln. Throughout their duel, Wade pitted his
strength against the President on issues of military strategy and
restoration of the seceded states. He did not doubt these were
congressional prerogatives, for the Constitution stated that
Congress and not the President should "make rules for the
government and regulation of the land and naval forces." The
source of authority made it very clear, he said, that "the President cannot lay down and fix the principles upon which war

shall be conducted. . . . It is for Congress to lay down the rules and regulations by which the Executive shall be governed in conducting a war." To demurrers about the President as commander-in-chief of the armed forces, he snorted that this was a "non-sequitur." He further construed the declaration "The United States shall guarantee to every state in this Union a Republican form of government" to mean that Congress should so guarantee. As a Whig, Lincoln also objected to executive invasion of the legislative function, reminding his subordinates that the Executive must not "expressly or impliedly seize and exercise the permanent legislative functions of the government." [23] Consequently, Lincoln's departures from this joint position seemed studied outrages to Wade. He very quickly developed the scorn for Lincoln that was widespread among antislavery Republicans. Lincoln was "a fool," he wrote his wife. Presidential policies were "over-cautious, timid and vacillating." The war, under such leadership, was "a rose-water war." [24] Respecting neither the Chief Executive nor a military leadership he saw tainted with "West Point proslaveryism," Wade turned the powerful Committee on the Conduct of the War, which he headed from 1861 to 1865, into an instrument for prodding the President and ousting dilatory generals. Through the committee he pressed for a more forthright prosecution of the war, a more advanced program of emancipation, admission of Negro fugitives within Army lines, use of Negroes as laborers and then as troops, dismissal of generals who refused to accept such policies, and retaliation for rebel atrocities and for conditions in rebel prison camps. He felt Congress should pick generals, determine strategy, and set policy. His committee examined nearly two hundred witnesses, half of them generals, and issued reports on the major battles in the eastern theater of war. These reports constituted a mighty propaganda effort, toppling McClellan at last. On the Senate floor Wade regularly assailed Lincoln's slowness in emancipation, his emasculation of the confiscation bill to seize Confederate property in slaves, and his unduly propitiatory policy toward the border states. He was scornful of the coalition policy and Lincoln's attempts to turn the Republican party into a Union party. A final clash on reconstruction came when, as joint sponsor of the Wade-Davis bill and co-author of the subsequent Wade-Davis Manifesto, he threw down a challenge to the President's plan for restoration, which he saw both as an unconstitutional usurpation of congressional authority and a violation of the principle of majority rule.

Wade's first connection with Lincoln had been as rival candidate for the nomination in 1860. Stephen Douglas expected Wade would be the candidate and "damned hard to beat." Both Old Abe and Old Ben were alike, said the Cincinnati journalist Murat Halstead, both symbols of opposition to the Nebraska Act and squatter sovereignty, yet both "representatives of the conservatism, the respectability, the availability, and all that sort of thing." [25] (Wade thought the three great pillars of the Republican party were protection, free homesteads, and non-extension of slavery into the territories.[26]) Wade's candidacy had "a brilliant and formidable appearance," scotching Chase's aspirations, a "betrayal" he never forgave Wade. Excepting himself, Wade would have preferred Seward; but he cheerfully took the stump for Lincoln, describing him as "the very incarnation of American labor." Throughout the interim between election and inaugural he remained favorable, expecting relief from the "treachery and imbecility of old Buck," whom he saw as "doubtless guilty of treason." [27]

He was at first disposed to discount threats of secession as "humbug." Southerners would "howl and rave, like so many devils," but in the end do nothing. The two sections "are married forever. . . . There can be no divorcement." But on December 17, 1860, the day set for the opening of South Carolina's secession convention, he addressed himself directly to the South. The slavocracy had controlled more than two-thirds of the Senate for many years past; at present it owned the cabinet and the President as much as it owned the servants on its plantations. If it persisted in a suicidal course and seceded, a new President would find it his duty to execute the law uniformly. The South, frustrated, would declare war. The North would quell the insurrection and the South end by losing everything, including slavery. Wade's speech, Lincoln's secretaries reported, became at once the Republican party's "unalterable position on the crisis." [28] Three days later, the Senate met the crisis by forming a Committee of Thirteen, scornfully christened the "Committee on Incubation" by Thaddeus Stevens. Wade and Seward were members. The border-state thinking of the Committee's chairman, Crittenden of Kentucky, appeared in proposals to permit slavery in territories south of 36' 30", and to enforce strictly the fugitive slave law Wade had urged Ohioans to disobey. Seward, in retreat from his "higher law" position, was inclined to temporize with slavery in the territories. "If we follow such leadership, we will be in the wilderness longer than the children of Israel under Moses," Wade complained. But from Springfield, Lincoln made it clear that there was to be no backing down on the territorial issue, the keystone of Republican policy. Republicans thereafter defeated Crittenden's conciliatory proposals, a rejection enormously popular with Wade's Ohio constituents. They agreed with his definition of compromise as "never founded on principle." In truth, Wade said later on the Senate floor, the South never would have been satisfied with conciliatory measures like Crittenden's, but only with a change in the northern attitude toward slavery. It was not personal liberty bills or the controversy over returning fugitives. "It was that we had institutions among us where our children were educated to hate slavery and oppression. . . . In the human heart lies the difficulty." [29]

Once in Washington, it seemed to Wade that Lincoln began to erode the effect of his principled stand. In his inaugural address he used Wade's metaphor of marriage for the warring sections, but his impartiality in treating northern and southern institutions was dismaying. Wade considered the cabinet "a disgraceful surrender to the South." Lincoln was also slow in reinforcing Major Anderson. Most serious, he was not treating the outbreak as an insurrection in spite of his own declaration to the special wartime session of Congress that secession was "an ingenious sophism" to cloak a rebellion. If he had closed the southern ports as Wade advocated in his December 17 speech instead of blockading them, the rebellion would never have turned into a civil war. If he had court-martialed resigning generals like Lee instead of permitting them to go south, the Confederacy would have been unable to create a military force. Stevens, who had seconded Wade's measure in January by proposing a bill to repeal the law creating ports of entry, cited these arguments in reproaching Lincoln for declaring a blockade. By recognizing the Confederacy, the President had allowed an insurrection like the Whiskey Rebellion to turn into a full-scale war. Lincoln had replied that he had left it up to Seward, convincing Stevens and Wade that Seward was the evil genius of a naïve President.[30]

Kenneth P. Williams and James Truslow Adams have wondered at the anomaly of accepting the resignations of officers solemnly sworn to defend the Union and then leaving to destroy it. Under existing regulations officers could have been held to their oaths of service. Acceptance of resignations was to Wade simply one more timid, if astounding, obeisance to the overweening arrogance and proslavery sentiments of West Point. No institution on the face of the earth or in the history of the world had ever turned out so many "false, ungrateful men." Nearly half the officers educated there went south. He declared that "if there had been no West Point Military Academy, there would have been no rebellion." Men got in by "mendicant solicitation" to "sponge" an education out of the government. He wanted to abolish the establishment he called "a blight, a mildew." It had created an "aristocratical" caste taught to despise the democratic section of the country, labor, and the simplicity of northern institutions, and to "admire above all things that two-penny miserable slave aristocracy of the South." Throughout the war he opposed all appropriations for West Point. Military tactics should be taught in the high schools and private military establishments. Military genius would spring out of the ranks, from civilian generals who learned tactics around the fume of the bivouac rather than from textbooks.[31]

When the South fired on Fort Sumter, Wade at sixty-one tried to enlist. He then went home and raised the Sixth Ohio Cavalry and saw Camp Wade named for him. He did join battle in an episode that made him a hero throughout the North, the rout at Bull Run Creek on July 21, 1861. Convinced the insurrection would be easily put down, Washington clerks, storekeepers, senators, and representatives went out to view McDowell's advance on rebel entrenchments at Manassas. Wade drove one of two carriages filled with congressmen. After an initial thrust by green troops, the battle scene suddenly changed as the Wade party met, first, fleeing Washingtonians, and then a full-scale retreat of hysterical troops. Ninety-day men, shouting their enlistment terms were up, fled toward the city. Throwing away blankets, canteens, axes, shovels, muskets, the panicked troops swirled past. Riderless horses circled about. Some officers tried to rally their troops; others merely ran. Onlookers left the field anyway they could (Senator Wilson found a stray mule). But Wade's party remained. Jumping out of his carriage at the foot of a long downgrade, he yelled, "Boys, we'll stop this damned runaway." Cocking his rifle, he bellowed to the onrushing soldiers to halt or lose their brains. His companions overturned the carriage, blocking the roadway, and holding back hundreds of fleeing soldiers until relieved by the Second New York Cavalry.[32]

This exploit on what Wade called the gloomiest day of his life turned him into a national hero, but Bull Run was a stunning blow to the North. In the sobering expectation that a long, hard war would require the broadest-based coalition, a subdued House and Senate hastened to pass a new Crittenden resolution declaring the war was not being waged to overthrow established institutions but only to preserve the Union. Only two legislators voted against the resolution, one of them Albert G. Riddle, Wade's biographer and the driver of the other carriage at Bull Run. The resolution infuriated Wade, but he voted for it on grounds of expediency, on the theory that it did not matter with what view the war was prosecuted. As he put it later, slavery had demonstrated its impotence. God and industrial progress had doomed it. Every labor-saving device was an abolitionist, every puff of an engine an antislavery sermon. The Ruler of the Universe was "at least a gradual emancipationist." [33]

In the wake of Bull Run, rumors of ineptitude and treachery among army officers flew. Why had General Patterson been unable to keep Joe Johnston bottled up in Winchester instead of allowing him to sweep in and overwhelm Union forces? Patterson, a West Point general, had lately angered antislavery men with his order to troops to suppress servile insurrection should occasion offer. Further suspicion of halfhearted conduct of the war rose with the disaster at Ball's Bluff in October. Here General Charles P. Stone, known like Patterson for returning fugitives, had ordered a senseless assault on a Confederate position atop a precipitous bluff. Among the wounded was a son of Oliver Wendell Holmes, and among the dead, a nephew of James Russell Lowell. Paul Revere's grandson had been captured and taken to Libby Prison, where he was sentenced to be hanged. The popular antislavery senator from Oregon, Edwin Baker, who had introduced Lincoln at his inaugural, died leading the charge. The rumor was that Stone's West Point hatred of a volunteer general plus his antipathy to Baker's advanced antislavery views had led him traitorously to sacrifice an aide. Further restiveness with conduct of the war developed as General McClellan, succeeding McDowell in command of the Army of the Potomac, conducted drills and dress parades rather than

an offensive. Wade, increasingly sarcastic about whether northern armies would ever move, said he did not wonder people
deserted to Jeff Davis: "I may desert myself." With his incessant
parading, McClellan was a "laughing stock" and a "byword,"
one of Wade's Ohio correspondents complained. "What, in the
name of God, are our one hundred and eighty thousand soldiers doing on the Potomac?" asked another.[34]

On October 25 Wade and two other Republican senators,
Chandler and Trumbull, faced McClellan. Writing his wife
about prospects for the visit, Wade was not hopeful. He had
already seen the President, Secretary of War Cameron, and
Jeremiah Black. ". . . All is gloomy & despondency here. All
are discouraged. Old Abe is a fool. And is under the entire
control of Governor Seward who is by nature a coward & a
sneak." Wade thought a majority of the cabinet was at heart
opposed to the war and favored putting the army into winter
quarters. "I hope to frighten & shove them into a fight. . . . But
no country was ever cursed with such imbecility." As he recounted the conversation later when he was opposing McClellan's bid for the Presidency, Wade berated the general for his
failure to move, quoting a French military commentator who
said no such aggregation of men and supplies as McClellan
commanded had ever been gathered before. McClellan disputed this, saying he did not have enough troops and that the
enemy had at least 220,000 men and was behind fortification as
strong as Sebastopol. If the rebels had been able to raise such an
army, Wade rejoined, they must "possess some of the qualities
of Christ in making bread." [35] The following two nights the
three senators met Lincoln, insisting he order McClellan to
move. Lincoln defended the general's slowness but was concerned enough to see him personally and report the complaint,
which he urged McClellan to regard as a "reality."

When December came with no improvement in the military
situation, dissatisfied Republicans decided to act. Democrats
opposed to an antislavery war commanded the two principal

armies. Of 110 brigadier generals, 80 were Democrats. In the east McClellan had promised to crush any attempt at a slave insurrection with an iron hand. In the west Halleck had ordered all fugitives within army lines ejected. But while McClellan's supercilious protégés were dallying on the Potomac and scoffing at antislavery sentiments, Lincoln had revoked Frémont's emancipation proclamation for the Department of the West and relieved him from command. The general had been widely criticized for failure to reinforce another commander, for his profligate military spending, inaccessibility, and the ostentation of his plumed and glittering guard of "foreigners." But why was an advanced antislavery man singled out for disgrace, while Stone remained uncriticized for his failure to reinforce Baker, members of the McClellan clique for their haughtiness, or the entire procurement policy under Cameron for its incredible wastefulness? A furious correspondent wrote Wade: "Do for God's sake, whip up the Pres. to call Frémont *with his bodyguard* to Washington and send McClellan and all the reviewing guards home." Wade himself was outraged. "No greater misfortune could befall the country" than Frémont's retirement. No man since Admiral Byng had been the victim of such summary treatment. Only a President with a "poor-white trash" background would treat Frémont so shabbily. He would expect to find the President recommending that every rebel be given 160 acres of land.[36]

However, it was less radical Republicans than Wade, such as Grimes, Fessenden, and Sherman, who were alarmed enough by military disasters to try to secure some congressional control of the war's conduct. If the "sore spots" were probed to the bottom by a congressional investigating committee, two of Wade's future enemies, Grimes and Fessenden, agreed, a new order of things might be instituted. Consequently, on December 5 a resolution was introduced into the House asking for information about the "most atrocious military murder in our history," i.e., Ball's Bluff. Simultaneously, Chandler in the Senate moved for an investigation of Ball's Bluff and Bull Run. John Sherman broadened the resolution to include inquiry into the general conduct of the war, including executive orders and policies. Thus not only would disasters be investigated, but the injustices done Frémont could be corrected and generals who ejected fugitives and protected rebel property disciplined. Both houses adopted the amended measure at once, and the civilian hero of Bull Run, known as "Old War Horse" and "Old Backbone," was named as chairman. His chief lieutenants were Senator Zachariah Chandler, equally zealous in the antislavery cause, and another future enemy, Andrew Johnson. George Julian, son-in-law of Wade's former law partner ex-Congressman Joshua Giddings, headed the House contingent, which included three other antislavery stalwarts, Daniel Gooch, John Covode, and Moses Odell.[37]

Thus originated one of the most controversial agencies in American history, "a force which was to have a great effect, for good or for evil," as Bruce Catton puts it. Opposition to the Committee at the outset centered on whether the war's conduct was congressional or executive business, the *Washington Intelligencer* charging that a division of responsibility would introduce confusion when unity was the supreme necessity. Throughout its existence the Committee nagged at and humiliated Lincoln. Behind much of its criticism of McClellan's "slows," was an even more devastating indictment of the President. Once, when they were both very angry, Wade told the President that he was the father of every military blunder in the war. Secretary of the Navy Gideon Welles saw the Committee as a "convenient machine" to cover up War Department errors, "a child of Stanton's . . . mischievous busybodies and a discredit to Congress." But Lincoln's personal secretaries thought that even though it was often "hasty and unjust" and questioned "soldiers and statesmen . . . like refractory schoolboys," it was "always earnest, patriotic, and honest" and merited more praise than blame. Newspapers and periodicals sometimes decried its methods as heavy-handed and inquisitorial, but these were generally Democratic or Copperhead journals. A majority of Republican papers, conservative and moderate as well as radical, agreed with its conclusions. Historians have tended to adopt the stereotyped "Star Chamber" committee of "Vindictives" and "Jacobins" initiated by its enemies, Senators Doolittle and McDougall. Woodrow Wilson shuddered at the prospect of its recrudescence in 1917. It is referred to among revisionists as a clumsy, ruthless, highly partisan body Lincoln should have disregarded. In the most extreme attack, the committee is spoken of as "paranoiac," conspiring with Stanton to "cripple" McClellan so that the Radicals' "vindictive" objectives might be attained. Most recently, the committee's materials have been used as source materials without characterization, indicating that the changes that prompted David Donald's reconsideration of the Lincoln image may ultimately rehabilitate some of his opponents.[38]

The committee had a fairly simple military philosophy: "In military movements delay is generally bad—indecision is almost always fatal." A responsible general would "march upon the enemy by the shortest route, assail, hang to him and lick him in the most direct way, and in the least possible time." He would solve problems in the field, not out of Jomini. He would live off the enemy. The committee wanted a Grant or Sherman. The only flaw in its thinking, as Bruce Catton has pointed out, was its assumption that only a politically sound general would possess traits of slashing aggressiveness and grinding inexorability.[39]

It was these traits that Wade, Chandler, and Andrew Johnson attempted to infuse into the parade of generals who came before them from December, 1861, to July, 1862. Through leading questions and exhortations, witnesses were grilled on two issues: why the Army of the Potomac did not move, and what policy generals pursued toward secessionist sympathizers living within their lines and Negroes seeking refuge. General

J. B. Richardson, appearing first because McClellan was ill, was non-committal. "Well, what advantage is there gained by delay?" Wade asked impatiently. Could the general think of any reason why a move had not been made? Chandler and Johnson asked about plans for going into winter quarters. Would the troops gain "much more by laying in camp than by smelling a little powder?" A second witness, old Indian fighter General Heintzelman, spoke unfavorably of General McClellan's aloofness and refusal to consult the senior commanders who advocated a more offensive policy. He agreed readily to Wade's suggestion that McClellan hold a council of war. Franklin, one of McClellan's youthful protégés, was stiffly reticent, objecting to Andrew Johnson's suggested military moves. "We must run some risk," Wade reminded him. It was unendurable to find the conduct of the war hanging upon one man who kept his counsels entirely to himself. If he were Bonaparte or Wellington, the country might well repose limitless confidence in him. But what if "we have no evidence that he is the wisest man in the world?" [40]

Other brigade members followed. General McDowell displeased the committee by insisting Virginia roads would soon be impassable and that any further losses like Bull Run would lower morale disastrously. "Of course, all war is more or less hazardous," Wade retorted. General Wadsworth claimed the roads were in good condition, thought winter quarters would demoralize the men, advocated reorganizing the Army into four or five corps that would give the anti-McClellan generals a deciding voice, and stated he never returned runaway Negroes. Quartermaster General Meigs argued against the corps proposal, recalling that Napoleon had never called a council of war. Fitz-John Porter, utterly devoted to McClellan, was the most recalcitrant witness, rejecting corps organization and refusing to comment on winter quarters. McClellan himself came before the committee on January 15 in a stormy six-hour session. No stenographic report was made, but Wade, Chandler, and

McClellan recalled it later. Wade and Chandler sneered at McClellan's insistence upon preparing adequate lines of retreat. "You want to be sure of plenty of room so that you can run," said Chandler. "Or in case you get scared," added Wade.[41]

Left gloomy by their examination, committee members had reported to the President early in January that McClellan had enough men to invade Virginia and that the roads were passable. Bluntly and undiplomatically, Wade presented the case that before any of the moves McClellan contemplated could be executed, the Union would collapse. Lincoln refused to be "disenchanted," claiming he neither knew nor thought he had the right to know McClellan's plans. But once again, he privately urged a forward movement on McClellan and issued his famous directive for a general movement of land and naval forces on February 22, plus a specific order to move south to Richmond. McClellan immediately countered with his own plan for an approach from the east, and Lincoln concurred. Wade was enraged. Confronting McClellan in the War Department on February 19—a meeting arranged by Stanton, who had replaced Cameron—Wade upbraided the general bitterly. McClellan once more argued he did not have adequate lines of retreat. Why always plan on retreat, Wade demanded. If Union troops could not lick the rebels, then "let them come back in their coffins." [42]

Throughout February the committee threatened Lincoln that if he did not force McClellan to move, a resolution would be offered in the Senate directing him to order an advance. Wade also urged reorganization of the army into corps. Lincoln asked for time on the order to advance but, without consulting McClellan, issued a reorganization directive. At this moment McClellan's prestige suffered another blow. The Confederate armies evacuated Manassas, before which McClellan had sat for months, paralyzed by "overwhelming forces" in the form of huge guns. They were nothing but logs painted black, a discov-

ery doubly disconcerting since McClellan had been fooled in
September by another "Quaker" gun. The committee quickly
sent in Bayard Taylor to describe what he saw. Going to the
President with this evidence, the committee was "surprised and
delighted" when Lincoln completely lost his temper. The result
on March 11 was a characteristic half-measure, however: sup-
planting McClellan with Halleck as general-in-chief, but retaining him in the Potomac command.[43]

A somewhat chastened McClellan began his crawl up the
peninsula, precipitating another quarrel with the President,
the committee, and Stanton, who decided he had not left Washington adequately defended. Lincoln, quite apprehensive,
recalled two of McClellan's divisions. McClellan and his partisans have argued this was a move designed with malice pre-
pense to "decimate" his army. It was the committee's and
Stanton's fault that he did not take Richmond. Four recent accounts of the controversy display an interesting variation. In his
account of the duel between the Radicals and Lincoln written
in 1941, T. Harry Williams accepted the McClellanite view
that Stanton and the committee had "engineered the intrigue
to cripple the Army of the Potomac" because they "wanted
McClellan to fail." Otherwise, they would not be able to carry
through their objectives of emancipation and confiscation. But
in 1952, writing about Lincoln and his generals, Williams
states that McClellan had played fast and loose with figures,
listing troops miles away in the Shenandoah Valley, and steam-
ing away from Washington before the President had a chance
to check his ambiguous statements. "Therefore, McClellan,
knowingly or unknowingly, did not obey the President's order.
. . ." Kenneth P. Williams' full-length appraisal of the military
campaigns of the war is as harsh on McClellan as the committee
ever was. He did not obey the President's orders; Lincoln
would have been fully warranted in recalling him. It is "cheap
fun" at Lincoln's and Stanton's expense to deride their concern
for Washington. Bruce Catton agrees that McClellan had not

done what he had been told to do by leaving only 28,000 men in and near the capital when 40,000 had been the agreed-upon figure.[44]

The late spring of 1862 passed with McClellan crawling toward Richmond, constantly crying for additional troops, settling down for long sieges whenever he found the enemy. In May, Lincoln allowed him to suspend the corps organization. A month later, Wade addressed a conclave of the angry senior generals. McClellan and his circle were trying the patience of the country, he said, according to the *Tribune,* but they could not last. Two weeks later, Lee and Stonewall Jackson turned on McClellan in the Battle of the Seven Days. McClellan fell back repeatedly, although a bolder stand at any one of several points could have turned the tide and sent the army into Richmond. This was the testimony the committee later heard officially from Heintzelman, Barnard, and Hooker. Meanwhile, Wade was learning that Heintzelman had pleaded to force enemy lines at Yorktown; that Barnard and Hooker had urged McClellan to push on into Richmond after Yorktown, Williamsburg, Fair Oaks, and Malvern. Instead, McClellan retreated steadily, a disaster, Hooker said, entirely due to "want of generalship on the part of our commander." Furthermore, McClellan had not been present during a single engagement, the senior generals stated. Learning of Jeb Stuart's daring raid around his army, he had panicked, sending a hysterical note to Stanton and ordering the destruction of all baggage, tents, and equipment. Hooker thought the retreat to the James, when 2,500 sick and wounded were abandoned, made the army look "like a parcel of sheep." [45]

The explosiveness of such information, received from the committee's confidants among the senior generals, Wade's son Jim, an officer in the Army of the Potomac, and various newspapermen, prompted a decision to rescind the committee's rule on secrecy. After July 15 members were privileged to use committee information in speeches, and on the following day Chan-

dler rose to arraign McClellan for his "do-nothing" strategy
and propensity for sitting down in "malarious swamps" where
"we have lost more men by the spade than the bullet, five to
one." In August, Wade ridiculed the general's compulsion to
lay siege. "Place him before an enemy and he will burrow like a
wood-chuck. His first effort is to get into the ground." To make
his point even clearer, Wade went to the War Office on a
perfectly sunny day carrying an umbrella. He explained that he
had heard the Army of the Potomac was in motion, and it
always began raining twelve hours after that army started to
move.[46]

Defenders of McClellan have accused the committee of providing an open forum for his enemies. It is true that Wade,
Chandler, and Julian listened raptly while Keyes and Hooker
expounded on McClellan's procrastination and with testy inattention while Porter and Franklin defended him. The senior
generals—Heintzelman, Sumner, Barnard, and Keyes—were
frequent witnesses, as were other anti-McClellanites like Sickles, Silas Casey, Abner Doubleday, and his son Charles. But
apparently McClellan's enemies were telling the truth. The
military studies previously cited concur generally with the committee's findings. Kenneth P. Williams' account of the Peninsula Campaign parallels the committee's on major points. The
committee had stated that at Williamsburg following Yorktown

there was no controlling mind in charge of the movements; there
was uncertainty in regard to who was in command; each general
fought as he considered best; and, by the time the general commanding appeared on the field, the principal part of the fighting
was over.

At Fair Oaks the corps commanders "each fought as he deemed
best." This pattern continued; corps commanders directed all
advances, retreats, and dispositions of troops without direction
from McClellan. Williams' summation is that

Sumner had fought the battle of Williamsburg while he [McClellan] was back at Yorktown. . . . Sumner and Keyes had fought the battle of Fair Oaks while he was indisposed at his headquarters. Porter had commanded at Gaines's Mill while he remained . . . in a panic preparing for an unnecessary retreat. Sumner and Heintzelman had conducted the affair at Savage Station, almost without orders. . . . Porter had commanded at Malvern Hill while he sat —part of the time at least—on a gunboat in the James.

McClellan had "little intellectual honesty," Williams states. He was "not a real general . . . not even a disciplined, truthful soldier." T. Harry Williams, for whom at one time no epithet was savage enough to describe the committee, does not characterize it at all in his second account. Instead, he cites committee reports frequently and lays heavy stress on McClellan's constitutional timidity, nervous panic, and inexcusable slowness. Catton also re-creates the McClellan of the committee, facing an imaginary enemy conjured up by Allan Pinkerton, whose spies reported the rebel forces as more than twice their actual size; never visiting the battlefield; frustrating his subordinates, until Phil Kearny cried out that the retreat from Malvern Hill could "only be prompted by cowardice or treason." [47]

Military critics tend to think McClellan's removal was a profound mistake, a bowing to a public opinion inflamed by such bodies as the committee. Adduced as proof are the weaknesses of McClellan's successors. But such a charge defies logic. The trouble with McClellan's successors was that they were too much like him. The committee was right about the kind of general Lincoln needed and finally got in Grant. It was their insistence upon ideological qualification that flawed their approach. At first, Wade, with his familiar mordancy, had demanded no qualification. *Anybody* was better than McClellan. Lincoln replied that he must have *somebody*. Wade's choice, then, was John Pope, victor from the West, ebulliently self-confident, sharing the committee's war aims. Appearing before the committee on July 8, just after the retreat to the James,

Pope said he meant to attack at all times he had the opportunity. The way to defend Washington was a direct attack on Richmond. He compared his stripped-down western troops to the oversupplied Army of the Potomac. In his command men went into action "with the locks of their muskets tied on with strings. I have seen them wearing overcoats to hide their nakedness, as they had no pantaloons." [48] The committee's urging of Pope coincided with McClellan's assertion to Lincoln that a declaration for emancipation would disintegrate the armies. The President knew his second revocation of an emancipation proclamation, General David Hunter's, was highly unpopular, that northern morale had never been at such a low ebb. McClellan's complete unawareness of northern sentiment dismayed him, and when the general had still not moved by late August, he named Pope chief of the Army of the Potomac.

Four weeks later came Second Bull Run, another disaster. In its report on Pope, the committee has been accused of whitewashing him and finding a scapegoat in Fitz-John Porter and his mentor, McClellan. But again, as Kenneth P. Williams points out, Pope emerges as superior in every respect to McClellan. He was aggressive, bold, responsible, and could have learned from defeat. He was shabbily dealt with when he was removed and McClellan reinstated. Williams concurs with the original findings that Porter sabotaged Pope by withholding troops from the field while McClellan was withholding three divisions. Sending them in could have won the day. A subsequent reversal of the verdict of guilty at Porter's court-martial does not clear him of dereliction. At the rehearing conducted during the Cleveland administration, it was claimed Porter had been given an order impossible to fulfil. But this claim was only hindsight. The order could not be fulfilled, but at the time Porter received it he did not know the strength of the Confederate forces he was facing. When he failed to attack, or even to inform General Sykes, who was with him, of the order to attack, it was not out of superior judgment but from habitual caution and in answer to McClellan's surly directive to let Pope "get out of his scrape" by himself. Catton says Porter did know that he was facing Longstreet and outnumbered three to one, but that he could not convince Pope. In his first account of the battle T. Harry Williams has Chandler convincing Pope that he has been "maliciously knifed" by Porter, who has been "pounced upon" by the Radicals as scapegoat for Pope's "tragic blunders." Ugly rumors that McClellan was delaying transference of troops to Pope had been circulating. Stanton "seized on these stories and ordered Halleck to substantiate them with official evidence." But in his second account Williams has Pope making his own charges against Porter, and grants that McClellan was guilty of inexcusable slowness in reinforcing Pope. It was not that "he wanted him to fail," as Lincoln put it. It was his constitutional inability to act in a crisis.[49]

McClellan's semi-victory at Antietam following Second Bull Run did not convince the committee that he should remain in command. Its report on the Maryland compaign found that the same mind controlled and the same general features characterized it that had made victory impossible for the Army of the Potomac. It was the old losing combination of delay, indecision, calls for more troops, and schisms between commanders. Hooker, Burnside, and Sumner had been active; Porter had not attacked at all. McClellan persisted in sending in troops "in driblets," thus permitting the enemy to get away. Catton, ranking Antietam high in battles ranged in the "magnitude of their calamitous stupidity," agrees with the committee that the engagement was fought in three separate, disjointed, almost totally unco-ordinated parts, while McClellan sat "like a bemused spectator," accepting the decisions of subordinates, watching the battle he had planned but not laying a hand on it. In his first account T. Harry Williams saw Antietam as a "dubious triumph," but a triumph nonetheless. His second version sees McClellan at the crisis of his career fumbling the moment completely.[50]

Such behavior sent Wade, Sumner, Stevens, and Chase to Lincoln in October with an ultimatum. Either he must fire the traitor or they would kill all appropriations. Stanton agreed, as did a conclave of Republican governors. Lincoln finally complied in November, naming Burnside.

Once again, disaster followed at Fredericksburg. On December 13 Burnside tried to cross the Rappahannock. It was Ball's Bluff magnified. 15,000 men—spread out like a pageant—were slaughtered by troops impregnable behind tiers of stone walls. Burnside became demoralized and incoherent, losing confidence and infecting his men with his panic. Once again, high-level incompetence had intervened when Halleck failed to supply the attacking forces with pontoons. Once again, a McClellanite general had failed to send in troops. Just after the battle, Wade and Chandler rushed to Burnside's camp to calm the mutiny brewing there. Formerly an ardent member of the McClellan clique, Burnside amazed the committee by his strong antislavery assertions. His reversal completely captivated Wade and Chandler, T. Harry Williams claimed while he was still intent on fastening the label of Jacobin double-dealing on the committee. Consequently, Williams charged in his first study, they whitewashed the convert and sought to "plaster an indictment" on Franklin. But once again evaluating Fredericksburg, Catton and Kenneth P. Williams find Burnside's plan not so suicidal. The first stage of the movement was "remarkably deft and speedy." Burnside "outgeneraled and . . . completely mystified" Lee for a number of days. If Halleck's pontoons had arrived in time, both agree, the "quick and bold plan" would have succeeded. T. Harry Williams, in his second account, also states that Halleck was largely to blame for the delays that ruined a plan dependent on speed of execution. As it was, Burnside was forced to wait until Lee became aware both of his plan and that he could not lose face by abandoning it. At that point, Catton feels, it was the act of a stupid general to march into a trap. In its report the committee placed major responsibility on Halleck's failure to send in the pontoons. Halleck was no committee favorite. He was so incompetent, Wade said, he couldn't scare "three setting geese" with an army of 25,000 men. The second factor was Franklin's failure to send in troops, attested by Generals Sumner, Hooker, Henry J. Hunt, Meade, and David Birney. If Franklin had renewed the attack, they claimed, a brilliant victory would have been achieved. Bruce Catton says Franklin's failure to reinforce Burnside illustrates once again the simple inability to use the English language that so many Civil War generals displayed. Burnside asked for full reinforcements; Franklin thought he meant a simple reconnaissance. But the committee attributed Franklin's failure to McClellan-inspired wilful disobedience, as did Lincoln.[51] Of Burnside's own demoralization, the committee said nothing; but it did comment on "interference" with his plans after Fredericksburg. Two generals in his command went to Lincoln to warn him of the Army's dispirited condition and the danger in attempting any new movement. Lincoln was alarmed enough to order Burnside to desist from further action, and Burnside distressed enough to issue a series of dismissals, death sentences, and orders for courts-martial. The committee did little but cite the facts of this imbroglio; but it made clear that Franklin and another McClellanite general, W. P. Smith, had known what tales the dissatisfied emissaries planned on bearing to Lincoln.[52]

Three days after Fredericksburg, a committee of Republicans went to Lincoln to stave off any possibility of his renaming McClellan. Wade was especially vehement in attributing Democratic victory at the polls in the fall to dissatisfaction with the President's policy of entrusting command of the armies to "bitter and malignant Democrats." [53] With the Democratic papers exhorting Lincoln to return McClellan to command, Wade's committee rushed to present the case against "McNapoleon" to the public. Through the spring of 1863 members worked feverishly to complete the report, holding hearings on the Peninsula

Campaign in February and March, and completing reports on First Bull Run, Ball's Bluff, and Frémont's command. Andrew Johnson, now governor of Tennessee, came in to assist. Frequent announcements to the press built up anticipation of startling revelations. Much of the testimony against McClellan was so discreditable, stories ran, that it could not be published but must be sealed in Senate archives. Finished, the report appeared on April 6 and was rushed to Burnside's mutinous army.

The report made it clear from the outset that it considered Lincoln's derelictions as grievous as McClellan's. Upon the war's conduct depended the future of the American experiment in self-government. Congress had "needed no prompting." It had fully and promptly supplied the administration, had clothed the Executive with the fullest power. The committee, a congressional body, had exercised its function of acquiring information the President and his cabinet could not obtain, and of advising of past mistakes and the proper course for the future. The committee's journal would show no opportunity had been neglected to present the Executive with its findings. What, then, had the Executive done? Readers should consider that "not upon those whose duty it was to provide the means necessary to put down the rebellion, but upon those whose duty it was to . . . rightfully apply those means . . . and the agents they employed for that purpose, rested the blame, if any, that the hopes of the nation have not been realized, and its expectations have been so long disappointed." Lincoln's agent, McClellan, had commanded an army "freely and lavishly" supported, singled out for special care to the point where western generals were slighted and all other military movements subordinated to it. Had that army fulfilled all that a generous and confiding people were justified in expecting from it, "this rebellion had long since been crushed and the blessings of peace restored to the Nation." Because of its failure, the war had been prolonged and the effect of the glorious victories in the West neutralized,

if not entirely destroyed. The report then recapitulated bitterly
the inaction of the army during the fall and winter of 1861–62,
McClellan's insistence "to himself manage this entire army,"
his failure to support a naval action to break the blockade on
the Potomac after twice promising to do so, his failure to leave
Washington adequately defended, his overestimation of enemy
troops, the episode of "Quaker" guns, his breaking of his snail's
pace up the peninsula with repeated sieges, his denials of requests by subordinates to force enemy lines, his panic at hearing of Jeb Stuart's raid, and his precipitous retreat to the
James. The committee then went on with his failure to back
Pope, Antietam, and the unending series of telegrams always
demanding more troops, more horses, until Lincoln finally replied: "Will you pardon me for asking what the horses of your
army have done since the battle of Antietam that fatigues
anything?" [54]

The report never charged outright that McClellan was a
traitor or secret sympathizer with the Peace Democrats. Wade
was less inhibited the following year when he spoke against
McClellan's bid for the Presidency. Quoting General Kearny,
Wade told a Cincinnati audience that a man like McClellan
"must be either a *coward or a traitor!*" He could not have
taken Richmond with all the troops in the world. The Confederate forces had laughed when they read how McClellan
had been fooled by the Quaker guns, a point Wade illustrated
with a miniature log painted black. When he started up the
peninsula, they had been ready to run; but when they saw him
"go into the swamps, bogs, and ague ponds to throw up entrenchments, they laughed and concluded they would take their
own time for running away." Outcries of "Shame!" and "Traitor!" came from Wade's audience at these revelations. [55]

The final section of the report was optimistic. Readers must
remember that war had broken out with treason in the executive mansion, in the Senate and House, army and navy, and
every government department. Great conquests had been made

in the West. If the deeds of the Army of the Potomac had at all corresponded, the rebellion would by this time be "well-nigh, if not entirely, overthrown." [56]

Union newspapers and periodicals generally applauded the report, overlooking its stricture on the President. Democrats disliked it, and the leading Copperhead journal called it the work of "a knot of malignant fanatics." But throughout the North, the Republican press, conservative to radical, spread the report over its front pages and endorsed it with enthusiastic editorials. Greeley thought it "a model of lucid, compact, and impregnable statement." The conservative *New York Times,* usually hostile to the Radicals, found, "Facts only were represented without color or bias." In reality, the report was not harsh enough, the *Times* thought. It had not set forth with sufficient vehemence the fact that McClellan was *"secretly in sympathy with the party aiming at peace."* [57]

Four days after the report on the Army of the Potomac appeared, the committee issued its findings on First Bull Run, Ball's Bluff, and the Department of the West under Frémont. Here the committee was considering foe and friend; charges of excessive partisanship may well be examined. If any scapegoat for First Bull Run was to be found, clearly Patterson with his secessionist sympathies was the candidate. But the committee's report did not throw the entire blame on him, nor did Wade and Chandler in cross-examination stress his West Point pro-slaveryism. In the early stages of the hearings, Wade hammered away at Patterson's failure to notify Washington that he could not hold Johnston, and the committee stated his failure to detain Johnston was "the principal cause of the defeat on that day [July 21]." Later Wade emphasized the bad timing of the move on Manassas, an emphasis that dominates the committee's summation. The "great error" had been General Scott's failure to occupy Manassas in May. Other causes of the disaster were: delaying a move until the enlistment stretch of ninety-day men was almost up; the greenness of the troops; unnecessary reconnaissance; prima donna quarreling over positions in the line of march; cooking breakfast; picking blueberries; "pottering along, pottering along," as General Andrew Porter put it— mistakes that no one could impute to Patterson in the Shenandoah Valley. As the evidence piled up, Wade clearly indicated he considered Scott and McDowell at fault in proceeding with the attack after it was known that Johnston had got away from Patterson, particularly when the sound of railroad cars bringing in Confederate troops could be heard all night. With this knowledge, it seemed to Wade that the battle should not have been fought that day at all. It was not "military prudence." By waiting a day or so, the "pell-mell" rout he remembered so vividly could have been avoided. To the implied accusation McDowell replied that the information about Johnston was indefinite, and Scott, that it came too late.[58]

Superficially, the verdict on the committee's favorite, Frémont, seemed to sustain the belief that he would receive unreserved support. The committee could "discover no cause of censure against him." His failure to relieve General Lyons could be explained by the haste forced upon him at the time, when Missouri was almost in anarchy. His loose handling of contracts was traceable to his own impatience with details and to a crooked quartermaster he had inherited from Frank Blair, one-time mentor, now enemy. He countersigned whatever was set before him, and he trusted unquestioningly some of his old California associates come to dip their hands in the procurement pork barrel. But the committee's statement that "much should be pardoned in one compelled to act so promptly" fell considerably short of unequivocal endorsement. Equally ambiguous was the statement that even if Frémont had "failed to do all that one under other circumstances might have done," much could be excused by the turbulence of Missouri affairs. Frémont's emancipation proclamation, whatever reservations might be entertained as to its premature issuance or its source, had been justified by the two subsequent proclamations of his

successor, General David Hunter, and the President. Thus Frémont "at that early day rightly judged . . . the most effective
means of subduing this rebellion." The Frémont administration had been "characterized by earnestness, ability, and the
most unquestionable loyalty." However, "the manner in which
that power was exercised was to be judged by results, and the
policy of continuing him in command was a matter for the
authorities above him to determine." This was a remarkable
concession on Wade's part.[59]

In the final report on Ball's Bluff, Wade and Chandler displayed once again a circumspection that was at variance with
their free-wheeling charges on the Senate floor. Furthermore,
time had presented them with a target more to their taste than
Stone—McClellan himself. The Stone case was the committee's
cause célèbre, the source of its "Star Chamber" reputation for
using *lettres de cachet,* which historians have so assiduously
kept alive. From its handling came charges that Wade was a
"Torquemada" and the committee an "Ottoman" or "St. Petersburg Court." However, when committee hearings began,
James Blaine reports that Washington generally believed that
General Baker's last words before charging the bluff were "I
will obey General Stone's order, but it is my death-warrant."
Stone had sacrificed Baker, it was widely believed, because he
resented Baker's declaration that the seceded states might have
to be reduced to a territorial status.[60]

Committee hearings began with a telegram from McClellan
stating he had not intended a crossing of the river in force. Two
other generals followed, testifying they had been baffled by
Stone's order to Baker and by his subsequent failure to reinforce his subordinate. Others—volunteer officers who disliked
Stone's West Point severity—followed. In response to leading
questions by Wade or other committee members, they agreed it
was shameful not to have reinforced Baker. Stone himself then
testified, laying the blame for the crossing on Baker. His order
had been discretionary, but Baker "chose to bring on a battle."

He was vague on why he had not reinforced him. At this point
Wade abruptly changed the tenor of the questioning, beginning a long grilling on Stone's habit of returning fugitives. The
general replied that he had merely obeyed War Department
directives, angering the committee by lumping together slave
runaways with murderers and thieves. A parade of witnesses
followed, testifying that Stone had "secesh" sympathies. He had
sent sealed letters across the river, provided escorts for relatives
of Confederate officers, and written assurances to the "strongest
and most notorious secessionists" in Maryland that their property would remain untouched by foraging parties. He had allowed a prominent Maryland planter to tend crops on the
Virginia side of the river and a flour mill allegedly supplying
the Confederate army to remain in operation. He had permitted the enemy to erect fortifications within range of his guns.
He had laughed and joked with rebel officers under a flag of
truce and had received "blackguard" letters from friends in
Virginia, one referring to Bull Run as the "Virginia races."
Many of his officers thought his secessionist sympathies, which
they discovered by opening his mail, strong enough to lead him
to treacherous conduct. Frequently, these came in answers to
questions like "It would be well . . . that I should ask you
whether there is prevailing—whether justly or not—a feeling of
suspicion in the army that General Stone is not entirely
loyal?" [61]

Outraged with the information it had received, the committee went to Stanton, and a warrant for Stone's arrest was issued.
McClellan asked that the accused general be given an opportunity to reply to charges, and on January 31 he appeared again.
He was informed in general terms of the accusations against
him but not of the names of his accusers, a practice Wade
defended by stating Stone would probably cashier them if he
learned their true identity. Stone tried to explain the charges.
Communicating under a flag of truce had been for purposes of
inquiring about, and sending supplies to, Union prisoners. He

had not razed the flour mill because its output was small, and
he did not like to destroy private property, even when Con-
federate-owned. He had planned on commandeering the Maryland planter's crops. The committee was not satisfied, especially
since Stone was still unresponsive on the reinforcement of
Baker. McClellan, not unwilling to sacrifice a subordinate
when the pressure grew great, issued an order for Stone's arrest
and the general went to prison for 189 days.[62]

The Stone case erupted on the Senate floor on April 15, 1862,
when McDougall of California denounced the treatment received by the general, comparing the committee to the inquisitorial Committee of Ten. To applause from the gallery, Wade
defended committee acts, stating that rather than being tyran-
nical, it had moved with discretion, moderation, and forbear-
ance. But only secret sympathizers with the Confederacy would
question arresting "a scoundrel when you know his heart is
with the enemy, but who meanly skulks from overt acts in their
favor." If any stain on the present administration existed, it
was that its members had been too lenient with traitors. No
doubt such mercy sprang from goodness of heart, but "mercy to
traitors is cruelty to loyal men." Six days later, Wade replied
again. Only "small" lawyers would "pettifog" the case of a
traitor or "mawkish sensibility" weep over him. With a degree
of wry satisfaction Wade defended Lincoln (who had refused
to intervene in the case) against charges of being a grand
inquisitor. He objected to efforts to brand a "mild, equitable,
just" President "who neither by word or deed or thought would
harm a hair of any man's head, who, of all men I know, is the
most reluctant to offend anybody." But "do you think that we
will stand by . . . while you fetter our legs, and bind our arms
with the Constitution of the United States that you may stab it
to death?" Wade's mail was filled with endorsements of his
stand. Typical was Judge Alphonso Taft's letter of May 14,
greeting "with greatest satisfaction" his speeches on the Stone
case.[63]

After his release Stone petitioned the committee to appear and came before it again for a third time on February 27, 1863. Bitter over McClellan's abandonment, he talked freely, no longer blaming the committee for his arrest. He explained for the first time why he had left Baker exposed by citing McClellan's order to hold all the ground he had on the Virginia shore and his promise to send reinforcements. Because of McClellan's instructions to "write nothing; say nothing; keep quiet," he had been equivocal in his answers before; and he had not asked for a court of inquiry because McClellan had shown him a letter to Lincoln stating he was "entirely without blame." He had talked to the relative of an old West Point acquaintance under a flag of truce, but had learned more than his companion. General Scott had countersigned some of the safe-conducts he gave to persons of known rebel connections. Recalled to the stand the next day, McClellan agreed that his order had been discretionary, but stated he had never contemplated a crossing, "merely to show a force in the vicinity of the river." [64]

Unlike their vociferations in the Senate, the report reflected Wade's and Chandler's final harmonious relations with Stone and their decision to shift much of the responsibility to McClellan. His dispatch had been unclear, and from it Stone "received no intimation" the movement was merely a reconnoitering one. Stone's testimony "would seem to indicate" that "under what he understood to be the circumstances," transportation for Baker was adequate, although "he left much to the judgment of others." Some witnesses supported Stone's contention that it would have been "extremely hazardous, if not impossible," to have sent reinforcements. With evidence "so very contradictory," the committee must "refrain from expressing any positive opinion. . . ." The committee's report to Stanton had been that evidence tending to impeach Stone's conduct was also "conflicting." Members had made no recommendation, although "they were satisfied that the information which they had furnished . . . had in all probability furnished some of the grounds upon which his arrest had been made." The order for arrest had been finally issued by McClellan upon the testimony of a Negro refugee from Virginia that tended to corroborate the charges. Why General Stone never received a copy of the charges against him, "your committee have never been informed." [65]

The Stone case convinced the committee that military lukewarmness was usually matched by softness toward rebels and harshness toward Negroes and Union troops. It heard much testimony about generals like McClellan's protégé, Andrew Porter, who stationed special guards before rebel households or guarded the cows of a "secesh" owner who sold milk for fifty cents to a dollar a pint to Porter's men. General McDowell had issued an order that property must be protected "even if it should be necessary to place a sentinel over every panel of fence." Wade immediately made a speech, asking his colleagues if they thought the war could be conducted by "sedulously" guarding the pigs and chickens of "your mortal enemies." McDowell, who defended his policy to the committee by claiming that whenever his men wanted anything from a house its owner was sure to be a "rabid secessionist," had removed General Doubleday for permitting pillage. Doubleday retorted that McDowell had guarded rebel households bursting with provender while Union soldiers were without rations for a week, and had told him "with a great deal of pride and satisfaction" that leading rebels acknowledged he guarded their property better than their own troops did.[66]

It was from Doubleday's son, Charles, and from General Dan Sickles that the committee received testimony about generals ejecting fleeing Negroes from their lines and welcoming "slavers." Hooker was one of the worst offenders. Furthermore, the committee learned in April, 1862, that the President had never transmitted to the army his revocation of Halleck's order not to allow fugitives within the lines. Typical of cases cited before the committee was the account concerning a General Lockwood who whipped a Negro found trying to enter his camp and assured planters that he was a slaveholder himself and would guarantee their property. Wade himself became personally involved when he tried to intervene with a Colonel Hazen who had threatened to flog Negroes. The U.S. District Attorney in Cleveland informed him that Hazen's commanding officer had claimed he could have Wade removed from the Senate any time, since he was "out clear in the cold with the administration." Wade's own personal mail corroborated committee testimony on the presence of "slavers" within Union lines. An Ohio major wrote:

All a rebel emissary has to do to get inside our lines & learn our strength, arms & efficiency is to claim to be hunting a negro and presto! his pass is forthcoming & he goes from camp to camp at his sovereign will, walking up to any officer's tent & Hallooing "got any runaway negroes here, let me see." [67]

Countering, generals who shared Wade's view devised various stratagems to hinder slave catchers and help Negroes. Charles Doubleday advised his pickets to obey the Dred Scott decision that a Negro was not a person. Laws pertaining to passage of "persons" in and out of the lines would then not apply. The "Abolitionist General" James Brisbin, Wade's great friend, after discovering that Kentucky slaveholders sent their Negroes away to prevent their listening to Union recruiting officers, issued an order that all Negroes found away from home would be considered "vagrants," subject to being taken into custody. Through such versatility Brisbin recruited 20,000 Negro troops. Both of Wade's sons served in his Negro cavalry regiment. Sickles told the committee of Zouaves—New York firemen—who would not allow "slavers" in camp and of angry soldiers who had thrashed slave catchers attempting to flog runaways. Sickles' own dismissal had come from ordering "well-known secessionists" in search of fugitives out of his camp, he thought.[68] General Butler pleased the committee by extending the term "contraband" from Confederate horses and mules to fugitives, whom he employed to build fortifications.

Wade, Chandler, Stevens, Julian, Owen Lovejoy, and other strong antislavery men had attempted to insert a provision in the second Confiscation Act to employ persons of African descent in putting down the rebellion. To gain support, they inserted "An Address to the People" in the *Tribune* on July 19, 1862. Employment of Negroes in labor details, they hoped, would lead to their use as soldiers. Negroes attempting to enlist were turned down generally throughout 1861 and early 1862, but in the summer of 1862 Massachusetts and Rhode Island formed Negro regiments. Wade knew problems of Negro recruitment first hand from both his sons and from General Brisbin, who complained that many officers were apathetic toward Negro soldiers. They used them only on labor details, maintained a pay differential, and refused to provide physical protection for recruiting agents. Wade used this information in 1864 to press on Stanton the issuance of a special order to commanders known like Sherman for their opposition to "eternal Sambo." [69]

The War Committee's most violent clash with Lincoln and the source of Wade's reputation as "Marat . . . brought from out the cellars of Paris" came on the question of retaliation for Confederate treatment of Union soldiers and prisoners and Negro troops. After First Bull Run the New York and Washington press had published accounts of mutilations of Union corpses. Demands for retaliation grew with news of conditions in Confederate prison camps and use of Indians at Pea Ridge. The committee began investigation of the mutilation charges on April 1, 1862. Fifteen witnesses appeared, among them ex-Secretary of War Simon Cameron, who had gone to the battlefield to recover his brother's body, and. Governor Sprague of Rhode Island, now a volunteer commander, seeking remains of members of his regiment. Residents of the area, a number of them Negro slaves, told them bodies had been burned or beheaded. The Sprague party, which included a physician and a clergyman, found a partly burned femur, vertebrae, and pelvic bones, and Sprague identified a shirt found with the bones. Cameron found his brother's body thrown with seven others in a common ditch. An old gentleman, whom a witness, the Reverend Frederic Denison, characterized as "highly esteemed by all who knew him," testified that he had heard that members of a Georgia regiment had carried a severed head south. Other witnesses related even more gruesome stories of brandy punch cups made from skulls and rings from bones; *Harper's Weekly* carried full-page sketches on June 7, 1862. An elderly planter, who owned most of the slaves appearing before the committee, attributed the atrocities to an irregular group called the Louisiana Tigers and asked that Confederate troops be not held responsible. One surgeon and a general told of bodies lying unburied for ten or twelve days while rebel women remained "entirely unmoved." (The committee itself in summarizing the evidence used the phrase "gloating over the horrid sight.") Attached to the report were affidavits charging that scalpings and other mutilations occurred at Pea Ridge. At the same time the committee had heard testimony on barbarous treatment and starvation of prisoners in Confederate camps. General Ricketts, held as hostage in Libby Prison by his West Point comrade, Beauregard, testified to having seen a Union soldier bayoneted fourteen times and bodies dumped unceremoniously in Negro burying grounds. After presenting evidence of crimes that "exceed the worst excesses of the Sepoys of India," the committee stated it advocated no retaliation. Let the Union side continue to furnish a contrast to such crimes. Northern armies should refuse to imitate the monstrous practices the committee had revealed.[70]

Two years later, the committee's sentiment about retaliation changed when the most frightful atrocity of the war took place at Fort Pillow, Tennessee. Negro and white defenders of the fort, attempting to surrender, were slaughtered wholesale until

Confederate General Forrest could boast that the river in front
of the fort was dyed with blood for two hundred yards. Holding
up white flags, Union soldiers were shot or hacked with sabers;
wounded were dragged out of the hospital; small children were
shot; tents where some cowered were set afire. Wade and Gooch
rushed at once to Tennessee, where they found "bodies still
unburied" and "could still see the faces, hands, and feet of men,
white and black, protruding out of the ground . . . still discol-
ored with blood." Of the 538 men at the fort (262 Negro)
"from 300 to 400 are known to have been killed at Fort Pillow," the committee's report declared, "of whom at least 300
were murdered in cold blood after the post was in possession of
the rebels. . . ." The two committee members examined sev-
enty-eight witnesses. Eight surgeons described the kinds of
wounds they treated, the first stating the men were the "worst
butchered" and "mangled" he had ever seen. Rebel soldiers
had entered the hospital, he said, and hacked at the head of a
sixteen-year-old Negro boy patient with their sabers, then cut
off one or two of his fingers. Survivors testified they had thrown
down their arms and torn pieces from their shirts to hold aloft.
One Negro soldier said, "I know General Forrest rode his horse
over me three or four times. . . . He said to some negro men
that . . . they had been in his nigger yard in Memphis." A
white soldier was told, "God damn you, you fight with these
damned niggers, and we will kill you." A Confederate officer
tried to rescue a Negro child, taking him up on his horse, but
his commanding officer, General Chalmers the witness thought,
pulled the boy down and shot him. Attempting to escape, white
and black troops ran for the river where, according to an
injured volunteer aboard the Union gunboat "Silver Cloud,"
bullets "rained as thick in the water as you ever saw a hail-
storm." Sent out to make burial arrangements, the "Silver
Cloud's" commander saw "bodies with gaping wounds, some
bayoneted through the eyes, some with skulls beaten through,
others with hideous wounds, as if their bowels had been ripped

open with Bowie knives. . . ." Lieutenant William Cleary of
the gunboat found "five negroes burning" the morning after the
attack. "I asked Colonel Chalmers, the general's brother, if that
was the way he allowed his men to do. He concluded that he
could not control his men very well, and thought it was justifia-
ble in regard to negroes; that they did not recognize negroes as
soldiers, and he could not control them." [71]

Testimony about forcing Negroes into tents or buildings and
then setting them afire varied. Generally, witnesses stated they
had heard about it but had not personally seen it. One Negro
survivor stated, "They nailed some black sergeants to logs, and
set the logs on fire." The committee found evidence of this in
"logs and trees which showed but too plainly the evidences of
the atrocities perpetrated there." It also stated that "the
charred remains of five or six bodies were afterwards found,"
all but one too disfigured for identification. The one of whose
"identification . . . there can hardly be a doubt" was named by
several witnesses as Lieutenant Akerstrom, a Tennessee con-
script who had run away from Forrest and charged him with
violating the rules of war by moving in under a flag of truce at
Paducah. (Testimony of Union officers at Paducah confirmed
his charges; Forrest's sharpshooters had also mingled with
women and children being evacuated, forcing Union troops to
hold their fire.) At Fort Pillow, Akerstrom had been "nailed to
the side of a house, and the house set on fire, burning him to
death," Lieutenants F. A. Smith and William Cleary stated,
furnishing affidavits from the wives of three privates, one of
whom positively identified the body as Akerstrom's, saying she
was "well acquainted" with him. The other two saw the
charred corpse of a white man and the nails, but had not
personally known Akerstrom. Major General Hurlbut stated he
"had no reason to doubt" a man had been so treated, but he
thought the identification doubtful. Eli Bangs, the acting master's mate from another gunboat, the "New Era," said he had
buried four burned bodies that he found in tents and that one

black man, parts of whose arms were burned off and whose "legs were burned nearly to a crisp," had been nailed to boards. Three other witnesses confirmed there were nails through his clothes and his cartridge box.[72]

In its report the committee found the atrocities at Fort Pillow were "not the result of passion excited by the heat of conflict," but of "a policy deliberately decided upon and unhesitatingly announced." Just after Fort Pillow, Lincoln had announced he would institute a system of retaliation if reports of the massacre were authenticated. The committee awaited his action, making no recommendation of its own. Meantime, Stanton had asked Wade to investigate the condition of returned prisoners at Annapolis. Here again, Wade made a personal trip. The prisoners were "living skeletons." Committee member Julian reported he found Wade "sobbing like a child." Wade heard from ten prisoners he examined and from four doctors, a nurse, and two chaplains grisly testimony of gratuitous cruelty: wanton killing for minor infractions; removal of blankets; forcing prisoners to sleep on the ground so that many froze; starvation to the point where filthy, lice-encrusted survivors had shrunk to gaunt, sunken-eyed wraiths. Wade attached to the report eight photographs that resemble strongly survivors of Dachau. The report charged Confederate officials, especially at Richmond, with following inhuman practices deliberately designed to render prisoners unfit for either further service in the field or, as Stanton added, "even to enjoy life." [73]

The committee's decision not to demand retaliation had changed. In the face of Lincoln's failure to carry out his pledge, Wade offered a resolution that inmates of Union camps receive the same treatment, rations, and clothing as Confederate prisoners. Speaking lengthily on rebel atrocities, Wade also flayed the administration for its failure to free the families of Negro soldiers. Some had been subjected to barbarous reprisals. At General Burbridge's camp Wade himself had seen a Negro woman whose face had been "whipped to a jelly," and a child, one of whose eyes had been gouged out and the other "attempted to be" by an infuriated mistress. If slavery was not to be abolished nor such practices abandoned, he hoped there would be no peace. If the war "continues thirty years and bankrupts the whole nation, I hope to God there will be no peace until we can say there is not a slave in this land." Democratic Senator Reverdy Johnson (Maryland) thereupon called Wade "vindictive" and reminded him that the President had stated the South might find peace at any time simply by submitting to national authority. Its institutions would remain intact. The President's statement, Wade replied, had no more force with him than that emanating from any "respectable source," although he expected the head of state to support retaliation and to free the families of Negro soldiers; if not, "it is so much the worse for the President." To unexpected opposition from Sumner, who regarded retaliation as "useless barbarism," Wade replied that he was not being merely vindictive. Washington had proved the practicality of retaliation when he told Gage and Howe that their conduct would govern his. General Butler had successfully practiced retaliation when he put captured rebels to work digging ditches; the next morning the enemy facing him had stopped using Negroes on labor details and effected an exchange of prisoners. Just recently, General Sherman had pledged to take five lives for one if anyone attacked a loyal man or Union soldier in Georgia. Wade was scornful of appeals to Christianity, observing little Christianity in war. His sense of humanity was "not merely" on the side of rebellion like those "old women" in the Senate guilty of "mawkish sentimentality." This statement caused several senators to react violently, including McDougall's frequently quoted comparison of Wade to "Marat . . . brought from out the cellars of Paris." [74]

Reading from the committee's report on prison conditions, Wade supported his argument for retaliation with an affidavit from a New Hampshire sergeant who had escaped from the

Confederate prison at Salisbury, North Carolina, together with reporters from the *Times, Tribune,* and *Cincinnati Gazette.* 10,600 men had been housed in a building fit for 2,000. (His figures were so precise because he had been in charge of issuing bread rations.) All blankets, tents, and knapsacks had been taken away, and then "one small wall tent" issued for each 100 men. For shelter men had to burrow into the ground in holes dug with pocket knives. Bread cost $20.00 a loaf. A fifth of the men died of starvation and diarrhea, nearly two thousand within a fortnight. Notwithstanding his evidence, the Senate refused to accept Wade's retaliation proposal, striking out specific items such as rations and clothing. Further amendments watered it down to a point where neither Wade nor Chandler would vote for it. As finally passed, it allowed the President to amend existing cartels so that commissaries of prisons might make suggestions for more humane treatment of prisoners. This was ridiculous, Wade charged. Jefferson Davis would "put your commissary in Libby before he had time to think." Many northern newspapers supported Wade's angry reaction. The *Tribune* had earlier found committee reports did not cite the full horror of the rebellion's "essentially barbarous conduct." The *Cleveland Leader* could not understand the Senate's indifference, declaring failure to retaliate was the Lincoln administration's greatest fault. The *Cleveland Herald* praised Wade for his efforts on behalf of those "dying by inches in Southern prisons." [75]

Meantime, Lincoln, Stanton, and the committee had been faced with continuing disasters in the Army of the Potomac. Hooker, once a target for allowing "slavers" in his camp, had succeeded Burnside. But his testimony against McClellan had won Wade's and Chandler's approval. Once again, they had to learn that political declarations did not guarantee military capability. After two months of McClellanite posturing, Hooker at Chancellorsville assumed the familiar role of a commander demoralized by responsibility. In its later review the committee minimized Hooker's ineptitude, recording Dan Sickles', Birney's, Butterfield's, and Hooker's own testimony that the intrigues of McClellan and Halleck and lack of support from jealous corps commanders were responsible for his difficulty. Lincoln also wrote Hooker that he had "painful intimations" he lacked the entire confidence of his corps commanders, a fact "ruinous, if true." Wade personally reprimanded Henry Ward Beecher for circulating the false story that Hooker had been drunk during battle instead of reeling from a blow caused by a collapsing pillar, and the committee chided Halleck for withholding from Hooker troops readily furnished his successor.[76]

Meade, who followed Hooker, was the fourth in a series of generals beset by vacillation when facing responsibility, and he received harsh treatment from the committee. They had never liked him as a West Pointer and brother-in-law of secessionist Governor Henry A. Wise of Virginia, and they were no more impressed by the official victory at Gettysburg than they had been by McClellan at Antietam. Witnesses before the committee testified to Meade's vacillations and his consideration of abandoning his position. They cited his directions to prepare for retreat on the second day when he was winning, an order he told the committee he had no recollection of ever having issued and, later, appeared to "utterly deny." There was also a strange assertion in the same order that the entire army should fall back if a single corps commander deemed it necessary. His failure to pursue Lee received special fire. Again, Kenneth P. Williams corroborates the committee's findings. Meade's army had been well concentrated on June 28; by June 30 he had succeeded in scattering it. "It is impossible to put any coherence and sense into the dispatches, circulars, and orders that Meade issued on the 30th. They show a vacillating, disturbed officer from whom all resolution and clear purpose had departed." "But the worst remains to be related." Writing to Halleck "as if in a dream," at the end of the second day, Meade wanted to retreat and was prevented from doing so only by the vote of his corps commanders. The army went ahead, smashing the last great assault—Pickett's. Then, as Lincoln put it: "We had them within our grasp. We had only to stretch forth our hands and they were ours. And nothing I could say or do could make the Army move." Catton, less critical, finds Meade "had not done too badly," but that the battle was won chiefly because of the fighting spirit of the troops. T. Harry Williams, who had once characterized committee hearings as a campaign to "destroy" Meade, the "inquisitors" using "Judas words" in their "double-dealing," merely cites committee testimony on several disputed questions in his second account. The evidence is equivocal, he finds. Meade fought well, but it was a completely defensive fight like McClellan's at Antietam.[77]

Directly after the testimony, the committee went to Lincoln, threatening to publicize charges that Meade had prepared an order to retreat and that only the action of the corps commanders in forcing a fight brought victory. Lincoln did not move at once, but eventually solved the matter with a characteristic gesture. He subordinated Meade to Grant, who had been brought in from the West to succeed Halleck as general-in-chief. Such a move satisfied the committee, once suspicious of Grant as a Democrat and unsure of his military ability at Pittsburg Landing, where, Lew Wallace intimated, he may have been surprised. This stung Grant. Sherman found him "almost weeping at the accumulated charges against him by such villains as Stanton of Ohio, Wade and others." Nevertheless, his definition of war agreed with theirs. At Vicksburg he had followed a policy of cutting himself off from his base of supplies and living off the country, a method Wade advocated in his cross-examination of generals. With Grant the policy of slashing, grinding total war was accepted, and the committee was at last satisfied.[78]

The committee had investigated several other areas: treatment of soldiers in Union convalescent camps, hospitals, and

bull pens; a massacre of Cheyenne Indians by Union troops at
Fort Lyons, Colorado; profiteering in ice contracts; naval infighting in the construction of light-draught monitors. Here,
Wade's old reform spirit asserted itself. The committee was
scarcely less vigorous in denouncing the callousness of Union
surgeons and jailers and those Colorado officials, including the
governor, and Army commanders responsible for the mutilations and castrations of nearly 500 Indians, than it had been in
describing Fort Pillow or Confederate prison camps. Wade and
his group also considered various lesser engagements in the
eastern theater, such as Ben Butler's ludicrous operations at
Fort Fisher, the Battle of the Crater at Petersburg, Rosecrans'
campaign in Tennessee, and Sherman's surrender arrangements with Joe Johnston. These reports, considerably briefer
than the extensive assessment of the Army of the Potomac,
displayed the committee's well-defined policy on military tactics
and Union objectives as well as its willingness to lead witnesses
and accept hearsay evidence.[79]

III

Wade's battle against "executive usurpation" reached its
grand climax with the publication of the Wade-Davis manifesto against the Presidential plan for restoring the seceded
states. From the first wartime session Radicals had quarreled
with Lincoln over whether the President or Congress should
determine policies toward the South. Confiscation and emancipation were especially sore spots. Of the confiscation bills offered in the special 1861 summer session, Wade favored Chandler's or Sumner's, seizing all property, slaves, and real estate,
of persons in rebellion. He would "go for the largest
forfeiture. . . . Yea, to the last dollar of these scoundrels."
Trumbull's less severe measure to free the slaves of every person convicted of rebellion was "a laughing stock," since it did

not confiscate real estate and, as Chandler put it, only freed the slaves of persons found guilty of aiding or abetting the rebellion "hereafter." Wade insisted upon a retroactive provision that the Senate and House adopted. Jocularly, he argued, according to Trumbull, that the contention that permanent forfeiture constituted a bill of attainder could be got around by offering the offender a choice between forfeiture and hanging, with his estate left clear to his heirs. Since property was so much more valuable than life, the rebel would elect to be hanged, and the estate would then be left to his heirs. With a retroactive provision and permanent forfeiture, he was willing to accept the measure, although he preferred the Judiciary Committee's "vigorous" and "masculine" bill, which would simply confiscate all property, slaves and real estate, used in pursuance of rebellion. At this point Lincoln let it be known that he would not accept the Trumbull bill. Emancipation by confiscation was a Presidential, not a congressional, prerogative. Wade, as usual, had claimed the opposite, insisting that attempts to invest the President with "despotic" and "irresponsible" power on this issue was a "most slavish and un-American doctrine." But Lincoln insisted that he would not accept the retroactive provision or permanent forfeiture; he would veto the bill unless these provisions were removed. Wade became violently angry when Fessenden conveyed this intelligence, accusing him of "mousing around" the White House. "We ought to have a committee on vetoes," he declaimed. "We ought to have a committee to wait on the President whenever we send him a bill, to know what his royal pleasure is in regard to it." He accused "privileged gentlemen who are charged with his constitutional conscience" of "creeping in at the back door," while others were "debarred all access" to the President. Wade's speeches on confiscation infuriated his colleagues, especially Fessenden and Trumbull, two of the "recusant seven" in 1868.[80]

But his constituents responded warmly, his old enemy Brother Ned writing that his confiscation speech was the best since the rebellion. Judge Alphonso Taft of Cincinnati, another regular correspondent, advised that "the country and Lincoln must be brought to the point of doing their duty." The higher law must be followed, not the lower expediency Lincoln operated on as he "petted" halfhearted supporters of the Union. General David Hunter sent his congratulations, along with a copy of his emancipation proclamation for the Department of the South. However, in spite of Wade's objections and the sweeping Republican majority in favor of the bill, Congress removed the objectionable clauses. After this gesture Radicals were doubly outraged when Lincoln sent over the veto message he would have issued if Congress had not complied with his request. Senators walked out while the message was being read, and the customary resolution to print it was not offered. According to Julian, "Mr. Wade said the country was going to hell, and that the scenes witnessed in the French Revolution were nothing in comparison with what we should see here." [81]

To Wade's mind the weakened confiscation bill, disappointing as it was, was greatly superior to the cautious and inoperative Emancipation Proclamation Lincoln finally issued two months later. He was dismayed by the puzzling declaration that its issuance did not change the character of the war, by its reaffirmation of compensated emancipation, and by its mode of operation that freed less slaves than the confiscation bill. By exempting from its provisions the areas controlled by Union armies, Lincoln freed the slaves where the proclamation could not be carried out and kept them captive where it could be enforced.

By the fall of 1863 the problem of reconstituting civil government in the seceded states became acute and the congressional-presidential issue flared again. Assuming that restoration was a congressional prerogative, the House appointed a committee of nine to consider a subject on which Radicals were by no means as monolithic as sometimes assumed. Sumner, Stevens, and Wade differed sharply. Sumner thought the states had committed suicide and ought to be reborn. Stevens held to the theory that they had reverted to a territorial status and must seek re-entry through the Committee on Territories. Wade was chairman of that committee, but he scorned Stevens' theory. He concurred with Lincoln's view that secession was illegal, but that the states remained as entities that could be restored through methods the Constitution had laid down. He differed from Lincoln in seeing Congress, not the Executive, as restorer. In other instances Wade's policy had approached Lincoln's. During the secession crisis he had publicly favored settling freed Negroes in some "congenial clime" such as Mexico or Central America. During the war he sometimes hedged on the question of equality, especially suffrage, accusing his Radical colleagues of being doctrinaire, and feeling he had "sufficient capital" invested in the Negro's cause to enable him to yield to expediency to get some justice done "if we cannot now do all the justice we want to do." [82]

Initial testing of reconstruction came in the Department of the Gulf, where Ben Butler, besides treating planters cavalierly, Confederate ladies ungallantly, and himself rather generously in the matter of cotton and sugar (the committee accepted unblinkingly his declaration that he had saved the government a considerable sum by sending ships to New York with sugar instead of sand as ballast), had also concerned himself with the freedman's status. He had appointed a general superintendent of Negro affairs; taken a census; provided shelter, medical care, and some schools; and allotted some land to Negroes for cultivating. Butler's transfer and N. P. Banks's appointment completely changed these tentative steps toward a new relationship between whites and Negroes. Banks created a commission of Army representatives and planters to draw up contracts. The army would enforce "perfect subordination . . . on the part of the Negroes." It was reconstruction "without destroying slavery," Henry Ward Beecher charged.[83]

The conflict accelerated in December, 1863, with Lincoln's

proposal of his own plan for restoration. Stating he would not modify nor retract emancipation, the President offered full pardon to all persons in the insurrectionary states willing to take an oath to support the Constitution, the Acts of Congress, and his Emancipation Proclamation. When in any state 10 per cent of the voters in 1860 took the prescribed oath, they could set up a state government and he would extend recognition. Radicals balked at the omission of a clause disfranchising Confederate officials and at the failure to insist upon state emancipation proclamations. What would stop the slaveholding powers from reinstating de facto slavery or from re-electing their old representatives? Once the slave no longer counted as three-fifths of a man, but as a whole man, Southern States would increase their representation in Washington.

To counter the administration's plan, Henry Winter Davis drew up a House measure that Wade then introduced into the Senate. The best speaker in Congress, Davis was a former Know-Nothing and abolitionist-baiter converted to the anti-slavery cause and enough of a daredevil to be chided by Stevens for his over-advanced position. Davis' measure directly opposed Lincoln's "hermaphrodite" (half-military, half-Republican) bill. It provided that a majority, not 10 per cent, of persons within the seceded states take the oath of allegiance. Such a body could then hold a state convention, excluding military or civil officeholders under the Confederacy. It must prohibit forever involuntary servitude. Here the measure struck down Lincoln's stratagem, derived from Banks, for sparing the southerners the ordeal of abolishing slavery themselves. The new state must repudiate any debt "created by or under the sanction of the usurping power." Negroes were to be protected by a habeas corpus clause and by a penalty of five to twenty years imprisonment and a fine to be imposed on anyone convicted of reducing a freedman to involuntary servitude.[84]

Sumner disliked the Wade-Davis bill because it made no provision for Negro suffrage, and Stevens disliked it because it

accorded partial rights to the rebellious states instead of reducing them to territorial status. Furthermore, it laid no ground-
work for confiscating real property to provide land for the
Negroes, a measure Stevens held more necessary than votes and
Wade considered "d——d foolery."

In debate Wade argued against both his friends. "I utterly
deny," he said, "the theory that States may lose their corporate
capacity by rebellion. . . . I hold that once a state of this
Union, always a State." It was unconstitutional to decide they
had been "obliterated, blotted out." As for the President, he
was undoubtedly acting from the best motives; but in the light
of American principles, his measure was "absurd . . . most
anti-republican, anomalous, and entirely subversive of the
great principles that underlie all our State governments and the
General Government. Majorities must rule, and until majorities can be found loyal and trustworthy for State government,
they must be governed by a stronger hand." The Constitution
expressly provided for exigencies like the present by stating
that the federal government should guarantee every state a
republican government. Here Carlile of Virginia interrupted
that Wade had misread "guarantee" to mean "impose." Citing
Madison in *Federalist* 43, Carlile argued that guaranteeing
meant no more than assuring the continuation of a pre-existing
government that had emanated from the people of a state.
Suppose the states were to set up a monarchy, Wade countered.
What, then, should the general government do? The basis for
his argument was always Section 3, Article IV of the Constitution. As Wade's colleague Henry Winter Davis saw it: "It is the
exclusive prerogative of Congress—of Congress and not of the
President—to determine what is the established government of
the state." Here, Wade and Davis were in substantial agreement with Congressman Samuel Shellabarger, who in a major
speech had quoted Chief Justice Taney: ". . . It rests with
Congress to decide which government . . . is the established
one." [85]

Eric L. McKitrick has recently stated that the Shellabarger doctrine represented the majority position in Congress on reconstruction. John W. Burgess, a leading congressional authority opposed to the Radicals, declared the doctrine of congressional reconstruction completely correct. It is exclusively a question for the legislature to decide "as to how the population in the rebellious districts shall be civilly organized anew." Congress "may fashion the boundaries of the district at its own pleasure. . . . These things are matters in which the President . . . cannot interfere." The Wade-Davis bill was "sound political science, and the President ought to have heeded its teachings." [86]

Sumner's opposition to the bill because it contained no Negro suffrage position posed a constant problem of conscience for Wade. The two men subsequently clashed on the bills admitting Montana and Nebraska. As chairman of the Committee on Territories, Wade argued that to insist on suffrage in a state like Montana, where there were no Negroes, was to deal in abstractions. He also opposed Sumner's attempt to establish Negro suffrage in the District of Columbia on the grounds that the proposal was temporary; only a permanent measure would do complete justice. Furthermore, why was it more antirepublican to exclude Negroes than women (he had just added a woman suffrage section to the bill)? Similarly, in the Wade-Davis bill, he argued, striking out the word "white" would jeopardize its passage. Public opinion was not yet ready to accept votes for Negroes. His argument convinced some of Sumner's lieutenants, but not Sumner himself, to waive their "conscientious scruples" and "go for expediency." [87]

Lincoln's response to the Wade-Davis bill, which passed a half hour before adjournment, was a pocket veto. Four days later, he issued a proclamation explaining why he did not endorse "one very proper plan" of restoration. It had good ideas, but he did not want to commit the government to any one inflexible plan, nor to set aside his own proposal. Furthermore, he could not concede to Congress "a constitutional competency" to abolish slavery. The longer route of a constitutional amendment would have to be sought. The proclamation enraged Wade, Davis, and other Radicals. The authors of the vetoed bill immediately framed a manifesto, which Greeley published on August 5. Addressing themselves to "Supporters of the Government," the manifesto's authors described themselves as impelled to "check the encroachments of the Executive on the authority of Congress." They questioned the propriety of a pocket veto accompanied by a proclamation, a document unknown to the laws and Constitution of the United States. Rather than being too weighty for quick decision, as the President explained in his unorthodox procedure, the contents of the bill had been known for months. Action on it had been "staved off" to the last moment by administration supporters so that the President might avoid the constitutional responsibility of a veto. The manifesto then attacked Lincoln for recognizing "those shadows of Governments in Arkansas and Louisiana . . . mere oligarchies imposed on the people by military orders under the forms of election, at which generals, provost-marshals, soldiers, and camp followers were the chief actors." In Louisiana, under cover of Banks's Red River campaign, the army perpetrated a "farce called an election." Probably one-third of the ballots cast were by Union soldiers. The same farce took place in Arkansas; only a military failure prevented it in Florida. The President held the electoral votes of the rebel states "at the dictation of his personal ambition." If Presidential electors were chosen in the 10 per cent states, "a sinister light will be cast on his motives." Congress had correctly refused to seat senators and representatives chosen under the 10 per cent plan, but he, disregarding their judgment and that of the Supreme Court, "strides headlong toward the anarchy his proclamation of the 8th of December inaugurated." Had not the President by emancipation freed a greater number of slaves than would be manumitted under the present congressional bill? Did the President suppose Congress would rest a discretion in him it could not exercise in itself? The public should mark the contrast between Presidential and congressional reconstruction. Congress required a majority; the President, one-tenth of the voters. The bill ascertained voters by registration, the President's plan by guess. The bill provided for government by law, the President for the "lawless discretion of military Governors and Provost-Marshals." The proclamation was silent on the Confederate debt and the exclusion of rebel leaders; it left slavery exactly where it was at the outbreak of the rebellion. The manifesto concluded by urging true friends of the government to assure that the President would "obey and execute, not make the laws." [88]

The manifesto was not well received. Even the *Tribune* and the *Intelligencer,* supporters of congressional restoration, were repelled by its vituperativeness, as were the antislavery papers. Lincoln's veto had been a "solecism in politics," but the manifesto's "severity" was objectionable. Assertions that Lincoln hungered for power were childish; their "envenomed hostility and ill-tempered spirit" unfitted either Wade or Davis to counsel the nation. The *Anti-Slavery Standard* felt it was regrettable the bill had not become law, but was even more concerned with "schisms in the party of Freedom" at a moment of military disaster. In an open letter to the manifesto's authors, the veteran abolitionist Gerrit Smith chided them for bringing about such a reduction in popular good will toward Lincoln. The Copperhead *World,* which had greeted both the Wade-Davis bill and the manifesto as a "humiliation" and "blow between the eyes" to Lincoln, thought Smith hypocritical. Obviously, Lincoln deserved impeachment for his usurpation. The *Times* thought it no surprise that the enemy should take delight in the manifesto; according to the *Times,* it was the "most widely circulated Copperhead document" of the war. Its real object was Lincoln's defeat. The President's invasion of congressional rights would never have disturbed Wade and Davis in the least if practiced on behalf of the slaves.[89]

Wade did not fare much better at home. His own district censured him in a formal resolution, calling the manifesto "ill-timed, ill-tempered, and ill-advised." This was a signal rebuke against a special favorite, commented the *Times*. If anyone had asked who of all men in Congress would be least likely to receive a reprimand from his constituents, it would be Ben Wade. James Garfield, accused of helping frame the manifesto, disavowed it passionately. Very likely, most congressmen felt as did James Blaine. Wade and Davis had no power. Even if the President were in error, it was better to follow him.[90]

Some evidence exists that Lincoln regretted the veto. Both Wade and Sherman cite Sumner's account of an interview he had with Lincoln in which the President expressed regret that he had not approved the bill; in Wade's version this becomes the "great error" of his life. He was deeply hurt by the manifesto, according to Carl Schurz, especially the accusation by "men who have been my friends and who ought to know me better, that I have been seduced by what they call the lust of power, and that I have been doing this and that unscrupulous thing hurtful to the common cause, only to keep myself in office!" [91]

Obviously, the manifesto had been issued with the intent of averting a second term for Lincoln. Reluctantly nominated in May, he faced three rivals: Chase, Frémont, and Butler, each of whom thought the President should step down. Disaffection with Lincoln, once a Radical monopoly, had spread to moderate Republicans. Wade made no public commitment and disassociated himself from a movement by Davis, Greeley, and William Cullen Bryant to ask Lincoln to step aside. His disavowal came after the Democrats had nominated McClellan on a peace platform written by the Copperhead chief Clement Vallandigham. Both Chandler and Wade agreed that anyone, even Jeff

Davis, would be preferable to McClellan. "Both are d——d traitors but give me a smart villain before a fool one," was Chandler's comment. Worried by third-party efforts, especially Frémont's, Chandler made a quick trip to Wade at home in Ohio to work out plans for dissuading the Pathfinder from challenging Lincoln. They would inform the President of their efforts, securing Montgomery Blair's dismissal from the cabinet as a guarantee that no soft peace would be tolerated. Wade's and Chandler's plans became incredibly snarled, faulty communication not being limited to generals; and Chandler, who had expected Wade to assail Frémont in New York, had to perform both halves of the operation. His Trojan efforts, especially in Washington, elicited lavish compliments from Wade for his success in "working on old Abe's fears." Wade would stump for the Republican party, not for Lincoln.

I only wish we could do as well for a better man. But to save the nation I am doing all for *him* that I possibly could do for a better man, were it not for the country there would be poetical justice in his being beaten by that stupid ass McClellan, who, he persisted in keeping in the service against all that you and I, and Andy Johnson could do, to have him removed and a live man in his place. That stupid wilfulness cost this nation more than a hundred thousand men, as you well know and when I think of those things, I can but wish the d——l had old Abe.[92]

Even though he stumped for Lincoln, Wade had no intention of permitting Presidential reconstruction to go unchallenged. He began hearings in December, 1864, on charges that Banks's Red River expedition, "a big cotton raid" for the benefit of speculators, had failed for two reasons. First, as Banks's archenemy Admiral David Porter testified, "cotton killed that expedition." Other officers testified to the abundance of rope and bagging, the presence of known speculators, there by Presidential permit, Wade emphasized, and connections between Banks's quartermaster and a "big cotton ring" operating out of New Orleans. Second, the campaign failed because the army stopped at intervals to hold elections under the 10 per cent plan. Less evidence substantiated the election charge, although Admiral Porter and a Colonel J. G. Wilson testified time had been lost in holding elections. Through this "farce . . . we lost, I think, two or three days," said Porter. For the first time the committee presented a majority and minority report. The majority finding asked why such an ill-advised expedition had been undertaken. Only, it would appear, to afford an egress for cotton and to establish a state government in Louisiana, "clearly a usurpation on the part of the military authorities, the execution of which was as weak and inefficient as the attempt was improper and illegal." Gooch's minority report saw no connection between the military fiasco and the elections and not much interference by cotton traders. Wade grew impassioned on the Senate floor, belaboring his old target—speculators—and denouncing the Louisiana elections as "the most absurd and impracticable that ever haunted the imagination of a statesman." He reported Andrew Johnson's fears that southern unionists would be annihilated when Army support was withdrawn. He accused Trumbull of Jesuit casuistry in reversing himself on Louisiana. He would continue to resist executive usurpation. "If the President of the United States, operating through his major generals, can initiate a State government, and can bring it here and force us, compel us, to receive on this floor these mere mockeries, these men of straw, who represent nobody, your Republic is at an end. . . ." As for the 10 per cent principle, "a more absurd, monarchical, and anti-American principle was never announced on God's earth." [93]

The last few months of Lincoln's life saw repeated warnings from Wade not to back out of his commitments. So consistent was the barrage that Senator Doolittle compared him to Herod or Pilate (it was never clear which) and asked that he not "in every speech that he makes on this floor, travel out of the record unnecessarily to denounce the Executive as wanting nerve,

wanting blood, [and] failing in the performance of his duty."
The negotiations at Hampton Roads prompted a resolution of
inquiry by Sumner said to have been suggested by Wade. He
wished to God, Wade said, that the President had not undertaken the negotiations. Not even the honor of the executive
office demanded that "we be his mere servants . . . obeying
everything that we may ascribe to his wish and will." If the
President betrayed the platform of 1864, he would be the "most
infamous man" ever to obtain the confidence of the people by
false pretenses. The last clash came just four days before the
President's death. With the news of Appomattox, Wade and
the committee had gone to Richmond to examine the rebel
fortifications McClellan had found so impregnable. There
they learned that General Weitzel, acting under Presidential
directive, had reconvened the rebel legislature, the body that
had voted secession. According to Julian, Wade's indignation
was "hot" and his words "wrathful," an emotion not much
dissipated when he returned to Washington to find that, although Lincoln had dismissed the Virginia legislature, he had
made a curiously Seward-like speech. Encouraging the band to
play "Dixie," he had urged a victory crowd on the White House
lawn not to concern themselves with whether the states had
ever been out of the Union. "Finding themselves safely at
home, it would be utterly immaterial whether they had ever
been abroad." The erring brothers must be welcomed back
under a benign Presidential, rather than a possibly harsh
congressional, policy. "We shall sooner have the fowl by hatch-
ing the egg than smashing it." Wade, whose taste in proverbs
would probably have run to revolutionary omelets that can't be
made without breaking a few eggs, was horrified at what he
deemed misplaced mercy for the war's instigators. There is a
"morbid sensibility," Stevens was to say later, "which has more
sympathy for the murderer on the gallows than for his
victim." [94]

In such an atmosphere, grief at the assassination would have been hypocritical, and Wade did not display any, agreeing with other members of the War Committee that accession of their old colleague would be "a godsend." The day after the inaugural, he told Johnson that he thanked God for his presence. "Lincoln had too much of the milk of human kindness to deal with those damned rebels." Attempts to soften Wade's contempt for Lincoln do not maintain. His biographer, Riddle, made a halfhearted attempt to indicate an empathy between the two. Carl Schurz thought Lincoln considered Wade his friend. Later on, Anna Ella Carroll and her supporters indicated close and friendly relations between Wade and Lincoln in Stanton's office as they listened to telegraph dispatches from the West. Wade himself, trying to be helpful to Miss Carroll's claims for having devised the strategy that led to the capture of Forts Henry and Donelson (she was a friend of his wife, and he supported the suffragettes), recalled frequent talks with Lincoln. But he was honest enough not to characterize them as particularly friendly. One account of a dialogue between the two men exchanged in 1862 may sum up their relationship. Wade told Lincoln he was the father of every military blunder made in the war and added that Washington at that moment was not one mile from hell. Lincoln retorted he thought hell was one mile from the White House [the Senate building].[95] Probably, Wade agreed completely with his friend Alphonso Taft's summary of Lincoln:

It is forever to be regretted that history should have to tell so many lies, as it will tell, when it shall declare Lincoln's intrigues and foolishness models of integrity and wisdom, his weak & wavering indecision & delay farsighted statesmanship, and his blundering usurpation of power, Jacksonian courage.[96]

Wade thought at first he had an ally in Johnson, his old War Committee colleague. Instead, he found himself facing the most extreme case of Presidential usurpation he had yet known. Julian had opposed Johnson from the start, finding from close association on the War Committee that he was "at heart, as decided a hater of the Negro and of everything savoring of abolitionism as the rebels from whom he had separated." But Wade persevered at first in explaining away Johnson's behavior, averting a distinct break between the Radicals and the new President in May. Johnson's amnesty proclamation the same month shook but did not shatter his confidence. He was disposed to see Johnson as responding mechanically to the intrinsic weakness of the American system. According to Gideon Welles, Wade "complains that the Executive has the control of the government, that Congress and the Judiciary are subordinate, and mere instruments in his hands; said our form of government was on the whole a failure; that there are not three distinct and independent departments but one great controlling one with two others as assistants." Three months after Johnson took office, he saw the issue less abstractly, writing Sumner that he and Stevens and Julian had been right. Johnson's course would result in nothing but "consigning the great Union or Republican party, bound, hand and foot, to the tender mercies of the rebels we have lately conquered in the field, and their Copperhead allies of the North." In February he proposed limiting the President to one term and providing that vice-presidents no longer be eligible for the office because of the President's death. Johnson had brought "the worst traitors, the leading traitors . . . unwashed and red with the blood of their countrymen" into the councils of the nation. Anyone so behaving is "a traitor in his heart." Was Andrew Johnson's policy any different from Jefferson Davis'? [97]

The story of Congress' duel with Johnson cannot be retold. But as new "Black Codes" were set up in the South, the condition of the Negro deteriorated to the point where Wade cried out in anguished hyperbole, "if by an insurrection [the colored people] could contrive to slay one half of their oppressors, the other half would hold them in the highest respect and no doubt treat them with justice." Gradually, he began to swing toward

Stevens' "conquered province" theory. When a whole state became contaminated with treason, he argued, he could no longer accept the perdurability of statehood. The southern states must be governed "equitably" until they should by petitions, speeches, and actions show they repented of their crimes. They must accept the principles of the Declaration of Independence, which would not cut off from the colored population of the South the right to participate in government. Congress certainly had the power to grant Negro suffrage if it felt freedom for the four million freedmen could be guaranteed no other way. When the Fourteenth Amendment was proposed, Wade made an important addition to the first section, substituting "persons born in the United States or naturalized under the laws thereof" for "citizens of the United States." This not only reflected his long interest in protecting the immigrant, but was an added safeguard to the Negro, who might not be considered a citizen if the Civil Rights Bill were declared unconstitutional. This was a significant change, according to Horace Flack. Wade also supported the Massachusetts proposal for literacy or property qualifications, but withdrew this part of his proposal after objections.[98]

While the Reconstruction Committee had been holding hearings, Johnson began his unprecedented string of vetoes. His advice to southern states to reject the Fourteenth Amendment after that compromise had been painfully hammered out made military reconstruction inevitable, Wade thought. Attempts by revisionist historians to present the Amendment as a "plot" on the part of Stevens & Company, never seriously intended as a final settlement, have the inherent difficulty of all conspiratorial theories: the non-monolithic nature of so-called blocs, and the inevitable backing and filling involved in developing any complicated constitutional change. Rejecting the conspiracy theory of Howard K. Beale and George Fort Milton, Eric McKitrick believes "throughout the whole process, chronology itself functions as a heavy balance wheel." Certainly,

Wade's case was illustrative of differences within the radical camp. In his proposal he left out the entire third section, disfranchising "all persons who voluntarily adhered to the late insurrection,"—the heart of the Amendment, according to Stevens. To Wade it did not "seem to amount to much," nor did he think it would be effective. Thus he supported the less punitive section to prevent such persons from office-holding unless Congress by a two-thirds vote removed the disability. He also furiously assailed Sumner for voting for the Amendment and then announcing he would insist on further conditions for readmission of southern states. He, Wade said, "intended to let them in on the terms prescribed. . . . If we did not mean that, I do not know what we did mean."

However, after every southern state except Tennessee rejected the Amendment upon Johnson's advice, military reconstruction passed. The impasse with Johnson worsened. Charges as to his unfitness for office had swelled ever since his unfortunate oath-of-office and Washington's Birthday speeches. According to James Blaine, the real reason for his impeachment was congressional belief that he was willing to return the representatives of the old slavocracy, only superficially purged, to their former eminence. With the ironic increased representation they had obtained through the Thirteenth Amendment, they would once again dominate Washington. Attempts by revisionists to present Johnson either as an agrarian Horatio at the bridge holding back the floodtide of northern capitalism or as a bulwark against imposition of a British parliamentary system have been thoroughly ventilated in the most recent study of the period. McKitrick's contention is: "There was a deep psychological need to eliminate Johnson from American political life forever, and it was principally Johnson himself who had created it." The best explanation for his behavior seems not economic or constitutional philosophy but "simple cussedness." Consequently, his successor was picked. On March 2, 1867, Wade was named president pro tem of the Senate, although apparently he was assured of his new post just after the fall elections that had proved so disastrous to Johnson. As early as December and January, Caroline was receiving letters rejoicing at the prospect of "Uncle Frank" as an "incorruptible" successor in case the President "is deposed," and prophesying that "when he and you are settled at the White House, I shall expect the poor negroes will have justice done them." [99]

And now at last Wade's temperament proved his undoing, as that astute observer, Colonel Alex McClure, observed from the beginning. His Kansas speech was haunting businessmen, editors, and colleagues. Even as an interim executive until Grant could succeed him, he might make some rash move. His proposed cabinet, including Ben Butler as secretary of state (or Sumner, as another version had it) reassured no one. At the moment of crisis the succession of enemies he had carelessly made over nearly two decades rose to defeat him. His ancient nosing out of Chase in 1860 and his more recent acidulous comments on a figure well known for his thin skin and capacity to nurse a grudge redounded against him as the chief justice worked feverishly to avert conviction.[100] Fessenden, the leader of the opposition against Wade (although ostensibly committed to conviction), Grimes, Trumbull, and Henderson, all bearing the wounds of Wade's outrageous barbs, were equally busy. Grimes's hostility to Wade had grown to the point, the *Washington Chronicle* observed, "that he finally fell in love with Andrew Johnson." As the trial progressed, stories of Fowler's and Trumbull's clashes with Wade were recalled, as was Fessenden's chagrin at not being chosen to preside over the Senate. Odds on the votes of senators committed to conviction and clearly unhappy over Wade's prospective elevation fluctuated from day to day. Enormous pressure was brought to bear—Greeley, Sickles, the National Republican Committee, the Union League, the Methodist church, and the antislavery papers leading the conviction forces; Chase, Thurlow Weed, the "Whiskey Ring," and various New York customs house

officials and Washington internal revenue agents working for
acquittal. When the vote was finally taken and the furor over
"apostasy" and "Judases" subsided, it became clear that Wade
never really had a chance of occupying the White House. At
least three other Senators stood ready to vote for acquittal,
perhaps even more. In any event, claims that constitutional
scruples governed voting were disingenuous, attesting to Toc-
queville's prophecy that democratic historians would tend to
seek great, overarching causes for events that were fortuitous
and personal. Senator Edmunds summed it up when he said
"but for distrust of Wade by the Senate, Johnson would have
been convicted." [101]

Wade was disappointed but not crushed. He still had his
Puritan conscience and his sense that he was on the side of the
Lord. These fortified him when he was passed over as Grant's
running-mate. Throughout the rest of his Washington career as
lobbyist and government director for the Union Pacific, advocate of the tariff interests, and as one of Grant's commissioners
to Santo Domingo, he continued to support a policy of "Thorough" for the South. He became an anachronism on the Washington scene, living frugally in cut-rate boarding houses and
making sardonic comments on Chandler's mansion and his
liveried servants. He was a hero to the suffragettes and the
freedmen, to land reform associations and eight-hour-day advo-
cates. He rejected repeated requests that he run for Congress or
governor of Ohio, stating the Republican party had "fallen so
low it was hardly worth saving." [102] His last public action when
he was seventy-six years old was to denounce Hayes's action in
withdrawing federal troops from Louisiana. He regretted that
he had seconded Hayes's nomination at the Republican convention in 1872. To have emancipated southern Negroes and
now leave them unprotected was "a crime as infamous as to
have reduced them to slavery when they were free." Contempla-
tion of Hayes's move left him filled with "amazement and
inexpressible indignation." [103] Many of his former allies had

decided that time was the great cure-all and Hayes a "healer of strife." The Negroes had not proved themselves, many northerners thought. But Wade, commented the *New York Times,* had not changed, recalling an old Lincoln story about the Wade-Davis bill. It had reminded him, the President had said, of the bed of Procrustes. Wade was still as rigid as Procrustes, the paper thought, and chagrin over Hayes's policy hastened his death. In December, 1877, he suffered a paralytic stroke; and on March 2, 1878 he died, an unreconstructed Covenanter to the last.[104]

History has not dealt kindly with "ignorant, profane" Ben Wade. Revisionists and followers of the Lincoln mystique alike have repeated without analysis the anti-Jacobin stereotypes of his enemies. Even his physical portrait is rendered inevitably in some such characterization as "hard eyes, thin lips, and mastiff-like jaws." Yet he was described by a friendly contemporary as having "sharp bright, eyes, and firm-set jaw. . . . A tender-hearted, gracious, and lovable man." His religious supporters could forgive even his incessant profanity; it guaranteed a perpetual allegiance to the rights of mankind. There was about it "a spontaneity and heartiness which made it almost seem the echo of a virtue!" [105] Just now, a little more than a century after the Emancipation Proclamation, Americans are deeply involved in re-examining their attitudes toward the Negro. A major re-examination of Civil War historiography has been in process for more than a decade. Perhaps it is time that Wade, along with Sumner, Stevens, and Stanton, be also re-examined.

1. David Dewitt, *The Impeachment and Trial of Andrew Johnson* (New York, 1903), p. 222. For Blaine's statement, *Congressional Globe,* 40th Cong., 1st Sess., Mar. 23, 1867, 317–18. Adam Badeau, *Grant in Peace* (Hartford, Conn., 1887), p. 137; Theodore C. Smith, *Life and Letters of*

224   BEN WADE

James A. Garfield (New Haven, Conn., 1925), I, 425–26; interview with
Stevens in *New York Herald,* July 8, 1867; Hugh McCulloch, *Men and
Measures of Half a Century* (New York, 1889), p. 400. Gideon Welles,
Diary of Gideon Welles (Boston, 1911), III, 293; Georges Clemenceau,
American Reconstruction (New York, 1928), pp. 106, 182.

Editorials from the *New York Tribune* are too numerous for individual
citation. Dispatches charging opposition to Wade appear almost daily from
March 5 until late May, 1868. I have also examined the files of the
Washington Intelligencer and the *New York Independent* for the period
of the trial. Both the *Tribune* and the *Intelligencer* made a practice of
reprinting editorials from other papers. On March 9 the *Intelligencer*
printed editorials from the *Providence Journal* and *Chicago Republican*
on the attempt to have Wade step down in favor of Schuyler Colfax. On
May 14 the *Tribune* printed comments on senatorial hostility to Wade
from the *Albany Evening Post* and *Cincinnati Gazette,* and on May 19
from the *Toledo Blade* and *Cleveland Leader.* Johnson was found innocent because Wade was "guilty of being his successor," claimed the *Detroit
Post,* quoted in the *Tribune,* May 19, 1868. In England the *Saturday
Review* on May 30, 1868, stated that dislike of Wade dictated the verdict.
The summing-up sentence is from the *Washington Chronicle,* quoted in
the *Intelligencer,* May 16, 1868; see also *New Haven Palladium,* same date,
and "Conspiracy in the Senate," *New York Independent,* May 21, 1868.

2. *New York Tribune,* July 19, 1867; William Dean Howells, *Years of
My Youth* (New York, 1916), p. 108; Andrew D. White, *Autobiography of
Andrew D. White* (New York, 1903), I, 503–4; *New York Times,* August
30, 1864. The typical Wade portrait, reprinted almost without variation in
standard texts is "profane, crude, and brutally sharp-witted." Benjamin
Thomas, *Abraham Lincoln* (New York, 1952), p. 287.

3. *New York Herald,* March 10, 1868; Joseph Savage, *Genealogical
Dictionary of New England* (Boston, 1862), IV, 377–79; interview with
Wade in *Cincinnati Commercial,* quoted in *Washington Daily National
Intelligencer,* November 8, 1867.

4. *Report of the Select Committee relative to the Annexation of Texas
to the Union,* Ohio Senate, January 12, 1838 (Cleveland: Wade Collection,
Western Reserve Historical Society); *Ohio State Journal,* Apr. 3, 1839;
Journal of the Senate of the State of Ohio, 40th General Assembly, 1st
Sess., 80; *ibid.,* 41st General Assembly, 1st Sess., 65, 246.

5. George W. Julian, *Political Recollections* (Chicago, 1884), p. 118.

6. *Ohio Daily Journal and Register,* Jan. 3, and Jan. 19, 1838; *Ashtabula Sentinel,* Feb. 2 and 17, 1838; *Cleveland Herald,* Mar. 15, 1838;
unfinished biography of Ben Wade, Wade Collection.

7. "Benjamin Wade," *Republic* (March-December, 1873), p. 314; *Journal of the Senate of the State of Ohio,* 41st General Assembly, 1st Sess., 259,
473, 566–68.

8. *Ashtabula Sentinel,* July 4, 1839; also Sept. 28, Oct. 5, Oct. 19, Nov. 9, Nov. 23. Ned Wade joined the Liberty Party in 1842, arguing against his brother's re-election as state senator on the grounds of Whig subserviency to slavery *(Ashtabula Sentinel,* Sept. 21, 1842). In 1848 Giddings criticized Whigs for supporting Taylor as Wade did (George W. Julian, *Life of Joshua R. Giddings* [Chicago, 1892], p. 241). In 1851 Giddings wrote Chase that antislavery men could "expect but little good to our cause" from Wade, who had demonstrated "past vacillation." (Giddings to Chase, Apr. 3, 1851, Chase Manuscripts, Pennsylvania State Historical Society, Philadelphia.)

9. Wade to Caroline Wade, Oct. 27, 1848, and Feb. 8, 1852, Wade Papers, Library of Congress.

10. Clipping from *Harper's Monthly,* date unknown, shown me by Mrs. Walter Woodbury of Jefferson, Ohio, Wade's grand-daughter; *Cleveland Plain Dealer,* Jan. 13, 1850; *Ashtabula Sentinel,* Oct. 28, 1850; *Cleveland Leader,* Nov. 8, 1850; Albert Riddle, *The Life of Benjamin Wade* (Cleveland, 1888), pp. 196–97. This is an expanded treatment, containing more material than the usually available 1886 edition.

11. *Cong. Globe,* 33d Cong., 1st Sess., Appendix, May 25, 1854, 763, 765.

12. Wade believed that after he extracted a promise from Scott "to keep his mouth shut," he had brought Washington Whigs to a "fierce & irrevocable decision" to repudiate the Compromise. (Wade to Caroline Wade, Dec. 10, 1851, and Feb. 8, 1852, Wade Papers). He was wrong, and his subsequent exaggeration of Scott's hostility to the Compromise brought on accusations by his brother Ned and other Free-Soilers of Whig double-dealing *(Cleveland Daily True Democrat,* July 30 and Aug. 21, 1852). The "funeral oration" *(New York Tribune,* May 24, 1854) appears in *Cong. Globe,* 33d Cong., 1st Sess., Appendix, May 25, 1854, 763–65.

13. For Wade on the Nebraska bill, see *Cong. Globe,* 33d Cong., 1st Sess., Appendix, Mar. 2, 1854, 299–300; Mar. 3, 1854, 310–13; for Lecompton, *ibid.,* 35th Cong., 1st Sess., Mar. 12, 1858, 1111–13, 1115, 1116; Mar. 15, 1858, 1123–24; Apr. 27, 1858, 1822–23; for Cuba, *ibid.,* 35th Cong., 2d Sess., Feb. 25, 1859, 1354. For Douglas as "dwarfish medium," *ibid.,* 33d Cong., 1st Sess., Appendix, May 25, 1854, 765; for "cannibalism," *ibid.,* 36th Cong., 1st Sess., Appendix, Mar. 7, 1860, 153–54; for John Brown and Hinton Helper, *ibid.,* 36th Cong., 1st Sess., Dec. 14, 1859, 141–42, 144.

14. Linus P. Brockett, *Men of Our Day* (Philadelphia, 1868), pp. 245–46; William Williams, *History of Ashtabula County* (Cleveland, 1876), p. 69; Julian, *Giddings,* p. 334; *Cleveland Leader,* May 28, 1856; Riddle, *Wade,* pp. 245, 247–51.

15. *Cong. Globe,* 34th Cong., 3d Sess., Dec. 4, 1856, 25; *ibid.,* 35th Cong., 1st Sess., Mar. 15, 1858, 1123–24; *ibid.,* 35th Cong., 2d Sess., Feb. 25, 1859, 1354; *ibid.,* 35th Cong., 1st Sess., Mar. 13, 1858, 1114–15.

16. *Ibid.,* 36th Cong., 1st Sess., Mar. 22, 1860, 1296; *ibid.,* May 9, 1860, 1997, 2009–10; *ibid.,* 37th Cong., 2d Sess., June 10, 1862, 2626; *ibid.,* June 19, 1862, 2807; *ibid.,* 38th Cong., 2d Sess., Mar. 3, 1865, 1353.

17. *Ibid.,* 33d Cong., 1st Sess., July 13 and 17, 1854, 1717–18, 1776. However, the distinctly antislavery character of Ohio Know-Nothingism in the fusion movement of 1854 counterbalanced Wade's declarations that "we are all immigrants ourselves." He had expected "Know-Nothings and Locos will postpone the thing until some bargain can be struck for somebody else," but he received all but one Know-Nothing vote in the Ohio legislature. Wade to Caroline Wade, Jan. 25, 1856, and Mar. 7, 1856, Wade Papers.

18. Wade's broader policies will be discussed in the second and third sections of this account. For his proposals on repealing the immunity provision, etc., *Cong. Globe,* 37th Cong., 2d Sess., Jan. 20, 1862, 387; *ibid.,* Jan. 21, 1862, 427; *ibid.,* Jan. 27, 1862, 490; *ibid.,* Jan. 28, 1862, 509, 511; *ibid.,* Feb. 25, 1862, 940–41, 959–60. He made his proposal for a lieutenant general clothed with "absolute and despotic powers" at a secret Republican caucus on December 15, 1862, according to Carl Sandburg, *Abraham Lincoln: The War Years* (New York, 1939), I, 638.

19. Carl Schurz, *The Reminiscences of Carl Schurz* (New York, 1907–8), III, 102; *New York Tribune,* July 19, 1867.

20. Ellis P. Oberholtzer, *Jay Cooke: Financier of the Civil War* (Philadelphia, 1907), II, 28; *New York World,* June 11, 12, 13, 14, 1867; *New York Times,* June 11, 13, 20, 21, 22, 1867; interview with Wade in *Cincinnati Commercial,* reprinted in *New York Times,* July 1, 1867; on July 20, 1867, the *Times* printed comments from both the American and British press, the latter being especially astonished at the speech.

21. *Washington Intelligencer,* Oct. 4, 1867; *New York Tribune,* Oct. 12, 1867; Samuel Bowles agreed in "Infidelity of Ohio," *Springfield Republican,* Oct. 14, 1867; Riddle, *Wade,* p. 234; *Cong. Globe,* 35th Cong., 1st Sess., Mar. 15, 1858, 1123.

22. *Cong. Globe,* 39th Cong., 1st Sess., Jan. 18, 1866, 293.

23. *Cong. Globe,* 37th Cong., 2d Sess., May 2, 1862, 1917; *ibid.,* 38th Cong., 1st Sess., July 1, 1864, 3451; David Donald, *Lincoln Reconsidered* (New York, 1961), p. 199.

24. Wade to Caroline Wade, Oct. 25, 1861, Wade Papers; *Cleveland Leader,* Sept. 10, 1862; *Cong. Globe,* 37th Cong., 2d Sess., Jan. 28, 1862, 511.

25. *Cleveland Leader,* Apr. 14, 1860; Murat Halstead, *Caucuses of 1860* (Columbus, Ohio, 1860), p. 122.

26. *Washington Intelligencer,* March 8, 1860.

27. Halstead, *Caucuses*, p. 143; Wade and Chase exchanged a series of mutually acrimonious letters on the alleged "betrayal." Chase to Wade, Dec. 21, 1860, quoted in Donnal V. Smith, *Chase and Civil War Politics* (Columbus, Ohio, 1931), Vol. II in "Ohio Historical Collections," p. 21; Wade to Chase, Dec. 29, 1860, Chase Manuscripts. For Wade on Lincoln, *New York Tribune*, Oct. 30, 1860; on Buchanan, Wade to Caroline Wade, Dec. 26, 1860, Wade Papers.

28. Wade to Trumbull, Nov. 14, 1860, quoted in Kenneth Stampp, *And the War Came* (Binghamton, N.Y., 1950), p. 14; *Cong. Globe*, 36th Cong., 1st Sess., Dec. 14, 1859, 145; *ibid.*, 36th Cong., 2d Sess., Dec. 17, 1860, 99–104; John G. Nicolay and John Hay, *Abraham Lincoln: A History* (New York, 1890), II, 412.

29. T. Harry Williams, *Lincoln and the Radicals* (Madison, Wisc., 1941), p. 20. Typical of letters urging Wade to stand fast were those of Jacob D. Cox, then a state senator in Columbus, Dec. 21, 1860, and Judge L. C. Turner, Dec. 24, 1860, Wade Papers. Wade's subsequent comments appear in *Cong. Globe*, 36th Cong., 2d Sess., Mar. 4, 1861, 1393.

30. For Wade's proposal to close southern ports, *Cong. Globe*, 36th Cong., 2d Sess., Dec. 17, 1860, 103–4. Stevens recounted his interview with Lincoln in *New York Herald*, July 8, 1867. Wade, who always thought in terms of absolutes and had little grasp of Lincoln's pragmatic attitude, could see no advantage in maintaining a dual policy—war as domestic insurrection and conflict with alien enemy—for the advantages to be derived from both positions.

31. Kenneth P. Williams, *Lincoln Finds a General* (New York, 1949), I, 121; James Truslow Adams, *America's Tragedy* (New York, 1934), p. 191; *Cong. Globe*, 37th Cong., 2d Sess., Dec. 23, 1861, 162; *ibid*, 37 Cong., 3d Sess., Jan. 15, 1863, 324, 332, 333.

32. Albert G. Riddle, *Recollections of War Times* (New York, 1895), pp. 46–57; Williams, *Lincoln and the Radicals*, pp. 30–31.

33. *Cong. Globe*, 37th Cong., 2d Sess., May 2, 1862, 1919.

34. Wade's remark is reported in Adam Gurowski, *Diary: March 4, 1861—November 2, 1862* (Boston, 1862), I, 90; A. Denny to Wade, Nov. 28, 1861; letter from Akron, name missing, Nov. 1, 1861, Wade Papers.

35. Wade to Caroline Wade, Oct. 25, 1861, Wade Papers, Benjamin F. Wade, *Facts for the People. Ben Wade on McClellan and Gens. Hooker and Heintzelman's Testimony. A Crushing Review of Little Napoleon's Career* (Cincinnati *Gazette*, Oct. 24, 1864, pp. 1–2).

36. Letter to Wade, signature missing, Nov. 1, 1861, Wade Papers; Wade to Frémont, quoted in Allan Nevins, *Frémont: Pathmaker of the West* (New York, 1939), pp. 545–46; Wade to Charles S. Dana and Chandler, quoted in Williams, *Lincoln and the Radicals*, pp. 41, 108.

37. Grimes to Fessenden, quoted in William Salter, *The Life of James W. Grimes* (New York, 1876), p. 156; *Cong. Globe,* 37th Cong., 2d Sess., Dec. 5, 1861, 16, 29–32.

38. Bruce Catton, *Mr. Lincoln's Army* (Garden City, N.Y., 1956), p. 82; *Washington Intelligencer,* Dec. 7, 1861; Nathaniel Wright Stephenson (ed.), *An Autobiography of Abraham Lincoln* (Indianapolis, 1926), pp. 416–17; Welles, *Diary,* II, 198, 226; Nicolay and Hay, *Lincoln,* V, 150–51; W. H. Pierson, "The Committee on the Conduct of the War," *American Historical Review,* XXIII (Apr., 1918), 550–76. For a typical hostile view: "Had he [Lincoln] ignored the Joint Committee . . . the Civil War might have been closed up six to ten months earlier" (George Fort Milton, *Conflict: The American Civil War* [New York, 1941], p. 132) ; Williams, *Lincoln and the Radicals,* pp. 65–76. The most recent use of the Committee's findings will appear later in this account.

39. *Report of the Joint Committee on the Conduct of the War* (37th Cong., 3d Sess., 1863), Part I, 63; Riddle, *Recollections,* p. 39; Catton, *Mr. Lincoln's Army,* pp. 204–5, 212.

40. *J.C.C.W.,* 1863, I, 116, 117–21, 122–30.

41. *Ibid.,* 131, 132, 140, 146, 149–50, 154–55, 159, 171, 175–76; Williams, *Lincoln and the Radicals,* p. 88.

42. Julian, *Recollections,* pp. 201–3; Pierson, "The Committee on the Conduct of the War," p. 567.

43. *J.C.C.W.,* 1863, I, 86, 246–47; Julian, *Recollections,* p. 205.

44. Williams, *Lincoln and the Radicals,* pp. 127–31; T. Harry Williams, *Lincoln and His Generals* (New York, 1952), pp. 78–81; Williams, *Lincoln Finds a General,* I, 159–60; Catton, *Mr. Lincoln's Army,* pp. 108–9.

45. *New York Tribune,* June 18, 1862; *Report of J.C.C.W.,* 1863, I, 346–47, 390–94, 575–80.

46. *Cong. Globe,* 37th Cong., 2d Sess., July 16, 1862, 3390–91; *Cleveland Leader,* Aug. 1, 1862; Sandburg, *Lincoln,* II, 554.

47. *J.C.C.W.,* 1863, I, 20, 22; Williams, *Lincoln Finds a General,* I, 340; *ibid.,* II, 479; Williams, *Lincoln and His Generals,* pp. 93, 95, 106, 114; Catton, *Mr. Lincoln's Army,* pp. 124–25, 132–33, 137–38, 149.

48. *J.C.C.W.,* 1863, I, 276–82.

49. The Committee stated that it would not comment on Porter's case, since a court-martial had been held; instead, it cites McClellan's excuse-filled telegrams and Halleck's statement that co-operation with Pope's forces would have brought victory. *Report of J.C.C.W.,* 1863, I, 32–37; Williams, *Lincoln Finds a General,* I, 357–58; 321–30; Catton, *Mr. Lincoln's Army,* pp. 35–36; Williams, *Lincoln and the Radicals,* pp. 174–76, 225; Williams, *Lincoln and His Generals,* pp. 158–63.

50. *J.C.C.W.*, 1863, I, 40–42; Catton, *Mr. Lincoln's Army*, pp. 305–6, 319; Williams, *Lincoln and the Radicals*, p. 181; Williams, *Lincoln and His Generals*, p. 168.

51. *J.C.C.W.*, 1863, I, 53–57, 657–60, 670, 690, 691, 706. Gurowski, *Diary*, p. 297; Williams, *Lincoln and the Radicals*, pp. 202–5, 268–69; Bruce Catton, *Glory Road* (Garden City, N.Y., 1956), pp. 33–34, 52–54, 74–75; Williams, *Lincoln Finds a General*, II, 501; Williams, *Lincoln and His Generals*, p. 196.

52. *Report of J.C.C.W.*, 1863, I, 57–60.

53. Francis Fessenden, *The Life and Public Services of William Pitt Fessenden* (Boston, 1907), I, 231–45 for a complete account of a Republican caucus and two interviews with Lincoln.

54. *J.C.C.W.*, 1863, I, 3, 4, 5–50.

55. Wade, *Facts for the People*, pp. 3–5.

56. *J.C.C.W.*, 1863, I, 60–62.

57. *New York World*, Apr. 4, 1863; Williams, *Lincoln and the Radicals*, p. 251; *New York Tribune*, Apr. 6, 1863; *New York Times*, Apr. 7, 1863.

58. *J.C.C.W.*, 1863, II, 3–8. In this paragraph I have summarized 251 pages of testimony by 38 witnesses. For Wade's specific comments on proceeding with the battle when it was known that Patterson had failed to hold Johnston, 151, 182; for McDowell's and Scott's rejoinder, 40–41 and 241–42. Williams agrees in *Lincoln Finds a General*.

59. *J.C.C.W.*, 1863, III, 1–6. For descriptions of Quartermaster McKinstrey, pp. 55–56; that Patterson was made a scapegoat for Scott's and McDowell's failures, I, 81–101; Blair's resentment at having a clothing contract for 40,000 men cut by two-thirds, III, 210–11; Blair's description of old California associates settling down "like obscene birds of prey," 177.

60. Williams, *Lincoln and the Radicals*, pp. 95–104. The charges of "lettres de cachet" and Turkish and Russian justice appear in *Cong. Globe*, 37th Cong., 2d Sess., Apr. 15, 1862, 1662, 1665; "Torquemada" and "the holy office," *ibid.*, Apr. 21, 1862, 1732; James G. Blaine, *Twenty Years of Congress* (Norwich, Conn., 1886), I, 382.

61. *J.C.C.W.*, 1863, II, 252, 255, 260–61, 288, 355. For Stone's testimony on the points at issue, 268–70, 276–77; on the question of his "secesh" leanings, 279–80, 295, 299–300, 302, 304, 328, 335–36, 338, 356–57, 370, 389, 397, 425. Four officers testified to the episode of the Maryland planter 343, 346–49, 372, 391–92; a grain broker, to the operation of the flour mill, 345–46; flag of truce, 372, 384, 385; "Virginia races," 299. Four witnesses stoutly fended off the Committee's leading questions, supporting Stone that the order had been discretionary and stating they found no signs of disloyalty or disaffection among troops, 316, 360–61, 365, 374, 413. Then

came General N. P. Banks, who, in spite of all Wade's questioning, adhered resolutely to non-committal officialese, 417–21. For the typical leading question cited, 306.

62. *Ibid.*, 426–33. For Wade's statement about keeping secret the identity of witnesses, 18.

63. *Cong. Globe,* 37th Cong., 2d Sess., Apr. 15, 1862, 1665–68; *ibid.*, Apr. 21, 1862, 1735–37. Alphonso Taft to Wade, May 14, 1862, Wade Papers.

64. *J.C.C.W.*, 1863, II, 486–96; 505–10.

65. *Ibid.*, 14, 17–18.

66. *J.C.C.W.*, 1863, I, 286–94 (Porter instance, 289) ; McDowell's order, *ibid.*, III, 448. Wade's speech, *Cong. Globe*, 37th Cong., 2d Sess., June 25, 1862, 2931. McDowell's testimony, *J.C.C.W.*, III, 442–49; Doubleday, 430–34.

67. *J.C.C.W.*, 1863, III, 632–43 (Sickles) ; 385–89 (Lockwood case) ; U.S. District Attorney R. F. Paine to Wade, Feb. 20, 1862, Wade Papers; Major A. B. Hall to Wade, Mar. 25, 1862, Wade Papers.

68. Col. Charles Doubleday to Hon. Robert Paine, Feb. 3, and Feb. 17, 1862, forwarded to Wade, Wade Papers; Gen. James Brisbin to Wade, Feb. 21, 1865, *ibid.; J.C.C.W.*, 1863, III, 638–39, 641.

69. Wade to Stanton, July 30, 1864, copy in Wade Papers.

70. *J.C.C.W.*, 1863, III, 458–60, 460–61, 461–63, 466–68, 468–71, 472–74, 474–76, 476–77, 479–80. For presence of Indians at Pea Ridge, 490–91. For treatment of prisoners in Confederate camps, 457, 461–65, 477–78, 485–87, 487–90. Committee summation, 449–57.

71. Forrest's remark quoted in Williams, *Lincoln and the Radicals,* p. 343. *Report of J.C.C.W.*, 38th Cong., 1st Sess., H. Rep. No 65, *Reports of Committees of the House of Representatives,* 1864, I, 5–6, 13–14, 18, 29, and 42, 51. Testimony of witnesses from gunboat, 48, 52, 100.

72. *Ibid.*, 5, 30; Forrest at Paducah, 78–80; statement of Smith and Cleary (spelled Clary in previous testimony about finding "five negroes burning") , 104–5, 107–8; Hurlbut, 67; Bangs and supporting witnesses, 91–92.

73. *Ibid.*, 2; Julian, *Recollections,* p. 239; *Report of J.C.C.W.*, 38th Cong., 1st Sess., H. Rep. No. 67, 6–30, 3–4.

74. *Cong. Globe,* 38th Cong., 2d Sess., Jan. 16, 1865, 267; for his often-quoted "thirty years" speech, Jan. 9, 1865, 161–62, 163–64, 165. Sumner opposition, Jan. 23, 1865, 381; Wade's reply, Jan. 30, 494; "old women," Jan. 26, 1865, 432; "Marat," Feb. 6. 1865, 497.

75. *Ibid.*, Jan. 27, 1865, 457, Jan. 30, 1865, 494–96; *New York Tribune*, June 3, 1864; *Cleveland Leader*, Jan. 25, 1865; *Cleveland Herald*, Jan. 25, 1865.

76. *Report of J.C.C.W.*, 38th Cong., 2d Sess., 1865, I, "General Hooker," 15, 37–38, 81–83, 175–78, XLIX–L, LIV–LV.

77. *Ibid.*, "General Meade," LV–LVI, LXIV; testimony of General Butterfield, 424–27; General Gibbon, 442; Gen. Seth Williams, 466; General Meade, 347–58; Williams, *Lincoln Finds a General*, II, 674–77, 680–81, 706–7, 730; Catton, *Glory Road*, p. 354; Williams, *Lincoln and the Radicals*, pp. 338–40; Williams, *Lincoln and His Generals*, pp. 263–65.

78. *J.C.C.W.*, 1863, III, 340. Wallace implies that Grant's commands were contradictory and that he was left completely on his own. Sherman to Mrs. Sherman, quoted in Williams, *Lincoln and the Radicals*, p. 334.

79. These reports appear in *J.C.C.W.*, 38th Cong., 2d Sess., 1865, 3 vols.

80. *Cong. Globe*, 37th Cong., 2d Sess., May 2, 1862, 1918; May 6, 1862, 1957, 1961; May 16, 1862, 2166, 2167–68, 2170; May 19, 1862, 2202–3; June 25, 1862, 2929–30; June 28, 1862, 3001; July 16, 1862, 3375.

81. S. Plumb to Wade, May 8, 1864; Ned Wade to his brother, May 11, 1864; Alphonso Taft to Wade, May 14, 1864; J. J. Elwell, "At the Request of Maj. Gen. Hunter," Apr. 20 and May 10, 1864, Wade Papers. Julian, *Recollections*, p. 220.

82. For Wade's earlier advocacy of colonization, *Cong. Globe*, 36th Cong., 2d Sess., Dec. 17, 1860, 104. "Sufficient capital," *ibid.*, 37th Cong., 2d Sess., July 1, 1862, 3038; argument with Sumner over Negro suffrage in Washington D.C., *ibid.*, 38th Cong., 1st Sess., May 26, 1864, 2486.

83. *Report of J.C.C.W.*, 38th Cong., 3d Sess., 1863, III, "Capture of New Orleans," 353–64; Banks's order quoted in Williams, *Lincoln and the Radicals*, p. 275; *New York Independent*, May 28, 1863.

84. *Cong. Globe*, 38th Cong., 1st Sess., July 1, 1864, 3448–49.

85. Wade's remarks on Stevens' confiscation proposal appeared in *Cincinnati Commercial* interview, reprinted in *Washington Intelligencer*, November 8, 1867; his answer to Stevens and Sumner, *Cong. Globe*, 38th Cong., 1st Sess., July 1, 1864, 3449–50, 3451–53; Davis' statement is quoted in Bernard Steiner, *Life of Henry Winter-Davis* (Baltimore, 1916), p. 249.

86. For a discussion of Shellabarger's speech, Eric L McKitrick, *Andrew Johnson and Reconstruction* (Chicago, 1960), pp. 113–14; John W. Burgess, *Reconstruction and the Constitution, 1866–1876* (New York, 1902), pp. 6, 17–18.

87. *Cong. Globe*, 38th Cong., 1st Sess., May 19, 1864, 2348–49; May 26, 1864, 2486; July 1, 1864, 3449; Wade and Sumner clashed subsequently on the same question over admitting Nebraska, *ibid.*, 39th Cong., 2d Sess., Dec.

14, 1866, 122; Dec. 20, 1866, 217–18; Jan. 9, 1867, 357; Wade made a long speech favoring woman suffrage, *ibid.*, Dec. 11, 1866, 62. It was John P. Hale, an old Free-Soiler, who waived his scruples, *ibid.*, 38th Cong., 1st Sess., July 1, 1864, 3449.

88. Nicolay and Hay, *Lincoln*, IX, 120–23; Wade-Davis Manifesto, *New York Tribune*, Aug. 5, 1864.

89. *New York Tribune*, Aug. 5, 1864; *Washington Intelligencer*, Aug. 10, 1864; *Harper's Weekly*, Aug. 20, 1864; *National Anti-Slavery Standard* quoted in *New York Times*, Aug. 13, 1864; Smith's letter, *ibid.*, Aug. 16, 1864; *New York World*, May 7, 1864; see also July 11, Aug. 5, and Aug. 15, 1864.

90. *New York Times*, Aug. 30, 1864; Smith, *Garfield*, I, 378–79; Blaine, *Twenty Years*, II, 44–45.

91. *New York Tribune*, Mar. 17, 1868, based on an interview with Wade in *Cincinnati Gazette; Cong. Globe*, 39th Cong., 1st Sess., Feb. 26, 1866, 1029; John Sherman, *Recollections of Forty Years* (New York, 1895), I, 361; Schurz, *Reminiscences*, III, 103–5.

92. William F. Zornow, *Lincoln and the Party Divided* (Norman, Okla., 1954), pp. 114–18; Winfred A. Harbison (ed.), "Zachariah Chandler's Part in the Re-election of Abraham Lincoln," *Mississippi Valley Historical Review*, XXII (Sept., 1935), 267–76.

93. *Report of J.C.C.W.*, 1865, II, "Red River Expedition," 270–72; 276–77, Porter's testimony; also 81–84, 208–9, 216, 224–27, 289–95, 302–3. For elections, 76, 280–81. Majority findings, XIV–XV; minority, XXXIII, XLIII–XLIV. *Cong. Globe*, 38th Cong., 2d Sess., Feb. 2, 1865, 599–60; *ibid.*, Feb. 25, 1865, 1128.

94. *Cong. Globe*, 38th Cong., 2d Sess., Feb. 3, 1865, 575, 580; Feb. 8, 1865, 660; Julian, *Recollections*, pp. 252–54; *Cong. Globe*, 39th Cong., 1st Sess., May 8, 1866, 2460.

95. Julian, *Recollections*, p. 255; Riddle, *Wade*, pp. 242, 316; Schurz, *Reminiscences*, III, 103–5 (prev. cited). Sidney and Marjorie Greenbie, *Anna Ella Carroll and Lincoln* (Manchester, Maine, 1952), pp. 368–69; Wade's efforts on behalf of Miss Carroll appear in H.R. Misc. Doc. No. 58 (1878) and H.R. Rep. No. 386 (1881); Stephenson (ed.), *Autobiography of Lincoln*, pp. 416–17.

96. Alphonso Taft to Wade, Sept. 8, 1864, Wade Papers.

97. Julian, *Recollections*, pp. 243, 263; Welles, *Diary*, II, 325; Wade to Sumner, July 29, 1865, copy in Wade Papers; *Cong. Globe*, 39th Cong., 1st Sess., Feb. 20, 1866, 931–32.

98. Wade to Sumner, Nov. 1, 1865, quoted in Howard K. Beale, *The Critical Year: A Study of Andrew Johnson and Reconstruction* (New York,

1930), p. 51. *Cong. Globe,* 39th Cong., 1st Sess., Jan. 18, 1866, 293–97; *ibid.,* Appendix, Feb. 14, 1866, 122; *ibid.,* May 23, 1866, 2768–70. Horace Flack, *Adoption of the Fourteenth Amendment* (Baltimore, 1908), p. 88.

99. McKitrick, *Andrew Johnson,* pp. 328–30; 359–63; *Cong. Globe,* 39th Cong., 1st Sess., May 23, 1866, 2667, 2769–70; *ibid.,* 39th Cong., 2d Sess., Dec. 14, 1866, 124–25; Blaine, *Twenty Years,* II, 377; McKitrick, *Andrew Johnson,* pp. 490, 499. Maggie Wade and "Your Aunty E.L.H." to Caroline Wade, Dec. 9, 1866, and Jan. 21, 1867, Wade Papers.

100. Alex McClure, *Recollections of Half a Century* (Salem, Mass., 1902), pp. 65–66; *National Anti-Slavery Standard,* Feb. 17, 1868; *New York Independent,* Mar. 26 and May 21, 1868; *New York Tribune,* May 14 and 18, 1868; "The Chief Justice's Little Game," *Washington Chronicle,* quoted in *Intelligencer,* May 16, 1868; Riddle, *Wade,* p. 356; Smith, *Garfield,* I, 426.

101. *New York Tribune,* May 6, 9, 12, 14, 16, 1868; *Washington Chronicle,* quoted in *Washington Intelligencer,* May 16, 1868; *Chicago Tribune,* quoted in *Washington Intelligencer,* May 20, 1868. "Impeachment Managers Report," *New York Tribune,* May 26, 1868, and July 4, 1868; William Dunning, *Reconstruction, Political and Economic* (New York, 1907 [vol. 22, *The American Nation,* ed. A. B. Hart]), p. 107; John B. Henderson, "Emancipation and Impeachment," *Century Magazine,* LXXXV (Dec., 1912), 208–9; Robert Winston, *Andrew Johnson: Plebeian and Patriot* (New York, 1928), p. 453.

102. Letters to Caroline Wade and from Susan B. Anthony, Lucretia Mott, Lucy Stone, Josephine Griffing, United Land Reform Association, National Executive Committee of Colored Men, Wade Papers, 1869; *Cleveland Leader,* June 10, 1871; Smith, *Garfield,* I, 432–33, 458–59; Wade to Caroline Wade, Dec. 24, 1874, Wade Papers.

103. Wade to his longtime confidant and frequent witness before the Committee, the reporter Uriah Painter, *New York Tribune,* Apr. 24, 1877.

104. Editorial entitled "A Scrap of Political History," *New York Times,* Apr. 25, 1877; *Nation,* Apr. 26, 1877; *New York Times,* Mar. 4, 1878.

105. Thomas, *Abraham Lincoln,* p. 287; Noah Brooks, *Washington in Lincoln's Time* (New York, 1896), pp. 25–26; *Christian Register,* no date, clipping from the Wade family scrapbook; Julian, *Recollections,* pp. 356–57.

FIVE

Charles P. McIlvaine

JAMES B. BELL

Charles P. McIlvaine played a prominent role in the diocesan and parochial expansion of the Protestant Episcopal church and was one of its chief intellectual figures between 1820 and 1873, notably during the High Church–Evangelical theological and liturgical controversy in the 1840's and 50's. He also exercised a significant diplomatic role in England on behalf of his country during late 1861 and 1862. Writing in 1862 about this later aspect of his career, McIlvaine remarked:

I have the greatest consolation in knowing that I am serving our dear country, and hence Ohio, and the Church, by being here, as (pardon me) no one else of America could, for no layman could go where I go, and no clergyman of our land has the acquaintances and the entrée among clergymen of all positions and religious laymen of all ranks, which God has given me.[1]

Politics was not a new and unfamiliar arena for the Bishop of Ohio: his family had long-standing interest in political affairs. The bishop's father, Joseph McIlvaine, a New Jersey lawyer, was a member of the United States Senate between 1823 and 1826, taking his seat on the Democratic party's side of the aisle. His mother's uncle, Joseph Reed, served as military secretary to George Washington during the first three years of the Revolutionary War and later held the posts of president of the

Supreme Executive Council of Pennsylvania (1778–81), delegate to the Continental Congress in 1777, and in 1784 was
elected to Congress, although poor health and finally death
kept him from taking his seat.

To his varied tasks throughout his lifetime Charles McIlvaine brought a background of intellectual distinction, preaching excellence, evangelical fervor, and, above all, commitment.
Born at Burlington, New Jersey, on January 18, 1799, he studied at the Burlington Academy before he matriculated at the
College of New Jersey at Princeton, from which, in 1816, he
graduated with high honors. In the autumn of 1817 McIlvaine
entered the theological school of the Presbyterian church at
Princeton, since the Episcopal church had not yet founded an
institution for the education of its clergymen. He was in residence at Princeton for about eighteen months when illness
forced him to withdraw and continue his theological studies in
private. Nonetheless, upon coming of age McIlvaine was or-
dained deacon in the Protestant Episcopal church on July 4,
1820, and immediately took up the charge of Christ Church,
Georgetown, near Washington, D.C. It was while holding that
position that his preaching, always imaginative and vital, attracted on Sunday mornings many of the leading political
figures in Washington. McIlvaine's pulpit eloquence was soon
publicly noted, and in 1821 and 1822 he was appointed to serve
as chaplain of the United States Senate. During his ministry in
Georgetown (1820–24), McIlvaine came to know the secretary
of war, John C. Calhoun, a member of his congregation; and it
was Calhoun who subsequently invited McIlvaine to move to
West Point as chaplain to the cadet corps. The Secretary was
reshaping the curriculum and staff of the Military Academy in
hopes of raising its standards of training, education, and moral
tone; hence, there was a need for a thoughtful and impressive
chaplain to complement the dynamic plans.

The warm humid climate of Georgetown affected the health
of the young priest, not yet twenty-six years old; and in Janu-

ary, 1825, he took up the post of chaplain and professor of geography, history, and ethics at West Point. Historians of the institution suggest that the spiritual life of the school was then, as it had been for some years, at a low mark, and that it modestly improved with McIlvaine's efforts. Certainly, his lively and forceful sermons, which on occasions continued for two hours, captivated the students.[2]

While at the Academy, McIlvaine, committed to the ideas of the nineteenth-century evangelical movement, instituted revivals of religion that profoundly affected many officers and cadets. This was something not only unusual at West Point, but not altogether pleasing to many members of the faculty who regarded with suspicion and guarded hostility the chaplain's "hellfire and brimstone" prayer meetings.[3] But the cadet body held him in high esteem. Indeed, a number of cadets who encountered McIlvaine's vivid, electric, and powerful preaching at chapel and his sense of personal religion at prayer meetings and in private conversations were converted to the faith.[4] Among the chaplain's pupils were Jefferson Davis, Robert E. Lee, Albert S. Johnston, Joseph E. Johnston, Charles F. Smith, Major Robert Anderson, and Leonidas Polk, all of whom were to play prominent roles either in the Union or Confederate armies during the Civil War. McIlvaine baptized Polk at the Academy, and on December 9, 1838, after Polk had abandoned a military career, preached the sermon at his service of consecration as missionary bishop of the Protestant Episcopal church in Arkansas, in Christ Church, Cincinnati.[5] Within ten years of McIlvaine's departure from West Point, nine cadets had retired from military life to prepare for the ministry and action in the church militant.[6]

The long shadow that the chaplain cast across the Academy was not restricted to his work as a preacher, priest, and evangelist, for he was one of the brightest, most vital and vigorous faculty members in the classroom, teaching history, geography, and a course in moral and political philosophy.[7] Furthermore,

McIlvaine, who was a man of wide reading and many interests, supported and assisted the Academy's superintendent, Sylvanus Thayer, in planning and implementing the curriculum reforms that occurred from year to year. He was a strong and valuable member of the faculty.

The chaplain's prominence in religious and educational affairs by 1827 radiated far from West Point and New York. During that year he declined the presidency of the floundering Episcopal church–related college at Williamsburg, William and Mary. Instead, he decided late in the year to return to the parish ministry and accepted a call to serve as rector of St. Ann's Church, Brooklyn, New York. The parish, which included many of the socially prominent business and professional people of the community, had in the past been served by men whose theological views were forthrightly evangelical. The rector fit this mold. Throughout his tenure as priest at St. Ann's, McIlvaine continued to teach part time and simultaneously held the appointment of Professor of the Evidences of Christianity at the University of the City of New York. In 1831 he delivered a notable series of lectures entitled *The Evidences of Christianity in Their External Division,* which were subsequently published in the United States and firmly established McIlvaine as the most theologically competent teacher of the evangelical faction within the Episcopal church.

Much of his life, from his days at Princeton Seminary till his death in Florence, Italy, in March, 1873, McIlvaine was pained and troubled physically and emotionally by the stress and anxiety of neuralgia and nervous exhaustion. On five occasions the severity of this condition prompted him to travel to England for quiet and rest. When McIlvaine arrived in England for the first time in the autumn of 1830, he knew nobody. However, his reputation as a preacher—in Georgetown, where many of the diplomatic corps were members of his congregation, including the British ambassador, Stratford Canning (Lord Stratford de Redcliffe), at the Academy, and at St. Ann's—complemented

by his skilful theological insights reflected in the lectures at
City University in New York, gave McIlvaine honor and praise
among churchmen on both sides of the Atlantic. Indeed, the
acquaintances he formed during his first journey abroad,
friendships that were to last till death, buttressed his lasting
attraction to England and Englishmen. During that first trip he
met many distinguished men: Lords Gambier (James Gambier) and Bexley (Nicholas Vansittart), the latter onetime
chancellor of the exchequer, both of whom were generous bene-
factors of Kenyon College in Ohio (which McIlvaine was soon
to serve as president); Lords Lorton of Boyle (Robert King)
and Mount Sandford of Castlerea (George Sandford), and a
number of prominent clergymen and military and naval leaders of the establishment.

Of course, it was to evangelical leaders within the Church of
England that McIlvaine was attracted during his visits. On his
journey in 1830 he met two of the most outspoken of the
evangelical party preachers in London, Daniel Wilson, later
bishop of Calcutta (1832–58), and Baptist Wriothesley Noel.
The latter was gazetted one of Queen Victoria's chaplains in
1840, but during the heat of the High Church controversy in
1849 he became a Baptist. There were others too: Dr. Thomas
Chalmers, professor of theology at Edinburgh University, the
bishops of Winchester (Charles R. Sumner), Chester (John B.
Sumner, the former's brother), and Lichfield (Henry Ryder),
and the dean of Salisbury. His friendships spanned the isle, and
nowhere were they more fascinating than at Cambridge University, where he was introduced to such prominent church
leaders and lecturers as the regius professor of Hebrew, Samuel
Lee, the foremost linguist and oriental scholar of his day; William Farrish, Jacksonian professor of natural and experimental
philosophy; and James Scholefield, regius professor of Greek,
all of whom were evangelicals and eminently learned. It was
through the respected encouragement and support of these
men, admirers of the theological resourcefulness of McIlvaine's

Evidences of Christianity in Their External Division, that the American lectures were reprinted in England.

In November, 1830, McIlvaine returned to his pulpit at St. Ann's, Brooklyn, and settled into his parochial and pastoral tasks with renewed health and keenness, although ten months later his life was to take a new course. On September 10, 1831, the diocese of Ohio elected McIlvaine bishop, and he was consecrated in the episcopal office on October 31, 1832, at St. Paul's Church, New York City. His memorialist claims that the thirty-three-year-old McIlvaine's acceptance of the Ohio post was, in comparison to the ease and social refinement of parish life in Georgetown and Brooklyn, and the chaplaincy at West Point, a "commitment of self-denial and endurance . . . in a frontier diocese." [8]

Regardless of the personal hardships, Bishop McIlvaine addressed himself to the tasks of a diocesan in a new state and to the appointment that accompanied his Episcopal post, the presidency of struggling and financially hard-pressed Kenyon College at Gambier. He remained in Ohio nearly twenty years, save for a journey to England in 1834 and 1835, again for his health.

From New York in April, 1853, the Bishop sailed for England, an American delegate to the jubilee meeting of the British and Foreign Bible Society in London. Once there, he renewed old acquaintances and participated in the consecration of John Jackson as the bishop of Lincoln at the request of his long-time friend John B. Sumner, the archbishop of Canterbury; but his signal honor during this tour was the conferral of the D.C.L. degree on him by Oxford University, June 7. He received his honorary degree at the Encaenia ceremony in the Sheldonian Theater along with such prominent members of the English establishment as Spencer Horatio Walpole, Benjamin Disraeli, and Thomas Babbington Macaulay. Cambridge University awarded McIlvaine a similar degree in December, 1858, when he again went to England for his health (which was indeed failing) and for what he thought was to be his final trip abroad.

However, his ties with England were now too firm and would soon follow him into his parlor in Cincinnati. The Prince of Wales, whom McIlvaine had met some years earlier, in 1860 undertook an extensive trip through Canada and the United States. He and his party—which included such distinguished government leaders as Sir Henry Holland, the Duke of Newcastle (Henry Pelham), Lord Richard B. P. Lyons, the British ambassador at Washington, and the Earl of St. Germans (Edward Granville Eliot), a prominent diplomatist, none of whom were known to the bishop—visited with McIlvaine at his home.[9] Several of these public figures were later to assist him while he was President Lincoln's quiet emissary to London.

It is not entirely clear when and how President Lincoln decided to send extraordinary deputies to the capitals of Great Britain and France in the autumn of 1861. He hoped to stem what he felt was an increasingly favorable sentiment within the governments of these nations toward the Confederate cause. Undoubtedly, Seward and Chase had a hand in the appointments, since at least two of the agents illustrated their loyalties. Lincoln named four men for the overseas assignments: Thurlow Weed, the veteran New York journalist and political king-maker, to whom the Secretary of State owed much; the Roman Catholic archbishop of New York, the Most Reverend John Joseph Hughes, a friend of both Weed and Seward; the aging "Old Fuss and Feathers," Lieutenant General Winfield Scott; and Charles McIlvaine. The Bishop of Ohio was a longtime friend of the Secretary of the Treasury, who was the nephew of McIlvaine's predecessor in the episcopal office. Possibly, as one commentator has pointed out, the President selected McIlvaine in order to preserve balance between the Seward and Chase factions in his cabinet.[10] In any case, for the job to be done, it was a thoughtful appointment.

These men were not to supplant but rather to supplement

the efforts of the American ministers in London and Paris.
However, they were not accredited to either the Court of St.
James or the Court of Napoleon III, nor were they under the
jurisdiction of the assigned minister of the United States government. They were agents of the government in Washington
operating outside the normal channels of diplomatic and
public communication. This arrangement, in the hands of less
sensitive men, might have been hazardous, as the American
minister to London Charles Francis Adams pointed out to
Secretary of State Seward. He strongly remarked that although
it was not his experience, two people pursuing a task in diplomacy might well initiate conflicts and contradictions between
themselves and others that could possibly result in the under-
mining of the role of the minister. Adams implied that the tasks
of McIlvaine and Weed should be distinctly defined and that
they should be accredited to the government before which they
appeared. Nothing came of this suggestion, however, and before July, 1862, had passed, both deputies had returned to the
United States.[11]

The President's appointees had much to do. Each deputy
had specially defined areas around which he would focus his
attention. Bishop McIlvaine was to make his appeal to the
British bishops, deans, and lesser clergy, while Weed, utilizing
his journalistic interest, was finally to wage a campaign against
Confederate propaganda in the columns of the London *Times*.
The other New Yorker, Archbishop Hughes, was to sway and
convey the Union's position at the courts of Napoleon III and
Pope Pius IX. General Scott arrived in Paris in early November, but returned to the United States soon after since it seemed
likely to him that an Anglo-American war would quickly follow the "Trent" crisis and that the French might join the
British.

Expenses of Hughes and McIlvaine, but not of Weed, whose
politics were especially disagreeable to certain antislavery
groups, were paid by the government. Consequently, to avoid

antagonizing the feelings of these factions at home, Weed met his expenses out-of-pocket. The bishop, on October 26, 1861, submitted a request for travel and maintenance funds to the secretary of the treasury, Salmon P. Chase. He understood that his role in England would necessarily "require as much mixing with the higher classes as possible, which involves a higher tariff for expenses." [12] His financial needs were modest considering the social circles in which he expected to move: he thought $480 and a credit balance of $500 at the Evans and Company Bank in Cincinnati would cover his expenses during five months abroad.

Secretary of State Seward telegraphed McIlvaine on November 8, urging his immediate preparation for departure to Europe. But before he could take leave from Ohio, he had to put his own house in order: diocesan affairs had to be arranged and placed in the appropriate hands, and the trustees of the college at Gambier advised of his departure. Of course he would go, but he felt uneasy about his mission. In a note to Chase the same day, he wondered if it was possible for him to travel to England without the slightest mention of his secret duties in the country's newspapers.[13] The bishop really feared a hostile response to his presence in England as a clergyman traveling actually as an informal government agent with government pay. Certainly, he suspected such an attachment would hinder his conversations and movements with appropriate English leaders. He much preferred to be invited by two or more friends, loyal to the Union position, who would ante up expenses, "to take such counsels with the government as for the Country's sake." [14]

Regardless of these qualms on the eve of his mission abroad, Bishop McIlvaine, accompanied by two of his daughters, left Cincinnati for New York in November, 1861, prepared to sail to England on his presidential assignment. En route he stopped at West Point to guide his children round where he once lived and worked, and while there, penned a note to Colonel Thayer illustrating feelings that were expressed again and again before the peace at Appomattox: "The more we love the dear land and the Union, the more we must suffer in heart till the great cause is triumphant." [15]

On December 7 McIlvaine arrived at Liverpool, about a month after the Trent episode. These were dark days in Anglo-American relations, so tense in fact, that the links between the two countries had been strained to the point that war seemed imminent. What had happened to disrupt United States ties with England? Briefly, it was this. James M. Mason and John Slidell had been charged by Jefferson Davis to serve as commissioners to represent Confederate interests in England and France. They left Charleston, South Carolina on a blockade-runner in early October and went to Havana, Cuba, where they took passage for England on the British mail steamer, "Trent." The U.S.S. "San Jacinto" at this time was putting in at a Cuban port, and there her commander, Captain Charles Wilkes, heard about Mason and Slidell. It was an accepted practice in international law that a nation at war had a right to stop and search a neutral merchant ship if it suspected that ship of carrying contraband. Wilkes reasoned that Mason and Slidell were in effect "personal contraband" and, therefore, he had a right to remove them. So on November 8, in the Bahama Channel, Wilkes stopped the "Trent" and removed the Confederate commissioners, returning them to the United States where they were jailed in Fort Warren, in Boston Harbor. At home Wilkes was applauded as a national hero while in London he was jeered as a wilful violator of maritime rights and the law.

Upon docking, the bishop, sensing the drama and import of the circumstances, arranged a series of meetings with several prominent government leaders in order to exchange views on the incident. On December 10, he met with the queen's physician extraordinary Sir Henry Holland, whom McIlvaine had first met in Cincinnati a year earlier; Arthur F. Kinnaird, a distinguished philanthropist, banker, humanitarian, and Liberal Member of the House of Commons; and finally with Antony Ashley Cooper, Lord Shaftesbury.[16] Whether he was influenced by public opinion, by the British press, or by these gentlemen regarding America's position in the Trent Affair is unclear; however, he did send a note to President Lincoln advising the release of Mason and Slidell in order to avert war.[17]

Crisis defined McIlvaine's purpose and role in London, and in a letter to a friend he wrote that it was "a most interesting and anxious time for me to be in England. Before that affair, the feeling of the great body of the nation was decidedly with the Union against the rebellion. At present, until the question of the release of the captured men is decided—that feeling is checked but not changed." [18] Furthermore, he felt persuaded that the English government would not attempt to intrude or interfere with the Union's blockade of the Confederate ports, unless the Trent Affair was not peacefully settled. The bishop perceived that the deep feeling of the British nation was against a war with the United States. Sermons on that theme were preached throughout the country, and prayer meetings were held in hopes of avoiding conflict. Besides, he felt the thinking Englishman realized that such a war would hardly be in the interest of one or the other of the nations, or for that matter, of any of the countries of the world.[19]

Although a preacher, theologian, and administrator of stature within the church, rather than a canonical lawyer, the legal subtleties involved in the American government's defense of Mason and Slidell's capture intrigued the bishop. He noted that British leaders recognized we had vindicated Captain Wilkes on the basis of international law, which applies only to belligerents, but the President regarded the seceded people of the Confederacy not as belligerents but as rebels, to whom, therefore, only our municipal law applies. McIlvaine argued that Mason and Slidell could not be treated as both belligerents and rebels, that we could not justify American intervention by both international and municipal law. But, let McIlvaine speak for himself:

Up to the Capture we had made our election and must abide by it. They are rebels—not belligerents in our sight—hence our act is indefensible—for we cannot invade a *neutral* ship to execute therein our *municipal* law—any more than we can invade England for such purpose. For this reason, not to speak of others, I cannot defend the capture—and hope the prisoners will be placed back again under English protection—and that *then* the question of international law, as to belligerents and neutrals, will be more clearly defined for the future. It will be a good time; for much of the complaint in England against the capture is an abandonment of what she has hitherto maintained, and an adoption of the precise ground which our government with France and etc., has for many years been trying to bring her to.[20]

The pressing question now was how the English and American governments would resolve their differences. The English lion's tail had been twisted; Uncle Sam's whiskers had been roughly tugged. Lincoln's temporary diplomat declared in the company of many people on various occasions that he regretted that Lord Palmerston (Henry J. Temple), the British prime minister, and his foreign secretary, Lord John Russell, had dispatched such a strong protest to Washington on November 30, requesting that Mason and Slidell be handed over to the British government. The message was received in the United States capital late at night on December 18; the secretary of state and Lincoln's entire cabinet studied the communication for several days. Bishop McIlvaine deplored the tone and urgency of Palmerston's message. More time to explore views was necessary, more time for a careful decision to evolve was essential: he wanted cautious rather than hasty negotiations. From his position in London, that seemed a small price for peace.

The prospect of the Union forced to enter war with England

over the Trent Affair disturbed and distressed McIlvaine. He
queried: Can the Union fight the Confederate armies and England's army, too? What about the difficulty of the North maintaining a naval blockade of southern ports as well as seaports in
England? How will Lincoln's government transport troops to
England, and what of the difficulties of financing such a costly
war? The bishop perceived that the English people were con-
templating a possible war, doubtless stirred up to that attitude
by the skilful propaganda of southern agents, and that if such a
war were precipitated and the English were victorious, it would
mean the setting up of a government based really and avowedly
on slavery. That kind of war and the consequence of war the
English, he felt, were earnest to avoid.[21]

Seward delivered the United States reply to Palmerston's
dispatch to the British ambassador, Lord Lyons, on December
27. In it, the secretary of state claimed Captain Wilkes was
justified in seizing the commissioners, but conceded that Wilkes
had made a regrettable error in releasing the "Trent" instead
of escorting her into port under the "contraband" doctrine for
adjudication in a prize court. Furthermore, the relative unim-
portance of Mason and Slidell no longer required their deten-
tion. They would be freed.

On January 9, 1862, McIlvaine learned the news and was
grateful that war between England and the United States now
had been averted. The American government's action, he believed, under the circumstances, was not only expedient but
right in itself.[22] The United States had lost nothing by its final
action on Mason and Slidell, the bishop claimed. Rather, it had
gained much. In the eyes of Lincoln's emissary, the government's moderate course had been fair, consistent, and just.
Moreover, he wrote, "a great [and] honorable reputation has
been given to a widespread and most dishonorable belief with
regard to us. The result [and] benefit are manifest here. The
reaction is wide [and] valuable. The capture had an evil influence on the public mind of England in reference to our war

with the rebellion. The release will have a stronger [influence] in the opposite direction." [23]

The passing of the Trent crisis neither diminished nor arrested Bishop McIlvaine's temperate though persistent diplomatic efforts. Instead, the pressure and gravity of his errand was considerably eased. He continued to move in prominent upper-class English social, political, and ecclesiastical circles, meeting, discussing, and informing his listeners of the Union's ideological attitudes and the course of the Civil War. At Hursely Park, the country estate of the bishop's old friend Sir William Heathcote, McIlvaine had the pleasure to make the acquaintance of Mr. Spencer Horatio Walpole, former secretary of state for the Home Department, who, the bishop noted, was "a very reasonable person to our side." [24] Later, he spent a week as a guest of his long-time friend Charles R. Sumner, the bishop of Winchester, in whose residence, Farnham Castle, he had constant opportunities to meet influential members of the church and government. During a brief excursion to Southampton, twelve miles distant, McIlvaine preached in the town church in the presence of the mayor and members of the town corporation. That occasion exposed McIlvaine to the pomp and color of local public and ecclesiastical ceremony when he walked from the city hall to the church in a procession of dignitaries led by two beadles—a distinct contrast to the untinged pageantry of diocesan and parish exercises in Ohio. We do not know the message of the bishop's sermon on that day, but we do know that local dignitaries and Captain Robert B. Pegram, bold commander of the blockade runner, the Confederate cruiser "Nashville," were in attendance. The following day McIlvaine and seventeen other gentlemen, among whom were six clergymen, two admirals, one general, one mayor, and two aldermen, breakfasted at the parsonage; and in response to the company's request, the bishop addressed them on American affairs. [25]

The bishop worked intensively at his tasks, traveling widely throughout the isle. In early February, 1862, he had visited the bishop of Rochester (Joseph C. Wigram) at his palace in the south of England, the bishop of Ripon (Robert Bickersteth) at his see about two hundred and fifty miles to the north, and spent a night at the stately home and seat of John James Strutt, Lord Rayleigh. After February 6 he was in London, where his work chiefly lay, for Parliament, about to debate American affairs, was sitting, and he had many opportunities to answer and enlarge upon inquiries of the "high ranked (Christian) people of England." [26]

At Fulham Palace, his official residence, Archibald Campbell Tait, the bishop of London, hosted McIlvaine and introduced him to a number of highly placed persons in the church and government. So too did Lord Arthur Fitzgerald Kinnaird, Lady Gainesborough (Francis Noel), and the keeper of the Privy Seal, the Duke of Argyll (George Douglas Campbell) and his duchess, whom the Bishop of Ohio found to be the most informed and sympathetic of the lay nobility toward the Union cause.[27] Through a leading member of the House of Commons, McIlvaine presented his views to a number of members of Parliament and to at least three of the prime minister's cabinet. Reporting to Secretary Seward, McIlvaine disclosed that his opportunities had much exceeded his expectations and that "everybody sees the change in public opinion, or expressions of it recently." [28] There was room for diversion and lightness too for McIlvaine, and as a prominent American bishop, he was a celebrity attractive to both the English and American communities. He had preached at the university churches in both Oxford and Cambridge, and at a special service of evensong on Septuagesima Sunday, February 16, 1862, the bishop delivered a sermon to a congregation of more than four thousand at St. Paul's Cathedral in the City of London. The following Saturday, February 22, he presided at a breakfast, attended largely

by Americans residing in London, in honor of the birthday of
George Washington, at the Freemason's Tavern in Great
Queen Street.[29]

For the next few months, there was much evidence and
assurance that English public opinion that had recently been so
hostile had shifted into the opposite direction.[30] The burden of
McIlvaine's obligation rested easier. His valuable diplomatic
efforts on behalf of his countrymen and his government had
won recognition abroad as well as at home, and it gave him a
deep sense of satisfaction that his modest involvement had been
effective. He and his two daughters, Nan and Anna, traveled to
the Continent for a holiday in France and Italy before returning to the United States in June.

McIlvaine estimated that his task in England had been useful. "It is impossible to doubt whether I should have come
here," he wrote. "People of high position say to me, 'How
thankful we are that you came at this time.' "[31] An archdeacon
of the Church of England told McIlvaine that the idea was
current in England that he came as an agent of the federal
government at a time when there was danger of trouble between the United States and England with the purpose to
"produce a quieting effect."[32] The bishop observed that he was
"regarded as an *expression* of pacific feeling at home—that the
bare facts of my coming *at such a season* [and] *juncture,* is so
read—[and] that there is no doubt, I have been instrumental in
keeping down a great deal of the froth that was rising, certainly
I could not have a warmer welcome or a wider field."[33] The
American minister, Charles F. Adams, with whom McIlvaine
frequently met during the winter of 1861–62 to discuss events at
home and to inform of his engagements, referred to the bishop's
services to Secretary Seward in December as "already [having]
been of material use and—will be of still more hereafter if
peaceful relations should be preserved."[34]

Thurlow Weed, who watched McIlvaine's proceedings firsthand, commented to Secretary of State Seward soon after the

bishop's arrival in England, that he "has been in the country
for more than a week, and remains several days longer, visiting
bishops and clergy, and doing good wherever he goes." [35] Later,
Weed wrote, "Bishop McIlvaine is doing vast good, in and out
of the City, and in influential quarters." [36] His opinion was no
less strong in April when again Weed emphatically declared to
Seward, McIlvaine "is a good man, and has done good service"
in England.[37] In Washington, Salmon P. Chase, who played a
significant and outspoken role in the sessions of Lincoln's cabinet during the weeks of intense agitation between England and
America generated by the Trent crisis, reported to his friend,
"you are doing a great work and a good one." [38]

After returning to the United States in June, 1862, McIlvaine continued to serve the Union's interest in Ohio and in
the country at large. In Cincinnati he assisted the local efforts
of the United States Christian Commission and the United
States Sanitary Commission to raise funds and supplies for aid
to be sent to the soldiers at the battlefronts. The bishop's
sympathies and activities, however, were more closely associated with the goals and work of the Christian Commission,
and with that agency he held a position of national prominence
and responsibility.

The Christian Commission was a private social agency
founded in New York in 1861 by prominent leaders in the
Young Men's Christian Association and the American Tract
Society. Also representing Protestant ministers, especially from
the rural areas of New England, the north, and from the urban
centers of the west, the organization's orientation was unquestionably evangelical in outlook; indeed, the society was motivated by a sense of religious enthusiasm. Its purpose was to
supply comforts and needs not furnished by the federal government to armies: clothing, food, medicine, prayer books, devo-
tional tracts, newspapers, and books. Though dispensing most
of these items to all soldiers, the Christian Commission really
was a Protestant society, since it would not purchase and dis-

tribute religious books and pamphlets to Roman Catholic combatants.[39]

Before he was elected a delegate of the Christian Commission (No. 2268) in 1864, Bishop McIlvaine had made two journeys from Cincinnati to northern Virginia battlefields.[40] General Winfield Scott, commander of the United States Army, in June, 1861, had given the bishop clearance and assistance to visit and preach among two Ohio regiments of the Union army at outposts not too distant from Washington. Another time, when he followed the maneuvers of the Army of the Potomac under the leadership of General Joseph Hooker, McIlvaine again, between May 15 and 25, 1863, carried his pastoral concerns and efforts to the front lines. Now a senior bishop of considerable stature within the Episcopal church, and one who also maintained active connections with various interdenominational societies, the Christian Commission on July 22, 1864, elected McIlvaine a member.[41] The post was quite similar in character and obligation to that of a director in other bodies, and he served until February, 1866, when the organization was disbanded.

He struck out in other directions though, too. Writing to President Lincoln during the triennial general convention of the Episcopal church in New York City in October, 1862, McIlvaine informed the chief executive of a pastoral letter strongly supporting his leadership and the Union's position in the Civil War that the house of bishops would deliver to the clergy and laity in attendance, and to church members throughout the United States at the close of the sessions.[42] This was an extraordinary change of events within the church's national administrative and legislative body. At the time of the "bleeding Kansas" issue in 1856, the convention in session in Philadelphia in October, heard a pastoral letter from the bishops that quite dramatically and pointedly ignored current public issues and crises that the people and the country were facing. In part, they said, that "the constituted rulers of the Church . . . are the ministry. With party politics, with sectional disputes, with earthly distinctions, with the wealth, the splendor, and the ambition of the world, they have nothing to do." [43] Secular and political affairs were matters of no concern to the church. Their debates and resolutions focused on the problems of drink, personal prayer life, and upholding the sanctity of family life and the home. For example, the Episcopal church never split on the issue of slavery because it refused at any time during the period to take any position on the controversy. With ten southern dioceses and ten southern bishops "temporarily absent," the way was clear in 1862 for the church to illustrate its patriotism without fear of schism within the ranks.

Never a trimmer, McIlvaine unabashedly informed Lincoln that the 1862 pastoral letter was his work: not only had he drafted the document, but he had also engineered the adoption of the letter in the house of bishops.[44] The sentiments feelingly expressed in this little-known address and delivered by the bishop from the pulpit of St. John's Church, New York City, on October 17, reflect in no uncertain ways the prospect of McIlvaine. The basic themes had already been spoken by him in a charge to his parishoners at Christ Church, Cincinnati, on April 19, 1861, seven days after the harbor batteries had opened fire on Fort Sumter.[45] Now the bishops, at McIlvaine's insistence, re-emphasized and expanded upon those principles: that Episcopalians are bound by Christian duty and national loyalty to obey and uphold the Constitution and government of the United States. The refusal of such allegiance, the prelates declared, would be held by them to be a sin, and when it is manifest in civil war it is not only a crime before the laws of man but also a transgression before the laws of God.[46] The tone of the message, which was required to be read by every minister to his congregation, was clear and unequivocal: the Bishop of Ohio had rallied the moral support of the Episcopal church to the side of the President and the cause of the Union.

Frequently during their acquaintance, which spanned Lincoln's four years in the White House, McIlvaine shared with the President a variety of matters. His letters mirror the high esteem he felt for the Chief Executive. Like countless other citizens, McIlvaine, too, asked Lincoln during the course of the war for special favors for his relatives. On one occasion he sought a military appointment for a nephew, and another time, in December, 1864, he requested a permit to allow his sister-in-law, Harriet C. Bledsoe, wife of Albert Taylor Bledsoe, professor of mathematics and astronomy at the University of Virginia and now assistant secretary of war under Jefferson Davis, to pass through the battlelines while en route from Philadelphia to her home and children in Charlottesville. McIlvaine constantly followed with interest and encouragement Lincoln's steps toward the Emancipation Proclamation, noting the sympathetic influence it would have on the Union's cause with the British government. Later, the bishop differed strongly and sharply with a decision of the Union's military leadership to place houses of worship in certain conquered southern towns under the jurisdiction of the provost marshal. Once he interceded at the final hour for clemency on behalf of Lieutenant S. Boyer Davis, a twenty-one-year-old Confederate spy who had been condemned to death. And he unfailingly followed and remarked upon the Union's progress on the battlefronts. One time though a letter carried a deeper and more personal message: a note of touching human tenderness and condolence was sent by the bishop during his assignment in London upon hearing of the death of Willie, Lincoln's son.[47]

He served the President for the last time in the spring of 1865. The bishop had traveled two hundred and fifty miles from Cincinnati to Cleveland to participate in that city's final rites for the murdered leader. In a pavilion especially erected in Public Square for the ceremonies on April 28, McIlvaine, reciting appropriate passages from the Burial Office of the *Book of*

Common Prayer of the Episcopal church, presided over the open coffin, while tens of thousands of men, women, and children standing in the rain surrounded the canopied catafalque. It was a heavy, sad day for McIlvaine, for he had deeply admired and respected the President, and the wantonness of the assassination at Ford's Theater puzzled and hurt him.[48] He spoke his part with "deep emotion and impressive fervor": his prayers for Lincoln, his petitions to the Almighty for blessings upon the life of the wounded secretary of state, for the preservation of the Union, and for President Johnson's guidance were vividly and movingly delivered.[49]

Tall, stately, handsome, a man of patrician appearance and bearing, McIlvaine's friendship with Lincoln was steadfast, his loyalty complete. Though a minor figure in the circle of presidential advisors and friends and in the events of the war, nonetheless, the bishop illustrated again and again between 1861 and 1865 his willingness to actively endorse principles and policies that he felt were right and would be helpful. Abroad in London, as well as at home in Cincinnati, or New York, he proved to be as skilled in the politics of international diplomacy as he was skilled in the politics of the church. His appreciation and understanding of political problems were never insular, provincial, or parochial. A breadth of vision and depth of compassion characterized his temperament and involvement in the contemporary affairs and issues that sharply tormented the national community and Ohio during those years. But he had set down his guidelines early in the war and had not deviated from his course. His address to the forty-fourth annual convention of the diocese of Ohio on June 5, 1861, became really his pledge, oath, and statement of fidelity to the Union: he declared to his fellow Ohioans that there is "no such thing as being neutral in this controversy . . . (there is) no middle ground between loyalty (to the) government and disloyalty. . . . Our duty in this emergency is steadily, bravely, earnestly to sustain our Government and its administration, in the use of all lawful means to preserve the integrity of the Union." [50]

1. McIlvaine MSS, Kenyon College Library, letter from Bishop Charles P. McIlvaine to Assistant Bishop Gregory T. Bedell, Danbury, Essex, Feb. 13, 1862. Hereafter cited as McIlvaine MSS.

2. Douglas Southall Freeman, *Robert E. Lee: A Biography* (New York, 1934), I, 59–60.

3. Ernest R. Dupay, *Men of West Point: The First 150 Years of the United States Military Academy* (New York, 1951), pp. 47–48.

4. William Carus (ed.), *Memorials of the Right Reverend Charles Pettit McIlvaine, D.D., D.C.L., Late Bishop of Ohio in the Protestant Episcopal Church of the United States* (London, 1882), chap. ii, *passim*.

5. Dupay, *op. cit.*, p. 209; Charles Pettit McIlvaine, *The Apostolical Commission: The Sermon at the Consecration of the Right Reverend Leonidas Polk, D.D., Missionary Bishop for Arkansas; in Christ Church, Cincinnati, December 9, 1838* (Gambier, Ohio, 1838).

6. Dupay, *op. cit.*, p. 48.

7. Hudson Strode, *Jefferson Davis, American Patriot: 1808–1861* (New York, 1955), pp. 43–44.

8. Carus, *op. cit.*, p. 65.

9. *Ibid.*, pp. 201–2.

10. Jay Monaghan, *Diplomat in Carpet Slippers: Abraham Lincoln Deals with Foreign Affairs* (New York, 1945), pp. 155–56.

11. Adams Papers (Microfilm; Boston: Massachusetts Historical Society), Part II, Reel 167, Charles Francis Adams, Letterbook, Jan. 11, 1862—June 23, 1862, letter to William H. Seward, London, Mar. 27, 1862, pp. 196–99. Hereafter cited as Adams Papers.

12. McIlvaine MSS, McIlvaine to Salmon P. Chase, Cincinnati, Oct. 26, 1861.

13. *Ibid.*, McIlvaine to Salmon P. Chase, Cincinnati, Nov. 8, 1861.

14. *Ibid.*

15. Carus, *op. cit.*, pp. 207–8.

16. *Ibid.*, p. 218.

17. *Ibid.,* p. 220.

18. McIlvaine MSS, McIlvaine to Bedell, Farnham Castle (Winchester), Dec. 23, 1861.

19. *Ibid.*

20. *Ibid.*

21. *Ibid.*

22. *Ibid.,* McIlvaine to Bedell, London, Jan. 13, 1862.

23. *Ibid.*

24. *Ibid.,* McIlvaine to Bedell, London, Jan. 14, 1862.

25. *Ibid.*

26. *Ibid.,* McIlvaine to Bedell, Danbury, Essex, Feb. 13, 1862.

27. *Ibid.*

28. Ibid., McIlvaine to Secretary of State William H. Seward, London, Feb. 21, 1862.

29. Adams Papers, Part I, Reel 77, Charles Francis Adams, Diary, Jan. 1, 1862—Apr. 30, 1864, Sunday, Feb. 16, 1862, and Saturday, Feb. 22, 1862.

30. Martin B. Duberman, *Charles Francis Adams, 1807–1886* (Boston, 1961), pp. 284–85; Ephraim Douglass Adams, *Great Britain and the American Civil War* (New York, 1958), pp. 237–43.

31. McIlvaine MSS, McIlvaine to Bedell, London, Jan. 14, 1862.

32. *Ibid.*

33. *Ibid.*

34. Adams Papers, Part II, Reel 166, Charles Francis Adams, Letterbook, Oct. 2, 1861—Jan. 18, 1862, letter to William H. Seward, London, Dec. 27, 1861, p. 318.

35. Weed MSS, The University of Rochester Library, Rochester, New York, Thurlow Weed to William H. Seward, London, Dec. 31, 1861.

36. *Ibid.,* Weed to Seward, London, Jan. 31, 1862.

37. *Ibid.,* Weed to Seward, Paris, Apr. 4, 1862.

38. Robert B. Warden, *An Account of the Private Life and Public Services of Salmon Portland Chase* (Cincinnati, 1874), p. 416.

39. Lemuel Moss, *Annals of the United States Christian Commission* (Philadelphia, 1868), *passim;* William Quentin Maxwell, *Lincoln's Fifth Wheel: the Political History of the United States Sanitary Commission* (New York, 1956), pp. 191, 192, 222.

40. Moss, *op. cit.*, p. 623.

41. *Ibid.*, p. 169.

42. Abraham Lincoln Papers, Library of Congress Microfilm, No. 19105, McIlvaine to Lincoln, New York, Oct. 20, 1862. (Hereafter cited as Lincoln Papers.

43. James Thayer Addison, *The Episcopal Church in the United States, 1789–1931* (New York, 1951), pp. 192–99.

44. Lincoln Papers.

45. Charles P. McIlvaine, *The Christian's Duty in the Present Crisis* (Cincinnati, 1861).

46. *Pastoral Letter of the Bishops of the Protestant Episcopal Church in the United States of America to the Clergy and Laity of the Same. Delivered before the General Convention, at the Close of its Session in St. John's Church, New York, Friday, October 17, 1862* (New York, 1862), pp. 8–10; *New York Times,* Vol. XII, No. 3454, Saturday, Oct. 18, 1862.

47. Lincoln Papers, No. 15244, McIlvaine to Lincoln, London, Mar. 27, 1862; No. 24697, McIlvaine to Salmon P. Chase, Cincinnati, July 6, 1863; No. 25164, McIlvaine to Lincoln, Cincinnati, July 27, 1863; No. 29232, McIlvaine to Lincoln, Cincinnati, Jan. 6, 1864; No. 30675, McIlvaine to Lincoln, Feb. 19, 1864; No. 31276, McIlvaine to Lincoln, Cincinnati, Mar. 4, 1864; No. 39422, McIlvaine to Lincoln, Cincinnati, Dec. 21, 1864; No. 40531, Isaac R. Trimble to McIlvaine, Fort Warren, Feb. 8, 1865; No. 40856, McIlvaine to Lincoln, Cincinnati, Feb. 20, 1865; No. 41116, McIlvaine to Lincoln, Cincinnati, Mar. 7, 1865.

48. Carus, *op. cit.*, pp. 252–54.

49. *Cleveland Plain Dealer,* Vol. XXI, No. 60, Saturday, Apr. 29, 1865; *Cleveland Morning Leader,* Vol. XIX, No. 103, Saturday, Apr. 29, 1865; *Morning Cleveland Herald,* Vol. XXXI, No. 102, Saturday, Apr. 29, 1865.

50. "Documentary History of the American Church. Views of the Bishops of Ohio and Louisiana upon the Secession of the Southern States, and Its Effects upon the Ecclesiastical Allegiance of the Dioceses," ed. Lawrence L. Brown, *Historical Magazine of the Protestant Episcopal Church in the United States of America* (Austin, 1962), XXXI, 290–91.

SIX

Miles Greenwood

CARL M. BECKER

As he journeyed along the National Pike in Ohio in 1817, the English traveler Morris Birkbeck depicted a panorama of America turning to the West. "Old America," he observed, "seems to be breaking up and moving westward. We are seldom out of sight, as we travel this grand track toward the Ohio, of family groups behind and before us." [1] Moving to Ohio in 1817 from Old America—though by flatboat down the Ohio River rather than by the "grand track"—were Miles Greenwood, Sr., his wife, Leah, and their ten year old son, Miles, Jr. Like thousands of Americans, the elder Greenwood was sloughing off the failures of an old life and setting for the promise of life in a New Canaan land yielding opportunities unnumbered to him who would dwell in its honeyed vales. His lot, though, would be one of failure; but his son would gather from the expanding West a full measure of success and fortune. As a Cincinnati ironmaster, he would expand his facilities and innovate with a kind of exhilarative vigor, becoming eventually the leading manufacturer in the leading industrial city in the west; as a civic leader, he would give his time, talent, and treasure to a variety of community enterprises redounding to his credit. And when the great civil war came to America, he would mobilize his intellect, energy, and facilities for the service of the

Union as though all he had accomplished hitherto had been but prelude—an "apprenticeship"—for a supreme endeavor.

I

Young Greenwood's origins and background presaged a life of novelty and entrepreneurship. Greenwood's father, born in 1769 in either Boston or Salem, Massachusetts, was a creature of mobility.[2] He left his home in Newbury, Massachusetts, at the age of eighteen, in 1787, to join an expedition of two vessels fitted out by Boston merchants for opening up the western fur trade. Under the command of Captain John Kendrick and Lieutenant Robert Gray, the vessels reached Nootka Sound in 1788. Greenwood evidently had a berth with Gray, whose ship, the "Columbia," sailed from the sound to Canton in China and returned to Boston in 1790 with a cargo of tea, the first ship to carry the American flag around the globe.[3] On a second voyage to the Northwest, in 1791, Gray discovered the river to which he gave the name of his vessel, "Columbia." Greenwood returned with Gray from one of these two voyages, locating shortly thereafter in Orange County in New York, where he taught school. There, in about 1797, he married a Mrs. Leah (Demarest) Gurnee, a daughter of a Revolutionary War veteran. In 1804 the Greenwoods moved to Paulus Hook, New Jersey; Greenwood kept a tavern near the ferry there, indulging behind the bar his avidity for reading. Near the scenes of revelry, Miles, Jr., was born in 1807, the third and last child of the Greenwoods; his two sisters, Martha and Mary, had been born in 1800 and 1801 respectively.

In 1808 Greenwood took his family to New York City. For eight years he was in the grocery business there, and for three years he operated a hotel. Failing to achieve any degree of material success in either venture, he set out with his wife and son in 1817 for Cincinnati, his two daughters remaining in the

East. Again he opened a tavern, but to little purpose, since his
stock drew few patrons through the swinging doors.[4] Closing his
establishment, he next essayed—for unknown reasons—the life
of a farmer, moving to a small farm about sixteen miles north
of Dayton, Ohio, on the Stillwater River. His stay there was
short—and unprofitable—but it did not diminish his desire to
till the soil. His wandering feet took him next to a "bush" farm
near Blaysdell's Mills, Indiana. He directed his son, now eleven
years old, to clear the farm. But the boy, finding the work too
difficult, demurred; and exhibiting a spirit of independence
hardly compatible with the image of the nineteenth-century
boy, ever obedient and hard-working as he followed the path to
success, he successfully persuaded the father—who may have
been deteriorating mentally—to return to Cincinnati in 1818.

Cincinnati was then developing its position as the "Queen
City of the West." An entrepôt tapping the produce of the Ohio
country and distributing it to the South, the city was seeking
commercial dominion over the West. As a manufacturing center, it was beginning to send its goods to Ohio Valley markets
and to southern consumers. And the city itself was a growing
market for goods and services, its population rising from 2,320
in 1810 to 9,642 in 1820 and to 24,831 in 1830. From its needs
and wants, mundane and otherwise, a resourceful lad might
wrest a living; and young Greenwood was looking to the opportunities around him. At first he sawed cordwood for household-
ers, earning a reputation for reliability that assured him a
steady market. Accumulating some savings, the boy, along with
his father, now a semi-invalid, opened a small store for the sale
of old books (surely the father's idea), fruit, and burnt coffee.[5]
He also circulated advertising bills for a local theater. After five
years in his dual pursuits, the boy turned to employment in a
drugstore for nearly two years. Altogether, he spent eight years
in his second residency in Cincinnati, finding employment in a
variety of occupations and unquestionably gaining valuable
knowledge of the business life of the community.

Barely subsisting despite young Greenwood's efforts, the father and son decided in 1825 to try their fortune at Robert Dale Owen's communal experiment at New Harmony, Indiana, a kind of project that had long appealed to the senior Greenwood. Mr. and Mrs. Greenwood separated at this juncture, apparently in disagreement over the wisdom of the new odyssey. From the hustling competition and attendant insecurity of a rising urban center, the two Greenwoods turned to the serenity and evident security of a communal village. It was a decision giving young Greenwood his real "start" in life. He expected to acquire at New Harmony an education that would lay the foundation for a career in business or one of the professions. Unfortunately, the school eventually opened by Owen was presided over by M. Phiquepal d'Arusmont, who, it appears, was an incompetent pedagogue. According to Owen, Phiquepal was "full of original ideas"; but he also was a "wrong-headed genius" who "gained neither the good will nor the respect of the pupils." [6] Certainly, he left no lasting and favorable impress on young Greenwood. But the New Harmony experiment offered a kind of education that proved to be of incalculable value to him.

At the village Greenwood first became acquainted with the emblems of the machine age. In the absence of a "more competent person," he was on his arrival at the community placed in charge of a steam engine used in the grist mill.[7] After a brief stint in that capacity, he carded wool, and then was introduced to the art of "striking" and "blowing" at the ax-making forge— now he had the smell of iron-working in his nostrils. Evidently impressed with the young man's work, Oliver Evans, a foundryman who had come to New Harmony from Philadelphia to erect a foundry, chose Greenwood to go to Pittsburgh to learn the foundry trade so that he could head up the New Harmony facility at its completion. The young man displayed his growing knowledge of iron work on the steamboat trip to Pittsburgh. At least as he remembered it nearly fifty years later, he forged

wedges for tightening the damaged paddle wheels of the steamboat and thus saved it from running aground. Though offered
$50.00 by the captain to stay aboard as a crew member, he went
on to Pittsburgh, working in one of the city's many foundries
for nine months. His training ended, he returned to New Harmony; and the fall of 1828 saw him operating a small foundry
in the village. Shortly thereafter, however, the communal program having failed, the foundry was closed. Greenwood, nonetheless, was determined to continue his life in the founding arts.

Shaking the dust of the unharmonious New Harmony off
their feet, the Greenwoods moved once more to Cincinnati.
The city was journey's end for the father, his death taking place
there in 1831. For the son it was the beginning of a journey in
iron entrepreneurship. Shortly after his arrival, he took employment in a small foundry owned by John and Thomas
Bevan.[8] His labor must have been productive for the partners:
he was hired at $1.25 a day, but by 1831, when the foundry was
destroyed by fire, he was earning $5.00 a day. His employment
terminated by the fire, young Greenwood—undeterred by this
example of entrepreneurial hazards—decided to open his own
foundry. Lacking sufficient funds, however, to enjoy the independence of a sole proprietorship, he resorted to the formation
of a partnership in 1832 with another young ironman, Joseph
Webb. They borrowed $500 and acquired a dilapidated build-
ing that was near the route of the Miami Canal. Here they
installed equipment for general foundry work. They hired two
boys and a man, borrowed more money—this time $5,000—as
initial expenses rose in a rapid wave, and awaited the verdict of
the market place on their firm, which they named the Eagle
Iron Works.

Greenwood must have had little doubt about the earning
capacity of the foundry. At least, he was willing to take on the
joys and burdens of matrimony in the year of his entrepreneurial debut. His marriage to a Miss Howard Wales Hills was
marred by tragedy; she and their two sons died early in the

marriage. He married again, in 1836, taking as his helpmate Miss Phoebe Jane Hopson, who bore him ten children, four girls and six boys, between 1836 and 1855.[9] She was as fecund as the Eagle Iron Works proved to be.

From a marketing and technological standpoint, the young men had chosen an opportune moment for entering the foundry business. The growing urban population of Cincinnati, young and willing to consume, supplied demand for uniform castings for domestic use—kitchen utensils, kettles, and so forth. A similar demand was developing among the farmers of the West and the planters of the South, who were being encompassed by a widening arc of river, canal, and road lines. Giving further dimension to the market for castings was the rapid rise of manufacturing in Cincinnati in the 1830's, which, of course, generated demand for producers' goods—shafts and casings for machinery, for example. The high cost of transportation of iron goods over the mountains from the East partially insulated western producers from the competition of efficient eastern manufacturers who otherwise might have exploited these markets.[10] Conjoined with increasing demand were significant changes in iron technology. The expanding use of new puddling and rolling techniques, well known to the Hanging Rock area furnaces that supplied much of the iron used by Cincinnati foundries, was increasing furnace capacity and providing foundrymen with a ready and reliable supply of scrap and pig iron.[11] Improved cupolas, introduced to foundries from 1815 on, were separating the functions of the blast furnace and the foundry, permitting the merchant pig-iron producer and the foundryman alike to move to more specialized and productive skills. The development of "Blackheart" malleable iron in the 1820's and the introduction of cast steel in the 1830's particularly opened innovative avenues to venturesome foundrymen.

Initially, the Eagle Iron Works produced a limited line of products for domestic use. According to advertising notices of later years, "the means of the proprietors would not admit of an extended business; and the articles of manufacture relied upon principally, were Stoves, Hollow Ware, Sad Irons, Dog Irons, Wagon Boxes, Plow Moulds, and some other ordinary articles in everyday use." [12] There was, of course, nothing unique in this line. Indeed, it was the characteristic output of the small general foundry of the day. The opportunities, however, for the expansive or specialized foundryman were proliferating as population increased and technological change accelerated. Foundries specializing in the casting of a single item—stoves or plow irons, for example—were on the rise in the 1830's. Large foundries fabricating heavy castings for engine works also were appearing.[13] A man on the make and given to novelty as he was, Miles Greenwood might well have eventually turned to one of a number of possible specialities. Or, located as he was in a rising commercial and industrial city serving a large regional market, he could have been content with increasing his general production to meet the needs of an expanding western population. Instead, he turned to a diversity of alternatives.

Though gradually enlarging their facilities and reaching beyond the Cincinnati market with their products throughout the 1830's, Greenwood and Webb remained undistinguished, though successful, iron founders. Their annual profits had reached twenty-eight thousand dollars by 1840 when Greenwood, apparently having accumulated substantial savings, bought out Webb's interest.[14] He soon gave his business a note of distinction and earned some slight repute as an innovator in the metal-working industries by introducing butt hinges to his line. "Mr. Greenwood, we think," as a contemporary recorded it, "was the first in this country to engage largely in the manufacture of Butt Hinges, having commenced it as early as 1840, which precedes, by at least two years, its establishment in Providence, Rhode Island. . . ." [15] Before 1840 only English firms and a few eastern foundries were supplying hinges for the Cincinnati market. Greenwood's hinge production rested no doubt on his experiential base in the manufacturing of stoves. Their manufacture required the casting of strong, irregular shapes, with particular allowance made for even shrinkage in cooling; these casting skills could be put to good usage in small hardware work. To capture a share of the Cincinnati market, Greenwood resorted to a simple but clever strategem, sending out a small army of friends from hardware store to hardware store to demand "Greenwood's hinges." [16] Dealers, responding to the artificial demand, soon were stocking his hinges. Demand was legitimate soon enough as builders became aware of their high quality. According to Charles Cist, the chronicler of life in mid-nineteenth-century Cincinnati, the Greenwood line was clearly superior to English hinges, which typically were "unequal in thickness, imperfectly jointed, and too light for heavy service." Greenwood's, on the other hand, were "substantial" and cast as evenly as if made by machinery.[17] Even English Commissioners at the New York World's Fair of 1852 acknowledged the excellent quality of Greenwood's hinges, noting, too, his ability to solve the problem of high labor costs always involved in small castings: "In the important item of Butt Hinges there can be no doubt of the great superiority of those manufactured by Messrs. Greenwood, alike as regards the general quality of the metal as in the adaptibility [sic] of strength or weight of material to size. In the finish of the joints great accuracy is obtained, whilst the labor of filing is saved by grinding the joints of the hinges on stones adapted to the purpose, and driven by steam power." [18] By the early 1850's, if Cist and Greenwood are to be believed, the Greenwood hinges had come to dominate the Cincinnati market. Their annual sales then were about $15,000. Admittedly, Greenwood could not assert any grand technological triumph in such a small hardware item as a hinge; but his success seemed to represent for Cincinnatians evidence of the innate genius of the West and its ability to develop a self-sufficient economy.

Succeeding in hinges, Greenwood took up the production of

an extensive line of hardware articles. To raise funds for this venture, he formed a partnership in 1844 with Charles Folger and Nelson Gates, whose contributions were largely financial rather than managerial.[19] The new concern, although organized as M. Greenwood & Company, was operated as a department of the Eagle Iron Works.[20] As the Hardware and Malleable Iron Department, it sent pendant pulleys, shutter lifts, shutter screws and catches, shutter slide bolts, sash weights, side and screw pulleys, locks and latches, and a host of other hardware items into thousands of homes in Cincinnati and the West. Like the butt hinges, these hardware articles won the acclaim of the English Commissioners, who reported that they were of a "superior character." [21] Butt hinges, it should be noted, continued to be manufactured in the Eagle Iron Works.[22] The Commissioners also had a word of praise for Greenwood's management: "Probably the most extensive, and certainly the best conducted and most systematically arranged establishment for the production of miscellaneous Hardware articles in the United States, is that of Messrs. Miles Greenwood & Co., Cincinnati, Ohio." [23] Besides producing hardware and a conventional line of saddlery, the department specialized in the manufacture of a variety of malleable cast-iron goods that had previously been formed from wrought iron. Greenwood was in the vanguard of foundrymen using malleable iron, for it was not in common use until the 1850's.[24] His usage probably was hastened by the availability of excellent malleable bar iron processed in the Scioto Valley region; that iron, said one observer, was superior to the fine Juniata iron of Pennsylvania.[25] Among the articles Greenwood cast with malleable iron were carriage wrenches, screw wrenches, staples, kettle-ears, table hinges, and tailors' shears. They were, noted the English Commissioners, "very excellent substitutes for the most costly wrought-iron articles." [26] The tailors' shears seemed particularly remarkable, one pair selling for $75.00 in England.

Throughout the 1840's, Greenwood sought to fashion a mul-

tifaceted foundry. Not satisfied with his success in hinges, he
looked, in 1843, to a heavier product than he had previously
cast, taking up the casting of iron house fronts, those facades
that emblematized the developing anonymity of urban life.[27] By
1846 he was turning to the production of steam engines and
mill gearing.[28] Though Greenwood was diversifying his output
in the 1840's, the array of articles emanating from the Eagle
Iron Works was yet characterized by small castings meeting
relatively simple needs. Indeed, Greenwood's advertising spoke
the language of the everyday, practical world: hinges and numerous other hardware items; plain, tinned, and Japanned
hollow ware; plow moulds; cooking and heating stoves; spit-
toons and tea kettles. Extolling Greenwood's work, Cist insisted
that many of these articles had until recent years been manufactured only in England and the East—and yet were often
superior to the products of those older industrialized communities.

If Cist's praise of the quality of Greenwood's output was
tinctured by a heady provincialism, surely the size of his works
demonstrated that the ironmaster was no ordinary man. His
establishment was the largest iron-manufacturing concern in
the West in 1850. In that year, the Eagle Iron Works employed
350 "hands," 250 in the main foundry and one hundred in the
malleable iron department.[29] No other firm in the city employed as many men; the second largest concern, Niles & Company, numbered its workers at about two hundred. In value
of annual production, the Greenwood works, according to
the original returns of the census of manufacturing, totalled
$238,000—$158,000 in the foundry and $80,000 in the malleable
iron department.[30] The capitalized value was $255,000, the
foundry accounting for $180,000 and the iron department add-
ing $75,000. Only two of the forty-four foundries in the city
could boast capitalization above $150,000, Niles and Company
at the $185,000 mark and the Globe Iron Works at $160,000.
The national average for capitalized value of foundries was

only about $11,000.[31] But nationally, the average capital investment of $773 per worker was above the $728 behind each Greenwood worker; and the average annual value of product of $1,053 per foundry employee was considerably more than the annual output of $681 for each Greenwood employee. The explanation for the apparent dichotomy between capitalization and value of product lies, possibly, in the nature of Greenwood's production, which had not yet extensively embraced castings for heavy producers' goods.

In any case, the small general foundryman of 1832 had become an entrepreneur, expansive and triumphant—the Tubal-cain of the West. But he was not content to rest on his oars, and as he entered the turbulent 1850's, he had before him pleasing vistas. His Cincinnati was a growing market, its population rising from 46,338 in 1840 to 115,430 in 1850. It had achieved, for the moment, by virtue of its connections with river, road, and canal traffic, commercial lordship of the West, its produce moving west and south in vast quantities to established markets: the value of its trade in dry goods, groceries, hardware, and so forth, in 1851 was $36,000,000, with only one quarter destined for local consumption, the bulk of the remainder going to markets ranging the Ohio and Mississippi river valleys.[32] As a manufacturing center, the city was becoming a colossus. Producing goods meeting a wide spectrum of human wants—shoes, shirts, trusses, caskets, candles, and so on—it had seen the annual value of its manufactures rise from about $17,000,000 in 1840 to $46,000,000 in 1850, ranking in the latter year as the third largest manufacturing city in the nation. And as Horace Greeley viewed the city, it was only beginning its ascent:

It requires no keenness of observation to perceive that Cincinnati is destined to become the focus and mart for the grandest circle of manufacturing thrift on this continent. Her delightful climate; her unequaled and ever-increasing facilities for cheap and rapid commercial intercourse with all parts of the country and the world;

her enterprising and energetic population; her own elastic and exulting youth; are all elements which predict and insure her electric progress to giant greatness. I doubt if there is another spot on the earth where food, fuel, cotton, timber, iron, can all be concentrated so cheaply—that is, at so moderate a cost of human labor in producing and bringing them together—as here. Such fatness of soil, such a wealth of mineral treasure—coal, iron, salt, and the finest clays for all purposes of use—and all cropping out from the steep, facile banks of placid, though not sluggish navigable rivers. How many Californias could equal, in permanent worth, the valley of the Ohio! [33]

The energetic, the enterprising Greenwood exemplified the qualities Greeley saw in the Cincinnati populace, and the ironmaster, like his city, was destined for industrial growth.

As Greeley suggested, manufacturers in Cincinnati enjoyed a low "customer risk" inherent in the widening market around them. By the mid–1850's, the population of the city was approaching 150,000. And as the English traveler Mrs. Isabella Bishop pointed out, Cincinnati was "the outpost of manufacturing civilization," fixed in the center of a circle of populous towns of the South, the lake country and the western territories, "with their evergrowing demand for the fruits of manufacturing industry." [34] The accumulating demand within this radius, noted William Chambers, a Scotchman on an American peregrination, had given rise to manufacturing establishments that made the city one of the "wonders of the New World." [35] Both commentators marveled at the size of the city's factories and the markets they reached. In the fabrication of iron stoves, locks and hinges, reported Chambers, "operations were on a . . . gigantic scale." Mrs. Bishop, surprised at the size of furniture factories, went on to say that "the manufactories of locks and guns, tools, and carriages, with countless other appliances of civilized life, are on a similarly large scale. Their products are to be found among the sugar plantations of the south, the diggers of California, the settlers in Oregon, in the infant cities of the West, the tent of the hunter, and the shanty of the emigrant: in one word, wherever demand and supply can be placed in conjunction." [36] Surely, large quantities of articles bearing the imprint of the Eagle Iron Works were reaching these diverse corners and consumers. Greeley's prophecy of industrial greatness for the city seemed to be coming to pass in the 1850's, and the elastic Greenwood was serving as a great instrument in its realization.

Almost compulsive in his impulse to expand, Greenwood looked to new technologies and products throughout the 1850's. He opened, apparently in the early 1850's, a steam and gas fitting department. One of the first iron entrepreneurs in the West to produce steam heating equipment, Greenwood had the department turning out a multitude of small castings: reducing couplings, plugs and bushings, elbows and bends, iron check valves, and so on.[37] Its larger castings—radiators and related equipment—appeared in factories, hotels, banks, and other public buildings in cities in Iowa, Missouri, Kentucky, and Ohio.[38] By 1851 Greenwood had initiated the manufacture of hydraulic presses and had found a ready market for them. He also was interested in hydraulic elevators, constructing one in 1858, but evidently finding no market for it.[39] Then, too, the founder was adding a host of miscellaneous articles to production. Ornamental screens, for instance, now were listed in his price catalogs, as were marbleized slates for covering steam radiators. Leafing randomly through Greenwood's catalog of 1855, a reader would have found ample evidence of versatility in iron; here were listed steam pumps, washing machines, glue heaters, grates, and so forth. Greenwood also outfitted a brass foundry in the 1850's, apparently as a unit in the steam department. There was nothing unique, of course, in this expansion; brass foundries often were associated with iron founding in the period. From the new facility flowed all manner of plumbing fixtures; steam cocks, bib cocks, check valves, oil cocks, cylinder cocks, and gauge cocks were but a few examples of Greenwood in brass.[40]

Perhaps it was the reputation of Greenwood as an innovator of capacity that prompted his friend, Hiram Powers, the noted Cincinnati sculptor, to solicit his assistance in a manufacturing venture. Writing to Greenwood from Florence, Italy, in 1858, Powers dramatically announced that he was the "fond Parent" of a child "naturalized" in three countries.[41] His "child" was a "powerful and simple" punching machine capable of punching holes rapidly through a sheet of one-quarter-inch iron. It weighed sixty-two pounds and could be produced for about $10, said Powers; its main usage would be punching hoops for cotton baling. Greenwood, Powers believed, was the American manufacturer to test and produce his remarkable device. Greenwood agreed, saying that he would be happy to receive the "machine of your invention." [42] Evidently, Powers sent a model to Greenwood, but whether he ever manufactured the machine is problematical.

Whatever the case, it would have been only a minor item in the mammoth output of the Greenwood works. By the end of the 1850's, the ironmaster had created a complex of founding activities that summarized nearly thirty years of innovation and expansion. In 1859, as reported by Cist, an "endless" number of castings—plain and ornamental, made from iron and brass, and ranging in size from one-twentieth of an ounce to ten tons—were fashioned in the Eagle Iron Works. It was the diversity of Greenwood's line that, asserted Cist, enabled the firm to maintain its labor force without layoffs during slack periods.[43] Afforded security by diversity were over five hundred mechanics and laborers who worked in the several departments or "branches," some of which supposedly were using techniques of assembly line production. With few exceptions, each department was turning out more production in its speciality than any other similarly specialized foundry in the area. Using the 1850 figure for capital invested per employee at the Greenwood works, one can estimate the capitalized value of the firm at $360,000.[44] The works covered about four acres.

The Steam Heating Department, organized in the early 1850's, was one of the prime departments. Here two principal types of heating equipment were produced. For purposes of high steam heating by "dried radiation," steam pipe arranged in coils was manufactured.[45] It was used usually in large buildings where a "practical engineer" was available. Low steam heating required the fabrication of radiators or cases, which could be covered with slabs of marble to enhance the appearance of the drawing room of the private residences where they were typically in use. In the manufacture of radiators, Greenwood was an innovator in the use of cast iron. "Here again," declared Cist, "the spirit of western improvement has displayed itself, in the introduction of *cast* instead of *sheet* iron radiators." [46] The cast iron was more durable than the sheet iron and distributed heat more uniformly. Cost of the steam heating equipment ran from $250 to $30,000 and more, depending on the size of the building in which it was installed. Another important department was the Machine Department. Here were produced a variety of stationary and portable steam engines, planing and saw mills, hydraulic presses, mill machinery, printing presses, and other producers' goods.[47] Castings of ten tons were not uncommon in the department. Yet another area working in large castings was the Iron House Fronts Department. Iron fronts for one to five story buildings took form here. For a one-story or a first-story installation, a front could be cast, fitted, and erected within a week after the order was received.[48] But for a five-story building with basement and subcellar piers, about three months elapsed from order to installation. Greenwood's fronts were adorning buildings in St. Louis, New Orleans, Chicago, Memphis, Nashville, and in many other cities in the West and South.

In several departments, Greenwood's technology in small castings reputedly was superb. Butt hinges, the sole castings of one department, were yet a source of glory for Greenwood, having driven imported hinges from the market as they earned

demand throughout the United States.[49] The parade of articles
produced in the malleable iron department almost defied classi-
fication: "ingenious" locks, wardrobe hooks and door bolts,
bridle bits and stirrups, piano stools and ottomans, shovels and
tong stands, garden seats, and furniture casters. The Steam
Heating Department was noted for its excellent iron and brass
valves, oil cups and globes, and the like. They were, said Cist,
as "perfect as possible" and superior to eastern production.[50]
For house furnishings and carriage trimmings, the Silver Plate
Department workers plied their trade.[51] Known for fine design
and finish were the Burton stoves cast in the Stove Department.
Also important to the comfort of the home was the equipment
manufactured in the Gas Apparatus Department.

As the Civil War approached, Greenwood, then, stood as a
giant among ironmasters of the West. He had become its
Hiram of Tyre. When the war came, he would be ready with
the physical capacity and the innovative drive to serve the
nation. He would be ready, flexible in mind and facilities, to
transform the Eagle Iron Works into a veritable arsenal for the
Union. Whether the nation would or could effectively utilize
his Eagle Iron Works was another question.

II

As he was making his mark in industry, Greenwood was
winning prominence as a civic leader. In civic affairs, as in his
industrial life, he was an able organizer and leader committed
to innovation. He was a many-sided man, set not in a Renais-
sance frame, but rather standing as an exemplar of the industrial prince of his day, privileged to demand status and to
accept responsibility in the throbbing life of the urbanized
order that he and other industrialists were creating.

His first important taste of community service came in 1840,
coincidentally the year of his new venture in the foundry trade,

when he ran for and won a seat on the city council.[52] He earned some repute as a poor man's advocate by opposing a proposal to charter a gas company, arguing that the company's ensuing monopoly power would result in raising gas prices beyond a point that poor people could afford to pay. It was a performance that must have endeared him to fellow Whigs, who were then challenging the Jacksonians for the role of champions of the masses. Otherwise, his record was undistinguished, and he decided not to run for re-election, evidently feeling that the politician's life was too circuitous for a forthright businessman.

Withdrawing from the political arena, Greenwood next entered the antiseptic world of academe. The board of directors of the Ohio Mechanics Institute, seeking a man of "influence" in the city, elected him president of the board in 1847.[53] Established in 1828 as a school for education in the mechanic arts, the Institute had led a marginal existence, occasionally enjoying a streak of prosperity but more frequently falling on hard times. Greenwood's election came as the Institute, having moved from building to building in the past, had resolved to raise funds for the acquisition of a site for a permanent home.[54] The next several years saw Greenwood engaged in a number of subscription drives on behalf of the school. Greenwood himself subscribed nearly $3,000 in the period and subsequently loaned the Institute over $12,000.[55] Though the directors unquestionably "used" him, he undoubtedly was sincerely interested in the "practical" education offered by the school. It was a day when businessmen were only beginning to develop a modicum of respect for formal education in business and engineering. As the Institute was attempting to solidify its position, another college dedicated to "practical" education—Farmers' College—was being raised on the outskirts of Cincinnati; and it, too, was soliciting the community for funds. But when Greenwood's active support of the Institute ended in 1855, it had achieved some degree of stability, derived in large part from the unselfish efforts of Greenwood.

While he was serving academe, Greenwood also was looking
to the welfare of homeless children. As a director and treasurer
of the House of Refuge, established in 1850 to care for or-
phaned and abandoned children, he persuaded skeptical directors to approve the organization of a children's band at the
House. To their contention that the House children would
enjoy greater privileges than the children of the common
schools received, he rejoined that the House of Refuge was an
"uncommon" school needing special privileges to lift the children's spirits. As Greenwood recalled it, the "music made a
wonderful change; the boys who played were as proud as could
be." [56]

Greenwood's most dramatic role in community life in the
1850's was played, suitably enough, against the background of
technological change and the rational organization of men and
machines. As an entrepreneur of the first order, he had ever
been concerned with innovation and efficient organization, and
it was only normal for him to bring these drives to any activity
in which he participated. From the 1830's on he had been
active in the independent volunteer fire companies of the city,
serving as president of the Fire Association on two occasions
and earning general recognition as the unofficial spokesman of
the volunteers. The companies, which operated under city sanction and, with the exception of two companies, used city buildings and apparatus, had served the community in a responsible
manner in their early years. [57] But by the late 1840's and early
1850's, as the older members ended their service and a younger
element assumed leadership, the position of the companies was
being challenged on a number of grounds. [58] Some critics complained that the young volunteers increasingly provoked fights
between rival companies at fires. Other observers indicted the
companies as quasi-political clubs to which politicians had to
pay an unhealthy obeisance. More moralistic men lamented
that the engine houses were becoming "nurseries where the

youth of the city were trained in vice, vulgarity and debauch-
ery." [59] Greenwood himself, acknowledging the correctness of
much of the criticism, recognized the deficiencies of the independent system and came to support reform measures.

Essential reform depended on control or operation of the fire
companies by the city government. Control, in turn, ultimately
turned on the question of whether the city should purchase a
steam fire engine being constructed by Abel Shawk and Alexander Latta, two mechanic-inventors who were using Greenwood's foundry for their work. Should the city acquire the
engine, it would be implicitly committed to organizing a paid
company to protect the belching monster from rowdy volunteers who saw in it a threat to their status. Its usage would
reduce the number of firemen needed, and, more importantly,
one paid company would set the precedent for organization of
the entire fire force under city control, thus enabling officials to
elevate the obstreperous volunteers to a manageable and perhaps virtuous position. Equating reform with the acquisition
of the engine, Greenwood the innovator pressed the city council
in 1852 and 1853 to make an affirmative decision. The council,
well aware of Greenwood's standing among the volunteers,
appointed him chairman of a committee of five councilmen
and five prominent citizens to observe a trial run of the engine.
Receiving a favorable report from the committee, the council
authorized purchase of the engine and then, after protracted
debate, enacted the measure creating one paid company—a
kind of select company—one of the first in the United States.

Greenwood's responsibilities did not end with the council's
action. The council, believing that only Greenwood could in-
duce the volunteers to acquiesce in the adoption of the new
engine, offered him the post of chief engineer of the fire department. Repeatedly urged by councilmen to accept the offer, he
finally yielded, insisting, however, that he be permitted to select
members of the company. The "machine will be attacked at the

first fire," he explained, "and I want to know whom I can rely on." [60] Despite his influence with the volunteers, Greenwood was correct in his prediction. At the scene of the first fire requiring the services of the select company, his men were set on by a volunteer group. But Greenwood was ready. Driving the engine in almost childlike exuberance, speaking to his newly uniformed men through a trumpet and bedecked with a brass helmet and red shirt, the muscular Greenwood directed the company and a phalanx of men from his foundry in a brief but bloody encounter that left the volunteers crushed. The fire, too, was subdued; and at one fell swoop the volunteers, so it seems, gave up their opposition, requesting in short order integration into the paid system and use of a steam engine.[61] Because of his total commitment to the system—for a period of eighteen months he gave all his waking hours to it—Greenwood had no time for his own business. At a cost of $1,500 he employed a man to run his foundry; when the council, which had failed initially to appropriate money for salaries of department personnel, finally paid him his salary of $1,000, he turned it over to the Ohio Mechanics Institute.

The department, according to Greenwood's reports, performed its mission orderly and effectively. Greenwood's data spoke particularly of the reduction of financial losses resulting from fires in the city. In 1853, for example, though the number of fires rose one third over the number in 1851, losses were reduced by about $455,000.[62] Greenwood cited as an important factor in the reduction the effectiveness of the steam engine in extinguishing fires before they could spread. The signal system he had improvised for alerting fire companies also contributed to effective fire fighting. He asserted, moreover, that the companies had been purged of their "vulgarity and vice"; he later argued that in abolishing the old-fashioned fire-engine house and its attendant vices, he had done more for the cause of morality than many preachers.[63] The engine itself, Greenwood told an amused Baltimore deputation, was a moralistic thing: "1. It never gets drunk; 2. It never throws brickbats, and its only drawback is that it can't vote." [64]

Greenwood served as chief until 1855, resigning when he believed the department to be on a firm footing. At his departure, a group of eminent Cincinnati citizens expressed their appreciation in a testimonial recognizing the excellent attributes of Greenwood: "The undersigned, Citizens of Cincinnati, deeply impressed with the value of the services rendered, by Miles Greenwood Esq. as Chief Engineer of the Fire Department, during the two years, he has acted in that capacity, propose to express, in some substantial testimonial, their regard for said services, and the energy and self-sacrificing spirit, with which they have been bestowed, and for that purpose agree to pay the sums annexed to their names. . . ." [65] At least sixty-eight signatures were attached, each signer pledging $25.00 or more. Throughout his involvement in the reorganization of the fire department, Greenwood had displayed his characteristic innovative and organizational drives, the qualities carrying him to prominence in the industrial world.

Greenwood's capacity for practical and novel answers also appeared in his work for the Covington and Cincinnati Suspension Bridge Company. Elected to the board of directors in 1856, serving for four years and then elected for another two years in 1862, he played a relatively modest part in the construction of the suspension bridge across the Ohio River—except in one critical aspect: his position in the community stamped the company with an imprint of stability that it could not otherwise have enjoyed. But his genius for novelty served the company in another way. Sometime after construction had begun (which was suspended from 1857 to 1863), John Roebling, the renowned civil engineer from the East who had been employed to build the span, came to Greenwood—so Greenwood later stated—admitting his inability to remove the water from the cylinders for the emplacement of the bridge pillars. As the Greenwood mind remembered it, the fumbling Roebling had

. . . put into the place a number of men, and they were dipping out with tin cups and buckets, and the water kept pouring in. One day Roebling came to my foundry and told me he could not get out the water for the placing of his pillars. I pointed to a little pump on my desk, and said to him if he had one made like that and with a cylinder large enough he could have the work done in a short time. He asked if it were patented. I said yes; to which he replied that he did not want anything of the kind. One day I told one of my men to make a pump of a certain size capable of throwing an immense volume of water. It was put near the foundry, and for weeks Roebling held out and would not use it. One day however, he came into the foundry, and taking off his hat and bowing low, said he would use the pump. I replied; now you see I was right when I told you we knew something this side of the mountains. Then I had the water pumped out and it took five hours.[66]

It was more than a triumph of the Greenwood genius; it was clearly a victory of western novelty over eastern tradition. As one observer saw it, Greenwood was exhilarated at the opportunity to humble Roebling: "The pump was put in position, and so anxious was the Ohio manufacturer, inventor and engineer to show the distrusting foreigner from the East what he could do, that he made ready the place for the towers in the night-time, in five hours." [67]

In his service in the governmental and educational fields, Greenwood manifested a real concern for the lot of the "plain" people. He displayed no trace of cant or self-seeking in this role; nor did he parade in haughty manner his service to the community. He was a successful entrepreneur whose business life did not separate him from the everyday life of the community. And yet his service was not motivated, perhaps, out of a generalized concept of duty to the community. Indeed, it sprang in part from duty to the self. For he was, it seems, a typical characterological product of mid-nineteenth-century America, a man who had to satisfy internalized goals of success. An "inner-directed" man, he thrived on the novel opportunities offered by rapidly changing economic and urban conditions

hardly susceptible to management by "tradition-directed" individuals. Still more opportunities for exploitation lay in the
Civil War. All his life hitherto seemed almost a prelude for the
struggle; the war of iron could give the man of iron yet another
dimension.

III

As the secession crisis mounted in 1861, Cincinnati merchants and manufacturers sounded calls for conciliation that
might preserve the status quo and thus spare them the loss of
southern markets on which much of their prosperity rested.
Annually, Cincinnati pork, beef, liquor, soap, iron goods, and
leather products moved in large quantities to the South via the
inland waterways; and the business community quailed at the
thought of the interdiction of the waterways. Besides economic
ties, social ties generated considerable pro-southern feeling in
the community.[68] Living in the city was the progeny of early
settlers who had migrated to Ohio from Virginia, North Carolina, and Kentucky. Sons and daughters of many leading Cincinnati families had been marrying the scions of the planter
aristocracy of the Black Belt, their marriages often taking place
in the plush hotels of the city. And further shaping a southern
tone in the city were the southern gentlemen who flocked there
during the summer months to taste the life of the rake in the
wicked city. These economic and social ties had no meaning for
Miles Greenwood. Though no abolitionist, he was a totally
dedicated Unionist. He had supported Lincoln and the Republican party in 1860, his enthusiasm for the ticket probably
heightened by the party's probusiness stance. When Lincoln
stopped in Cincinnati in February of 1861 on his way to Washington, Greenwood was the grand marshal of the procession in
which the rail-splitter rode through the Queen City.[69]
The coming of the war saw the fears of the business commu-

nity realized. With the closing of the Mississippi River, trade fell off appreciably. Merchants and manufacturers alike felt the impact of loss of the Dixie markets. According to Chamber of Commerce reports, general iron goods producers, as well as furniture manufacturers, ceased all capital investment as they looked fearfully to the future.[70] Receipts in the iron industry were off 70 per cent in 1861, would lag in 1862, and would not begin to recover noticeably until 1863.[71] But good times or bad times, the protean Greenwood was on the move. Indeed, the war set him on a course of innovation, experiment, and expansion. Unlike other foundry proprietors of Cincinnati and the Miami Valley, he was able and willing to transform his facilities into a virtual arsenal. Other valley founders, perhaps enjoying a war-sustained demand for consumer goods, did not give their resources over to efforts that might require pouring of unfamiliar castings and the fabricating of related flasks and cores. In fact, proprietors of foundries and machine shops, the best-suited establishments for arms production, were almost oblivious to the tools of carnage.[72] (Of course, some westerners alleged that the War Department favored eastern manufacturers in awarding contracts.) Before ascribing unalloyed patriotism to Greenwood, one should note that his large-scale operation permitted reasonably easy organization of resources for production of military matériel.

The first two years of the war—the period of improvisation and search for a coherent organization of the war effort—truly were the vintage years for Greenwood. His opportunities emanated, in part in fact, from the inchoate nature of mobilization for war as both state and national governments girded for action. In 1861 the bulk of his work served state governments, which, of course, early in the war were vigorously—if somewhat flailingly—engaged in procurement of supplies for state militia forces.[73]

Greenwood's first important war project was a characteristic effect of the improvised war, and it was a characteristic triumph of the ironmaster's flexibility. Only a few days after the firing on Fort Sumter, the state of Ohio, taking on the burden of raising and equipping volunteers, called on the Eagle Iron Works to "modernize" a large stock of flintlock muskets (.69 caliber Springfields) that had been provided to the state by the national government.[74] To recondition the muskets, percussioning, rifling, and sighting were required. For the rifling, Greenwood designed and constructed machines supposedly capable of working up three thousand pieces a day.[75] His machinists took up the task with patriotic fervor, and the reconditioned muskets were soon being turned out. Testing of a run took place in June of 1861, with reportedly excellent results. According to the *Cincinnati Commercial*, the Greenwood weapon was pitted against Enfields, Colts, and United States regulation muskets firing from a ninety-foot distance at a three-eighths-inch sheet of steel; the Greenwood rifle, said the *Commercial*, proved superior to its competitors in accuracy and penetrative force.[76] The *Commercial* story was picked up by *Scientific American*, which reported Greenwood's success to the nation.[77] Later tests demonstrated conclusively that firing would not burst the barrel, as some experts feared, and that the recoil action would not injure the user.[78] Evidently, soldiers at Camp Dennison, near Cincinnati, did not read either publication. There, one regiment, promised "modern" rifles, was issued the "Greenwood rifles," as they were often called; at first the men flatly refused to accept them, and only the oratorical skills of an officer brought them to a more reasonable state of mind.[79] As the war progressed, the rifle apparently won considerable respect among troops. In 1862 the quartermaster general of Ohio reported that in "precision and range it is said to be fully equal to the celebrated 'Enfield,' while it carries a much heavier weight of metal, and is consequently much more destructive." [80] Virtually the same language was employed after the war by Whitelaw Reid, the chronicler of Ohio in the Civil War; the rifle was, he wrote, "held by the troops the equal of the Enfields in precision and range, and more destructive, inasmuch as it carries a heavier weight of metal." [81] It should be noted, however, that in 1863 nearly four thousand reconditioned muskets were listed by the quartermaster general as unserviceable; presumably these pieces were Greenwood's production, since no other contractor rifled appreciable numbers for the state.[82]

It must have been a rewarding task for Greenwood—both from a patriotic and monetary standpoint. In all, he altered 26,533 muskets at $1.25 a piece.[83] He also was paid $1.75 for each breech sight added to one-twentieth of the total number rifled, or approximately 1,326 sights. Though rifled originally for Ohio, 3,040 of the Greenwood rifles were sent to the state of Indiana in September of 1861; and apparently about two thousand were delivered in October to Major General John Frémont, whose Western Department desperately needed arms.[84] Including a cost of $4,259.94 for the rifles sent to Frémont, Greenwood was paid a total of $37,726.48 for his reconditioning work.[85] The bill ultimately was paid by the national government, which assumed responsibility for state commitments.

Greenwood followed completion of his rifling work with several proposals to recondition more muskets for Ohio and the national government, meeting rejection in every case. He was suggesting to Ohio in January of 1862 that a smooth bore percussion gun—of unidentified caliber—would make an excellent weapon if rifled; the adjutant general's office believed the caliber, whatever it was, to be too large for effective rifling, and Greenwood's proposal was dismissed.[86] To the national government, he proposed in February of 1862 the percussioning and rifling of 2,250 muskets at the Pittsburgh arsenal at $3.00 each.[87] He particularly noted his rifling capability, explaining that the "rifling is done with three grooves, which we consider better than most, as the gun can be kept clean much easier." [88] His technology did not impress the Ordnance Department, and nothing came of his bid. He was similarly rebuffed in a proposal to alter flintlocks captured at Fort Donelson.[89] Likewise, his offer in July of 1862 to recondition a large stock of muskets—about twenty thousand—at the St. Louis arsenal was turned aside.[90] Unfortunately for Greenwood, the government was then receiving adequate numbers of new .58 caliber Springfield rifles, the basic weapon of Union infantry.

In addition to "modernizing" muskets for Ohio, Greenwood's Eagle Iron Works in 1861 and 1862 was casting smooth bore and rifled bronze cannon. At the outset of the war, Governor William Dennison rejected Greenwood's offer to cast guns for the state, saying that the state, having already purchased twenty-four six-pound rifled cannons, had no further need for field artillery.[91] But by September—after Bull Run— Greenwood had received an order from the state for forty-three six-pound bronze rifled cannons; [92] and by December his orders totalled thirty six-pound smooth bore and forty-three six-pound rifled cannons.[93] Greenwood's charge was fifty cents a pound for the smooth bores and fifty-eight cents for the rifled guns (they typically weighed 870 pounds each) ; later these prices evidently were scaled down by four and six cents a pound. Some confusion attended Greenwood's contractual responsibilities, Greenwood believing that his work did not require sighting of the cannon but the adjutant general's office contending—and successfully so—that it did include sighting. By July of 1862, Greenwood had cast all the cannon, receiving eventually $31,556.76 for his work.[94]

Greenwood also was performing work of an emergency nature in 1861 and 1862 for clients outside the state. For Indiana, whose governor, Oliver Morton, held Greenwood in high regard, he was casting in July of 1861, vaguely reported a Cincinnati newspaper, "two batteries of brass cannon." [95] By the end of 1861, so an analysis of Ordnance Department records indicates, he had turned out for the state fourteen six-pound smooth bores, eight six-pound rifled cannons, and twelve twelve-pound howitzers, their cost totalling $13,430.73.[96] Referring to a lot of these guns twenty years later, Greenwood proudly recalled that "we made the guns for Morton's men, the first who were ready for the fight."[97] Probably, too, Greenwood delivered to the state in 1862 two more six-pound smooth bores and two twelve-pound howitzers costing $1,573.54. He also supplied the state with at least six six-pound gun carriages in 1861—at a price of $1,710.[98] And in 1861 he produced at a price of $102.23 a small quantity of cannon balls and canister.[99] In addition to supplying Frémont with rifles, Greenwood manufactured for him on twenty-four hours' notice twelve anchors for pontoon bridges;[100] and he also was asked in September of 1861 to cast cannon for Frémont's command—but it is not apparent that he did so.[101] So great had demand for his war matériel become by late 1861 that Greenwood introduced gas lighting to the first three floors of his main building; his labor force, now numbering over seven hundred, was set to work through the evening hours until 9:00 P.M.[102]

As a contractor for the national government, Greenwood ran a course of success, then frustration, and finally failure. His first substantial contract, issued in February of 1862, called for the manufacture of fifty twelve-pound bronze field guns, known usually as "Napoleons." The negotiation of the contract represented a tribute to Greenwood's reputation—or friendship with influential men. Initially, the Ordnance Department proposed a price of forty-six cents a pound for the guns.[103] Replying to Brigadier General James Ripley, chief of the Department, Greenwood pointed out that since he had last cast a lot of bronze guns, the price of copper had advanced from twenty-two cents a pound to twenty-eight cents and tin from twenty-seven cents to thirty-six cents.[104] He could not, explained Greenwood, accept an order of forty-six cents a pound in the light of such increased costs. Greenwood went to Washington to present his case to General George B. McClellan, then commanding all Union armies. McClellan, who, as president of the eastern division of the Ohio and Mississippi Railroad, had known Greenwood in Cincinnati in the late 1850's, took the ironmaster's arguments to the secretary of war, Edwin Stanton, who had but a short time earlier asked Greenwood to inspect the Washington Arsenal for him.[105] McClellan believed Greenwood's word to be beyond question and recommended approval of the request for an increase to fifty-two cents a pound.[106] "Mr. G's well known reputation induces me," he told Stanton, "to give full credit to his statement without further enquiry." Perhaps not wishing to seem imperious, McClellan acknowledged that the secretary ought to satisfy himself as to the correctness of the price. He further supported his recommendation by stressing that it was important for the government to develop cannon-making capacity in the West. Within two days after receipt of McClellan's letter, Stanton approved the issuance of a contract incorporating the increase in price.[107] At the time no contractor in the nation was receiving more than forty-six cents a pound for twelve-pounders, and none would receive more until September of 1862.

Perhaps McClellan's intervention bore other fruit for Greenwood. In his beseeching letter to Stanton, McClellan had noted Greenwood's capacity for producing gun carriages, remarking that it was "a matter of great interest & importance." Only three days after approval of the gun contract, Greenwood received an order for the manufacture of carriages and related equipment—fifty gun carriages, fifty caissons, eight forges, and eight field battery wagons.[108] By October of 1862 nearly all the contracted items—guns and complementary gear—had been completed at the Eagle Iron Works, inspected, and turned over to the army. For the carriages and caissons, Greenwood was paid $43,593.60.[109] His payment for the guns was $31,482.36. For artillery of all sort produced for Ohio, Indiana, and the national government, his payments totalled $84,157.68.[110] Altogether, in 1861 and 1862, the only years in which he cast cannon, Greenwood produced forty-six six-pound smooth bores, fifty-one six-pound rifled guns, fifty twelve-pound Napoleons, and fourteen twelve-pound howitzers. He thus cast 161 field pieces of the some eight thousand pieces produced in the North during the war. Small though his contribution was, it did come during the early years when the need was acute. And judged by one simple standard, his cannon work was impressive: no other contractor in the West supplied cannon to the government. But in ordnance work for the national government, two western firms producing projectiles and small arms—Thomas Howard & Company of St. Louis in shells and case-shot and Kittredge & Company of Cincinnati in rifles—were recipients of larger contracts, totalling $130,344.56 and $160,581.00 respectively. Of course, Greenwood's contract work of all kinds exceeded these figures. In the East several cannon men dwarfed Greenwood, Robert Parrott of New York, for instance, manufacturing Parrott guns costing in excess of $4,000,000.

As he pursued his rifling and cannon work, Greenwood also was urging the national government to consider the merits of several experimental and innovative projects. Early in the war, he requested the Ordnance Department to undertake a "practical" testing of a model of a breech-loading cannon—possibly Walter Sherwin's Cincinnati Breech-loading Cannon.[111] Ripley, the conservative head of the department, was almost intransigent in his opposition to breech-loaders; and, not surprisingly, Greenwood's request apparently was shunted aside. His proposal to cast iron cannon—a proposal that Greenwood viewed as innovative—met a similar fate. In early February of 1862, he indicated to McClellan that he stood ready to manufacture "heavy" iron guns.[112] The casting of large iron guns—twenty-pounders, for instance—was not commonplace in the day. It required the use of superior pig iron, which was not easily obtainable owing to the still imprecise state of the metallurgical arts. It entailed problems in the cooling and shrinkage of the iron cast, which gave rise to defects revealed often only when the gun blew up. And it involved not insignificant outlays for new cores and flasks. Greenwood, nonetheless, would assume the risks of production if an order of sufficient quantity would be given. He carried his offer to Ripley, describing his facilities—shops, tools, machinery, and so forth—for manufacturing.[113] He would, he said, use the best quality iron procurable in the West. Before he could consider turning to such a project, however, he would have to know at what price and in what quantity the government would order the guns. Greenwood also noted that because of the scarcity of timber for gun carriages he wished to call Ripley's attention to the "propriety" of making the carriages of wrought or cast iron or of steam-seasoned timber. The ironman did not specify what size gun he had in mind, but it probably mattered little. Ripley, a champion of bronze guns, was averse to the use of iron and steel cannon;[114] and Greenwood's offer came to naught, receiving scant attention from Ripley.

Frustrated in innovation, Greenwood turned to more conventional proposals only to meet with bureaucratic repulse, his connections with the War Department serving him little purpose. Shortly after negotiation of the contract for the Napoleons, he sought a contract for the production of one hundred ten-inch Columbiads, promising to deliver the guns at the rate of three a week.[115] But for reasons unrevealed in Ordnance Department correspondence, no contract was issued. (The silence of Ordnance contract records is eloquent testimony of rejection.) Then, his work on the Napoleon contract nearly completed, Greenwood attempted to secure a contract in August of 1862 for the delivery of fifty more twelve-pounders and complementary equipment.[116] Ripley promptly and curtly informed him that all carriages and related equipment would henceforth be produced at government arsenals, with no contracts to be farmed out.[117] As to the guns, Ripley would make no assurances, stating only that Greenwood would have to indicate the *lowest* price at which he would furnish the guns. His price, whatever it was, availed him nothing; once again a cannon contract was denied him. Perhaps his prices were above those of eastern manufacturers, as had been the case in early 1862; or perhaps the increasing output of easterners that rendered needs less urgent diminished the image of Greenwood in bureaucratic eyes.

In late 1862, despite Greenwood's inability to secure all the contracts he desired, the Eagle Iron Works was pouring forth a torrent of military goods. As described by an exulting *Cincinnati Enquirer* newsman, it was virtually an armory. Small but essential items being produced under contract included bridle bits, stirrups, and musket sights.[118] Under government order, 150,000 bayonet sheath tips were being manufactured. At a cost of $30,000, 130 gun carriages were being produced for the navy. Brass guns of "beautiful finish" were being rifled. A "number of steel guns" were being cast for experimental purposes; these guns were testing satisfactorily, while those cast in the East and sent to Greenwood for finishing had exploded (another western triumph!). An ironclad gunboat was also being constructed.[119] The works, reported the *Enquirer*, had already turned out nearly two hundred bronze cannons of various types—a slight exaggeration—and the total value of production for government agencies had passed $250,000. Though an impressive gathering of production, except for the ironclad monitor and the cannon, not one of the items listed can yet be accounted for in ordnance, quartermaster or navy records; but surely the *Enquirer* man had some reliable evidence on which to base an account of such panoplied production. The Eagle Iron Works, in any case, was the setting for an exemplification of the industrial might that the North could muster for war; and it was a representation of the entrepreneurship that had molded sinews of strength.

Notwithstanding the press of government commitments, Greenwood was willing to give his attention and support to a venture in innovation promising little immediate rewards. In 1861 Richard Gatling of Indianapolis, a former resident of Cincinnati, sought Greenwood's assistance in testing his ideas for the development of a rapid-fire gun, which, of course, would become in elaborated form the celebrated Gatling Gun. According to Gatling, he "had a loyal friend in Miles Greenwood, and he was a friend in time of need." Short of funds, Gatling "confided in him and he gave me liberties in his plant. . . . The Greenwood Plant was working full capacity and it was with difficulty that good men could be spared from their own departments for experimental work, but Mr. Greenwood gave me access to lathe or force as the necessity required. . . ." [120] Thus assisted, Gatling was able to cast a prototype. Tested before a gathering of army officers, the model fired over two hundred rounds per minute, later firing over one thousand rounds. The model was then placed on exhibition in the foundry, its appearance winning the acclaim of Cincinnati newspapers.[121] As the *Cincinnati Gazette* reported it, Greenwood had begun production and would be ready to supply one a day to the army at the issuance of a contract. By December six guns had been cast, but a fire in the same month, ignited by sparks from a furnace, destroyed Gatling's "revolving rifles" and his drawings. Gatling then took his idea to another Cincinnati firm, which finally cast thirteen guns. He later declared that "the fire that burned the Greenwood Plant saved many lives." [122] His weapon did not, in fact, gain much attention until near the end of the war.

Failing to secure additional contracts from the War Department in 1862, Greenwood successfully offered his services to the navy for construction of a sea-going ironclad monitor. Probably, he had become interested in ironclads in early 1862. Stanton, in March of 1862 (a few days after the "Merrimac-Monitor" engagement), had requested the president of the board of trade in Cincinnati to find three men who were familiar with steamboats and engine-building and who "from patriotic motives" would give thirty days to "purchasing and preparing" means of defense on western waters against ironclads.[123] Among the three men appointed was Greenwood, who surely gave the assignment his customary verve. Possibly it gave him an inside track in seeking a monitor contract. In any case, he was awarded a contract in September of 1862 for the construction of the U.S.S. "Tippecanoe," a single-turret monitor to be completed within six months.[124] Initially authorizing an expenditure of $460,000, the contract easily was the largest issued to Greenwood during the war and provided his firm with the bulk of its work in 1863 and 1864.

If Greenwood regarded award of the contract as a great tribute to him, he soon found it to be a Pyrrhic victory. As he recalled the course of the work, navy engineers assigned to develop plans for the monitor "blundered outrageously." Incompetent men, they committed design and construction errors that prolonged work and as a result saddled Greenwood with costs, particularly wages, far beyond the contracted sum.[125] The government, said Greenwood, refused to accept responsibility for the additional expenses; but he continued with construction. To acquire funds for completion of the work, he sold a part of the foundry. When he finished the monitor, Greenwood did not submit his claims to the government because it was financially "burdened" at the time! Eventually, he sought relief but never received adequate compensation, and the resulting loss acted as a drag on the Eagle Iron Works for many years. As the *Commercial* remarked, it was an ironic turn of events: "The manufacturers of shoddy goods grew rich; the patriotic, enterprising genius and constructor of the most terrible engine of the war was ruined, almost, in his country's interests." [126] Patriotism, it seems, was its own reward. That a competent, experienced businessman should have hesitated to present legitimate claims to the government seems incredible. His failure to seek payment suggests, of course, that Greenwood was in some way at fault.

Yet Greenwood's self-justification and view of bureaucratic incompetence had some validity when set in the light of navy records. In the performance of work for the army—which always was satisfactory—Greenwood enjoyed a free hand, only submitting his cannon to army inspection at their completion and otherwise going about his business without interference. But in the construction of the "Tippecanoe," a sophisticated vessel for its day, he was subjected to constant inspection by navy personnel and was innundated by a stream of orders for alterations of design and construction details. He had hardly started work when the flow of corrections and modifications of drawings began. First, in October of 1862, a minor correction calling for armor boltheads to be applied flush to armor rather than as "button-heads" was issued by the general inspector's office.[127] Then changes in the timber within the sponsors, the sponsor plate, and in the sponsors were ordered.[128] Other modification orders followed in pell-mell fashion. At the suggestion of John Ericsson, the great designer of the "Monitor," alterations were required in March of 1863 in the design of gun carriage friction gearing; a year later the original drawings were substituted for the altered plans.[129] In the meantime, the changes in the carriages had necessitated changes in outside gun slides.[130] In April orders were sent to Greenwood to lengthen armor stringers, to alter armor attached to the overhang aft, and to change check valves.[131] At one point, in February, the navy, questioning whether Greenwood could manufacture pumps for use in the propellor engines, insisted that he purchase them from Henry Worthington, a hydraulic engineer in New York; two months later, the navy reversed its stand, saying that acquisition of Worthington's pumps had been delayed and requesting that Greenwood build his own pumps.[132] Now that the matter was in Greenwood's hands, noted the general inspector's office, there would be no delay. Greenwood must have come to dread opening mail from that office of indecision!

In June of 1863, when completion of the "Tippecanoe" was already overdue, Alban Stimers of the general inspector's office called for a number of substantial changes in turret-house construction. Resulting from defects revealed in monitors "now afloat," the modifications applied to the "Tippecanoe" and eight other monitors under construction by contractors in the

North, including the Niles Works, which was building the "Catawba" and "Oneota." [133] According to the instructions, the "system of bolting" used on the plates forming the turret was to be changed to a "system of riveting." The railway bars used on the roof of the house were to be replaced by forged rectangular bars. The armor of the pilot house was to be ten inches thick instead of eight inches. The cover of the house was to be three inches thick instead of two inches. The grates on the smoke pipe were to be moved so that another breadth of plate could be added. And the recitation continued on. If the contractors felt aggrieved, they could take consolation in the inspector's need for a listing of the expenses entailed in the changes. "You will greatly oblige me," he wrote, "if you will examine at once into the expense of making the changes directed in this letter and send me the bill, with each item in detail."

After the issuance of the June edict, the navy circulated in the next few months a variety of orders for minor changes.[134] Often, the changes set Greenwood in a haggling match with the general inspector's office. His request, for instance, for $496 for proposed alterations in the iron work around the gunports met a curt pronouncement that the maximum payment for the work would be $495.[135] If Greenwood would not make the changes at that price, the navy would find someone who would. Greenwood did the work at $495. He was similarly treated in his proposals for changes in port-stoppers, though the difference of $130 seemed to justify the Navy's position.[136]

The "Tippecanoe" work must have been a stifling experience for a man who had characteristically been a creature of action and independence. It involved him in a sea of paperwork arising from design changes and other problems. In the world of iron, Greenwood was at home; but in the world of paper, he was at sea. In December of 1862, for example, the navy was asking him for estimates of increased costs incurred in modifications; in April of 1863, it was still asking for them; and in July, it was still seeking them.[137] Nearly eight months after

Stimers had requested Greenwood to supply credentials for his engineer, N. G. Thorn, the navy yet awaited them; Stimers finally moved Greenwood by saying that Thorn's correspondence would not be "noted" until the papers were provided.[138] More importantly, Greenwood's freedom of action was reduced to a nullity as he awaited orders from navy engineers. Greenwood could not, said Stimers, launch the "Tippecanoe" without the boilers on board; he could not suspend work on the pilot house shaft—he could not do this—he could not do that—and so it went.[139] In a more tangible way, the "Tippecanoe" was a burdensome weight for Greenwood. For the additional costs incurred in performing modifications, both for materials and labor, he was paid $173,327.84 (making a total expenditure of $633,327.84), an amount that he contended was far below his actual expenses.[140] In his opinion the navy failed to give proper account to the serious problems he had faced. The interruption to work occasioned by the approach of Morgan's raiders to the doorsteps of Cincinnati in 1863 and the delays caused by the navy, so he alleged later, had come at a time when inflationary pressures were driving up prices of material and labor beyond the levels at which the navy calculated his increased costs.[141] In the decade after the war, as will be noted later, Greenwood persisted in this argument.

As the changes and costs mounted, time passed while the navy awaited delivery of the "Tippecanoe." At the end of 1863, it was not finished; and at the end of 1864, it remained landlocked at the Eagle Iron Works. Evidently, the main obstacle to completion then was a labor shortage. In early January of 1865, the general inspector of steam machinery for the navy, his attention called to the "deficiency" of workmen, politely informed Greenwood that he hoped the government would not be kept waiting because of "non-employment of hands." [142] With less restraint, he reminded Greenwood in late January of the navy's urgent need for the "Tippecanoe." [143] By June of 1865, the vessel was still unfinished, and not until March of

1866—some few months after the war had ended—was it finally delivered to the navy. Displacing 1,034 tons, it was later named the "Vesuvius," then the "Wyandotte"; in 1873 and 1874 it was rebuilt at a cost of $196,250.[144]

His work for the government, inherently productive of new managerial problems, gave rise to another problem that Greenwood had not encountered as a producer for the market place. Known as an ardent Unionist, he was subjected to harassment by some pro-southern men in the city, who, rumor had it, frequently set fires at his works. "When the friends of the Southern Confederacy," recounted a contemporary historian, "found that neither their entreaties, nor threats of the loss of Southern custom, could prevail upon him to forbear in aiding the Government, by furnishing warlike material, they resorted to intimidation, setting the establishment on fire three several times, involving a loss of $100,000; but the attempt, so far from inciting timidity, tended to arouse his courage and renew his energy." [145] Reporting one of the fires, an "extensive blaze," the *Gazette* limned Greenwood as one who "seems invincible, and [who] will proceed immediately with both repairs and business." [146] In the eyes of some viewers, his business was political in orientation. According to a Copperhead newspaper, Greenwood used his employees for political purposes. A Union demonstration in Cincinnati, sneered the Hamilton *True Telegraph,* was attended only by "Protestant priests, boarding-house pimps, Miles Greenwood's slaves." [147]

Greenwood's employees certainly were not "slaves," and apparently Greenwood never had any serious disputes with his labor force over wages and hours or other issues. Yet, as intimated by the view of him as a despot over his workers during the war, Greenwood tended throughout his life to assume paternal authority over them and other men coming under his direction. Possessed of an excellent physique and leonine in aspect, he was almost naturally given to the role of the "father-person" and in fact was generally known among his

employees as the "Old Man." [148] In a directive way, for instance,
he used his workers to assist him in putting down the unruly
volunteer firemen; and to make direction effective, he insisted
on personally selecting members of his fire company. As the
solicitous patriarch, he gathered his tribe around him to celebrate his triumphant days in industry, holding a dinner and
dance for about a thousand employees and their families on the
occasion of his fifty-fifth birthday and thirtieth anniversary in
the foundry business. He acted the role, one Cincinnati historian has said, of Fezziwig, Scrooge's employer.[149] As a protec-
tor of the working class, he sought to keep gas prices at a
reasonable level, and it was often for the benefit of working-
class sons in military service that he supported the Western
Sanitary Commission. He exerted his protective influence especially on behalf of children, as evidenced, for example, by his
service to the House of Refuge. For the "many boys" employed
at his works at the end of the Civil War, supposedly because
they had been thrust into the breadwinner's place by the death
of their fathers on the battlefield, he provided, for a while,
educational instruction; when they resisted his well-meaning
efforts, his "feelings were badly wounded." He was also concerned for the moral welfare of his boys, urging them to forgo
the use of whiskey and tobacco—particularly when his largess
might contribute to a moral lapse. As one of the boys described
it, "There were more than a hundred boys employed about the
various departments. During my five years' apprenticeship he
never failed to present every boy in his employ with spending
money every Christmas and every Fourth of July. . . . He did
not omit the usual injunction: 'No whiskey, no
cigars. . . .'" [150] In the context of inner-direction, his "paternal regard for young employees" probably flowed from a sense
of duty to implant in their minds ideals of correct behavior.
(To "be good" was standard counsel set before children by
inner-directed adults of the day.)

Greenwood's propensity for the directive part had been af-

forded full play during the Civil War, but it also had been
restrained at one critical point by external, bureaucratic controls. But the ironmaster had served the nation well in a great
crisis, one that had given him the opportunity to exercise his
entrepreneurial genius and to utilize his physical facilities in
the name of patriotism. At once it had been a rewarding and
frustrating experience. He had reached dazzling heights in
1862, his Eagle Iron Works then turning out a vast array of war
matériel. But the unhappy monitor work begun in that year
marked, unfortunately, the decline of Greenwood and his Eagle
Iron Works.

IV

The tag end of the Civil War and the ensuing years saw
many changes in ownership of Greenwood's facilities, stemming
in part probably from the financial reverses arising out of the
monitor fiasco and the subsequent need for operating funds.
The foundryman sold a portion of his foundry in 1864. His
association with Gates and Folger as Greenwood and Company
was terminated in the same year, T. B. Paddock and P. Y.
Brown becoming his new partners.[151] In 1866 he sold a share of
the malleable iron branch to his son William, and in that year
he found purchasers—Charles Wilson and James Paddock—for
a part of the steam-heating department, which they operated
for a few years as the Greenwood Pipe Company. Greenwood
still had expansive ideas, though, entering into a partnership
with Palmon Powell in 1867 for the manufacture of railroad
car springs. The venture fared badly, however, and the partnership was dissolved within a year. He then borrowed $5,000
from the Ohio Mechanics Institute to expand his foundry capacity. The loan availed him little, for his old enemy, fire,
destroyed a part of the foundry in 1869. Determined as ever, he
rebuilt the burned-out area. In 1869 or 1870 he also organized

the Greenwood Stove Company, apparently taking over the facilities of the S. H. Burton Company for the new operation. In these years he also was giving the Eagle Iron Works a minor innovative note: under a license obtained from James Leffel, an inventor and foundryman of Springfield, Ohio, the works began to manufacture Leffel's celebrated water turbine wheel, the American Double Turbine.

By 1871 the process of fragmentation had been arrested. Wilson, Brown, and the Paddocks had left the Greenwood businesses. Greenwood and his sons now enjoyed complete ownership of three firms. Greenwood himself was the sole owner of the Eagle Iron Works and the Greenwood Stove Company, and his sons William, Charles, and Edmund had joined him in the ownership of M. Greenwood and Company, which was producing goods formerly turned out by the pipe company and the malleable branch. As the decade began, the Greenwoods presided over a manufacturing complex yet imposing in dimension. In capitalized value, the Eagle Iron Works was estimated by census officials in 1870 to be worth $250,000.[152] It gave employment to 235 men and seventy-five children. The various departments were units within two divisions, the foundry and machinery divisions. Value of annual product for the foundry, which still produced a wide variety of small castings, was $170,000. For the machinery division, which turned out various types of presses, mills, and steam engines, it was estimated at $350,000. The per capita output of the 173 workers in this division was about $2,000, which, though far above the average output of 1850, was not unusual for the period. The lower product of approximately $1,200 for foundry employees very likely reflected the greater complexity and sophistication of the heavier producers' goods manufactured in the machinery division. For the stove company, which employed sixty men, the capital value was $55,000 and annual output was $20,000. Greenwood and Company had a work force of thirty, capital value of $75,000, and annual value of product of $60,000.

Altogether, then, the Greenwood works employed four hundred workers, had a capital value of $380,000, and yielded an annual product of $600,000. Compared with its position in 1850, the works had increased its labor force by fifty and could boast a substantial rise in capital value and annual value of product.[153] But since the early 1860's it had declined. Its work force had fallen off by at least three hundred, and its capital value had diminished by perhaps $100,000—that is, if the increases in employment during the Civil War years were at least partially matched by additional capital investment. In relation to other firms in the city, the Greenwood works certainly had lost ground. A number of concerns in several industries, but particularly in the metal-working industry, had outstripped it in capitalized value. To name but one, the Globe Iron Works, capitalized at $160,000 in 1850, was valued at $606,000 in 1870.

The Eagle Iron Works continued operations through the 1870's and early 1880's. But it was no longer the giant in the metal-working industry, which was now coming under the dominion of machine tool men, who looked with some disdain on the founding arts. And its great proprietor was losing much of his élan, his vitality. Little of the expansive and innovative drive that had marked his course down through the years asserted itself. Almost coincidental with his deterioration, the "Tippecanoe" problem—Greenwood's one great failure—was now resolved, but evidently in an unsatisfactory way for him. After the war, in June of 1865, various ship contractors had received in excess of $2,000,000 for costs incurred through government delays. The "Tippecanoe" being unfinished at the time, Greenwood presented no case to the Senate committee hearing testimony.[154] Then under an act of 1867, a navy board was authorized to investigate contractor's claims for losses, but the board allowed Greenwood nothing. But in 1871 Congress adopted a joint resolution calling for the "relief of certain contractors for the construction of vessels of war and steam machinery." Included among the "certain" contractors was

Greenwood. Grant vetoed the resolution, however, arguing that
it did not specify that payment would be made only when it was
clear that "ordinary diligence and prudence" had been exercised by the contractors to avoid the costs of delays. Greenwood
next asked for enactment of a private bill permitting the
United States Court of Claims to take jurisdiction of his case.
Introducing the bill for Greenwood was Senator James W. Nye
of Nevada, who, noting the protracted history of his claims and
describing him as an "upright and meritorious man," stated
that the government ought to bear the costs of navy-imposed
changes in plans, as it had in similar cases.[155] The senator did
not specify what amount of settlement Greenwood believed to
be fair. In fact, at no point in advancing his claims did Greenwood seem to stipulate approximate or exact figures. Whatever
the case, a private bill was enacted on his behalf in March of
1873. It gave him six months to submit his claims to the Court
of Claims.[156] It specified that the court could ascertain additional costs borne by Greenwood by reason of the Navy's modifications. The court could not, however, make any allowance
for any rise in the price of materials or labor unless it clearly
occurred during the "prolonged term" needed for completion
of the "Tippecanoe"—and then only if the cost could not have
been avoided by the use of "ordinary prudence." At this point,
the records are silent, nothing in the Court of Claims docket
showing that Greenwood submitted his claims. One might spec-
ulate that the conditions designated by Congress were too re-
strictive—hedged too much—and that as a consequence Greenwood the forthright decided to give up his contest with the
paper knights.

If the Greenwood works had any real possibility for renewed
growth in the 1870's, it depended probably on a successful
conclusion to Greenwood's appeal for compensation. Whether
or not the failure to initiate a claims action was a telling factor,
the Eagle Iron Works was decaying in the 1870's. The Greenwood genius was not genetic, his sons giving the firm no new

thrust. Indeed, the firm apparently was undergoing a disman-
tling process. By 1879 its capitalized value had fallen to
$25,000, its employees numbered but thirty-five and its value of
annual product was but $59,800.[157] It was almost moribund,
and its proprietor was now a mere mortal. Nevertheless, he
contemplated in the early 1880's the erection of a new foundry
for manufacturing a cooking stove that would "revolutionize"
the kitchen.[158] Nothing came of his planning, which probably
was but an old man's dreamy attempt to recapture a sense of his
former greatness. Miles Greenwood, for all his ingenuity, was
an aging man whose role of innovator had been assumed by
younger, more energetic men who were better attuned to the
new technologies of industry. Perhaps it was a source of pride
for Greenwood to observe the progress of some of his former
employees who were making their mark in the machine tool
industry in Cincinnati.

As a civic leader, too, Greenwood was no longer the giant. As
president of the board of trustees of the Cincinnati Southern
Railroad from 1870 to 1880, he was involved in the expenditure of millions of dollars in public funds for the construction
of a railroad from Cincinnati to Chattanooga.[159] He proved to
be somewhat less than wise in the discharge of his duties. His
name linked with alleged bribes of Kentucky state legislators
whose support was needed for the granting of a right of way
through the state, he appeared to testify before an investigating
commission. Though emerging with his reputation for honesty
intact, he clearly had not acted prudently. His standing as a
trustee was shaken, too, by revelations that he and railroad
employees had woefully misestimated construction costs. Of
more serious import, he and other trustees were also accused of
graft in taking bids for railroad work. They were exonerated
but were criticized for mismanagement. Greenwood's reputation as a civic servant consequently lost some of its sheen—at a
time in his life when he surely would have preferred to be
viewed as the apotheosis of wisdom and virtue.

Greenwood's death in 1885, occurring shortly after his retirement from the Eagle Iron Works, commanded lengthy columns of newsprint, his obituaries reciting in reverential language the qualities and achievements of the ironmaster.[160] Unhappily, though almost fittingly, the Eagle Iron Works fell into bankruptcy within three years after its founder's death. Without question, Greenwood had been an industrialist of imposing stature; *prima inter pares* could well have been his epitaph. He embodied many of the classic traits of the successful nineteenth-century entrepreneur: steadfastness of purpose and effort, resilient energy and optimism, and drive for productive expansion and efficiency. He had appeared at a time in American history when economic growth and the industrial entrepreneur were in happy juxtaposition. Rising market demand, an improving transportation network, accelerating technical change, all were strands in the fabric of economic opportunity. The entrepreneur given to novelty and expansion could prosper in the market place and in community repute; indeed, America required and rewarded commensurately the man who could exploit the opportunities around him. Such a man was Miles Greenwood, and prosper he did.

Yielding further glory to him was the Civil War, which was a kind of showcase for the display of his talent and capacity. Yet the war, exhilarating though it was for Greenwood, represented a total political and economic effort that in some ways diminished him as an individual. It took him out of the market place, interposing between him and the user of his products wearisome bureaucracy—ordnance personnel who rejected his innovative ideas, navy engineers who controlled his work—and vitiating in the process the free play of individuality. In Greenwood's case, it tended to sacrifice the individual ethic to the demands of the organizational ethic; it tended to subject the "inner-directed" man to stifling, external controls, as particularly expressed through the maze of "Tippecanoe" paper. Besides eroding individuated values, the Civil War, for Greenwood and many other established entrepreneurs, heralded the transition from a proprietary to a corporate economy, leaving the older industrial entrepreneurs marking time as their glory faded and impelling the corporate organizers—the Carnegies, the Rockefellers—to the industrial apex. It left Greenwood an aging man with no great plans for industrial organization spanning the nation. He had no visions of vertical or horizontal integration that might have sustained him in his greatness. He was, as he was before the war, committed to localism in production. And his spirit of innovation, nurtured in the founding arts, had less relevancy in an age when the machining arts were emerging as the aristocracy of the metal-working industry. Cast in another day, Greenwood's invincibility in iron was the relative invincibility of a unique time and place. Greenwood, like the metal he worked with, was tough and malleable; but, even like that metal, he could not resist the ineluctable rust of time.

1. Morris Birkbeck, *Notes on a Journey in America* (Dublin, 1818), p. 35.

2. For the life of the elder Greenwood, see Isaac J. Greenwood, *The Greenwood Family of Norwich, England, in America* (New York, 1934), pp. 202–4. See also Frederick Greenwood, *Greenwood Genealogies* (New York, 1914), pp. 459–60.

3. When the expedition left Boston, Kendrick commanded the "Columbia," Gray the sloop, "Lady Washington." They exchanged vessels at Nootka Sound in the fall of 1788.

4. M. Joblin & Co., comp., *Cincinnati Past and Present* (Cincinnati, 1872), p. 101. A compilation of short biographies of prominent Cincinnatians, this book, unfortunately, seems to be the only source bearing on the Greenwoods in the years immediately following their arrival in Ohio. Greenwood the son probably provided the information for his biographical sketch, which is quite reverential in tone. See also J. Fletcher Brennan (ed.), *A Biographical Cyclopaedia and Portrait Gallery of Distinguished Men, with an Historical Sketch of the State of Ohio* (Cincinnati, 1879), p. 344; Cincinnati *Daily Times Star*, November 6, 1885; and Cincinnati

Commercial Gazette, November 7, 1885. These sources are largely based on the Greenwood biography in *Cincinnati Past and Present.*

5. *Cincinnati Past and Present,* p. 101.

6. Robert Dale Owen, *Threading My Way* (New York, 1874), p. 283. If Phiquepal was eccentric, he was surely no more so than Greenwood's father, whose behavior at New Harmony must have been a burden on the son. On one occasion, as Owen described it: "We had, during the summer of 1826, several terrific thunderstorms such as I had never witnessed. . . . It was during one of these storms . . . that I saw old Greenwood, thoroughly drenched, and carrying, upright as a soldier does his musket, a slender iron rod, ten or twelve feet long. He was walking in the middle of the street, passed with slow step the house in which I was, and, as I afterwards learned, paraded every street in the village in the same deliberate manner. Next day I met him and asked an explanation. 'Ah, well, my young friend,' said he. 'I'm very old; I'm not well; I suffer much: and I thought it might be a good chance to slip off and be laid quietly in a corner of the peach orchard. . . . You see I don't like to kill myself— seems like taking matters out of God's hands. But I thought He might perhaps send me a spare bolt when I put myself in the way. If He had only seen fit to do it, I'd then have been at rest this very minute; all my pains gone; no more trouble to anyone, and no more burden to myself.' "—Owen, *Threading My Way,* pp. 282–83.

7. *Cincinnati Past and Present,* p. 101.

8. *Ibid.,* p. 102. Gilbert F. Dodds, *Early Ironmasters of Ohio* (Columbus, Ohio, 1957), p. 13.

9. William L. Downard, "Miles Greenwood, An Active Cincinnati Industrialist" (Master's thesis, University of Cincinnati, 1964), p. 9.

10. A brief description of the iron business in the period may be found in Francis P. Weisenburger, *The History of the State of Ohio: The Passing of the Frontier, 1825–1850* (Columbus, Ohio, 1941), p. 77.

11. On economic and technological development in the foundry trade in the first half of the nineteenth century, see Victor S. Clark, *History of Manufactures in the United States* (3 vols.; New York, 1929), I, 412, 416, 502 ff.; John W. Oliver, *History of American Technology* (New York, 1956), p. 167; and Bruce L. Simpson, *Development of the Metal Castings Industry* (Chicago, 1948), pp. 191 ff. The Hanging Rock furnaces as suppliers of the Cincinnati market are described in Wilbur Stout, "Charcoal Iron Industry of the Hanging Rock Iron District," *Ohio State Archaeological and Historical Quarterly,* XLII (1933), 72–104. Also see James Hall, *The West: Its Commerce and Navigation* (Cincinnati, 1848), pp. 281–82. According to Hall, ton prices of iron from the region transported to Cincinnati typically ran four dollars under prices in Pittsburgh.

12. Advertising Notice of Eagle Iron Works (n.d.), Cincinnati Historical Society Picture File (hereafter abbreviated as CHS). Unsubstantiated but possibly correct is the assertion that the firm was "Commenced with a view of making principally heavy castings for mill work. . . ." J. Leander Bishop, *A History of American Manufactures from 1608 to 1860* (3 vols.; Philadelphia, 1866), III, 382.

13. Clark, *History of Manufactures,* I, 502 ff.

14. *Cincinnati Past and Present,* p. 102.

15. Bishop, *A History of American Manufactures,* III, 383.

16. *Cincinnati Past and Present,* p. 102.

17. Charles Cist, *Sketches and Statistics of Cincinnati in 1851* (Cincinnati, 1851), p. 195. Advertising notice of the Eagle Iron Works in the Cincinnati Historical Society. Recently, the Society received an inquiry from a New York resident, evidently a connoisseur of antiques, concerning hinges manufactured by Greenwood that had been found on a desk. According to this writer, the hinges were unusual in structure: the ends were of molded iron and no pins showed through them (Sara Pekarsky to the Cincinnati Chamber of Commerce, July 7, 1965, CHS).

18. Quoted in Bishop in *A History of American Manufactures,* III, 383.

19. Charles Cist, *Sketches and Statistics of Cincinnati in* 1859 (Cincinnati, 1859), p. 281.

20. For a few years the new company and the Eagle Iron Works occupied the same building. But even after their physical separation, observers viewed them as one firm—Greenwood's works.

21. Quoted in Bishop, *A History of American Manufactures,* III, 383.

22. Cist and some other sources seem to suggest that the butt hinges were produced in the Hardware and Malleable Iron Department. But the original census returns specifically include the hinges as a product of the Eagle Iron Works.

23. Quoted in Bishop, *A History of American Manufactures,* III, 383.

24. Clark, *History of Manufactures,* I, 416.

25. Hall, *The West: Its Commerce and Navigation,* p. 282.

26. Quoted in Bishop, *A History of American Manufactures,* III, 383.

27. Cist, *Sketches and Statistics of Cincinnati in 1859,* p. 279.

28. *Cincinnati Directory for 1846* (Cincinnati, 1846), p. 505. A listing of Greenwood's production in the early 1840's may be found in Charles Cist, comp., *The Cincinnati Directory for the Year 1842* (Cincinnati, 1842), p. 311.

29. Seventh Census of the United States, Schedule 5, Fifth Series, Production of Industry, Hamilton County, in State Library of Ohio.

30. *Ibid.*

31. The national averages were developed from census figures found in Bishop, *A History of American Manufactures*, II, 454.

32. Cist, *Sketches and Statistics of Cincinnati in 1851*, p. 262.

33. Quoted in Cist, *Sketches and Statistics of Cincinnati in 1851*, p. 257.

34. Mrs. Isabella Bird Bishop, *An Englishwoman in America* (London, 1856), pp. 121–22.

35. William Chambers, *Things as They Are in America* (London, 1854), p. 151.

36. Bishop, *An Englishwoman in America*, p. 123.

37. *Catalogue and Invoice Prices of Welded Wrought Iron Pipe: Boiler Flues, Steam and Gas Fittings . . . Manufactured by Miles Greenwood* (Cincinnati, 1855), pamphlet in CHS.

38. *Ibid.*

39. Frederick V. Geier, *The Coming of the Machine Tool Age* (New York, 1949), p. 14.

40. *Catalogue and Invoice Prices.*

41. Hiram Powers to Miles Greenwood, May 13, 1858, Hiram Powers Letters, CHS. Powers did not patent his machine in the United States until 1861.

42. Miles Greenwood to Hiram Powers, June 24, 1858, Hiram Powers Letters, CHS.

43. Cist, *Sketches and Statistics of Cincinnati in 1859*, p. 279.

44. Quite unfortunately, the original schedules of the census of manufactures for 1860 have been lost or destroyed.

45. Cist, *Sketches and Statistics of Cincinnati in 1859*, p. 280.

46. *Ibid.*

47. *Ibid.*, p. 279.

48. *Ibid.*

49. *Ibid.*

50. *Ibid.*, p. 280.

51. *Ibid.*, p. 282.

52. Downard, "Miles Greenwood, An Active Cincinnati Industrialist," p. 9. It was probably during the election campaign that Greenwood boasted that as a general he could outrank anyone in the city; he went on to explain that he referred to his experience as a "General Bill Poster." *Cincinnati Past and Present*, p. 105.

53. *Cincinnati Enquirer,* Apr. 19, 1922.

54. George W. Kendall, *A Sketch of the History of the Ohio Mechanics Institute* (Cincinnati, 1853) , pp. 3 ff.

55. Subscription List for the Ohio Mechanics Institute, April, 1847; July, 1847, in Miscellaneous History File, Ohio College of Applied Science Library. Also see Dana B. Hamel, "A History of the Ohio Mechanics Institute" (Doctoral dissertation, University of Cincinnati, 1962) , pp. 18 ff.

56. *Cincinnati Commercial,* Mar. 20, 1882.

57. A lucid explanation of the relationship between the companies and the city government may be found in George Escol Sellars, "Early Engineering Reminiscenses," *American Machinist,* XII (1889) , 1–2.

58. The description here of fire department problems generally follows Downard, "Miles Greenwood, An Active Cincinnati Industrialist," pp. 15 ff.

59. Quoted in Henry Howe, *Historical Collections of Ohio* (2 vols., Cincinnati, 1902) , I, 820.

60. *Ibid.*

61. *Ibid.,* pp. 419–20. See also John Faig, "The Steam Fire Engine," typed MS, Feb., 1940, John Faig Papers, Ohio College of Applied Science Library.

62. Miles Greenwood, *Report of the Chief Engineer of the Fire Department, for Six Months Ending October 1, 1853* (Cincinnati, 1853) , p. 5.

63. *Appleton's Cyclopaedia of American Biography* (6 vols.; New York 1888–91) , II, 758.

64. Quoted in *Cincinnati Past and Present,* p. 104. See also John Bunker, "Fire Department Highlights," *Bulletin,* Historical and Philosophical Society of Ohio, IV (1946) , 5–17.

65. Testimonial to Miles Greenwood, Apr. 3, 1855, in the Miles Greenwood Collection, CHS.

66. *Cincinnati Commercial,* Mar. 20, 1882. A search through the *Index of Patents* has thus far revealed nothing relating to Greenwood's patent. No reference to Greenwood's pumps is found in Harry R. Stevens' *The Ohio Bridge* (Cincinnati, 1939) .

67. *Cincinnati Commercial,* Mar. 20, 1882.

68. For a description of the pro-Southern atmosphere, see Louis L. Tucker, *Cincinnati during the Civil War* ("Publications of the Ohio Civil War Centennial Commission," No. 9 [Columbus, 1962]) , pp. 8–9.

69. Robert Gray Gunderson, "Lincoln in Cincinnati," *Bulletin,* Historical and Philosophical Society of Ohio, VIII (1950) , 258–66.

70. William Smith (ed.), *Annual Statement of the Commerce of Cincinnati for 1861* (Cincinnati, 1861), p. 7.

71. Smith (ed.), *Annual Statement . . . for 1862*, p. 27; *Annual Statement . . . for 1863*, p. 28.

72. For some statistics, see Carl M. Becker, "Entrepreneurial Invention and Innovation in the Miami Valley during the Civil War," *Bulletin*, Cincinnati Historical Society, XXII (1963), 5–28.

73. Ohio's problems in the procurement of supplies are described in Harry L. Coles, *Ohio Forms an Army* ("Publications of the Ohio Civil War Centennial Commission," No. 5 [Columbus, 1962]), pp. 16 ff.

74. There are numerous sources describing this work. See particularly Annual Report of the Quartermaster General of Ohio, 1861, *Executive Documents*, Part 1 (Columbus, 1862), p. 587; Whitelaw Reid, *Ohio in the War* (2 vols.; Cincinnati, 1868), I, 60; and the *Cincinnati Commercial*, Nov. 7, 1885.

75. *Appleton's Cyclopaedia of American Biography*, II, 758.

76. *Commercial*, June 12, 1861.

77. *Scientific American*, July 6, 1861.

78. *Commercial*, Aug. 9, 1861.

79. Stephen Z. Starr, "Camp Dennison, 1861–1865," *Bulletin*, Historical and Philosophical Society of Ohio, XIX (1961), 167–90.

80. Annual Report of the QMG, 1861, p. 587.

81. Reid, *Ohio in the War*, I, 60. See also Harry L. Coles, "Raising an Army," *Museum Echoes*, XXXIV (1961), 27–30.

82. Annual Report of the QMG, 1863, Part 2 (Columbus, 1864), p. 624.

83. Annual Report of the QMG, 1861, p. 587. Several sources state that Greenwood altered forty thousand, but no state or national records substantiate the figure. See, for example, Howe, *Historical Collections*, I, 820.

84. *Enquirer*, Oct. 23, 1861. Record of Issues of Ordnance Stores, Ordnance Department of Indiana, p. 90, bound manuscript in Archives Division, Indiana State Library.

85. These figures, which include $782.40 for cleaning muskets, were derived from a variety of files of the Ordnance Department in the National Archives: Abstract of Purchases, July 1, 1862—Dec. 31, 1862, p. 5; Abstract of Purchases, 1861–1862, p. 76; Statement of Contracts No. 9, p. 84; Statement of Contracts No. 10, p. 59; Statement of Contracts No. 16, p. 63; Miscellaneous Letters, Mar. 29, 1862—Aug. 17, 1862.

86. E. P. Jones to George B. Wright, Jan. 15, 1862, Adjutant-General's Ordnance Letterbook, Oct. 10, 1861—Jan. 28, 1862, State Archives of Ohio.

87. Miles Greenwood to James Ripley, Feb. 11, 1862, Box 201, Letters Received, Ordnance Department. All Ordnance Department records cited are in the National Archives.

88. Miles Greenwood to James Ripley, Feb. 21, 1862, Box 201, Letters Received, Ordnance Department.

89. Miles Greenwood to [?], Feb. 21, 1862, Register of Letters Received, 1862, Ordnance Department.

90. Miles Greenwood to Col. F. D. Callender, July 9, 1862, Box 201, Letters Received, Ordnance Department; Miles Greenwood to James Ripley, July 28, 1862, Box 201, Letters Received, Ordnance Department. Greenwood's price had risen to $3.60 for these muskets.

91. William Dennison to Miles Greenwood, July 10, 1861, Letterbook, Apr. 1—Aug. 8, 1861, in Governor's Official Papers, Ohio Historical Society.

92. D. L. Wood to Miles Greenwood, Sept. 13, 1861, Adjutant-General's Ordnance Letterbook, June 28, 1861—Oct.11, 1861, State Archives of Ohio.

93. George B. Wright to Miles Greenwood, Dec. 10, 1861, Adjutant-General's Ordnance Letterbook, Oct. 10, 1861—Jan. 28, 1862, State Archives of Ohio.

94. Various sources were consulted and analyzed to arrive at this figure. A basic source is the statement of purchases found in H.R. Exec. Doc. No. 99, 40th Cong., 2d Sess. (1867–1868) (Washington, D.C., 1868) p. 754. The table presented here, unfortunately, does not distinguish between work done for the state government and the national government. The tabular figures were studied in light of various Ordnance Department records to determine payments made for state work. These records include the following files: Statement of Contracts, No. 9, p. 84; Statement of Contracts, No. 10, p. 59; Abstract of Purchases, 1861–1862, p. 70; and Miscellaneous Papers, Oct. 24, 1861—Mar. 26, 1862.

95. *Enquirer,* July 10, 1861.

96. Statement of Contracts, No. 9, p. 84; Abstract of Purchases, 1861–62, p. 70. Figures in these records were studied in context of total Greenwood production of cannon as listed in H.R. Exec. Doc. No. 99, p. 754.

97. *Commercial,* Mar. 20, 1882.

98. Abstract of Purchases, 1861–1862, p. 74; Open Purchases, 1861–1867, p. 5.

99. Voucher 3932, October 21, 1861, Archives Division, Indiana State Library.

100. *Appleton's Cyclopaedia of American Biography,* II, 758.

101. *Enquirer,* Sept. 15, 1861.

102. *Commercial,* Oct. 30, 1861.

103. James Ripley to Miles Greenwood, Jan. 16, 1862, Miscellaneous Papers, Oct. 24, 1861—Mar. 28, 1862, Ordnance Department. See also H.R. Exec. Doc. No. 99, pp. 148–49.

104. Miles Greenwood to James Ripley, Jan. 28, 1862, copy in Greenwood Collection, CHS; Miles Greenwood to James Ripley, Jan. 26, 1862, Box 201, Letters Received, Ordnance Department.

105. Robert V. Bruce, *Lincoln and the Tools of War* (Indianapolis, 1956), p. 93.

106. George B. McClellan to E. M. Stanton, Feb. 5, 1862, in Greenwood Collection, CHS.

107. James Ripley to Miles Greenwood, Feb. 7, 1862, in Greenwood Collection, CHS.

108. James Ripley to Miles Greenwood, Feb. 10, 1862, in Greenwood Collection, CHS. See also entry of Feb. 10, 1862, in Register of Contracts made by the Ordnance Department.

109. Statement of Contracts, No. 10, p. 59, Ordnance Department.

110. H.R. Exec. Doc. No. 99, p. 754. This figure includes a payment of $6,200.00 for 2,500 lances supplied to an unidentified purchaser.

111. Miles Greenwood to the War Department, June 1, 1861, Classified Register of Improvements, Construction Division, No. 2, Ordnance Department. For the history of Sherwin's cannon, see Bruce, *Lincoln and the Tools of War,* pp. 126–28, 184–86, 201–2.

112. George B. McClellan to E. M. Stanton, Feb. 5, 1862, in Greenwood Collection, CHS.

113. Miles Greenwood to James Ripley, Feb. 11, 1862, in Greenwood Collection, CHS. Greenwood's emphasis on the unusual character of his proposal raises the remote possibility that he was referring to cast-steel guns, which were rather unusual at the time; many foundrymen of the day did not differentiate carefully between cast iron and cast steel.

114. For a brief commentary on Ripley's attitude, see Allan Nevins, *The War for the Union: War Becomes Revolution* (New York, 1960), p. 469.

115. Miles Greenwood to James Ripley, Feb. 20, 1862, copy in Greenwood Collection, CHS; Register of Letters Received, 1862, Feb. 20, 1862, Ordnance Department.

116. Miles Greenwood to James Ripley, Aug. 9, 1862, in Greenwood Collection, CHS.

117. James Ripley to Miles Greenwood, Aug. 18, 1862, in Greenwood Collection, CHS.

118. All these figures come from the *Cincinnati Gazette,* Dec. 15, 1862.

119. *Gazette,* Oct. 14, 1862; Dec. 15, 1862.

120. Quoted in Vincent Brown, "A Sketch of Dr. Richard Gatling and His Great Invention," typed MS in CHS.

121. *Gazette,* Sept. 15, 1862; *Commercial,* Sept. 15, 1862.

122. Quoted in Brown, "A Sketch of Dr. Richard Gatling and His Great Invention."

123. Edwin M. Stanton to president of the Board of Trade [Joseph Butler], Mar. 26, 1862, *The War of the Rebellion: A Compilation of the Official Records of the Union and Confederate Armies* (Washington, D.C., 1891), Series III, Vol. I, pp. 949–50.

124. Record of Payments on Contracts for Ships, Bureau of Ships, p. 308, in National Archives. See also *Official Records of the Union and Confederate Navies in the War of the Rebellion* (Washington, D.C., 1921), Series II, Vol. I, p. 224.

125. See the *Commercial,* Mar. 20, 1882, for Greenwood's rather vague explanation of the situation. See also George M. Morris to John Faig, Jan. 22, 1924, in Greenwood Folder, Ohio College of Applied Science Library.

126. *Commercial,* Mar. 20, 1882.

127. Alban Stimers, General Inspector's Office, Iron Clad Steamers, to Miles Greenwood, Oct. 18, 1862. Letters Sent to Contractors, Sept., 1862—June, 1865, Circular Letters Sent to Contractors, in National Archives. All navy letters cited below come from this file, a microfilm copy of which has been used.

128. Alban Stimers to Miles Greenwood, Jan. 15, 1863.

129. Isaac Newton to Miles Greenwood, Mar. 24, 1863; Alban Stimers to Miles Greenwood, Mar. 19, 1864.

130. Isaac Newton to Miles Greenwood, Mar. 25, 1863.

131. Isaac Newton to Miles Greenwood, Apr. 11, 1863; Alban Stimers to Miles Greenwood, Apr. 23, 1863; Apr. 29, 1863.

132. Alban Stimers to Miles Greenwood, Feb. 9, 1863; Isaac Newton to Miles Greenwood, Apr. 10, 1863.

133. General Inspector's Office to Harrison Loring, Superintendent, City Point Works, Boston, Massachusetts, June 18, 1863. This circular letter was sent to Greenwood on June 22, 1863.

134. These changes are detailed in letters of July 29, 1863; Aug. 5, 1863; Aug. 31, 1863; Sept. 10, 1863; Oct. 7, 1863; Oct. 23, 1863.

135. Alban Stimers to Miles Greenwood, Mar. 7, 1864.

136. Alban Stimers to Miles Greenwood, Jan. 8, 1864.

137. Alban Stimers to Miles Greenwood, Apr. 21, 1863; July 1, 1863.

138. Alban Stimers to Miles Greenwood, Oct. 25, 1862; May 14, 1863.

139. Alban Stimers to Miles Greenwood, May 14, 1863; Jan. 9, 1864.

140. Record of Payments on Contracts for Ships, p. 308.

141. Report on Claim of Miles Greenwood, Feb. 12, 1873, S. Rep. No. 422, 42d Cong., 2d Sess. (Washington: Government Printing Office, 1873), I.

142. William W. Wood, General Inspector's Office, Steam Machinery for the Navy, to Miles Greenwood, Jan. 13, 1865.

143. William W. Wood to Miles Greenwood, Jan. 31, 1865.

144. *Official Records of the Union and Confederate Navies in the War of the Rebellion*, Series II, Vol. I, p. 224.

145. Bishop, *A History of American Manufactures*, III, 384.

146. *Gazette*, May 23, 1864.

147. Quoted in Hamilton *True Telegraph*, Apr. 30, 1863.

148. Henry Gabel, "Reminiscenses of Miles Greenwood," *Quarterly Journal of the Ohio Mechanics Institute*, IV (1908), 71–76.

149. Alvin F. Harlow, *The Serene Cincinnatians* (New York: E. P. Dutton, 1950), p. 275.

150. Gabel, "Reminiscenses of Miles Greenwood."

151. For this change and others of the period, see Downard, "Miles Greenwood, An Active Cincinnati Industrialist," pp. 32–33.

152. Figures cited here were taken from the Ninth Census of the United States, Schedule 4, p. 9, in State Library of Ohio. The Greenwood Pipe Company, in which Greenwood may have retained an interest, was capitalized at $75,000 and employed thirty workers.

153. For the 1850 statistics, see pp. 268–69 above.

154. Exec. Doc. No. 18, 39th Cong., 1st Sess. (Washington: Government Printing Office, 1866), p. 11.

155. Report on Claim of Miles Greenwood, Feb. 12, 1873.

156. *The Statutes at Large of the United States of America* (Boston, 1873), XVII, 764.

157. Tenth Census of the United States, Schedule 3, p. 39, in State Library of Ohio.

158. Brennan, *A Biographical Cyclopaedia and Portrait Gallery of Distinguished Men,* p. 344.

159. This material is based on Downard, "Miles Greenwood, An Active Cincinnati Industrialist," pp. 34 ff.

160. *Cincinnati Commercial Gazette,* Nov. 7, 1885; *Cincinnati Daily Times Star,* Nov. 6, 1885.

BIBLIOGRAPHICAL NOTE

Manuscripts Collections

DENNISON, WILLIAM. Official Governor's Papers. Ohio Historical Society.

FAIG, JOHN. Papers. Ohio College of Applied Science.

GREENWOOD, MILES. Manuscripts Collection. Cincinnati Historical Society.

GREENWOOD, MILES. Manuscript Folder. Ohio College of Applied Science.

Miscellaneous History File. Ohio College of Applied Science.

POWERS, HIRAM. Letters. Cincinnati Historical Society.

Official Records and Documents

Adjutant General of Ohio, Ordnance Letterbooks (1861–1865). State of Ohio Archives.

Annual Reports Made to the Governor of the State of Ohio. Annual Report of the Quartermaster General for the Year 1861. Part 1. Columbus: Richard Nevins, 1862.

Annual Reports Made to the Governor of the State of Ohio. Annual Report of the Quartermaster General for the Year 1862. Part 2 Columbus: Richard Nevins, 1863.

Annual Reports Made to the Governor of the State of Ohio. Annual Report of the Quartermaster General for the Year 1863. Part 2. Columbus: Richard Nevins, 1864.

Census of Manufactures. Seventh Census of the United States. Original Returns. Fifth Series. Production of Industry. State Library of Ohio.

Census of Manufactures. Ninth Census of the United States. Original Returns. Schedule 4. State Library of Ohio.

Census of Manufactures. Tenth Census of the United States. Original Returns. Schedule 3. State Library of Ohio.

Executive Documents Number 18, First Session of the Thirty-ninth Congress. Washington: Government Printing Office, 1866.

Executive Documents Number 99, the House of Representatives, Second Session of the Fortieth Congress. Washington: Government Printing Office, 1868.

GREENWOOD, MILES. *Report of the Chief Engineer of the Fire Department, for Six Months Ending October 1, 1853.* Cincinnati: Daily Enquirer, 1853.

Ledger, Ordnance Bureau. United States Navy, 1862. National Archives.

Letters Sent to Contractors, September, 1862–June, 1865. Circular Letters Sent to Contractors. Bureau of Ships. National Archives.

Official Records of the Union and Confederate Navies in the War of the Rebellion. Series II. Vol. I. Washington: Government Printing Office, 1921.

Ordnance Department Files (1861–1865). National Archives. Abstract of Purchases; Classified Register of Improvements, Construction Division; Letters Received; Open Purchases; Miscellaneous Papers; Register of Cannon; Register of Letters Received; Statement of Contracts.

Record of Issue of Ordnance Stores. Ordnance Department of Indiana. Archives Division, Indiana State Library.

Record of Payments on Contracts for Ships. Bureau of Ships. National Archives.

Report on Claim of Miles Greenwood, February 12, 1873. *Senate Reports Number 422, Third Session of the Forty-second Congress.* Washington: Government Printing Office, 1873.

The Statutes at Large of the United States of America. Vol. XVII. Boston: Little, Brown & Co., 1873.

The War of the Rebellion: A Compilation of the Official Records of the Union and Confederate Armies. Series III. Vol. I. Washington: Government Printing Office, 1891.

Newspapers and Periodicals

American Machinist.

Cincinnati Commercial Gazette.

Cincinnati Daily Times Star.

Cincinnati Enquirer.

Cincinnati Gazette.

Hamilton *True Telegraph.*

Scientific American.

Books

Appleton's Cyclopaedia of American Biography. 6 vols. New York: D. Appleton & Co., 1888–91.

BIRKBECK, MORRIS. *Notes on a Journey in America.* Dublin: Thomas Larkin, 1818.

BISHOP, MRS. ISABELLA BIRD. *An Englishwoman in America.* London: John Murray, 1856.

BISHOP, J. LEANDER. *A History of American Manufactures from 1608 to 1860.* 3 vols. Philadelphia: Edward Young & Co., 1866.

BRENNAN, J. FLETCHER (ed.). *A Biographical Cyclopaedia and Portrait Gallery of Distinguished Men, with an Historical Sketch of the State of Ohio.* Cincinnati: John C. Yorston & Co., 1879.

BRUCE, ROBERT V. *Lincoln and the Tools of War.* Indianapolis: Bobbs-Merrill Co., 1956.

CHAMBERS, WILLIAM. *Things as They Are in America.* London: William and Robert Chambers, 1854.

Cincinnati Directory for 1846. Cincinnati: Robinson & Jones, 1846.

CIST, CHARLES (comp.). *The Cincinnati Directory for the Year 1842.* Cincinnati: E. Morgan, 1842.

CIST, CHARLES. *Sketches and Statistics of Cincinnati in 1851.* Cincinnati: William H. Moore, 1851.

CIST, CHARLES. *Sketches and Statistics of Cincinnati in 1859.* Cincinnati: Moore, Wilstach, Keys & Co., 1859.

CLARK, VICTOR. *History of Manufactures in the United States.* 3 vols. New York: McGraw-Hill, 1929.

COLES, HARRY L. *Ohio Forms an Army.* ("Publications of the Ohio Civil War Centennial Commission," No. 5.) Columbus: Ohio State University Press for the Ohio Historical Society, 1962.

DODDS, GILBERT. *Early Ironmasters of Ohio.* Columbus: Franklin County Historical Society, 1957.

FITE, EMERSON D. *Social and Industrial Conditions in the North during the Civil War.* New York: Macmillan Co., 1910.

GEIER, FREDERICK. *The Coming of the Machine Tool Age.* New York: Newcomen Society of England, 1949.

GREENWOOD, FREDRICK. *Greenwood Genealogies.* New York: Lyons Genealogical Company, 1914.

GREENWOOD, ISAAC J. *The Greenwood Family of Norwich, England, in America.* New York: Lyons Genealogical Company, 1934.

HALL, JAMES. *The West: Its Commerce and Navigation.* Cincinnati: H. W. Derby & Co., 1848.

HARLOW, ALVIN F. *The Serene Cincinnatians.* New York: E. P. Dutton, 1950.

HOWE, HENRY. *Historical Collections of Ohio.* 2 vols. Cincinnati: C. J. Krehbiel & Co., 1902.

Joblin, M., & Co (comp.). *Cincinnati Past and Present.* Cincinnati: Elm Street Printing Co., 1872.

KENDALL, GEORGE W. *A Sketch of the History of the Ohio Mechanics Institute.* Cincinnati: A. Pugh, 1853.

NEVINS, ALLAN. *The War for the Union: War Becomes Revolution.* New York: Charles Scribner's Sons, 1960.

OLIVER, JOHN W. *History of American Technology.* New York: Ronald Press, 1956.

OWEN, ROBERT DALE. *Threading My Way.* New York: G. W. Carleton, 1874.

PRATT, FLETCHER. *Civil War on Western Waters.* New York: Henry Holt, 1956.

REID, WHITELAW. *Ohio in the War.* 2 vols. Cincinnati: Wilstach & Baldwin, 1868.

SIMPSON, BRUCE L. *Development of the Metal Castings Industry.* Chicago: American Foundrymen's Association, 1948.

SMITH, WILLIAM (ed.). *Annual Statement of the Commerce of Cincinnati for 1861.* Cincinnati: Gazette Co., 1861.

SMITH, WILLIAM (ed.). *Annual Statement of the Commerce of Cincinnati for 1862.* Cincinnati: Gazette Co., 1862.

SMITH, WILLIAM (ed.). *Annual Statement of the Commerce of Cincinnati for 1863.* Cincinnati: Gazette Co., 1863.

TUCKER, LOUIS L. *Cincinnati during the Civil War.* ("Publications of the

Ohio Civil War Centennial Commission," No. 9.) Columbus: Ohio State University Press for the Ohio Historical Society, 1962.

WEISENBURGER, FRANCIS P. *The History of the State of Ohio: The Passing of the Frontier, 1825–1850.* Columbus: Ohio State Archaeological and Historical Society, 1941.

Articles

BECKER, CARL M. "Entrepreneurial Invention and Innovation in the Miami Valley during the Civil War." *Bulletin,* Cincinnati Historical Society, XXII (1963), 5–28.

BUNKER, JOHN. "Fire Department Highlights." *Bulletin,* Historical and Philosophical Society of Ohio, IV (1946), 5–17.

COLES, HARRY L. "Raising an Army." *Museum Echoes,* XXXIV (1961), 27–30.

GABEL, HENRY. "Reminiscences of Miles Greenwood." *Quarterly Journal of the Ohio Mechanics Institute,* IV (1908), 71–76.

GUNDERSON, ROBERT GRAY. "Lincoln in Cincinnati." *Bulletin,* Historical and Philosophical Society of Ohio, VIII (1950), 258–66.

SELLARS, GEORGE ESCOL. "Early Engineering Reminiscenses." *American Machinist,* XII (1889), 1–2.

STARR, STEPHEN Z. "Camp Dennison, 1861–1865." *Bulletin,* Historical and Philosophical Society of Ohio, XIX (1961), 167–90.

STOUT, WILBUR. "Charcoal Iron Industry of the Hanging Rock Iron District." *Ohio State Archaeological and Historical Quarterly,* XLII (1933), 72–104.

Unpublished Papers

BROWN, RICHARD S. "A History of the Machine Tool Industry of Cincinnati." Thesis, University of Cincinnati, 1927.

BROWN, VINCENT. "A Sketch of Dr. Richard Gatling and His Great Invention." Typed MS, Cincinnati Historical Society.

DOWNARD, WILLIAM L. "Miles Greenwood, An Active Cincinnati Industrialist." Master's thesis, University of Cincinnati, 1964.

FAIG, JOHN. "The Steam Fire Engine." Typed MS, 1940, John Faig Papers, Ohio College of Applied Science Library.

HAMEL, DANA B. "A History of the Ohio Mechanics Institute." Doctoral dissertation, University of Cincinnati, 1962.

Miscellaneous

Advertising Notice of Eagle Iron Works (n.d.), Cincinnati Historical Society Picture File.

Catalogue and Invoice Prices of Welded Wrought Iron Pipe; Boiler Flues; Steam and Gas Fittings Manufactured by Miles Greenwood. Cincinnati: No publisher, 1855. Cincinnati Historical Society.

Illustrated Catalogue of Ornamental Iron Work Manufactured by M. Greenwood. Cincinnati: No publisher, 1871. Cincinnati Historical Society.

Subscription List for the Ohio Mechanics Institute, April, 1847; July, 1847. Miscellaneous History File. Ohio College of Applied Science Library.

SEVEN ★

Murat Halstead

DONALD W. CURL

Although he was still a young man when the first shots were fired at Fort Sumter, Murat Halstead was already one of the best known reporter-editors in the West. After graduating from Farmers' College at College Hill, Ohio, in 1851, he had decided to become a writer. The literary capital of the West in the fifties was Cincinnati, and Halstead easily traveled the six miles from College Hill to his new life. Besides six English and four German newspapers, Cincinnati could boast forty-three other publications in 1851 ranging from the temperance journal, *The Western Fountain*, to *Dye's Counterfeit Detector*.

From the first, Halstead found editors eager to publish his work; but since most of the newspapers and periodicals struggled along on meager budgets, they were unable to pay him well. It was only natural that the young writer should desire a more assured income and should eventually seek employment on the staff of one of the newspapers. After short stints on the *Atlas*, a small afternoon daily, and the already powerful *Enquirer*, Halstead joined the staff of the *Commercial*, the city's leading morning journal, in March, 1853. This association was to last for nearly half a century.[1]

The *Commercial* was owned in 1853 by the firm of Potter and Lee. Martin D. Potter, a printer turned publisher, was in charge of the business and printing aspects of the business;

Richard H. Lee was editor-in-chief.[2] Halstead's first job for the
Commercial was that of exchange, or "scissors," editor. Western
newspapers published many columns that they reproduced ver-
batim from eastern journals. It was Halstead's job to choose the
material to be included in these columns. Journalism itself was
a leisurely field, and the general rule for Cincinnati newspapers
was that they would publish nothing that arrived in the city
after ten o'clock in the evening. Halstead was responsible for
disturbing these easygoing habits and for raising the circulation
of the *Commercial* in his first few months as a reporter. He
would sit up until two o'clock in the morning when the last
train from the East arrived at the Cincinnati depot. He would
then rush to the *Commercial* office with the latest eastern papers. Working quickly with scissors, he would make up one or
two columns under the heading "Midnight Mail Matter," and
have them ready before the paper went to press.[3] He was able to
bear the reproaches showered upon him by his fellow journalists for being in such an "atrocious hurry" when it became
evident that the good citizens of Cincinnati preferred purchasing a morning paper with the latest news and when his initiative found an appreciative response from his employers.[4]

Within a few months of Halstead's coming to the *Commercial,* he had started to write paragraphs about various issues of
the day. Most of these found their way into the editorial page of
the paper, and Lee started asking him to contribute more. His
vigorous and forceful style, and the initiative he had shown in
scooping the other sheets on late news, resulted in his being
asked to take on more and more duties of an editorial nature.
When Lee fell ill in the late summer of 1853, at a time when
Potter was vacationing in the East, Halstead was asked to submit a daily news summary for the paper along with a leading
editorial. Lee's illness proved fatal, and when Potter returned
in August, he found the paper virtually under the direction of
the young reporter who had been hired just six months before.
Potter was impressed by Halstead's capabilities, and when the

company was reorganized in the spring of 1854, Halstead was made a one-sixteenth partner in the new firm of M. D. Potter and Company. The young editor was able to pay for his five thousand dollar interest in the paper out of his share of the profits in just four years.[5]

Potter took a fatherly interest in the bright young man and marked him at an early date as his successor as the *Commercial*'s publisher by insisting that Halstead learn the business side of the operation of a newspaper.[6] Potter's interest was also reflected in the shift in party loyalties of the editor. Although Halstead had been exposed to several abolitionist professors in college, his father was a strong Jacksonian Democrat, and Halstead had followed his father's politics. During the early fifties the editor had some second thoughts about his political alignment, since he felt the southern wing of the Democratic party had become too strong; but it was not until Potter converted to the rising Republican party that the editor also announced his decision to join.

When Potter decided that the *Commercial* should become a Republican newspaper, Halstead cheered the decision. All his life he was an enthusiast. Whenever he gave his support to something or someone, it was wholehearted. Being zealous, and seeing the large circulation of the *Commercial* as providing a fertile field on which to commence his missionary efforts for the Republican party, Halstead wished to launch an all-out campaign in its columns. Potter, on the other hand, felt that Cincinnati, and in particular Cincinnati business interests who through advertising were the main support of the paper, would not support such a campaign. As Potter controlled a majority of the stock of the company, he was able to keep the paper moderate in its tone. Though sometimes straining within this harness of moderation, Halstead nonetheless came to recognize the wisdom of the older man's policy.[7]

Halstead's long career as political reporter and commentator might be said to date from the first Republican national convention, which met in June, 1856, in Philadelphia. Potter decided to attend the convention and invited Halstead to join him to write firsthand reports for the *Commercial*. To Halstead the great question before the convention was whether slavery should be extended into the territories. He had voiced fears that both the Republican and Democratic politicians would try to avoid the question. He feared that they, in a search for winning candidates, would come up with weak nominees who would offend no one, since the politicians to him were all "trucklers, temporizers and compromisers." [8]

Halstead's first choice for the nomination was the Cincinnatian Salmon Portland Chase. Chase had served as a senator from Ohio from 1849 until his election to the governorship in 1855. Opposed to the Compromise of 1850 and the Kansas-Nebraska Act, he was the kind of no-nonsense candidate that Halstead thought would give the people a fair test of the "Great Question." Although certainly an early front-runner for the nomination, Chase lost out partly because the Whig element in the party found it too hard to forget him as an old political opponent. In fact, the polyglot nature of the new party made it impossible for the convention to agree on any of the old political leaders; and instead, a figure of romance and adventure, John G. Frémont, captured the nomination. [9]

The editor could claim that his low opinion of politicians had been justified by Frémont's nomination; he said the voters were once more given a popularity contest and not a clear trial of the issues at stake. Nonetheless, Halstead and the *Commercial* supported Frémont in the election; and the editor stated privately that should the Republicans lose, the nation would soon be involved in civil war. [10]

The country disagreed with Halstead, and Potter sent the editor to Washington to cover Buchanan's inauguration. It must be admitted that the *Commercial*'s reporter in Washington was not an unprejudiced observer. In his reports Buchanan became the overly nice "Jeems," a man for whom Halstead could have no respect. "It would appear from the exquisite polish upon him and the expression of his lips, that he must sleep between rose leaves with a little lump of fresh butter in his mouth. . . ." [11] Moreover, he found the pomp and circumstance surrounding the ceremony too elaborate for his republican tastes. Halstead did not comment on the major political questions of the day in his reports—he had been married the night before his departure and the trip was far more important to him as a honeymoon—but his increased acquaintance with politicians and events on the national scene gave a breadth to his later editorials and increased his stature as a commentator with his Cincinnati readers.

On January 15, 1859, Potter appointed Halstead editor-in-chief and permitted him to purchase another one-sixteenth interest in the firm. [12] While remaining strongly Republican, the newspaper under Halstead developed the position that the outstanding problems between North and South could be solved by means short of disruption of the Union and war. It was under such conditions that on the night of October 16, 1859, an event occurred that would have great portent for both the nation and for Halstead. John Brown and eighteen followers attacked and captured the federal arsenal at Harpers Ferry, Virginia. His raid electrified the South. A complete failure, it nonetheless seemed to prove to many southerners that they were right about the length to which the abolitionists would go in attacking their institutions. Northern Republican newspapers such as the *Commercial* were embarrassed by the raid, but like the *Commercial,* could claim with much justification that it was the act of a madman and that Brown had not had the support of the more rational elements in the North. [13]

After a speedy trial, Brown was sentenced to be executed on December 2, 1859. Many editorials in the *Commercial* had been particularly critical of the outcry in the southern press against Brown and against the support the South felt he had in the North. In one editorial Halstead said that the southern

editors were as "mad as March hares—mad as Old Brown." [14]
All told, the position of the *Commercial* on this issue was not
one that would recommend itself to what Halstead proposed.
As the date set for Brown's execution drew near, the editor
decided to go to Harpers Ferry and witness the event. He had
planned to go to Washington for the opening of what he felt
would be an important and exciting Congress, and stopping at
Harpers Ferry would mean only a short delay.

As the execution date approached, Halstead's friends argued
that the position of the *Commercial* was known in Virginia,
and if his life was not in actual danger, there was at least a
chance that he would be mobbed, or possibly arrested. Halstead
refused to listen to these warnings. On board the train to
Virginia rumors were afloat that no one would be allowed to
leave the cars at Harpers Ferry and that all the passengers
would be searched when the train crossed the state line. [15] The
Master of Transportation for the Baltimore and Ohio Railroad, an old friend of the reporter, happened to be aboard the
train. He promised to introduce Halstead to the road's special
agent at Harpers Ferry. Thus when the train arrived, Halstead
received his introduction and was greeted cordially. He was
vouched for by the agent to the commander of the military
contingent at the terminal, and taken to the Wagner House, a
local hotel, for the evening. [16]

On the morning of the second Halstead arose early and went
to Charlestown to see the field in which the gallows had been
built. The hanging was to take place in the center of a thirty-
acre clover field. On returning to town, he discovered that the
general commanding the forces had decided to give the press
special privileges. A list had been made of the reporters present
who would be permitted to witness the hanging. Halstead was
told later that several of the reporters charged with making the
list had not wanted to include his name. They feared the
general would decide that rather than let a representative of

the *Commercial* into the area close to the gallows he had better not let any of the reporters enter.[17]

The Cincinnati editor's name was included, and a few minutes before the appointed time, a military escort came to take the reporters to the field for the execution. When Brown arrived, Halstead was most impressed by his great dignity. He saw an old man with white hair and beard, sitting very straight and riding on his own coffin in a small cart. In contrast, the officers with their plumes and highly polished sabers and the long ranks of soldiers seemed pretentious and completely unnecessary. The hanging itself was over in a minute.

There was a moment of intense stillness, a sudden movement, a sharp twang of the rope, a creaking of the hinges of the trap door, and at fourteen and one-half minutes after eleven the old man, indomitable to the last, swung between the sky and the soil of the Old Dominion. As he dropped, he turned sharply round and faced North.[18]

The sympathy that Halstead felt for Brown did not interfere with his evaluation of the execution. No one, Halstead declared, could say that Brown had not received a fair trial, or that his conviction and sentence were not completely in accord with Virginia law. The tragedy in the situation for the reporter was that Virginia, in doing only what her laws demanded, increased Brown's importance in the eyes of the nation and the world, and assured his niche in history.[19]

Halstead's reports were widely reproduced by other newspapers in the North. The *Commercial's* man had been the only reporter of a Republican paper at Harpers Ferry. To his worried friends he might complain that the *Cincinnati Enquirer's* dispatches—the *Enquirer* was a Democratic newspaper—were approved by the commander of the troops and telegraphed back to Cincinnati, whereas he could only telegraph his family that he had arrived safely; but he also had to admit that he was treated kindly and shown many courtesies. His reports, only

three days delayed, were published in the *Commercial* beginning on December 5, while he was in Washington for the
opening of the winter session of Congress.[20]

Halstead found further cause to distrust politicians in Washington. The fanaticism, indulged in on both sides, appeared to
him to make a rational settlement of outstanding differences
between the two sections impossible. He reported that there
was already talk that the election of a Republican President
was to be the signal for the withdrawal from the Union by the
southern states. Conversations with leading men from the
North convinced him that the unreasonable demands of the
South could not possibly be met. Halstead was also critical of
the Republicans in the House of Representatives. The most
serious controversy that the editor witnessed was the election of
a new speaker of the House. His candidate was John Sherman,
his fellow Ohioan. If the Republicans had been organized and
not disputing among themselves for leadership, Halstead
claimed Sherman could have won the post on the first
ballot.[21]

Halstead's coverage of the John Brown execution and the
opening sessions of Congress had made his name well known in
the West, but his rise to the front ranks of western reporters
came with the conventions of 1860. The *Commercial* decided it
could accomplish a great coup by sending the young editor to
all the conventions. When the plans were drawn, a tight schedule for the three expected conventions resulted; but before
Halstead returned to Cincinnati in late June, after an absence
of two months, he had actually attended seven. These included
the Republican and Constitutional Union conventions, two
"Northern" Democratic conventions and three "Southern"
Democratic conventions.

Apprehensions arose similar to those when Halstead went to
Virginia to witness the hanging of Brown. Though the people
of Virginia had treated him as politely as could have been
expected, the Democratic convention of 1860 was to be held in

Charleston, and as his friends warned him, hatred of the North and of Republicans in particular was much more intense in South Carolina than in Virginia. Nonetheless, when the convention opened on April 23, Halstead was at his seat in the reporters' gallery. When he arrived in Charleston, he had spent his time interviewing various delegates and mingling with the politicians in the crowded hotel lobbies and on the streets, and was prepared to report the convention in depth, analyzing the significance of various maneuvers, and predicting what their instigators had in mind.[22]

Douglas was front-runner among the candidates, but his position on slavery in the territories made him unpopular with the southerners. Oregon and California delegates voted with those from the South to make a majority of the resolutions committee anti-Douglas. The platform that was then brought in was the antithesis of popular sovereignty, declaring that it was the duty of the federal government to protect slavery in the territories. A minority report of the Douglas faction was also read that called for the reaffirmation of the platform of 1856, which had endorsed the Kansas-Nebraska Act, with the added proviso that the party would abide by Supreme Court decisions on the right of property in the territories. Halstead did not like either platform, but he thought the majority recommendations at least had the virtue of honesty, whereas the minority report was "a miserable and cowardly evasion." [23] After a long and bitter debate, the Douglas platform was carried by the convention as a whole. By this time Halstead had decided it was the "most uncouth, disjointed, illogical, confused, mean, cowardly, and contemptible thing in the history of platforms. . . ." [24]

With the Douglas platform ratified, the southern extremists seceded from the convention. Until the secession, Halstead had claimed in his correspondence that the preponderance of brains in the convention was with the South. Now he decided that if this was the case, it had not been apparent in the action of the extremists. He reported that the citizens of Charleston were jubilant over the secession and turned out enthusiastically for a mass meeting to support the action of the extremists.[25]

With the southern delegates gone, and the two-thirds rule of the Democratic party held to apply to the total vote of the convention, it was impossible for the Douglas supporters to muster enough votes to nominate their candidate. Calling for the southern states to fill the vacated seats with new delegates, the convention was adjourned to meet again in Baltimore on June 18. The seceders met and adopted the platform that the regular convention had rejected, but also adjourned before nominations were made, planning to reconvene on June 11 in Richmond.

Leaving Charleston on the last day of the conventions, Halstead felt that the sectional cleavages he had witnessed proved the "false pretence" of the Democratic party and were a portent of its final dissolution. Nothing could be more fervently wished for than this by the Republican editor, who spitefully wrote: "May it die hard." [26]

The old church in which the Baltimore convention met seemed appropriate to Halstead for the Constitutional Union party. He found its delegates all fine looking and "eminently respectable" gentlemen, but he found their convention unanimated and the great issues of the day ignored. Fully resolved to save the country and devotedly patriotic—the church had been decorated with a full-length painting of Washington, a carved American Eagle, two great flags, and masses of smaller flags and tricolor drapery—the convention stressed the fraternal feelings that united the Union but did not take into account or attempt to resolve any of the issues that divided it.[27] The most exciting occurrence that Halstead could report during the two-day meeting came during the balloting for a presidential nominee and had nothing at all to do with the issues before the convention. While the votes were being changed to give John Bell of Tennessee the nomination at the end of the balloting, there was a sudden crash, and everyone believed that the overcrowded balconies of the old church had given away. Panic resulted, and there was a great rush for the doors and windows. It was then learned that only a bench had broken. When the delegates and visitors realized that there was no peril, Halstead reported the crowd stared at each other with "white faces and laughed." [28]

The editor heaped as much scorn upon this convention as on the Democratic one. The platform, which called for the support of the constitution, and the candidates, who were old-time conservatives, drew this scathing summary from him:

The whole talk was of the Constitution, the Union and the laws, of harmony, fraternity, compromise, conciliation, peace, good will, common glory, national brotherhood, preservation of the confederacy. . . . The Constitution, the Union, and peace between the sections would appear from the record of proceedings to be in the exclusive care of, and the peculiar institutions of, the no-party and no-platform gentlemen here assembled.[29]

The Baltimore convention ended on the eleventh of May, and the Republican convention began on the sixteenth. Thus Halstead found himself rushing to Chicago to be on hand for the opening gavel. Chicago had gone all out to play host to her first national convention. The "Wigwam," a ten-thousand-seat wooden auditorium costing seven thousand dollars, had been specially built to house the proceedings, and every effort had been made to house the delegates comfortably in Chicago's many large hotels.

Halstead arrived in Chicago a firm supporter of William Seward of New York for the nomination, and was thus greatly disappointed that the Ohio delegation, which he argued could hold the balance of power in the convention, was divided. The Chicago reports were as telling as those Halstead had previously sent from Charleston and Baltimore, with the faults of the convention pointed out to his readers; but it was also obvious that Halstead was a partisan, supporting this conven-

tion, and supporting and hoping for Seward's victory. Moreover, he failed to see, or at least report, the significance of the
platform. Seward and his supporters were most closely associated with the old abolitionist wing of the party, but the
platform was a victory for those who wished the party to rest on
a much broader base than the issue of slavery. The "Dutch
Planks," which opposed any change in the immigration laws
and demanded passage of a homestead act, and other planks
that supported river and harbor improvements and a federal
subsidy for a Pacific railroad could be said to have made the
platform sectional (these were things the southern representatives in Congress had voted down) but certainly not abolitionist. In fact, the old abolitionist wing had to be content with the
"inalienable rights" statement of the Declaration of Independence.[30]

On the eve of the balloting Halstead was still predicting that
Seward would win the nomination. Thus he was bitterly disappointed when at the end of the third ballot (Seward led on the
first two, but Lincoln pulled within one and a half votes of
nomination on the last), a delegate from Ohio arose and gave
Lincoln four additional votes and the nomination. The "Stop
Seward" movement among those who felt he was too closely
identified with the abolitionist wing of the party had been successful, and Halstead felt he saw another reason for condemning
party conventions as a means of choosing candidates and writing
platforms. He concluded:

The fact of the Convention was the defeat of Seward rather than the
nomination of Lincoln. It was the triumph of a presumption of
availability over pre-eminence in intellect and unrivaled fame—a
success of the ruder qualities of manhood and the more homely
attributes of popularity over the arts of a consummate politician and
the splendor of accomplished statesmanship.[31]

The southern Democrats, or Constitutional Democrats as
they preferred to be called, met in Richmond on June 11, and
Halstead was again at the reporters' table to witness the pro-

ceedings. Attendance was very small (even though the convention was held in the capital of Virginia, only one Virginia delegate was present), and after two days of what Halstead thought was inconsequential debate and much talk about defense of the constitution, the meeting adjourned until after the regular Democratic convention, which was to meet on the eighteenth in Baltimore.[32]

The second half of the Democratic convention in Baltimore proved to be as stormy as the first half in Charleston. The seceders, under the leadership of William Yancey, demanded readmission to the convention, and this was agreed upon except in the cases where state action had been taken and the seats of those who had left in Charleston filled by new men. This provoked a new secession that left only northern and border-state delegates and a few of the southern replacements, who nominated Stephen A. Douglas for the presidency on June 23. On the train from the convention Halstead met a northern Douglas delegate who told him that the northern Democrats were angry with the South, and had insisted, for once, that the northern wing of the party have its way. As far as he and many other northern Democrats were concerned, the South could act completely on her own. Halstead was convinced that this conversation represented the feeling of the majority of the northwestern delegates.[33]

The seceders met on the last day of the regular Democratic convention and nominated the Vice-President, John C. Breckinridge of Kentucky, a man who was considered a border-state moderate, for President. The now greatly diminished Richmond group confirmed the Baltimore seceders' nomination and adjourned. Halstead did not return for the Richmond rump meeting since the action that they would take was known beforehand, and there was little interest in their actual meeting. Moreover, Halstead had been on the road for two months, with only a brief rest in Cincinnati, and he was anxious to return home.[34]

Halstead had reason to be satisfied with his reports of the conventions. He had written the most complete eye-witness account of all the conventions but the last Richmond meeting and had scored a major coup for his newspaper. Not even the larger eastern journals could boast of such coverage. He received the great compliment of having his reports copied by many of the northern and northwestern newspapers. Usually, these newspapers gave the author full credit for his work, though in one case a paper claimed that the reports were from its own special correspondent. This newspaper, the *Herald,* of Cleveland, changed a few words here and there and then signed their columns with an "S." [35] The *Commercial* had to defend editorially the attacks from other newspapers who felt its "On the Circuit of the Conventions," as Halstead's newsletters were called, were too long. The *Commercial* claimed that it was greatly complimented by the copying and criticism of the reports and felt much more amusement than annoyance at the harping of those journals whose jealousy at a job well done had prompted the attack. The most annoying feature to the *Commercial* was their habit of criticizing prognostications made in the reports and playing up the wrong guesses made by the author, but never mentioning the times when his guesses turned out to be correct.[36]

Nonetheless, the criticism and the copying all proved that many had read the reports with interest, and many had obtained all their firsthand information of the conventions from the pen of Murat Halstead. The worth of these interesting and informative reports was also noted by the enterprising publishing firm of Follett, Foster and Company, of Columbus, the publishers of the Lincoln-Douglas debates, who quickly brought out the Cincinnati journalist's correspondence in book form as a companion piece to William Dean Howells' campaign biography of Lincoln, which they also published in 1860.[37] Halstead's often sarcastic and biting commentary did not find particular favor with the politicians of 1860, but it has become a basic source for historians. Halstead himself believed the publishers did a very poor job, both limiting the number of pages and marring the narrative with serious omissions. In 1887 when Nicolay and Hay quoted from it in their biography of Lincoln, he received many requests for information about the book, which he answered by saying that it could be found only in libraries with large collections of pamphlets and documents and was regarded as a curiosity.[38] Nonetheless, this curiosity has been quoted by almost every major historian writing about Lincoln or the Civil War years, and with only a few exceptions, Halstead's reporting ability has always been given credit.

In 1960 William Best Hesseltine, the biographer of Grant, brought out a revised edition of the 1860 work, calling it *Three against Lincoln*. Professor Hesseltine pointed out in his introduction that the main point of the original reports was almost completely ignored at the time. Halstead felt the conventions of 1860 had proved that the "caucus system" was a failure and that it defrauded the American people of their effective rights of suffrage. "King Caucus," the editor claimed, permeated American political life with his corruption. All decisions were made in government with an eye to his next meeting, and the nominees were thus only his "obsequious viceroys." Halstead warned his readers that a bonfire must be made of "King Caucus's throne" if the country was to retain a republican form of government.[39]

Halstead did not easily overcome the keen disappointment that he suffered when Seward failed to receive the Republican nomination; but the principles of the party held his whole-hearted support, and so he worked hard for Lincoln's election. The jubilation he felt after the election was great, but it was more for the triumph of the party than the triumph of the man. In fact, it would be only after Lincoln's death that Halstead would appreciate those qualities that made him a great President.

As the southern states began passing ordinances dissolving

the union between them and the other states, Halstead began
to have second thoughts about the complete justice in the
northern cause. Cincinnati had many close ties with the South.
Many of her citizens were of southern origins; many of her
leading businessmen were engaged in trade with the southern
states; and only a river separated her from a state where slavery
was still legal. Though these close ties had convinced many
Cincinnatians that all compromise was impossible, Halstead
urged that the national government take no coercive steps
against the South. He proposed as the best solution to the
problem a national convention that would find a compromise
solution or end the old union on lines satisfactory to all the
states.[40]

The firing on Sumter ended Halstead's agitation for a national convention. The Union had been attacked, and he and
his fellow Cincinnatians did not hesitate in declaring their
complete loyalty to the national government. Potter had not
shared Halstead's apprehensions as far as Lincoln was concerned, and so the *Commercial* had been willing generally to
give him every chance to prove himself in office. Although
Halstead still felt that Seward and Chase were greater men
than Lincoln, he had been determined from the beginning of
Lincoln's term to support his administration and the cause of
the Union.[41]

Though the events of the day had a personal meaning for the
editor of the *Commercial,* Halstead's uppermost concern was
the meaning they had for his newspaper. It is often said that a
revolution in journalism took place with the coming of the war.
Although this is certainly true, it is also true that for several
years Halstead had been introducing into the news-gathering
practices of the *Commercial* many of the innovations that were
now to become general in the American newspaper world. The
most important of these innovations was a result of the necessity for prompt reporting and publishing of events soon after
they occurred. A newspaper might still remain a sounding

board for its editor's opinions, but if it did not carry up-to-the-minute news, its public would find another source of information. As sons and brothers, husbands and fathers, marched off to join the crusade for the North or for the South, those people left at home became more and more insistent that the progress of the army be followed—and not followed several weeks later in the stilted prose of a war historian, but followed by a man on the spot whose reports could at least vicariously recreate for the reader the action, the suffering, and the valiant efforts found on the fields of battle.[42]

For several years the *Commercial* had received brief telegraphed reports of the latest New York and Washington news. Halstead had felt that it was necessary to supplement these brief telegrams with longer articles from the latest editions of the exchange newspapers or with reports sent by railroad from special correspondents. Now, with speed one of the newspaperman's greatest concerns, the telegraph achieved a far greater importance. Many editors complained bitterly about this necessity to rely upon the telegraph. Reports carried over its wires were relatively expensive, and at the beginning of the war the reports that were most often telegraphed were sensational and often not verified by the reporters. It was not long, however, until the telegraph wire became the news editor's best friend.[43]

Though most newspapers either had their own special correspondents at Washington or shared one with another paper, the idea of large numbers of reporters in far-flung corners of the country writing regular reports of the happenings in their area was rather foreign to American newspaper life. Now all this was changed by the war. All the major journals found it necessary to have a full staff with each army. To bring the reading public the complete picture of a battle meant that reporters had to be on the front lines with the men, at the army headquarters with the commanders, and at points of vantage to be able to see the whole sweep of the fighting. Few newspapers were able to fulfil all these requirements, but as a goal of good reporting, many tried. The *Commercial* was not able financially to attempt to compete in this manner with the leading eastern papers, but it did have at least one correspondent with all the major armies most of the time. Often, arrangements were made with reporters from the New York newspapers, like the *Tribune* or the *Times,* to send articles to the *Commercial;* and often, Halstead himself would take on the role he had assumed at Harpers Ferry, at Buchanan's inauguration, and at the conventions of 1860, and become a special correspondent, reporting the news from Washington or from a battlefield near Washington.[44]

Halstead spent most of the month of June, 1861, in and around Washington, sending a daily newsletter to the *Commercial*. In his first dispatches written soon after the outbreak of hostilities, Halstead began the criticism of the actions of officers and governmental officials in waging the war that later caused his journalistic rivals to bestow upon him the title of "Field Marshal." Arriving in Washington, Halstead was immediately struck by the terrible June heat and the clouds of dust that the heat and lack of rain helped form on the streets. The large number of troops that had been sent into the city were encamped in a ring about two miles from the Capitol; but even so, he found the most distinctive feature of the downtown area to be the great numbers of men in uniform.

One of the first things Halstead did after his arrival was to visit the camps of the Ohio regiments. After passing the camps of beautifully uniformed and plentifully supplied volunteers from other states, he was mortified to come upon the Ohio soldiers. He found them demoralized and in ragged condition. Writing indignantly that they had been hurried out of the state unprepared, he said that once they had left Ohio a dispute arose between state and federal officials over whose responsibility it was to provide for them. While the argument was still in progress, Halstead reported that some uniforms had been sent but that they were of the worst possible material, in many ways comparable to paper. The seams of the trousers, he wrote, "could be pulled open with the fingers. . . ." Since Ohio had appropriated a million dollars for her troops, he asked why it was necessary for them to be styled paupers by the other regiments? The men themselves blamed their misfortune on Ohio's adjutant general, H. B. Carrington, and were convinced that he allowed some of the contractors to make money from their distress.[45] Halstead insisted that he was not reporting the plight of the Ohio soldiers to create a sensation but to let every citizen of Ohio know that the state was being disgraced.[46]

Halstead's fighting newsletters, and the protests of Ohio officials in Washington, were successful. By June 10 he was able to write that the troops had been supplied with new uniforms and that they would receive a month's pay the next day. He declared that if the government granted a liberal furlough policy the men would find nothing more to complain about during their service and would probably stay in the army until the end of the war.[47]

During the month Halstead was in Washington, hardly a day passed that he did not find some bit of military strategy that required modification or correction. One basic recurring theme was found in his suggestion that the motto "Delays are Dangerous" should be posted on all the desks in the War Department and in adjutant general offices across the country. "Time," he wrote, "is the most costly of all human possessions. . . ." Yet while he thought minutes were important to the war effort, he found hours and days wasted. He claimed that "Circumlocation Offices" in the War Department and the red tape and other delays found in other departmental offices caused hardships on the soldiers, and kept the army from making progress.[48] Although he was fairly critical of Secretary Gideon Welles's handling of the Navy Department (Cincinnati boat-builders

were not receiving their fair share of the contracts), Halstead's
pen fairly dripped with venom when he wrote of Simon Cameron in the War Department:

No one ever suspected Cameron of honesty, but there were hopes that
he had business capacity and that . . . he would make a reputation
for integrity. In truth, however, he is very incompetent. . . . Cameron attends to the stealing department. . . . It would be of greater
advantage to the country than to gain a battle, to have Cameron
kicked out of the cabinet.

Specifically, Halstead charged that Cameron was incapable of
running his department and that most of the work was being
done by General Winfield Scott and Secretary of the Treasury
Salmon P. Chase. Moreover, he said that Cameron's relatives
had all been placed in the War Department in lucrative jobs or
were selling goods to the army at highly inflated prices.[49] Halstead reported that he had met a fellow Cincinnatian in Washington who had come to the capital city to gain a contract for
his foundry to cast cannon balls for the army in the West. The
foundry man was told by Cameron that he had already decided
to give the contract to some Pennsylvania foundries, and the
cynical Halstead concluded that the Pennsylvania foundries
that would get the work probably were those belonging to a
man named Simon Cameron. The editor's charges were widely
echoed in the press and in the halls of Congress.[50]

About the only person in the cabinet that Halstead did not
complain about was the Cincinnatian, Chase. Not only did
Halstead say that Chase was doing the work of the secretary of
war, but he also claimed that Chase was the driving wheel of
the whole administration.

Halstead constantly complained that every politician who
could make a stump speech thought he deserved a commission
in the army. Moreover, if the politician held enough political
power, he usually received one. Halstead also claimed that
these "political soldiers" were advanced in the ranks when

more worthy officers, of proven performance but without political power, were more deserving of recognition.[51] He elaborated, "I know of several instances in which perfect boobies have been given commissions, while most meritorious applications are unheeded." Moreover, the Ohio editor claimed, "A word from a silly Congressman has often gone farther than the highest grade of merit in securing appointments." These appointments had the positive good of creating and maintaining national unity, but Halstead, like other critics, saw them as only political pay-offs.[52]

During this first wartime visit to Washington Halstead made several excursions into the surrounding area. Though he did not witness any battles, these trips provided him with the knowledge of the area that later made his editorial writing on the progress of the Union forces lively and vivid. On one visit he toured Robert E. Lee's estates and inspected the fortifications and camps established to protect Washington from a Confederate invasion.[53] On another trip he went down to Alexandria, a city of almost eleven thousand before the war, but now practically deserted.[54]

The farthest that the Cincinnati reporter went into Confederate territory during this period was to Fortress Monroe, an outpost still held by the national government at the mouth of Chesapeake Bay, between the James and York rivers. The government was running a daily steamer from Baltimore to the fort, and permission to make the visit was easily obtained. Fortress Monroe was considered of the greatest strategic importance in commanding the waterway system of Virginia, and would often figure in reports from correspondents during the war; but Halstead's visit was during a period of calm.[55]

The most personally galling of all of Halstead's complaints in Washington was that as a newsman in the city to gather information for his Cincinnati readers, he was unable to find a source of reliable news. The War Department, which he said should be the greatest source of information, was staffed with

particularly uncommunicative officials. Even when he was able
to learn some particular intelligence about a battle or a troop
movement, he found he had to contend with a censor in the
telegraph office. Halstead realized that the enemy might gain
valuable information from the reports of resourceful newsmen
who were able to learn advance army plans, and he was not
hostile to the idea of keeping this information from the telegraph. His main criticism was that the censorship rules were
applied in such ways that the reporter could never really be
sure which dispatches would pass and which ones would not.[56]
The problem was extremely serious. Commanders claimed that
through knowledge that was gained from northern newspapers,
the southern army leaders were able to escape traps or prepare
for actions when surprise was the major element in the northern plans. On the other hand, Halstead and the northern editors in general claimed that the reading public had a right to
know what was happening in the army. The principal problem
seemed to be that the censors themselves were too ill informed
to make intelligent decisions on what news to release and what
news to withhold. The end result was controversy and bad
feelings between the reporters and the War Department. The
situation was so bad that some commanders even found it
necessary to bar reporters from their camps.[57]

Halstead's most serious conflict with a northern general
came in December, 1861. Henry Villard, a German immigrant
who had covered Lincoln's campaign for the *New York Herald*
(and was later to gain control of the Northern Pacific Railroad), was at General William Tecumseh Sherman's headquarters in Louisville representing the *Commercial*. In November,
Secretary of War Cameron arrived on an inspection visit. For
several weeks guests at the hotel where Sherman made his
headquarters had noticed the general pacing up and down the
corridors hour after hour, so preoccupied that he did not seem
to notice his surroundings. This preoccupation had led to gos-
sip, and it was soon whispered about that Sherman was having

mental difficulties. When Cameron arrived in Louisville, Sherman asked him for a private interview to discuss the military situation in the West. Cameron had traveling with him a special correspondent for the *New York Tribune,* and he allowed this correspondent to attend the meeting with Sherman. During the course of the talk Sherman told Cameron that he would need at least two hundred thousand men to march South. The *Tribune* man later told Villard of this figure and said that he felt the general must be "unhinged." [58]

When this news became known in Louisville, many people, remembering the reports of Sherman's strange behavior in his hotel, concluded that he was insane and should be removed from command. The rumor soon spread that he was frightened of a southern invasion and might take his army into Indiana, abandoning the loyal people of Louisville. Since the people of Louisville feared that any accusations they would make about Sherman's mental health would be attributed to southern leanings, they contacted Villard and asked him to return to Cincinnati and report the whole situation to Halstead, a man whose loyalty to the northern cause could not be questioned.[59] The end result of this was a *Commercial* headline, "General Sherman Insane." [60]

Sherman may well have needed a rest, but it was quite evident to those who were close to him that he was not insane. Asking to be relieved of his command, he returned to his Lancaster home for a few weeks and then went to St. Louis, where he was placed in a subordinate position. Sherman was livid with anger about the whole situation and quite rightly blamed the press, and Halstead in particular, for most of his problems. In his memoirs he said:

The newspapers kept up their game as though instigated by malice, and chief among them was the Cincinnati *Commercial,* whose editor, Halsted [*sic*] was generally believed to be an honorable man. P. B. Ewing [Sherman's brother-in-law], being in Cincinnati, saw him and asked him why he, who certainly knew better would reiterate such a damaging slander. He answered, quite cavalierly, that it was one of the news-items of the day, and he had to keep up with the time; but he would be most happy to publish any correction I might make, as though I could deny such a malicious piece of scandal affecting myself.[61]

Sherman had never trusted reporters and had often lectured them on what they could and could not say about his plans and ideas. After this incident the life of a reporter in Sherman's army was almost impossible, and many, in fact, were ordered from his camps. As can be imagined, reporters from the *Commercial* were not well received from this time on in Sherman's headquarters.[62] Once, he asserted, "I never see my name in print without a feeling of contamination, and I will undertake to forego half my salary if the newspapers will ignore my name." [63]

Though Sherman never really forgave him for his part in the insanity stories, Halstead and the general became friends in later years and often corresponded. When Sherman's memoirs were published, Halstead wrote to him about the above passage. The general said that he had no feelings of malice in publishing the story, but thought it might be useful to others. If Halstead desired, he promised to withdraw his name from the second edition. While there is no reply available from Halstead, the later editions of the memoirs all include the passage with his name.[64] Many years later, Halstead appeared on the same program with Sherman at a dinner at Delmonico's given by the New York Press Club. Halstead, who spoke first, recalled that Sherman had run a school of journalism in the West, a humorous reference to the general's action in running reporters out of his camps. Along the same line, the man introducing Sherman said that this was the perfect time should he wish to apologize to the press for his treatment of their representatives during the war. The old general, in less than humorous mood, settled old accounts by his opening sentence, addressed to

Halstead: "You ought to have been put into Fort Lafayette—and you know it." Halstead admitted that this may have
been true and said that something of the sort was probably
needed by many of the editors and reporters of the era. The
general, making his last public appearance on this night, soon
found himself in a more mellow mood and, dropping the press
business, gave a talk on the old army before the war.[65]

Throughout 1861 Halstead continued to combine the jobs of
editor and special correspondent. Returning to Cincinnati at
the end of June, he spent the month of July editing the *Commercial* and writing strong editorials in support of the Union.
At the same time he often printed editorials that condemned
the administration's handling of the war effort. In fact, the
rival Democratic *Enquirer* felt called upon to defend the administration from Republican papers like the *Commercial*
after some of its comments had appeared on how the war
should be handled.[66]

In the fall Halstead attended both the Democratic and
Union party conventions in Columbus. As was the case with the
national Democratic conventions in 1860, the editor's Republican-Unionist predilections made it impossible for him to send
completely unbiased reports from the Democratic meetings;
but he happily reported that the "secesh sympathizers" wing of
the party seemed to be in the minority, thus making the platform less violent on the war question than it would have been
without the presence of so many War Democrats.[67] The tame
platform, according to Halstead, still should not obscure the
fact that because of the peril that the country faced, the Republican party had invited the Democrats to unite with them and
nominate one combined ticket. That they refused and nominated their own ticket meant to him that they were willing to
sacrifice their country for the benefit of their party. Their
platform claim that the Democratic party, since it had always
opposed sectionalism, could not be counted responsible for the

war, brought Halstead's most scornful comment on the convention: "The Democratic party not responsible for sectionalism indeed!" [68]

"The intelligent, honest and patriotic people of Ohio" looked with more hope and confidence, Halstead insisted, on the Republican-Union convention that met a month later in September. He characterized the delegates as a "very good class of men" and felt that the large turnout of Douglas Democrats assured the party's success.[69] Halstead believed that David Tod of Youngstown, a Douglas Democrat, was a wise choice for the Union nomination for governor, and he applauded the decision to divide the nominations for the other state offices between the Republicans and War Democrats. The convention's resolve to fight the campaign entirely on the lines of support for the Union and the constitution met his wholehearted approval.[70]

Halstead's reports were always marked with a completely personal approach that not only combined firsthand news of the convention but also gave his readers a picture of the behind-the-scenes activities. An example of this would be his complaint that Columbus was no place in which to hold a convention of any size. The fire that had leveled the Neil House and consumed "an infinite assortment of roaches" had left the city without a decent hotel or one that was capable of lodging any number of delegates. In fact, he said there was not a hall in the city large enough to accommodate the meetings. The Republican convention was actually held on the east steps of the capitol. The theater for which it was first scheduled produced the same scare situation as that which Halstead had described at the Baltimore meeting of the Constitutional Union party. An old building packed with people and the rumor that the floor was settling set the stage for a panic. The panic came when a man mounted a bench and asked if a certain doctor was present. A piece of plaster fell from the ceiling onto his hat and there were immediate screams that the ceiling was falling. In seconds the supposedly dignified representatives of the people of Ohio were "leaping with the agility of cats over chairs and benches, and tumbling over each other down the stairway." As had been the case in Baltimore, the building was discovered to be safe, and the embarrassed delegates returned, but decided to adjourn to a location where they might feel more comfortable and less fearful for their safety.[71]

Editorially, the *Commercial* supported the Union ticket, taking the line that a vote for the Democrats was a vote for treason. Although the *Commercial* did not claim that all Democrats were traitors, it did say that all the traitors in the state were Democrats. Thus Halstead insisted that loyal men, who hoped and prayed for the success of the Union cause, could do nothing less than vote for Tod and the complete Union ticket.[72] The election returns gave Tod a fifty-thousand-vote majority over his Democratic opponent, but the more than 150,000 votes polled by Ohio Democrats showed they were not willing to give up their party organization.[73]

The outbreak of the war found the people of Cincinnati in a state of near panic. There was great fear—particularly if Kentucky should secede—that the city would be seized by the Confederates. The measures taken for the city's defense included the mounting of huge guns in the surrounding hills and the establishing of a military camp in the near vicinity. Yet the fear of a southern attack proved virtually groundless.[74] With Kentucky remaining in the Union, Cincinnati was no longer a border city and her safety was threatened only three times throughout the war. Two of these threats came in 1862. The first, in July, was the least serious. It was the result of a raid by Colonel John Morgan into Kentucky. Morgan's cavalry came through Kentucky wrecking railroad lines, destroying bridges, and in general interrupting communications and throwing many of Cincinnati's citizens into a panic. Halstead felt that the situation was alarming and entitled a *Commercial* editorial "TO ARMS!" He called upon all citizens capable of bearing arms to turn out for the public defense.[75] Morgan, after inflicting much property damage, turned southward again after reaching Paris, Kentucky.[76] The panic over, Halstead chastised the citizens of the city and their officials for what he termed their disgusting reaction to the attack threat. When the enemy was near he said that, instead of the strong united stand that was necessary to meet the attack, everything was in confusion and nothing was done except a vast amount of talking. He claimed that everyone had his own theory of what to do, and consequently, nothing was accomplished. What the situation demanded, according to the *Commerical*'s editor, was a military system that could be placed in immediate operation should the city be threatened by another attack.[77]

The second alarm came just two months later and was certainly the most serious of the three threats to Cincinnati. General Kirby Smith with a force estimated at between ten and fifteen thousand men was marching northward through Kentucky. Halstead blamed those in authority for this second possible raid. He claimed that if the city officials had followed his advice in July, the city would have been adequately defended and the Confederate armies would not dare even threaten it. Since his earlier advice had not been followed, he insisted that the present invasion made it necessary to call out every citizen in the city capable of bearing arms. He argued that this plan would save the city and that after these men had been drilled, they would always constitute a ready reserve for future emergencies.[78]

Halstead's proposal was followed. General Ben Wallace, the commander of the military district that included Cincinnati, declared martial law, and the mayor suspended all business in the city so that the men might be used for defense purposes. Those men who did not willingly volunteer for service were impressed. Though Halstead himself had recommended this plan, he nonetheless felt compelled to complain when he found the provost guards, who had been organized for the impressments, were over-zealous in their search for delinquents. He claimed many of them took "keen enjoyment" in their work and impressed some who were too old or too ill for work on the trenches.[79]

With business suspended, gangs of men working on the city's defenses, others drilling, and regiments pouring in for the rescue, Halstead thought Cincinnati seemed very much like Washington in June of 1861. "All day the city resounded with the measured tread of armed men. . . . The din of drum and the piercing notes of the fife, were constantly heard, far and near. . . ." [80] Added to the more military-like aspect of the city was a group of men who had shouldered their own guns and had come from various parts of southern Ohio when they heard of the invasion threat. Their unmilitary appearance and the variety found in their firearms soon earned them the name "Squirrel Hunters." The first week of September witnessed the massing of many volunteers and the building of many additional defenses around the city.[81] Then the rumor was started that the alarm was false, and many of the Squirrel Hunters began returning to their homes. Halstead felt compelled to try to counteract the rumor. He stated editorially that the announced purpose of Kirby Smith was to take Cincinnati and that the city had to be ready for him. Between the sixth and eleventh of September, as more and more of the volunteers abandoned their posts, Halstead's editorials stressed Cincinnati's real danger and the need for preparedness. Halstead maintained that the fortifications should be pushed forward as if there were only a few hours left in which to prepare to defend the city and that the Squirrel Hunters should hold themselves as "minute men" ready at an instant's notice to return.[82]

On the tenth the military authorities sent out the alarm once again. They were convinced that the rebel forces were massing for an attack just ten miles from the Queen City. The prompt answer that the Squirrel Hunters gave the call and the improved fortifications surrounding the city convinced Halstead that the enemy would not succeed, but he still called for more volunteers. By this time he not only wanted to save Cincinnati but also to inflict a damaging blow to the invading army.[83] On the twelfth the Confederate army was "almost within rifle cannon range of the City," Halstead reported, but it commenced an almost immediate retreat. Actually, only a few companies out of Smith's army had advanced close to Cincinnati, and these only to cover the retreat of the main force. Thus on the thirteenth Halstead predicted that the "state of seige" would soon be over, and congratulated the Cincinnatians on the record they made in defending their city.[84]

Even after the withdrawal of the southern army, martial law was retained throughout most of the month of September, and until the twenty-fourth all business was suspended at four o'clock for daily drills. Since the regular drilling of every able-bodied male in the city had been one of Halstead's demands, he was quite pleased, and claimed that the orders placed the city in shape to ward off any future attack.[85]

The final panic came in July, 1863, and cannot really be termed a serious invasion threat. Once again, as in the previous July, it involved a raid by Colonel John Morgan. The raid was of slight military importance, but it did give southern Ohio its only taste of the war. Martial law was proclaimed as Morgan with a force of 2,460 men crossed the Ohio River into Indiana and blazed a crescent-shaped trail across the southern part of Indiana and Ohio. The *Commercial* claimed that Morgan had a force of nearly 5,000 men (other reports ran as high as 10,000) and again called upon the citizens of the Queen City to help intercept and destroy him. Though even an army of 5,000 men would not have been able to take Cincinnati, the fact that he was in Ohio and less than a day's ride from the city frightened many people.[86] While Halstead and most of Cincinnati's citizens were fearful of an attack, Morgan was taking his troops on a forced march to avoid the city. With just over 2,000 men left in his army, the general knew he was no match for the almost 30,000 soldiers and volunteers that had been called to Cincinnati's defense.[87]

The raiders were soon pursued by the federal cavalry. After Morgan's group had inflicted damages of over half a million dollars to Ohio's citizens, the leader was captured on July 26.[88] Halstead said the raid had caused little more damage than would have been done by a well-organized band of horse thieves, and in the long run he felt a positive good might result. That Morgan was able to cross the whole state was proof to him of the lack of preparedness of the local militias. The raid, he said, had called to people's attention that they were in a state of war and had convinced many that every township should have a company of well-armed and well-drilled militia ready for instant action.[89]

In all of the emergencies martial law or its threat brought with it military censorship of the newspapers of Cincinnati. Halstead did not complain of the censorship as he had done earlier in Washington. As the news items and the editorials in the local press reveal, the military officials were extremely lax in their control. Moreover, by the summer of 1862 Halstead had learned the importance of self-censorship. Thus while the *Commercial* gave as complete a picture as possible of the position of the enemy and its probable strategy and told of local plans for defense, it never gave details of these designs nor told of movements of the Union army. Time after time an editorial would end, ". . . for the obvious reason that publication of the state of our defenses would be far more interesting to enemies than to friends. . . ."[90] or, "The publication of details of the military preparations made in this quarter would be improper, and we only give such points as are requisite for the public information."[91]

From the outbreak of the fighting Halstead and the *Commercial* supported the war and the Union completely. As we have seen, this did not mean blind support for party. Halstead

reserved the right to criticize both friend and foe. His only
loyalty was to what was best for the war effort and what would
save the Union. Allegiance to these two principles brought him
into conflict with many in Ohio, but particularly with Clement
Vallandigham, a Democratic congressman from Dayton, and
the *Enquirer,* a Democratic newspaper and the *Commercial's*
most serious rival. The Peace Democrat position that Vallandigham and the *Enquirer* upheld naturally conflicted with Halstead's uncompromising support of the Union. Thus as early as
July, 1861, Halstead called Vallandigham and the editor of the
Enquirer "semi-secesh," and began a course of almost daily
abuse directed against the Dayton congressman and the entire
staff of the *Enquirer.*

Halstead did not dislike all Democratic newspapers, though
he said the dissolution of that party would best promote the
general welfare of the country. He just disliked the "pitiful,
whining, sneaking, snarling" of the *Enquirer.*[92] Halstead constantly complained that the *Enquirer* was doing serious injury
to the national cause. Its daily manifestations of sympathy with
the South were calculated, he declared, to encourage that section to carry on the war and to cause trouble in Kentucky.
Whenever there was a rumor afloat of a disaster to the Union
armies, and whenever politicians "whose tongues are uttering
. . . treason" made a statement, he claimed the *Enquirer*
could be counted upon to spread the sensational exaggerations
all over the paper. The effect of this type of editing, Halstead
thundered, was to deceive the South with the impression that
the great masses of northern people were not loyal to the
Union. Nothing could be further from the truth, since there
was an "inexorable resolution to wipe out in blood the inso-
lence of the rebels."[93]

Halstead could not understand why the federal authorities
allowed the *Enquirer,* an "organ of the traitors . . . the border guerrilla sheet, the comforter of assassins, the solace of
horse thieves, the favorite of house burners," to be published.

He thought it would be suppressed at once by the military if it were published on the other side of the Ohio River. The encouragement it gave to the enemy, he ominously concluded, meant that the war would be prolonged, and that more young men fighting under the Union's flag would be murdered.[94]

Part of Halstead's criticism of the *Enquirer* was a result of that newspaper's support of the Peace Democrats and Vallandigham in particular. The Peace Democrats, or Copperheads as they were soon called—Halstead claimed they were venomous and crawling creatures who were "sticking their heads out of their holes, and darting their forked tongues as if they would like to bite"—felt that a peaceful solution might be found to end the conflict between the two sections.[95] The Copperheads insisted that the use of force for the preservation of the Union was both unconstitutional and futile. They argued that only a "Union of hearts and hands" could endure. Largely of Irish-American or German-American heritage, or transplanted southerners on the lower rungs of the economic ladder, they represented a conservative force that feared the competition from free Negro labor.[96]

Halstead said the question was between peace or the preservation of the Union. Between the two, he claimed, there was no compromise. According to the Cincinnati editor, Vallandigham, with his concern over the shedding of blood between brothers, was a hypocrite. Where was he, Halstead asked, when the secessionists were seizing United States forts, robbing United States arsenals, or firing on Fort Sumter? At times when the Union was in danger and its loyal supporters were being killed, Halstead found him "exceedingly calm and philosophic." It was only when the nation had assumed an attitude of self-defense and he could see that the demands of justice were to be executed that Vallandigham became excited. "The blood of the innocent victim didn't disturb [him], but the hanging of the criminal was frightful." [97]

Halstead was particularly upset when he discovered that,

under the influence of men like Vallandigham and the publishers of the *Enquirer,* the Peace Democrats were working in Cincinnati to stir up dissatisfaction with the war and to keep young men from volunteering for the army. One of the arguments they used was that it was a "nigger war," and that a white man from the North should not become involved.[98] Halstead had insisted from the first that the question of slavery was secondary to that of the preservation of the Union. Although he had become an abolitionist and did believe the war would result in the crushing of the institution of slavery, the real objective of the war for him was to vindicate the laws of the nation.[99] In fact, he was as critical of what he called the "rabid anti-slavery agitators" as he was of the Copperheads. He claimed that the antislavery men's criticism of the administration often furnished the Copperheads their best material in their war against the government.[100]

As the time for the fall elections of 1862 approached, Halstead became more and more convinced that the real danger was not, as he said, "that the armies of the Union will fall in a fair fight," but that the internal dissensions raised by such demagogues as Vallandigham would shatter the confidence of the people in their government. Democratic criticism of the administration in such times of peril was to him a blunder, and, while not necessarily treason, it was a mistake that had all the consequences of a crime.[101] He did not feel that all the nominees of the Union party were the best possible men for the jobs, but he said they were pledged to support the administration and to preserve the Union, and as such deserved the support of all loyal citizens. The Democratic nominees, though he admitted some were personally fine men, were dedicated to the embarrassment of the administration, and as such would, if elected, give comfort to the enemy.[102] The campaign that the *Commercial* waged most vehemently in the fall of 1862 was for the defeat of Vallandigham's re-election to Congress. Vallandigham's district was gerrymandered by the state legislature to include the overwhelmingly Republican Warren County. It was thus assumed that he would be defeated, but the Democrats claimed it was possible only by these rather shoddy methods. To overcome this criticism, Halstead called for his defeat in the old district as well as the reorganized one. If he could not be beaten, Halstead said, the disgrace would be "black, burning, and infinitely shameful." [103]

Vallandigham was defeated, but the over-all result, both in Ohio and in the country in general, was a defeat for the Union party. George Pendleton, the Democratic congressman from Cincinnati's First District, was re-elected, even though Halstead had editorialized that Pendleton invariably voted with Vallandigham and that his speeches were "tinctured with a tender feeling towards the rebel in arms." [104] Halstead found many reasons to explain the action of the American people at the polls. He felt that many had voted for the Democrats with the mistaken idea that their victory would in some way bring the war to an end. To him it was a mistaken idea because the war would only end with the defeat of one side or the other. Many others, he claimed, had been dissatisfied with the administration's conduct of the war and had voted Democratic as a protest. Others, he said, were influenced by the race prejudice that the Democrats had inflamed during the campaign. Finally, he said that many thousands of soldiers who would have supported the Union ticket were in the field and unable to vote.[105]

Though Halstead insisted that the country's best hope was still found with the Union party and the existing administration, he did believe that much of the criticism of the administration's war effort was valid. He said that the people were restless under the prospect of an indefinite prolongation of the war; of a system where victories were rarely followed up; of battles without decisive results; and of months of inaction on the part of large segments of the army. He admitted that many factors and individuals were to blame for this situation, but he said that under the American political system the administra-

tion must take the responsibility when the situation was bad if
it was to receive the credit when that was due.[106]

Vallandigham, who felt that his defeat, especially at a time
when so many of his party had been elected, was particularly
unfair, became even more defiant in his speeches. He continually urged peace between the two sections by conciliation and
bitterly denounced what he called the unconstitutional measures of the Lincoln administration. Halstead, as earlier stated,
felt that his utterances were treasonable, and General Burnside, commander of the Department of Ohio, obviously agreed
with the editor. In General Order No. 38, Burnside announced
his intention to arrest anyone who declared his sympathy for
the enemy. In a speech at Mt. Vernon, Vallandigham not only
denounced the war as he often had before but also attacked
General Order No. 38, declaring his authority was "General
Orders No. 1—the Constitution." Burnside had him placed
under arrest, and after a trial by a military commission whose
authority Vallandigham refused to recognize, the former congressman was sentenced to prison for the duration of the war.
The trial and conviction made him a martyr to the Peace
Democrat cause and increased his popularity in Ohio im-
mensely. Lincoln realized that Burnside had blundered but felt
that since the action had been taken, he must uphold the
military's decision. He finally decided to change the sentence to
exile to the Confederacy. Vallandigham was consequently sent
to Tennessee, from where he later went to Canada. The Ohio
Democratic convention, which met in June, 1863, in a reaction
against what was considered the unconstitutional manner of
Vallandigham's trial and sentence, nominated him as their candidate for governor.[107]

Halstead approved of Vallandigham's arrest and conviction.
It was, he said, "high time that the loyal sentiment of the
people of the northwest was making itself felt." [108] Thus when
the Democratic party made its gubernatorial nomination, he
declared that the issue between the two parties was squarely

joined and that the people of Ohio would not allow the calamity of Vallandigham's election to take place.[109] Halstead's choice for the Union party's nomination was John Brough, a former Democratic state auditor who had retired from politics to take over the presidency of a railroad. The *Commercial* published a strong Union speech that Brough delivered at Marietta and in an editorial declared that "the coming man has arrived." Brough's former support of the Democratic party, his vigor in upholding the Union cause, and the enthusiasm that the Marietta speech inspired all over the state convinced Halstead that he had found the candidate who would and could win in November.[110] Brough's support spread rapidly, and he was nominated on the first ballot by the Union convention.

During the campaign Halstead attempted through his *Commercial* editorials to emphasize the traitorous activities and the fanaticism of the Democratic candidate. The old issue of Vallandigham's sympathies for the South was again raised, and Halstead declared that Ohio was on trial. Should Vallandigham win, the editor prophesied that the victory would be hailed by southern rebels, British Tories, French interventionists, and northern traitors—by all the enemies of America—as their victory. It would, his gloomy prediction concluded, "[presage] the irretrievable downfall of the Union." [111] It was in the midst of the campaign that Halstead first recognized that perhaps General Burnside's action in arresting the Democratic candidate had been a mistake. He thought that Vallandigham was a much more imposing person in exile than he would have been campaigning in the state. Brough's majority would be increased many thousands, the editor claimed, if Vallandigham was in Ohio on the stump. Moreover, he asserted that the Democrats realized this also and refused to accept the liberal terms that Lincoln imposed for removing the obstacles in the way of his return. These terms were that the committee petitioning the President for his return agree to support the war. This they refused to do.[112]

As election day approached, Halstead's editorials against the Democratic candidate became increasingly more vehement. His election, it was claimed, would seal the doom of the Union and spark civil war in Ohio.[113] Personally, he was called a traitor, an assassin, and a "malignant and atrocious wretch." [114] The greatest disgrace, the editor declared, was that one single Ohio voter might cast his ballot for the southern sympathizer. On election day, after a campaign marked by its viciousness, Halstead asserted that Vallandigham would be defeated; but by now he felt his defeat was not enough. Now he demanded the people of Ohio give Brough at least a 100,000 majority, a majority that would inspire the American people from Maine to California and that would show the Union armies that the people of Ohio were with them.[115]

Thus it was with great jubilation that Halstead announced Brough's victory. Brough received over a 100,000 majority, and the relieved editor said it proved that Ohio was wholeheartedly in support of the Union. This victory, he declared, would, by showing the South that the North was united, have the effect of proving the absolute hopelessness of the rebellion and shorten the war.[116] The result had probably really been determined by the Union victories at Gettysburg and Vicksburg, which proved that the North was capable of military successes. With its defeat in the election, Copperheadism was no longer a serious threat to the Union. Vallandigham also lost much of his influence in the Democratic party; and when he illegally returned before the end of the war, the government, rather than give him added publicity and notoriety, chose to ignore his presence.

Halstead again traveled to Washington for the December 1, 1862, opening of Congress. Arriving a few days early, he was the guest of Senator Pomeroy at a Thanksgiving Day dinner for Negroes who had escaped to Washington from the South. Among the other guests was Harriet Beecher Stowe.[117] Halstead found Washington changed from his last visit. The crowds were as great as they had been on his first wartime trip, but he missed the old faces. He thought that the old stock had seemingly perished, both at social gatherings, on the streets, and in Congress. Those leaders of old Washington society, so often southern in sympathy, were nowhere in evidence.[118]

As on his earlier visit, Halstead secured a pass and rode out to inspect the fortifications around the city. He found every eminence for miles around crowned with a fort. Acres of underbrush had been cleared and the fences all removed. What had only two years before been rich farm land was now a vast waste dotted by the encampments and forts. The forts were connected by long lines of rifle pits with occasional placements of batteries of siege guns. From what he saw, Halstead concluded that Washington was reasonably safe. He thus wondered why it was necessary to retain such large numbers of troops for defense when they could obviously be used to better advantage—as, he queried, "Why not use [them] to take Richmond?" [119]

This was a time when northern editors were urging the government to march on the Confederate capital, and Halstead was no exception. All the editors and reporters had their plans as to how Richmond would be taken, and again, Halstead was no exception. He asserted that there was only one sensible way of taking the rebel city, and that was to use the Union's command of water transportation in Virginia to move the northern armies to the closest point possible and then to march on the city.[120] He claimed the reason that Richmond had not already fallen was that the nation did not have a man at the head of its military affairs who was quick to take responsibility, or who could promptly and competently dispatch executive business.[121]

After much difficulty, Halstead was able to secure a pass to join the Army of the Potomac. He had heard rumors of approaching action, and his newspaperman's instincts demanded that he be where he could get the best story. When General McClellan was relieved of command of the Army of the Potomac and General Burnside appointed as his successor, Halstead had doubts as to whether the situation had been improved; but he defended the President's action. Democratic newspapers complained that Lincoln had succumbed to radical antislavery pressure in his removal of the conservative McClellan, but Halstead said that this had not been the case. The President wanted a man of action, and Halstead declared he hoped such a commander would be found in Burnside. When it looked as though the long awaited march on Richmond might start, the Cincinnati editor planned to be with the new commander's army.[122]

He wrote rather bitterly that he had spent two days getting his pass, but that it stayed folded in his pocket from the time he left the War Department in Washington until he reached General Burnside's tent with the army in Virginia. Traveling by boat from Washington to Acquai Creek, a sixty-mile journey, then by a military train for the remainder of the trip, Halstead reached the army on December 13.[123] On the boat from Washington to Acquia Landing he learned that a reporter friend of his was with the army, and since he had few supplies or friends at the camp, he decided to try to find his friend. He found the encampment as confusing as a large city, but after trudging through deep mud long into the night, he found the right tent but not his friend. He was made welcome, but was told that the southern armies would begin their bombardments in the morning, and that the Union army was determined to force the passage of the Rappahannock the next day. Warned of the dangers, he was given permission to stay if he wished. The next morning, an hour before dawn, operations commenced. The troops, taking up their haversacks and cartridge boxes fell in at the call of the bugle to march silently off to the Battle of Fredericksburg.[124]

Halstead was not a trained military reporter, but he quickly realized that the Battle of Fredericksburg was a "blunder and disaster," a judgment with which later historians would agree. Randall calls it one of the "colossal blunders of the War." [125] In a signed editorial—one of the few in all the files of the early *Commercial*—that he telegraphed from Washington, Halstead said the battle was hopeless from the beginning. The rebels commanded a formidable natural position, had a large army, and were supplied with well-placed artillery. The whole situation, he concluded, "was an enormous trap, and the Union army had to withdraw at once or worse would yet come." [126] Ohio regiments suffered heavily. Some of Halstead's friends were among the casualties, and he experienced for the first time a sense of guilt for not being in the ranks with them, instead of merely looking on from a semi-sheltered location with a pair of field glasses. Potter, a semi-invalid by this time, had prevailed upon him not to enlist for military service, saying that the *Commercial* needed him and that as an effective writer, he could do more for the Union with his pen than with a gun. [127] A disheartened Halstead returned to Cincinnati after the battle. He was still determined that the North must be victorious, but his private confidence in the Lincoln administration and the ability of the Union army was greatly shaken. Thus when the report of General Burnside's resignation of the command of the Army of the Potomac reached Cincinnati, Halstead commented that this was certainly good news. Burnside's successor, General Hooker, was declared to be a fighting man who could restore the confidence of the army. [128]

Although Halstead supported the Union cause and the administration, from more than ample evidence it can be shown that he felt Lincoln was a poor President and that his management of the war was not the best; but the editor's desire to show an undivided front to the South restrained his editorial criticism of the President. As Halstead said, "It did not seem to me there was any other way of going on. If the country was gone, why chaos and black night would come." [129] It is unfair to say, as one history of Cincinnati does, that the *Commercial* far outdid the *Enquirer* in vilifying Lincoln or that Halstead was a badly balanced, pugnacious firebrand who allowed his dislike of Lincoln to color his editorials. The *Commercial's* columns often contained criticism of the administration, and this criticism was often unfair; but it was no worse than the criticism of many Republican papers of the era. It was not in the *Commercial* that Halstead gave his true impressions of the wartime President but in his private correspondence. Thus the quotation, "There could not be a more inefficient man President of the United States than Abraham Lincoln . . . the poor, silly president sucks flattery as a pig sucks milk," which is used to justify the claim that the *Commercial* was worse than the *Enquirer* in its criticism, came from Halstead's private correspondence. It would never have been published as his editorial opinion.[130]

Halstead believed that Chase would have made a better President, and he believed that he was the strongest member of the Lincoln cabinet. Chase encouraged Halstead in this belief, and the correspondence between the two Cincinnati men was most unflattering as to Lincoln's abilities. Chase related his opinions of the administration to many men in the North. He complained that it was next to impossible for him to maintain the public credit in face of what he called the inadequate administration. He said Lincoln appointed unfit men to high command, and this, plus his unwillingness to heed Chase's advice, had prolonged the war by years.[131] To Halstead he complained that he had no voice in the management of the war. The three people most responsible for its management—the President, the commanding general, and the secretary of war—all displayed the greatest differences in temperament, wishes, and intellectual characteristics that, he claimed, made it unreasonable to expect the war to be conducted in a wiser manner.[132]

With such criticism coming from a high-ranking member of the cabinet, it was no wonder that Halstead's private opinion of the President was so low. Chase was Halstead's principal source of Washington information. Moreover, Halstead considered himself a close friend of the secretary, and he admired him greatly. Thus the aristocratic, cultivated, and ambitious Chase, who was doubtless envious of Lincoln, convinced Halstead of the President's inferiority and his basic inability to cope with the problems of the war.[133] Halstead's opinions can be best seen in a group of letters that he wrote to Timothy E. Day, a Cincinnati congressman during the first years of the war. In their harsh and unrestrained manner, they show how contemptuous Halstead was of the president. In one he said:

Lincoln is simply of no account. He is a little in the way, that's all. He don't [sic] add anything to the strength of the Government— not a thing. He is very busy with trifles, and lets everybody do as they please. He is opposed to stealing, but can't see the stealing that is done. I use the mildest phrase when I say he is a weak, a miserably weak man; the wife is a fool—the laughing stock of the town, and her vulgarity only the more conspicuous in consequence to her fine carriage and horses and servants in livery and fine dresses, and her damnable airs.[134]

The author of the biography of Day, in which these letters are printed, said that Halstead wrote his comments privately —and with "hasty rashness," and that he did not give them to the press. Nonetheless, she says the scorn that the letters show must have made Halstead's press treatment of Lincoln less than fair.[135] This, to a certain extent, may have been true. When he wrote of Lincoln's first message to Congress, he was more snippy than critical as he commented, "As for its style—enough is said when we observe that Mr. Lincoln certainly wrote it himself," or, "While it is plain, that an honest man whose intentions are excellent, is the occupant of the Presidential chair, it is equally clear that he brings to the aid of the country no such thing as first rate executive ability." [136] While Halstead probably never really appreciated Lincoln's abilities until after his assassination, the harping tenor of the early editorials did not continue. The closest to personal criticism of the President that Halstead reached was an editorial about a "gay and festive" White House party given by the Lincolns during the war. He claimed in the editorial that the plain people disapproved of the costly and gaudy demonstration that Mrs. Lincoln made of her party and said that when thousands of brave men were out dying for their country it was deplorably wrong to have the White House connected with feasting and dancing. Mrs. Lincoln herself, he said, would be better off employed in promoting the comfort of the sick soldiers than in "driving out in her fine carriage and presiding at ostentatious carousals." It was unfortunate, Halstead declared, that Mrs. Lincoln had "so poor an understanding of the true dignity of her position." [137] Several important journalists, Halstead among them, had received letters from her dealing with political matters. Thus part of Halstead's dislike may have stemmed from what he thought was her meddling in the nation's political life.[138]

Halstead's strongest criticism was directed at the activities of various members of the cabinet. Much of his information of course came from Chase, of whom he was never critical, and it can be assumed that his editorial pronouncements against such cabinet members as Simon Cameron and Gideon Welles expressed Chase's opinions. The official and personal relations between Chase and Lincoln were severely strained during the later part of 1863 and early 1864. Many people by this time felt that Chase had been guilty of many things unworthy of a man of his position.[139] Even though Chase had felt forced to resign from the cabinet, when Chief Justice Roger Haney died, in October, 1864, Halstead and many other Ohioans still called upon Lincoln to appoint the former Secretary to the vacancy. Halstead argued that in the matter of the appointment it did not matter that the President and Chase were personally uncongenial. He said that the people wanted Chase, and that since Lincoln had a higher duty than to just award friends and punish enemies, he was sure Chase would get the appointment. This was particularly true, he felt, because Chase was the only one talked about for the position who was qualified.[140] Since Lincoln was a good politician and realized that it might be well to have Chase as far removed from political life as possible, he yielded to the onslaught from the Ohioans and made the appointment.[141]

As the war progressed, Halstead's personal and private criticism of the President became less and less frequent. He was a supporter of Lincoln's nomination for a second term and once again used the full weight of the *Commercial* to help in his re-election. From the beginning of the campaign he felt Lincoln's victory was assured; but he called for more than just a victory. Halstead felt that as in the case of the 1863 state elections, the presidential election had to serve as a symbol of American loyalty to the government and leaders. He declared that the election had to prove to America's enemies, whether foreign or domestic, that the people would stand by the Union at all costs and hazards until once again the constitution's authority was recognized throughout all the land.[142] This position was really not a change from Halstead's earlier attempts to gain public support for the administration, but throughout 1864, in editorials and letters, a definite softening of his personal hostility to Lincoln and his government may be seen. During the early months of the year there was less of a critical nature in the *Commercial* about the administration and the army, and more about Congress and congressional interference in the conduct of the war. In one editorial Halstead asked the congressmen of the Committee on the Conduct of the War whether they did not know they were impairing the discipline of the army, and perhaps endangering its very existence.[143] Lincoln's post-election speeches were termed "magnanimous in sentiment" and praised for their conciliatory tone.[144] The inaugural message was called a "sensible, quaint, brief document, expressing deep religious feeling as well as patriotic sentiments." [145] With the second inaugural, Halstead felt there was now additional cause for rejoicing in Lincoln's good health and reason to wish for his continual occupancy of the presidential

chair. Though he praised Andrew Johnson's wartime record
and said that he deserved the respect of all loyal citizens, he
could not help but think the country had made a mistake in
electing him vice-president. Halstead claimed Johnson lacked
any sense of propriety, and said his drunken condition at the
inaugural was in the worst taste.[146] In a later editorial Halstead
was also solicitous of the life and comfort of the President and
suggested that he take refuge with one of the armies until the
horde of office-seekers had disappeared from the Washington
streets.[147]

It was a jubilant Halstead that was able to write the editorial
in April of 1865 entitled, "The Surrender of Lee!" For once, it
looked as though the nation would again be able to enjoy a
period of peace and prosperity. The job for the country, he said,
was to clear away the ruins of the war and to rebuild, enlarge,
and strengthen the country.[148] But in the midst of the joy over
the southern surrender came the word of Lincoln's assassination. No longer did Halstead feel the contempt for the President that he had at the beginning of the war. Now he could
write that in all the world, no life had proved so valuable to the
people as Lincoln's. He said that the President had matured
under his great responsibilities and with his new maturity,
good sense, and kindness of heart, had been the hope of the
nation.[149]

Many people blamed the critics of Lincoln for inflaming
passions and ultimately causing his death. Halstead felt that this
was wrong, but he also felt that the story of Lincoln could teach
the country's politicians and journalists a great lesson. This
lesson was that they should weigh their words more carefully
before giving them publicity. He explained:

History will decide our capacity for self government more by the
measure of restraint we place upon our passions in the consideration
of political questions and acts, than by any event affecting the lives
and fortunes of individuals and parties. We shall but demonstrate
our ability to govern ourselves, and any provocation which moves

men from their balance, and incites them to use unmeasured language and perform unlawful acts, is to be deprecated.[150]

Years later, in 1888 at the first Ohio Lincoln Day Banquet at Columbus, Halstead, in recalling the war years, said that his love and admiration for Chase had blinded him to the "serious greatness" of Lincoln. When he looked back on the Lincoln administration, he found that many of the differences between the two men were a result of their vastly different personalities. Chase, he said, was the more brilliant—and the more rash; but Lincoln was the less emotional and the more patient. In summary he quoted Chase, who had said, "I do not know but he was wiser than all of us." [151]

Halstead proved himself even more independent of the Republican mainstream during reconstruction than he had during the war. He refused to endorse the Radicals' impeachment of Johnson; and while the *Commercial* supported Grant's election in 1868, by 1872 the editor had become so disenchanted with the President that he was one of the leaders of the insurgent Liberal Republican movement.

The continuing revolution in journalism with its ever-increasing costs hit the *Commercial* particularly hard, since Halstead had always demanded the use of the most modern techniques and processes. By 1884 the financial structure of his newspaper (he had become owner of the *Commercial* on Potter's death in 1866) was so unstable that he was forced to merge it with Richard Smith's *Gazette*. Even this merger did not solve the *Commercial*'s or Halstead's financial problems; and when the editor died in 1908, he had but a slight interest in the *Commercial*, which was then owned by his old rivals, the McLeans of the *Enquirer*.

Perhaps it may be said that the war and reconstruction brought out the best in the editor. His unquestioned patriotism, his desire to save the Union at all costs, and his later demand that the defeated South be dealt with fairly, gave his reporting and editing a vigor that he would never equal in his later years.

Halstead was one of the last of the giants of "personal journalism." He—like Greeley, Bowles, Medill, Reid, and Watterson, the other giants—believed in liberty and democracy, the freedom of the press, and, most importantly, the duties of the press. Their personal integrity and forceful journalism had an influence on public opinion and the affairs of the nation far greater than their local reading public would warrant.

Many of these men had strong connections with Ohio journalism, but only Halstead spent the prime years of his editorial life in Ohio, editing an Ohio newspaper. In 1928 the Cincinnati editor was among the first eight to be elected to the newly established Ohio Journalism Hall of Fame. His place among the great journalists of Ohio would have been secure without the election to the Hall of Fame, but the election gave a deserved honor to one of Ohio's most distinguished sons.

1. Murat Halstead, "History of the Cincinnati *Commercial*," Murat Halstead Papers (Cincinnati Historical Society).

2. *Ibid.*

3. Murat Halstead, "The Varieties of Journalism," *Cosmopolitan Magazine,* XVL (Jan., 1892), 205.

4. Murat Halstead, "Early Editorial Experiences," *Lippincott's Monthly Magazine,* XLIX (June, 1892), 714.

5. Halstead, "History of the Cincinnati *Commercial.*"

6. *Ibid.*

7. *Ibid.*

8. *Cincinnati Commercial,* Apr. 29, 1856 (Ohio Historical Society); Murat Halstead, *Trimmers, Trucklers and Temporizers: Notes of Murat Halstead from the Political Conventions of 1856,* ed. William B. Hesseltine and Rex G. Fisher (Madison, Wisc., 1961), p. v.

9. Wilfred E. Brinkley, *American Political Parties: Their Natural History* (New York, 1954), pp. 207–8; *Commercial,* July–November, 1856, *passim.*

10. Murat Halstead to T. C. Day, June 30, 1856, in Sarah J. Day, *The Man on a Hill Top* (Philadelphia, 1931), p. 172.

11. *Commercial*, Mar. 10, 1857. The delicacy that the young reporter noted in Buchanan seems to have been at least partially the result of illness. The President had fallen victim to the "National Hotel Disease," a kind of dysentery accompanied by diarrhea, brought on by a failure in the water supply of the hotel (Philip S. Klein, *President James Buchanan: A Biography* [University Park, Pa., 1962], pp. 268–72).

12. *Commercial*, Jan. 15, 1859; William L. Halstead Manuscript (Cincinnati Historical Society), p. 70.

13. *Commercial*, Oct. 19, 1859. While the issue of Brown's insanity has yet to be settled, most northerners of the time, like Halstead, were eager to repudiate his raid and claim he was mad. Louis Filler, *The Crusade Against Slavery: 1830–1860* (New York, 1960), p. 273.

14. *Commercial*, Oct. 25, 1859.

15. *Ibid.*, Dec. 3, 1859.

16. *Ibid.*, Dec. 2, 1859.

17. *Ibid.*, Dec. 5, 1859.

18. *Ibid.*

19. *Ibid.*, Dec. 6 and 7, 1859. Professor Morris disagrees with the editor's contention that Brown received a fair trial. He claims that Brown's lawyers were given no time to familiarize themselves with the case and that Brown could not have been guilty of the crime of treason against the state of Virginia as charged because he was not a citizen of that state. Richard B. Morris, *Fair Trial* (New York, 1953), pp. 259–60.

20. *Commercial*, Dec. 7, 1859.

21. *Ibid.*, Dec. 9 and 15, 1859; Eugene H. Roseboom, *A History of Presidential Elections* (New York, 1957), p. 173; Henry H. Simms, *A Decade of Sectional Controversy: 1851–1861* (Chapel Hill, N.C., 1942), pp. 155–57.

22. *Commercial*, Apr. 23, 1860; Halstead's reports of the conventions can also be found in Murat Halstead, *Caucuses of 1860: A History of the National Political Conventions of the Current Presidential Campaign: Being a Complete Record of the Business of all the Conventions; with Sketches of Distinguished Men in Attendance upon them and Descriptions of the Most Characteristic Scenes and Memorable Events* (Columbus, Ohio, 1860), and Murat Halstead, *Three Against Lincoln; Murat Halstead Reports the Caucuses of 1860,* ed. William B. Hesseltine (Baton Rouge, 1960).

23. *Commercial*, Apr. 28, 1860.

24. *Ibid.*, Apr. 30, 1860.

25. *Ibid.*; Eugene H. Roseboom, *The Civil War Era* (*The History of the State of Ohio*, Vol. IV, ed. Carl Wittke [Columbus, Ohio, 1944], pp. 364–65).

26. *Commercial*, May 2, 1860.

27. *Ibid.*, May 10, 1860.

28. *Ibid.*, May 12, 1860.

29. *Ibid.*

30. Eugene H. Roseboom, *A History of Presidential Elections* (New York, 1957), pp. 177–79.

31. *Commercial*, May 20, 1860.

32. *Ibid.*, June 13, 1860.

33. *Ibid.*, June 26, 1860.

34. Halstead, *Three against Lincoln*, pp. 277–78.

35. *Commercial*, May 26, 1860.

36. *Ibid.*

37. Halstead, *Caucuses of 1860*.

38. Cincinnati *Commercial Gazette*, Sept. 27, 1887.

39. Halstead, *Three against Lincoln*, p. 279.

40. Roseboom, *The Civil War Era*, pp. 373–74; Alvin F. Harlow, *The Serene Cincinnatians* (New York, 1950), p. 224; David M. Potter, *Lincoln and His Party in the Secession Crisis* (New Haven, 1942), p. 53.

41. Halstead, "History of the Cincinnati *Commercial*," Halstead Papers; *Commercial*, Mar., 1861, *passim*, and Mar. 6, 1861, in particular.

42. Louis M. Starr, *Reporting the Civil War: The Bohemian Brigade in Action, 1861–1865* (New York, 1962), p. 9.

43. *Ibid.*, p. 6.

44. J. Cutler Andrews, *The North Reports the Civil War* (Pittsburgh, 1955), pp. 6–34.

45. *Commercial*, June 3, 1861.

46. *Ibid.*, June 6, 1861.

47. *Ibid.*, June 13, 1861.

48. *Ibid.*, June 12, 1861.

49. *Ibid.*, June 14, 1861; in fairness to Chase, he did write to Halstead in defense of Cameron claiming the Secretary was a patriotic man and was

just not receiving the support he desired and needed to carry on the work of his department. Chase to Halstead, December 25, 1861, J. W. Schuckers, *The Life and Public Services of Salmon Portland Chase, United States Senator and Governor of Ohio: Secretary of the Treasury, and Chief-Justice of the United States* (New York, 1874) p. 381.

50. *Commercial,* June 24, 1861; Burton J. Hendrick, *Lincoln's War Cabinet* (Garden City, N.Y., 1961), p. 264.

51. *Commercial,* June 17, 1861.

52. *Ibid.,* June 6, 1861; T. Harry Williams, *Lincoln and His Generals* (New York, 1963), p. 10.

53. *Commercial,* June 20, 1861.

54. *Ibid.,* June 24, 1861.

55. *Ibid.,* June 17, 1861.

56. *Ibid.,* June 8 and 13, 1861; Andrews, *The North Reports the Civil War,* p. 649; Starr, *Reporting the Civil War: The Bohemian Brigade in Action, 1861–1865,* 30–32; Emmet Grozier, *Yankee Reporters: 1861–65* (New York, 1956), pp. 86–88.

57. *Commercial,* June 27, 1861; Starr, *Reporting the Civil War: The Bohemian Brigade in Action, 1861–1865,* pp. 64–68.

58. *Ibid.,* 69–70; B. H. Liddell Hart, *Sherman: Soldier, Realist, American* (New York, 1960), pp. 106–11; Lloyd Lewis, *Sherman: Fighting Prophet* (New York, 1958), pp. 194–96.

59. Murat Halstead, "Recollections and Letters of General Sherman," *The Independent,* LI (June 15, 1899), 1612–13.

60. *Commercial,* Dec. 12, 1861; Crozier feels that the entire incident may have been a result of Villard's unfamiliarity with the American idiomatic use of the word "crazy." He claims that when the *Tribune* reporter told him Cameron thought Sherman was "crazy," he was only using hyperbole, but that Villard, who had learned English only a few years before, believed he meant "insane." Crozier explains the month-and-a-half delay between the time Villard told Halstead the story of Sherman's "insanity" and the *Commercial* article by saying the editor was personally aquainted with the Sherman family and wished to be sure the story was correct. Halstead felt the facts had been verified when the general was relieved from duty. Crozier, *Yankee Reporters: 1861–1865,* pp. 176–78.

61. General William T. Sherman, *Memoirs of General William T. Sherman* (New York, 1875), I, 216.

62. Harry L. Coles, "General William T. Sherman and the Press," unpublished paper delivered before the Southern Historical Association,

1962, *passim;* Lewis, *Sherman: Fighting Prophet,* pp. 190–91; Crozier, *Yankee Reporters: 1861–1865,* p. 173.

63. Hart, *Sherman: Soldier, Realist, American,* p. 103.

64. Murat Halstead, "Recollections and Letters of General Sherman," *Independent,* LI (June, 22, 1899) , 1683.

65. *Ibid.,* p. 1685.

66. *Cincinnati Enquirer,* September 1, 1861.

67. *Commercial,* Aug. 8, 1861; though Halstead did not emphasize the fact in his dispatches, Hugh J. Jewett, the Democratic nominee for governor, was a strong Union man (Roseboom, *The Civil War Era,* p. 390) .

68. *Commercial,* Aug. 8, 1861.

69. *Ibid.,* Sept. 5, 1861.

70. *Ibid.,* Sept. 7, 1861; Joseph P. Smith (ed.) , *History of the Republican Party in Ohio and Memoirs of its Representative Supporters* (Chicago, 1898) , I, 135.

71. *Commercial,* Sept. 7, 1861.

72. *Ibid.,* Aug. 17, 1861; Oct. 3 and 8, 1861.

73. Eugene H. Roseboom and Francis P. Weisenburger, *A History of Ohio* (Columbus, Ohio, 1956) , p. 188.

74. Roseboom, *The Civil War Era,* p. 386.

75. *Commercial,* July 18, 1862.

76. Roseboom, *The Civil War Era,* p. 397; J. G. Randall and David Donald, *The Civil War and Reconstruction* (Boston, 1961) , pp. 406–7.

77. *Commercial,* July 22, 1862.

78. *Ibid.,* Sept. 4, 1862.

79. *Ibid.,* July 23, 1862.

80. *Ibid.,* Sept. 5, 1862.

81. Harlow, *The Serene Cincinnatians,* pp. 232–33.

82. *Commercial,* Sept. 6–10, 1862.

83. *Ibid.,* Sept. 11, 1862.

84. *Ibid.,* Sept. 13, 1862.

85. *Ibid.,* Sept. 24, 1862; Roseboom, *The Civil War Era,* pp. 398–99.

86. *Commercial,* July 13, 1863.

87. Allan Keller, *Morgan's Raid* (New York, 1962) , pp. 142–43.

88. Roseboom and Weisenburger, *A History of Ohio,* pp. 194–95; Roseboom, *The Civil War Era,* pp. 423–25.

89. *Commercial,* July 16, 1863.

90. *Ibid.,* Sept. 5, 1862.

91. *Ibid.,* July 13, 1863; one Cincinnati newspaper, the *Times,* was temporarily suspended during the panic for printing an article accusing the government of manufacturing the scare. Andrews, *The North Reports the Civil War,* p. 291.

92. *Commercial,* July 11, 1861.

93. *Ibid.,* July 16, 1861.

94. *Ibid.,* July 31, 1862.

95. *Ibid.,* July 13, 1861; Roseboom, *The Civil War Era,* pp. 408–9.

96. Carl M. Becker, "The Genesis of a Copperhead," *Bulletin of the Historical and Philosophical Society of Ohio,* XIX (October, 1961), 235.

97. *Commercial,* July 14, 1861.

98. *Enquirer,* Oct. 8, 1863.

99. *Commercial,* Oct. 10, 1863.

100. *Ibid.,* June 3, 1863.

101. *Ibid.,* Sept. 27, 1862.

102. *Ibid.,* Oct. 4, 1862.

103. *Ibid.,* Oct. 14, 1862.

104. *Ibid.,* Oct. 6, 1862; Frank L. Klement, *The Copperheads in the Middle West* (Chicago, 1960), pp. 124–25.

105. *Commercial,* Oct. 16, 1862.

106. *Ibid.,* Oct. 21, 1862.

107. Klement, *The Copperheads in the Middle West,* pp. 87–95; Roseboom, *The Civil War Era,* pp. 411–15.

108. *Commercial,* Feb. 18, 1863.

109. *Ibid.,* June 12, 1863.

110. *Ibid.,* June 13, 1863.

111. *Ibid.,* Aug. 26, 1863.

112. *Ibid.,* Aug. 8, 1863; Klement, *The Copperheads in the Middle West,* p. 130.

113. *Commercial,* Sept. 30, 1863.

114. *Ibid.,* Aug. 5 and Oct. 10, 1863.

115. *Ibid.,* Oct. 13, 1863.

116. *Ibid.,* Oct. 14, 1863; Klement, *The Copperheads in the Middle West,* pp. 132–33; Roseboom, *The Civil War Era,* pp. 421–23.

117. *Commercial,* Dec. 2, 1862.

118. *Ibid.,* Dec. 4, 1862.

119. *Ibid.,* Dec. 13, 1862.

120. *Ibid.,* Dec. 4, 1862.

121. *Ibid.,* Dec. 11, 1862.

122. *Ibid.,* Nov. 17, 1862; Williams, *Lincoln and His Generals,* 178; Chase had defended McClellan to the editor, but in this case Halstead did not agree with the secretary's judgment. Chase to Halstead, May 24, 1863, Schuckers, *The Life and Public Services of Salmon Portland Chase,* p. 436.

123. William L. Halstead MS, p. 98; Andrews, *The North Reports the Civil War,* p. 323.

124. *Commercial,* Dec. 18, 1862.

125. Randall and Donald, *The Civil War and Reconstruction,* p. 312.

126. *Commercial,* Dec. 17, 1862; Andrews, *The North Reports the Civil War,* pp. 331–32.

127. William L. Halstead MS, p. 100.

128. *Commercial,* Jan. 27, 1863.

129. Murat Halstead, "Weakness of Journalism," Halstead Papers.

130. Harlow, *The Serene Cincinnatians,* p. 230; the quotation is from one of Halstead's letters to Congressman Day. Day, *Man on a Hill Top,* p. 247.

131. Donnal Vore Smith, *Chase and Civil War Politics* (Columbus, Ohio, 1931), pp. 50–51. In one letter Chase claimed the war would have been more efficiently managed if the cabinet members had been allowed to run their own departments without constant interference. This was a not too veiled hint that Lincoln was the one interfering. Chase to Halstead, December 25, 1861, Schuckers, *The Life and Public Services of Salmon Portland Chase,* p. 281.

132. Chase to Halstead, Sept. 21, 1862, in Robert B. Warden, *An Account of the Private Life and Public Services of Salmon P. Chase* (Cincinnati, 1874), p. 549; the same letter is also published in Schuckers, *The Life and Public Services of Salmon Portland Chase,* p. 393.

133. William L. Halstead MS, p. 97.

134. Halstead to Day, June 8, 1861, in Day, *Man on a Hill Top,* p. 243.

135. *Ibid.,* 240.

136. *Commercial,* Dec. 4, 1861.

137. *Ibid.,* Feb. 10, 1862.

138. James E. Pollard, *The Presidents and the Press* (New York, 1947) .

139. William Henry Smith Papers, Vol. XLIII, 15 (The Ohio Historical Society) .

140. *Commercial,* Dec. 2, 1864.

141. Smith, *Chase and Civil War Politics,* p. 159.

142. *Commercial,* Nov. 8, 1864.

143. *Ibid.,* Mar. 25, 1864; Halstead's criticism was probably justified, but Randall points out that ". . . in a democratic society civilians must exercise control over the military, even during times of war." Randall and Donald, *The Civil War and Reconstruction,* p. 281.

144. *Commercial,* Nov. 12, 1864.

145. *Ibid.,* Mar. 6, 1865.

146. *Ibid.,* Mar. 9, 1865. Although it was unknown to Halstead, Johnson's drunken condition at the inaugural was a result of his recent bout with typhoid fever and an overheated capitol, and was not a "normal" condition for the man. Margaret Shaw Royall, *Andrew Johnson— Presidential Scapegoat: A Biographical Re-evaluation* (New York, 1958), p. 51; Randall and Donald, *The Civil War and Reconstruction,* pp. 586–87.

147. *Commercial,* Mar. 31, 1865.

148. *Ibid.,* Apr. 10, 1865.

149. *Ibid.,* Apr. 15, 1865.

150. *Ibid.,* Apr. 22, 1865.

151. *Ohio State Journal* (Columbus) , Feb. 14, 1888.

EIGHT

John Sherman

JEANNETTE P. NICHOLS

Ohio is a state of many minds. Of this challenging fact her new "junior" senator must have been acutely aware on the morning of Saturday, March 23, 1861, as he vacated his seat at the head of the table in the room of the august Committee on Ways and Means and cleared out his papers from the precincts of the House of Representatives. Turning northward, the tall spare sedate figure in the dark frock coat (and bow tie) may have seemed to observers older than his thirty-eight years, as he soberly trod the five hundred feet of marble corrridor stretching up to the farther end of the Capitol.

There awaited him in the Senate Chamber the place held for two days earlier this month by Ohio's ambidextrous ex-Governor Chase, before he was translated by Lincoln to the throne of the Secretary of the Treasury a mile down Pennsylvania Avenue.[1] John Sherman had won, just the past Wednesday, a Republican majority in the Ohio legislative caucus for senator; and this was but the first of six times (over a span of thirty-six years) that he would wrest election from this normally temperamental body. Just how temperamental may be judged by the fact that in all that time the legislature gave him but two Republican colleagues, choosing rather to send to Washington four different Democrats.[2]

As he finished his walk this Saturday to the entrance of the

Senate Chamber, whence he would be escorted to his swear-
ing-in by Senator Wade [3] (whose supporters had opposed
Sherman's election), Sherman could reflect that he might not
have been taking this walk if he had not ventured a far more
hectic journey to Columbus the weekend before. There the
Republican caucus had been of so many minds that they bal-
loted more than seventy times (while "senatorial groceries"
flowed freely) without coming up with an agreed nominee for
senator. At one juncture his own chances had seemed so slim
that his name had been withdrawn. At another, his chief com-
petitor, Governor Dennison, might have won the prize if over-
zealous or clever partisans had not twice stuffed the box with
more ballots for him than there were members actually present
to cast them! [4]

Back in Washington Sherman himself had not been wholly
of one mind—for while he was writing Ohio supporters regarding his chances, he was aware that he was practically assured
the speakership if he did not leave the House. Over the weekend urgent telegrams from his own partisans for his presence in
Columbus moved him. He went, arriving Monday evening, the
eighteenth. On their seventy-ninth ballot the caucus had allowed him the forty-two votes needed for a majority. That
night, victorious members had sought him out for a jollification. But Sherman, they found, was going to bed, doubtless
quite fatigued by triumph. [5]

It is indeed tiring to live a life of uncertainty, as this ex-
representative well knew. Luckily, he had gambled wisely on
the power potential of a new political party. After winning
election to Congress on an anti-Nebraska platform in 1854, he
had presided the next year at Ohio's first Republican state
convention; and under this new banner he had won election
from the Thirteenth Congressional District three more times,
although his home county of Richland never went for him
after 1854. From this week's senatorial caucus he could take
further instruction, for its members had been inclined to pass

by candidates thought of as too conservative (such as Delano, Horton, and Schenck), and Dennison had been regarded by some as too "radical." The members had fallen back on Sherman as a compromise, a "moderate." [6]

But what did Ohio politicos of the moment mean by "moderate"? Moving from a constituency of four counties to one of some 2,400,000 persons (Ohio then boasting the third largest population in the United States) meant much more of a problem for a senator than a simple increase in numbers, for Ohio was sharply regionalized. She was recognized as embracing numerous enclaves differentiated by places of origin of her settlers, who had brought into the state attitudes and opinions on politics nurtured elsewhere. To this ingrained diversity now was added the stress of civil war and of economic and political change.[7]

So, citizens of Ohio would amply prove that theirs was a state of many minds as they reacted to such issues as secession, the Negro, Lincoln, Republicanism, Copperheads, money and banking, taxation and the tariff. The political power structures in various parts of the state must tax the ingenuity of any senator to reconcile pressures upon him.

In this situation Sherman's course would be affected by the fact that in addition to his two major political obligations—to his state and to his party—he recognized two other broader and, perhaps, more complex obligations. These two were an obligation to the Union—to the nation as a whole—and an obligation to his private sense of proper demeanor. The first of these two symbolized Sherman's quality as a statesman, moving him on some crucial issues to alienate special interests in Ohio for the sake of the body politic; this did not, in the long run, militate against his chances for continuing as a senator, but it did contribute later on to defeat of his ambition for the presidency.[8]

His fourth obligation, that to his private sense of proper demeanor, proved a political handicap always. He was so con-

stituted that he was incapable of exuding great warmth of
personal feeling toward adult associates.[9] He would not assume
such a display; evidently he thought that solid attainments
would compensate for this lack. But it made it less likely that
people who respected his attainments would exert themselves
for his advancement against opposition from more outgoing
competitors. Since he could not deliberately inspire an infec-
tious enthusiasm for him as a person, people sometimes failed
to go down the line for him in crucial situations.[10]

His concept of proper demeanor, unfortunately, included
also an abiding contempt for broad humor; an earthy story
seemed to him a mark of ill-breeding rather than a display of
camaraderie. Worse, a habit of recognizing and flavoring ridiculous aspects of human behavior seemed to him to betoken an
undignified, irresponsible attitude toward serious problems—a
suspect habit.[11] Thus Sherman, like Chase and Wade, knew
little of the emotional solace and sustaining power of a strong
sense of humor.

This made it all the more remarkable that he escaped the
fate of many an undemonstrative politician relegated to the
rear. His re-elections tended to be hard to win, a fact he was
loathe to admit; [12] but he developed some phenomenal skills
especially designed to work through Ohio's many-mindedness.
Most important, he was rising to the challenge of the Civil
War. Those four years would provide the crucial test of Sherman's capacity for leadership, as he strove to function as both
politician and statesman.

II

The next-to-the-youngest member of the Senate faithfully
followed the dictum of new-member-silence during the five days
remaining of the special session, and then sought some relaxa-
tion at his home in Mansfield, Ohio, the calm center of rural

Richland County. His quietude was rudely shattered a fortnight later when a mysterious April 11 telegram summoned
him back to Washington.[13] Before dawn next day—a most unlucky Friday—Sumter was attacked, and on Monday Lincoln
called for 75,000 three-month volunteers, to preserve the
Union.

Sherman answered the call with mind, heart, and body, not
for three months, but for the duration. The statesman in him
knew well that to admit the right of secession would be to
destroy the nation; and so this moderate man had been working as a House member of a compromise committee seeking
peaceful means to avoid a split. His reward had been criticism
from two of the divisive elements in Ohio—those sympathizing
with the South and slavery and those eager for her subjection
and abolition of slavery.[14]

The issues were all confused and entangled, but on two
points John was clear: secession must not succeed, and it probably could not be a short and easy contest, contrary to the
confident optimism of Lincoln and many northerners at the
moment. Into this dire emergency Sherman poured his energies
and won such gratifying results as must have given him a sense
of self-fulfilment. Perhaps this was the most satisfying period of
his life.

At once he engaged in encouraging enlistment, helping to
build up Company I of Mansfield volunteers and other groups
over the state. Equipment and supplies proving very hard to
come by in the disorderly haste to get troops to Washington, he
took it upon himself to become an interstate expediter of military equipment for Ohio volunteers. He found his way through
bureaucratic channels in Pennsylvania, New York, and Washington, having the forethought and courage to offer to sign his
personal note as a guarantee of ultimate payment for requisi-
tions. Within another fortnight he was bringing to Ohio volunteers stalled at Lancaster, Pennsylvania, the joyful tidings that
more equipment was on its way. There he joined Company I as

a private, and this 6 feet 1½ inch tall enrollee was straightway
and unanimously elected standard-bearer by the company.[15]

The next day he was off to Washington as "bearer of des-
patches" to Secretary of War Cameron. From that interview he
emerged with the rank of colonel, through the medium of a
commission as volunteer aide (without pay or rations either)
to General Robert Patterson, the seventy-year-old commander
of the Military Department of Washington, with headquarters
in Philadelphia. At a local race track there he located Company
I and other Ohio units among volunteers gathered in improvised barracks; through his efforts he diminished their discom-
forts. He found time also to visit a Philadelphia tailor and to
buy a colonel's insignia, complete with sword and sash—
evidence of status reported at once in the Ohio press.[16]

The spanking new outfit came in very handy when the secession of Virginia brought down from Philadelphia to frightened
Washington two regiments of Ohio volunteers. Lincoln reviewed them, and who should walk beside the President but the
volunteer colonel! As they approached Company I, he drew the
attention of the Commander-in-Chief to Mansfield's own Captain Laughlin, he of the flowing white hair, and a greeting and
handclasp capped the climax. To these Ohioans now biv-
ouacked west of Washington the colonel rode out daily,
through mud on rainy days and dust on dry; they well knew
that they ate, slept, and drilled better for his efforts, and they
named their abiding place Camp Sherman.

Less gratifying and more difficult was the task of assigning
officers among the ten new regiments of three-year recruits, now
being added to the regular army because in May it was realized
that this war might be no three-month picnic. Under a wither-
ing political fire the administration labored over first lieutenants, captains, colonels, and field officers. Like many another
man in Washington, John was besieged not only by ambitious
constituents but also by a plethora of his own relatives and
kinsfolk by marriage.

His West Point–trained older brother, William Tecumseh, had delayed re-entry into the army, despite weeks of urging from John, until he finally took a commission as a colonel in the regular army; and "W.T." 's wife Ellen imagined that the Senator could get whatever he liked for them. The pressure on John can be surmised from a letter of his eldest brother Charles to "W.T.," reporting assignment of two captaincies, a paymaster, and an assistant quartermaster, and closing triumphantly, "so you see the family is provided for." [17]

This kind of task was scarcely one that could be performed on horseback. In fact, no less a person than the Commander-in-Chief preferred that the volunteer colonel now dismount, discard his military insignia, and don the senatorial toga; for Lincoln had summoned Congress to legislate in special session on war appropriations and executive powers, which he badly needed. John had proved his legislative expertise; as Chairman of Ways and Means during the previous session, he had forced needed appropriations through the House against heavy odds. Now, the national welfare, Lincoln suggested, required John's skills in the Senate. The politician should employ his talents as a statesman for the benefit of the nation and the sorely pressed standard-bearer of the Republican party.[18]

The volunteer colonel acceded to this request from the highest level. He gave his two horses, his cherished sword, sash, and other equipment to his brother, and climbed back up Pennsylvania Avenue to the Capitol. Oddly enough, on arrival he was reminded that New York and Massachusetts volunteers but lately had been quartered there; from their emergency ovens installed in the basement rose the homelike aroma of freshly baked bread.

When senators assembled July 4 at noon to hear Chaplain Byron Sunderland, D.D., intone the opening prayer, John was standing at his desk, tall and erect, in civilian clothes. Not so two other Ohioans later rewarded. That same afternoon, at Camp Chase just four miles west of Columbus, Ohio, Major

Rutherford B. Hayes was standing in a hollow square formed
by the 23rd Ohio Volunteer Infantry, reading to the regiment
the Declaration of Independence; among the privates there
assembled, an eighteen-year-old named William McKinley
stood listening.[19]

III

Ohio at this Congress had a chance to exert more influence
than ever before. Departure of southern brethren had shifted
the dominant influence in a shrunken Congress: in the Senate,
to the Middle West and New England; in the House, to the
Middle West and Pennsylvania. The most important state of
the Middle West was Ohio, and because of her chronic disunity
she would retain, though the next sixty years, first rank as a
political uncertainty.[20] The question was whether she could
send to Washington politicians capable of retaining enough
independence to exercise statesmanship.

To this special session Ohio contributed contrasting personalities. In the Senate middle-of-the-road Sherman was junior to
fiery Benjamin Franklin Wade, of ten years' tenure, wont to
take his mandate from the most radical wing of their party. In
the House eight of her twenty-one-man delegation were Democrats, including such colorful personalities as "Rise-up" William Allen, "Sunset" Cox, "Gentleman George" Pendleton,
and the rabid pro-southerner Clement Vallandigham.

Fortunately, for the nonce most members felt more the necessity to extinguish a rebellion already ablaze than to ignite fires
of partisanship. Dire necessities somewhat discouraged partisan
bickering. So in the thirty-three days before they quit on August 6 to go home and feel the pulse of their constituencies, they
fumblingly provided a framework for expanded military services and started the financing of them by passing loan, tariff,
and taxing bills.[21] In this work Sherman's reputation enabled

him to be much less inconspicuous than was normal for a freshman senator. Allowed the second place below the chairman on the vital Finance Committee, and intimately concerned in administration programming, he became privy to important conferences between senators, representatives, and members of the administration, especially Secretary of the Treasury Chase.

Economy, order, and uniformity in federal outlays were three of Sherman's continuing objectives throughout the war; in these meritorious attempts he proved sometimes naïve and mainly futile, although he persisted in opposing the corruption and extravagance endemic in prolonged war. He had the courage to go against the current also in defense of regular army officers, the favorite whipping boys of partisans like Wade who blamed them for the fact that raw recruits cannot overnight become seasoned veterans, nor victories ensue on premature campaigns demanded by an impatient public. Here time tended to support Sherman's position as officers named to satisfy mere political demands effectively demonstrated their incompetence.[22]

Really outstanding achievements by Sherman at this short session were twofold: one concerned emergency powers of the Executive, the other defining the purpose of the war. On both he fought hard and persistently to make congressional action conform to the realities of the situation, so as to strengthen the Union.

Between Sumter (April 12) and the meeting of Congress (July 4) the President had assumed emergency powers, not all constitutional, some infringing upon the powers of Congress; and underlings had conspicuously abused those powers. Questions of constitutionality and infringements so agitated Democrats and other opponents of Lincoln and of the war that the session neared its end without the indispensable congressional validation of Lincoln's acts. Lawyer Sherman was uncomfortable but also realistic. He freely admitted that the Constitution gave the power of suspension of the writ of habeas corpus, and enlargement of the army also, "to Congress alone. . . . I cannot here in my place, under oath, declare that it was strictly legal." But, he added, he approved the President's acts "as a matter of public necessity. He did precisely what I should have done if I had been in his place." [23] The question was, how to get the Senate to act?

Ingenuity became indispensable. A group consisting principally of two New Englanders, Senators Wilson of Massachusetts and Fessenden of Maine (chairman of the Finance Committee), and Sherman, summoned the ingenuity the day before adjournment. They managed to tie a more vaguely worded validation measure to another (introduced for the purpose) raising the monthly pay of the lowest military ranks by two dollars. Wilson even allowed it to go up to $4.00. What member could go on record as voting against that pay raise if it were tied to validation phraseology that was not too precise? The Senate passed this device 33–5. In the House Vallandigham's effort to strike out validation was defeated 19–74, and Thaddeus Stevens of Pennsylvania sugared the plum by adding a provision that all wartime volunteers should receive a back-pay allowance that Ohioans already had been given.

After the amended bill reached the Senate, it gave place to a new bill in which the pay raise was back to $2.00, which John preferred, and the back-pay plum was included. To this, Wilson added validation phraseology as an amendment, and so the package passed the Senate late that evening, without debate, 37–5; next morning before adjournment the new measure was put through the House by a two-thirds vote, against Vallandigham's attempt to kill it. Thus Lincoln got his validation, the soldiers an increase, and the freshman senator some practice in the high art of legislative maneuver.[24]

The President already had good reason for gratitude to the ex-colonel for support, since the question of the object of the war was also a burning issue. Some Radical Republicans liked to proclaim triple objectives: preservation of the Union, abolition of slavery, and subjugation of the South. Lincoln and the moderates feared that the last two would drive the four border states—Delaware, Maryland, Kentucky, and Missouri—into the arms of the Confederacy. They insisted that the sole objective was preservation of the Union. This position Sherman supported with unwonted heat, despite bitter denunciation from Ohio Radicals. He denied the right of secession (as did the majority of the Ohio legislature), and he had opposed the spread of slavery. But he had not demanded abolition of slavery where it existed, and he would not interfere with it unless abolition proved essential to preserving the Union. Yet his earlier involved statements on these complex issues furnished opponents with ammunition.[25]

Finally, on July 25, in the closing debate on the objective, the opposition stung him to a ringing ten-minute declaration of faith. The accusations "I know, will excuse even the youngest senator on this floor for saying a few words in reply." The North's purpose is "to preserve this Union; to maintain the Constitution as it is in all its clauses, . . . all this claptrap about subjugation, it seems to me, ought to be dismissed from the Senate. . . . Everything depends upon subduing the disunionists. . . . If we divide into two sections now, soon we shall be divided into three or four or five. . . . I for one am for this war; for its active, vigilant and determined prosecution." [26]

That day the Senate, 30–5, declared that preservation of the Union was indeed the sole objective. Yet, in time fate would move Lincoln, Sherman, and many other Republicans to accept emancipation as a means to preserve the Union.

Sherman's eventual espousal of emancipation was hastened by the quickening reversal of Ohio majority opinion. The first constitution had come close to allowing a limited form of slavery, and subsequent legislatures enacted "Black Laws" restricting immigration, employment, status before the law, education, poor maintenance, and suffrage. These laws, however, were interpreted variously, some counties even permitting Negro suffrage. By 1847 a delicate balance of power in the legislature enabled Free-Soilers to get repeal of most of the "Black Laws," and by 1855 a Republican party majority was enacting three "Personal Liberty" laws protecting free blacks and hindering the return of fugitive slaves.

But the next legislature had a Democratic majority, which repealed two of the "Personal Liberty" laws and decreed disfranchisement of anyone with a "Visible Admixture" of Negro blood. Definition of the term "white," however, inclined to be liberal when the state Supreme Court got a Republican majority. Debate was waxing hot, over black immigration, slavery abolition, and Negro suffrage. It depended on whether one was alarmed by the presence in Ohio of an estimated 36,673 Negroes by 1860, due largely to an estimated 40 per cent increase in immigration since 1850.[27] Or one might be committed to the Underground Railway's efforts to flout the federal Fugitive Slave Law. Or one might pooh-pooh both extremists, arguing that the Negroes were too few to constitute a real problem, and that with emancipation all blacks would go away, preferring the warm southern climate. While Sherman was in the House, he had opposed interference with slavery in the District of Columbia, and he carried into the Senate a feeling that dislike of Negroes was strong in Ohio.

But by early spring of 1862 he had concluded that emancipation was coming ultimately, that most northern constituents opposed slavery and were not going to change their opinion; in this mood they would agitate for emancipation in the District of Columbia until it was accomplished there. He assured opponents it would be a good move, economically and politically: the few slaves remaining in the District since the southerners left were the property mostly of southern sympathizers; removal of slave labor would entice to Washington productive free labor, increase population and property values, and light the experimental way for emancipation in the border states, come the end of the war. So he gave his support to the April 16 law freeing slaves in the District, and many Ohioans approved.[28]

Whether sweet reasonableness on emancipation would prevail in a congressional election year in Ohio was another matter. The fiction that abolition could not be a general federal objective was in fact being undermined by majority action in Congress and in the states, and Sherman himself was abandoning it. Emancipation gathered momentum because wherever the war effort turned it was confronted by the continued existence of Negroes held as property. So slavery increasingly obtruded into military, diplomatic, economic, social, and moral problems. It suffused politics all the more as the prize of Richmond continued to elude Union generalship: frustration must have an outlet. Debate on the necessity of emancipation filled page after page of the *Congressional Globe,* members' correspondence, and back-home newspapers.

It furnished yet another issue on which Congress and the President got into arguments over jurisdiction and timing. Lincoln's principle of *gradual* emancipation under state authority, with federal compensatory funds, had won qualified congressional endorsement in a resolution passed the week before the District of Columbia got *immediate* emancipation with $300 allowed for each slave, and Congress was decreeing other varieties of compensation. Sherman was troubled by costs, and Lincoln was emphasizing that if compensation ended the war, it would indeed save lots of money.[29]

However, congressional insistence upon its own right to force quicker, more inclusive emancipation multiplied the number, and increased the severity, of both confiscatory and emancipatory measures. An example involving both Shermans was two laws aimed to encourage the tendency of some army officers to free slaves found within their lines and to discourage others who returned them to their owners; the later practice was one on which Colonel "W.T." had been criticized, to John's embar-

rassment. July brought from the congressional hopper a confiscation bill that attempted (in effect) to extend property loss
beyond rebels to their descendants; this brought a showdown
with Lincoln, and Congress, to avoid a veto was forced to join
in an official denial that the law could function to that effect.
Thus emerged the Confiscation Act of July 17, 1862.[30]

But this was also an emancipation act; it carried clauses
declaring that anyone hereafter adjudged guilty of treason
could suffer death and his slaves should be made free. This
might be said to make a presidential pronouncement a duplica-
tion; but the Act did not provide for effecting the emancipation, and Lincoln determined to issue his own version anyway,
although his cabinet, including Chase, disapproved. Into this
situation he injected his September 22 notice (following the federal victory at Antietam) that as of January 1, 1863, he would
proclaim slavery abolished in Rebel territory.

Unfortunately, the date for Ohio's election of members of
Congress was but twenty-two days away. Politicos in Washington and in the states were watching her as an omen for November voting everywhere else. Republican chances were not rosy
in many-minded Ohio, where a mass of general dissatisfactions
was building, with active encouragement from Peace Democrats. The majority did not wish a southern victory, but they
were torn by active dislikes on such things as political unrest,
administrative mismanagement, the inconclusiveness of the war,
federal defeats, and Negro immigration.

The emancipation issue aggravated the political unrest.
Radical Republicans said Lincoln had moved too slowly. Conservative Republicans and War Democrats inclined to think he
had moved too fast. In this parlous situation a "union" ticket of
Republicans and Democrats was contending with a Democratic
ticket invitational to all sorts of malcontents. When the polls
closed October 14, Ohioans had elected to Congress fourteen
Democrats and only five Republicans; when the national tally

ended in November, the Republican-Unionist majority in the House had been reduced by thirty-two.[31]

Ohio stood forth as the state that had most decisively repudiated Lincoln. But John Sherman was imprecise in blaming it partly on the Republican decision to eschew a separate Republican organization. Where he showed real acumen was in assigning blame also to the general dissatisfaction with the war. The election demonstrated Ohio many-mindedness reigning supreme.[32]

A most amazing fact emerges from all the political infighting. Of course, nation and state had to take time out for the habitual election calendar, not always helpful to broader objectives and sometimes damaging to performance; but despite ordinary political virulence and extraordinary wartime stresses the first regular session of the Thirty-seventh Congress (meeting December 2, 1861–July 17, 1862) achieved an outstanding legislative record unsurpassed during the nineteenth century.

IV

The challenge of the emergency was met mainly because the shock of a civil war called forth the loyalties of a few leaders (none then very outstanding) and because the previously acquired momentum of national growth was strong enough both to support the war and to continue growth during it. So while Congress was passing measures concerning Negroes and rebels, it seriously concerned itself with financing the most expensive civil war the world had seen, with stimulating further long-range growth for a nation already growing faster than any other, and with expanding cultural opportunities for a people considered by foreigners to be uninterested in culture.

After all, if one believes, as did Sherman in 1862, that the

Chief Executive has "neither dignity, order nor firmness" and if one is conscious of possessing these qualities himself and sincerely wishes to serve his nation and state, he will assume responsibilities in any field he considers vital.[33] That field in Sherman's case was finance—paying for the war and building foundations for national economic advancement. But in these endeavors he did not get eager co-operation from either Lincoln, his congressional colleagues, or the Ohio legislature. The President not only left economic legislation usually up to Congress, but he also failed to create a Lincoln machine geared to secure enactment of administration-accepted policies by that body. Its Republican majority was not unaware that departure of southerners and many Democrats gave them an unprecedented opportunity to exercise power; but their formulation of statesmanlike objectives for which to use that power was sadly hampered by rivalries between conservative and radical factions, conflict with President and cabinet, and pressures from wartime immediacies demanding hasty action. Lacking abundant, gifted leadership, politicians were striving to carry on.

The Ohio legislature was, for its size, even more distraught than Congress, because Democrats there had a higher potential in clashes between radical and conservative factions and much hung on how a "Union" party was working out. But a majority sometimes proved obtainable to endorse particular policies dear to Sherman, and "Peace Democrats" never succeeded in winning a majority for a demand that war with the South end before its defeat.[34]

Sherman was in an anomalous position. His objective was basically conservative—establishment of a prosperous Union of reunited states. But familiar means for reaching that end were grossly inadequate. He must associate himself in devising new means with legislators of like talent and intention. Together, they must make do with findable materials in their political environment, overcoming such opposition as they could. The upshot would prove to be a revolutionary alteration in the pattern of some relationships between the government and the economy. Here, in Sherman, it was the statesman coming to the fore.

Instant attention must be paid to devising new methods of financing the war economy, for the credit of the nation was being undermined by adherence to a decrepit specie (i.e., gold) doctrine, incapable of supplying an adequate circulating medium. The government was back on pay due contractors for war matériel, pay they needed to manufacture more things for the war effort, while Chase was trying to run the nation's business on a peacetime specie basis. The incoming gold supply was being reduced by a fall in receipts from customs and from the sale of government bonds, while foreign creditors were taking out what gold they could.

Congress, wiser than Chase, in the special session had suspended the requirement that all Treasury transactions be in gold, empowering Chase to pay creditors in paper—"demand notes"—but had not made them legal tender nor provided that interest be paid on them.[35] Neither the banks nor anyone else had to accept what was not legal tender, and state laws variously required banks to pay in legal tender and maintain gold reserves. But Chase would not accept bank paper, insisting upon specie, of which the banks were unwilling to suffer further losses. The upshot was that the banks (on December 30, 1861) and the Treasury (on January 6, 1862) suspended specie payment. Ohio bankers were among the last to suspend.

Yet Chase held out stubbornly against Sherman and others arguing for emergency issue of legal tender paper. As late as mid-January, the Secretary still clung to the traditional opinion that the government should not substitute for gold its own authority. He even made an accord with a minority faction of bankers that the government would continue to rely on bond sales at whatever the market would bring, as a source of funds. Other more influential bankers rejected the accord, as did Sherman and other congressmen with whom the bankers had met on January 11 in Chase's office.[36] Late in the month, as nearly empty treasury vaults stared Chase in the face, and as banks approached the point of refusing to accept demand notes, Chase finally faced reality and listened to Sherman and his collaborators.

He grabbed a lifeline thrown to him by three business-oriented, ex-Whig Republicans (whose old party in its heyday endorsed paper issues) ; they were helped by a few associates. Representatives John B. Alley and Samuel Hooper of Massachusetts, and John Sherman of Ohio, all knew from personal experience the credit needs of manufacturers and the uncertain values of many kinds of notes issued by banks.[37] They with a few others exhibited the temerity to sponsor a revolutionary proposal. Instead of simply multiplying issues of demand notes, they insisted that the notes constitute issue of legal tender paper, backed not by gold but by the general credit of the government. Thus the government would be shouldering a role formerly allowed the banks, but most of the bankers whose co-operation was essential to Treasury operations saw the need and plumped for an emergency, legal tender issue. As Sherman put it, "every organ of financial opinion . . . in this country agrees that there is such a necessity." Incidentally, he had just received an endorsement of his position from the chamber of commerce of Ohio's largest city, Cincinnati.[38]

Competent leadership was essential, of course, to get the innovation through Congress, for it went against the widespread conviction, sanctified by time and the Democratic party, that anything other than "hard" money, which you can feel and hear, was an evil thing. Elbridge G. Spaulding of New York, another ex-Whig, who had worked with Sherman on the House Committee on Ways and Means and who had graduated to chairmanship of it, introduced a bill written by Alley, and Alley and Hooper took the strongest laboring oars in the House.

At the other end of the Capitol Sherman had to handle the

laboring oar, both in private conferences of the Finance Committee and on the floor of the Senate Chamber. In both, another Republican ex-Whig—no less than the committee chairman himself, Fessenden of Maine—put up "a most able and determined opposition," so able it stuck in John's memory ever after. Fessenden, strongly backed by Collamer of Vermont, strove to keep demand notes from being made legal tender, which Sherman argued would make them a "ridiculous" currency. They took their stand on Lincoln's birthday, Wednesday, February 12. Next day (the second of the two allotted the bill for formal Senate debate), John met the opposition head on. With utmost vigor and conviction he insisted that the emergency required legal tender status. Sherman defeated the opposition's amendment by five votes, as it lost, 17–22. Further, as other amendments stipulated payment in "coin" for customs duties and for the principal and interest of government bonds, the final vote for the bill as a whole rolled up to 30–7, with Fessenden, but not Collamer, in the majority. In this emergency solution that challenging Thursday, Sherman took great pride.[39]

The achievement had also a long-term significance which then, and for near a half-century thereafter, was ill-appreciated. In the legal tenders this nation for the first time got in circulation national paper money as the standard of value. Other important nations had not been so slow in recognizing its usefulness as a permanent economic instrument. The Congress continued to think in emergency terms as it added to the $150,000,000 authorization of February 25, 1862, $150,-000,000 more on July 11 and yet another $150,000,000 under a joint resolution of January 17 and a law of March 3, 1863. The increase to a total of $450,000,000 made Sherman and a few others uneasy, although it was below one-sixth of the total public debt at the end of the war.[40] Trouble would arise when the legal tender, known as "greenbacks," became a prime political instrument. As such they would cause Sherman untold campaign misery, for he was basically a conservative and always clung to ultimate redemption in gold; as he told the Senate the day it passed the first legal tender bill, "I dislike to vote for it. I prefer gold to paper money. But there is no other resort. We must have money or a fractured government." [41]

V

When Senator Sherman was pushing enactment of the bill for a legal tender paper currency, he was keenly aware that it was but one of the four principal means that they were using to finance the United States during this war. Unlike the revolutionary "greenbacks," the others were traditional—loans, taxes, and tariffs. Recourse to them all was frequent; in addition to the three *principal* measures for greenbacks, there were five on loans, four on taxes, and four on tariffs, besides innumerable clauses inserted in other measures.[42] All of them required that congressional permission be given to the Treasury, and the outcome hung on what permissions the Treasury requested, what Congress voted, and how they were used. Throughout the negotiations politics and personalities became deeply involved.

What would be the relation of John Sherman to all of this? He was in a peculiarly difficult position because his approach was that of both a statesman and a politician. As statesman, he read and studied with keen interest the "science of political economy," as it was termed in that day; this made him aware of problematical aspects of pending measures that did not rise to trouble the dreams of less-informed colleagues. In fact, he sometimes revealed in Senate debate a grasp of economic principles that find recognition in the best mid-twentieth-century texts.[43] On the other hand, as politician, he could legislate only as wisely as current political realities permitted. Therefore, he sometimes acted like what might be labelled a "practicing economist." Even his opponents, in Ohio and in Washington, could be moved to grudging tribute to this quality in him. He had demonstrated it, for example, on the legal tender issue.

The upshot was intimate involvement of John Sherman in the most challenging financial problems facing the United States since the days of Hamilton. His leadership would command recognition because of his acknowledged familiarity with the field, because of his influential status on the Finance Committee, and because of his closeness to the Secretary of the Treasury—especially to Chase, who held the office until July 1, 1864, and afterward to Fessenden, stepping up from the chairmanship of the Finance Committee. His leadership would meet strong opposition because he hoped Congress would adopt two primary objectives: to meet government costs as speedily, economically, and efficiently as possible, and at the same time to erect firm economic foundations for postwar prosperity. These sound objectives flew in the face of current wartime pressures, and Sherman would suffer frustrations.

From where would the frustrations arise? They would come when he sought to inject efficiency into politics, when he urged innovations that frightened important conservatives, when an imperceptive Secretary of the Treasury clung to outmoded or inappropriate practices, when Congress took as a guide to policy the fiction that the war soon would be over, when Sherman gauged public tolerance differently from his colleagues, and when he moved too far ahead of his time. The politician would have to accept much less than he sought; the statesman, persisting in some of his objectives, would obtain a few of them. The irony of it was that this politician-statesman who sometimes associated with Radicals disliked to go as far as they did; he was most comfortable using the instruments of change for basically conservative purposes.

Efficiency of administration was meaningful to him under all circumstances, and so he had entered the Senate determined to reduce government waste. He caused to be created, and chaired, a commission for collection of data looking to es-

tablishment of better budgetary responsibility—a bold stance
for any politician at any time and impossible to follow up in
wartime. Nevertheless, apprehending that the cost of this war
could escalate beyond any limits imaginable to his colleagues
(which it did), he persistently objected to ill-planned expendi-
tures and usually went down in defeat.[44]

On the larger question of how to adapt traditional means of
government finance—such as loans and taxes—to this hard-
fought, interminable war, a big obstacle was the Secretary of
the Treasury. Chase initially saw the war as a short one, loans
as capable of carrying the major cost of it with little recourse to
taxes, and the government securities market as rather amena-
ble to his wishes. John Sherman (impressed by the southern
will to resist as described to him by "W.T.", who had been head
of a Louisiana military academy) saw victory as hard-bought,
taxes as a necessary strong adjunct to loans, and the securities
market as a barometer of Treasury policy.

These two Ohioans conferred continually, the ex-Independ-
ent Democrat and ex-Whig, the loan man and the tax man. Chase
possibly visited the Capitol as often as Sherman the Treasury.
Very frequent notes passed between them. In the jumble of loan,
tax, tariff, and legal tender legislation that spilled from the legislative mill, Congress and Secretary often combined in a single
measure several different types of recourse; it became humanly
impossible for either Treasury or Congress to keep a clear idea
of where the finances stood. As long as Chase remained firmly
wedded to loans—and to loans on his own terms—and the war
went badly for the North, the marketing of bonds, certificates,
notes, and other "loan" securities remained a costly undertak-
ing.[45] Sherman was troubled by the impact of interest payments, conversions, refunding, and other compulsory Treasury
operations upon the national credit.

He was not wholly without satisfactions, however. One of his
revolutionary ideas was that a modest but uniform income tax
should become an established feature of internal revenue prac-

tice; Congress adopted an income tax in August, 1861, but did not make it uniform, setting it at 3 per cent on incomes above $800; by 1865 it was 5 per cent on that between $600 and $5000 and 10 per cent above $5000. Also, Congress quit avoiding real tax increases, although fumblingly; Sherman criticized the 1862 bill for taxing a multitude of employments, which would amount to but small sums and be hard to collect, when scientific tax policy dictated taxes on a few things such as manufactures, luxuries, fair-sized incomes, and railroads, which would bring in large sums and be readily collectible.

As he put it, "This bill, if it was reduced to a few simple propositions, would be an excellent tax bill." "You tax almost every kind of employment, from a juggler up to a lawyer, if there is any gradation between them; some people think there is not. (Laughter)." "I think it is an invidious kind of tax." It would strike at horse-traders, which most Ohio farmers were. But he would not tolerate any accusation that Ohioans were shirking war taxes.

I certainly do not object to my constituents paying their share of taxation. I not only expect them to do it, but I know they are ready and anxious to do it. . . . They are all willing to pay taxes, so far as I know. I have heard no complaint. Indeed, the heaviest tax on this bill is a tax on one of the chief productions of our State— whiskey made out of corn.[46]

The state legislature had not done badly, but it could not quite keep up with John Sherman. It met Ohio's share of the 1861 federal direct tax on real estate, amounting to the tidy sum of $1,567,089.33, with retrenchment in local outlays. But it memorialized Congress to replace the new income tax with a direct tax on land. In general, war-tax outcries were not loud in Ohio. There they had increased activity in manufacture of military equipment, clothing, and cured meats; although the manpower drain cut crop totals greatly, special crops and new enterprises made some localities better off than before, with

Cleveland apparently the greatest gainer. Even Cincinnati recovered from an early war slump, after the river was opened up
by the military successes of "W.T." and another son of Ohio,
U. S. Grant. The annual reports of the state auditor showed that
even this predominantly agricultural state was increasingly
prosperous.[47] The North as a whole, especially the industrial
areas, was justifying Sherman's economic forecasts; war production, spurring popular enthusiasm, spurred the tax potential.

Congress came to a like conclusion when the war looked
black in 1864. A new tax measure vastly expanded the number
of items on the list; the yield doubled. As Sherman recalled, "So
sweeping were the provisions that it was frequently a matter of
joke as well as comment. Someone remarked to Senator Collamer that everything was taxed except coffins. He rejoined:
"Don't say that to Sherman or he will have them on the tax list
before night." The Civil War thus in yet another way was
having a nationalizing effect, by inaugurating a nation-wide
internal revenue system. On loans versus taxes Sherman had
the satisfaction of observing that whereas the ratio of loans to
taxes during 1861–62 was $8.52 of funds from loans to $1.00
from taxes, by 1864–65 it was $2.95 to $1.00. This last was much
nearer the two-to-one ratio that John had hoped for.[48]

Loans, however, remained the Treasury's main reliance
until by December of 1862 an impasse had grown up between
Chase and the banking community; out of a current authorized
issue of $500 millions, all but $23.7 millions remained unsold.
Retreat by the Treasury and Congress was in order. It came
with a January 17 abandonment of the insistence that bonds be
sold only at their par value and a March 3 law announcing that
permission to convert greenbacks into bonds would end July 1.
More important than these steps by far was the fact that
another son of Ohio had come to the rescue of the Treasury.

The Cooke family of Sandusky, with the active intercession
of John Sherman, became enlisted in a project for sale of
government bonds to the general public. Jay Cooke was now a

Philadelphia banker who shared Sherman's optimism regarding the growth of the economy and who was absolutely certain that the general public could be persuaded to buy bonds. An expert advertising campaign worthy of the finest on Madison Avenue emanated from the staid old city of William Penn, with an assist from brother Henry Cooke, conveniently conducting a banking house in Washington. As Sherman put it, the issue of five-twenties was made to stare "in the face of the people in every household from Maine to California." It was a masterly operation and went over the top handsomely to the great delight of the Cookes, Sherman, and Chase—no mean Ohio aggregation.[49]

The one element in the quadruple financial program that did not greatly complicate life for Sherman was the tariff, because industrialization had not advanced far enough in Ohio to build much protectionism. Ohio iron interests and their coal associates in two southern districts had been inspired by the 1860 tariff plank to put that area nicely in Lincoln's column, and Sherman the next year was safeguarding them from possible fraudulent imports hidden behind ad valorem rates.[50]

In tariff debates during the Civil War, Sherman's participation included rather routine watchfulness over Ohio's iron and wool industries. Over-all, he appears to have subscribed to three basic principles. These emerge in the *Congressional Globe* and are enumerated in his *Recollections*: duties should be imposed according to the "pecuniary wants of the government"; luxury items consumed by the rich should have "a higher duty than upon an article in general use"; and "articles should be classified in schedules, so that the rate of duty on a single schedule, or on many schedules, could be advanced or lowered without disturbing the general scheme of taxation."[51]

Of these principles, one stands out as most important—that duties should be imposed in consonance with the financial needs of the government. During the 1862 debate his general position was one of maximizing tariff collections without regard to protection. He opposed prohibitive tariffs because they reduced revenue. For example, mistakenly assuming that the rag rate was being raised, he said, "Now, I ask whether to protect a small, narrow interest you would dispense with a mere revenue duty of 10%. This bill proposed to increase the duty to 30%." [52]

In 1864, when Congress moved toward a huge increase over the modest "Compensatory" rates (which in 1862 had aimed to offset for domestic producers the effects of heavy internal taxation), Sherman absolved himself of extreme protectionism. It was then not favored in Ohio. He states, "I am actuated simply by the desire to get money into the Treasury . . . without regard to protection." [53]

Yet another important contribution to the war, in the opinion of Sherman, was his position on the conscription bill. He told the Senate, "I do believe if this law had been passed at the beginning of this rebellion the rebellion would now be over. If the people of the United States show the spirit and determination to enforce this law fairly and rigorously this war is no longer of doubtful result." He wanted conscription carried out on scientific principles; he urged dividing men subject to military duty into age classifications and marital status, drafting men of appropriate age, preferably over age twenty-one but under thirty, and only single men where possible.[54] On such matters Sherman conferred with Secretary of War Edwin M. Stanton, another Ohioan at the center of the wartime administration.

VI

Ohio co-operation in statesmanship found its best wartime demonstration in an achievement for which John Sherman, more than any other one person, deserves the credit. This achievement was the National Banking Act, in which Sherman,

Chase, and the two Cookes were among the prime movers; and at the critical juncture, it was Sherman who brought it off. The Secretary, the Senator, and the two investment bankers, approaching the proposition from three different angles, finally converged their efforts on a law that set the general pattern of American banking for the next fifty years. No less.

When Chase first sat down at the ponderous desk in the august office of the Secretary of the Treasury, one mile down Pennsylvania Avenue from the Capitol, he hoped his management of the nation's financial affairs might proceed along the austere lines of the sacred Independent Treasury Act of 1846. He would like to (1) keep the Treasury relatively uncontaminated by banks and (2) stay on a specie basis. War outlays quickly vetoed both. He had to become a very frequent suppliant before the bankers for their purchase of government securities; and soon, neither Treasury nor banks would be remaining on a specie basis.[55]

The conservative Chase—in his 1861 report—had asked Congress for a banking revolution. Authority over the credit circulation of the nation should be shifted in part from the 1,600 private corporations issuing bank notes under the laws of thirty-four different states to the government. Note issue should depend on bank purchase of government bonds, on a percentage basis, with a specie reserve required. Thus would Americans use a more uniform currency, one cementing national feeling and based on the credit of the government.[56]

Evidence of the need for safer paper money filled a black notebook cherished by John Sherman. In it he had kept track of the shifting value of bank notes in the days before Ohio got her 1845 law restricting the number of banks and safeguarding their note issues. The firm where he had worked as a law student then got its major income from debt collections; knowledge of which banks were sound had been indispensable then and there, and remained so in states where flimsy banks could cheat with irredeemable paper. So Sherman from his youth

knew the need for an end to the existing state bank issues, but
realized the tremendous political power of the state bank interest and of those opposed to innovation, especially the weak
banks. In 1861 he was not yet sure what to do.[57]

The opposition loomed so large that the first bill prepared in
line with Chase's recommendation for introduction to the
House was not pushed; and other drafts were labored over
during discussions among Sherman, Chase, and Representatives
Hooper and Spaulding. The latter essayed a second national
bank bill that they managed to get through the Ways and
Means Committee and to report to the House only five days
before members ended the second session of the Thirty-seventh
Congress and dashed home to campaign.

Sherman, meanwhile, had been interested in trying for legislation to discourage spurious note issues—this was in line with
a Chase recommendation of a year earlier for a tax on state
bank circulation. At one point Sherman "gave the number of
banks issuing notes in 1862 as 1,500, while the number whose
notes were not counterfeited was only 253; of the various kinds
of imitations, alterations and counterfeits there were more than
6,000." The Senator offered an amendment to the 1862 revenue
bill for a 2 per cent tax on state bank notes; in his presentation,
not wishing to stir up hornets, he was "carefully avoiding reference to the National Bank Bill," as he explained to his wife.
His finesse did not succeed. He lost, 27–10.[58]

When Congress reassembled December 1, Chase, Sherman,
Hooper, and Spaulding, still not wholly agreed, got an assist
from Lincoln. The President's annual message, like Chase's
report to Congress, advocated organization of banking associations under a general act of Congress, well guarded in its
provisions; thereby, said Lincoln, uniform, secure, and convert-
ible notes "would at once protect labor against the evils of a
vicious currency, and facilitate commerce by cheap and safe
exchanges." Unfortunately, Lincoln's advice on finance then
had little weight with those Republicans and Democrats who

were fighting the administration; Sherman for his part had then a very low opinion of the President's judgment in general.

The Senator was feeling his way along. His speech of the previous July urging taxation of notes had attracted correspondence with some favorable comment, and it induced in him much further study. Sure that "my remedy for paper money is, by taxation to destroy the banks and confine the issue to Government paper," [59] he was undecided about the best means of achieving this.

In this uncertain state of affairs Henry Cooke stepped into Chase's office. He emerged with an appeal from Chase to John: Would the Senator please remodel the bank bill to satisfy his own views and take charge of it in the Senate? As Fessenden was opposed to Chase's ideas, the chairman of the Finance Committee could not be utilized. John wrote his wife that he had reached the judgment

that it was a public duty to risk a defeat on the Bank Bill. I thoroughly convinced myself, if I could not convince others, that it was indispensable to create a demand for our bonds, and the best way was to make them the basis of a banking system. When you reflect upon the magnitude of the interests involved you will be impressed what a task this was. Not a step could be taken without a contest with local banks of great power and extensive ramifications. However, I carefully examined Chase's bill, made several important alterations and restrictions and introduced it. . . .[60]

During the struggle Sherman "was very anxious and scarcely slept." This bank legislation became a maze of confusion. On the same day, January 26, 1863, Hooper brought a bank bill into the House, and Sherman brought into the Senate one "a little different," *S.486.* Cabinet members climbed the hill to support one or the other. Both served as targets for marksmen perfecting their skills: such marksmen as antiadministration Republicans and Democrats, "more-greenbacks" men led by

Thaddeus Stevens of Pennsylvania, Constitution-protectors like Fessenden and Collamer, representatives of little banks cherishing their freedom to issue weak currency and of big banks opposed to government controls over their strong currency, all groups fluid, crossing regional and sectional lines. Sherman, scanning the newspapers and his correspondence, sought a steady stance in the tornado of opinion, feeling, and influence.[61]

He got his *S.486,* amended in the Finance Committee, to the printer Monday, February 2, and on Wednesday arranged to have it taken up on the ninth. That next Monday an incident threatened his success; only by the narrow margin of one vote did he prevent a Navy bill from preceding his own. However, the senators accepted the committee amendments that day without demanding roll calls, and he got a significant assist when Chairman Fessenden spoke up to assure objectors that the bill was permissive, not obligatory; in fact, he gave Sherman his vote on every roll call in the three hectic days that followed.[62]

What chance had Sherman to push into enactment—in a Senate calendar badly overcrowded with tax, loan, military, and end-of-the-session appropriation measures—a bill strongly opposed by local bank interests? He judged, evidently, that there was enough general anxiety over currency depreciation to give him a chance.

On Sherman's exhausting fight to get at least a permissive national bank act based on government bonds, the skills of the politician fortified the basic objective of the statesman. In this midwinter of 1863 he was holding to a practical technique characteristic of most of his forty-three years at the nation's capital. If he could not win support for his position on some patricular aspect of a bill that he felt should not be allowed to fail, he would yield that part for the sake of the larger whole, and accept disliked amendments to keep the core.

Also, he could accede to nearby enactment of diverse measures, to content warring factions. Thus while the bank bill was cooking, a pot of loan bills and another of legal tender bills was coming to a boil over the congressional fire. In fact, Sherman had to tend the bank bill so watchfully that his pet proposition—taxing the state bank circulation—got pushed aside. Such a "powerful combination of bank interests" opposed it that it could not be passed separately, or as an insertion in other bank, loan, or legal-tender bills. For his tax provision, Sherman had to wait two years more.[63]

As debate closed that Monday, Sherman announced, "I shall hope to get a vote on this bill tomorrow." On the morrow he opened debate with a powerful speech, one of the best of his entire career. He summoned the wisdom of the Senate to decide between a permanent system of safe national currrency and a system of paper money without limit as to amount. "In the consideration of such a question we surely should sacrifice all local interests, all pride of opinion, and, . . . we should bring to our aid all the wisdom of united counsels, and all the light which the experience of former generations of men can give us." [64]

But the question remained: how united were the counsels on *S.468*—for, or against? During a prolonged session that Tuesday, the senator was kept busy answering objectors. His following was tested in six roll calls. He got defeat of opposition amendments objectionable to him by votes of 14–22, 9–27, 11–"noes not counted," 19–21, and 6–31. He got reconsideration of an objectionable amendment, accepted while his attention had been diverted, by 21–16. In four cases he got rejections without a roll call. But at a late hour they had not moved to a final vote; so he made sure *S.486* would come up as the unfinished business on Wednesday. On the one tight question of the day thus closed he had won only by 19–21. Could he hold a majority on the next tomorrow? [65]

Collamer of Vermont was determined that he should not. Much of Wednesday had to be given to argument with him over the threat to local banks and the relative importance of opponents and proponents of the measure. Sherman waxed sarcastic.

The honorable Senator, however, seems, from the whole course of
his argument, to have had only in view the interests of local banks
and bankers. If he can refer to their interests, and appeal to us in
eloquent terms to protect them from the doom that the sons of
Jacob believed was about to fall upon Benjamin, and almost excite
our sympathy to tears in view of the afflictions we are about to put
upon local banks; if he can cite the opinions of those who have
charge of them, surely I may cite the opinions of grave and honorable men who are charged with the responsibilities of administering
the Executive Departments of the Government.[66]

Thus was Wednesday consumed by Collamer and his cohorts.

They summoned the senators to five roll calls. Sherman won
against the opposition five times: 13–23, 18–18, 15–23, 14–22,
7–28. The worrisome fact was inconstancy in the lineup; five
men whose support Sherman might need on a final vote broke
away from him on some tallies or did not show up for the roll
call on others. Four were Republicans, one a Democrat.[67]

The five could not in any real sense be called a bloc. They
were Harding and Nesmith of Oregon, Howard of Michigan,
Howe of Wisconsin, and Wilmot of Pennsylvania. None of
them had served with Sherman in the House, although two of
them had been there earlier. None had been in the Senate
before 1861, and only two were destined to have more than one
term there. Only one hailed from a state on the Atlantic seaboard. Three of them had voted on the opposition side at one
time or another, and the other two had not bothered much
about voting at all. They were alike in but one respect—a lack
of distinction (unless the ex-Democrat, David Wilmot, may be
so honored for his Free-Soil fame). But Senate votes are
counted numerically, not weighted by prestige.[68]

It was likely that the number of members voting on Tuesday
and Wednesday (varying from thirty-five to forty) would be
exceeded on Thursday, what with the importance of the bill
and the fact that a definite hour—1:00 P.M.—had been set. It
seemed unlikely that Lincoln was offering patronage plums for

bank votes, for the Senator had made no secret of his contempt for the President. It was certain that party "discipline" could not be invoked, for it was non-existent in a Senate with only ten Democrats out of forty-eight members, and with a record of factionalism exceeded only by its record of achievement. So the outcome was anybody's guess.

Thursday came, and the hour of one. The presiding officer intoned:

The Chair will state the question to the Senate. The special order of the day is the unfinished business of yesterday, which is the bill (S. No. 486) to provide a national currency, secured by a pledge of United States stocks, and to provide for the circulation and redemption thereof. The question is on the passage of that bill. Is the Senate ready for that question?

The yeas and nays were ordered, and the voting began, "Anthony, yea"; and on through the Senate alphabet. It stood 7–7, when Harding was called and voted aye making it 8–7. It stood 10–9 when Howard was called and made it 11–9, and Howe following made it 12–9. It stood 14–13 when Nesmith was called and made it 15–13. It was 19–19 when Wade was called and made it 20–19. It was 21–20 when Wilmot was called and made it 22–20. Two names remained; if both went to the opposition, it would be a tie. But they divided, one to each. Thus, Sherman ended up with a safe 23–21.

Safe, because conditions in the House were not quite so harrowingly close, and because there was at least a degree of co-operation between the House Ways and Means Committee and the Senate Committee on Finance. Although the bill had to go through the House and other procedures delaying enactment until February 25, the *Congressional Globe* of February 13 spoke truly when it said of that day, "So the bill was passed." [69]

The end product could not wholly suit anyone; certainly not Sherman, partly because it did not end state bank issues. But it

did project a more secure currency—about which he cared
greatly—based on government bonds and reserve requirements; in fact, the gold premium had fallen temporarily in
connection with presentation of the bill. Further, Sherman had
hopes that a uniform currency would tend to lessen the divisive-
ness in the nation. The Treasury, particularly, should be
helped: by better bond sales, by the banks becoming public
depositories, and by the acceptability of bank notes submitted
in payment for sums due the government. Altogether, the
statesman in Sherman had good reason for content. War emergencies had enabled him to participate in a long-term financial
benefit to a growing nation.

Sherman paid heed in more than one way to national growth
during this phenomenally energetic Congress, despite such clam-
orous problems as military defeats, enlistments, an impover-
ished Treasury, the Negro, and political feuding. However, on
the other growth legislation—especially, two transcontinental
railroads, free homesteads, and land grant colleges—it was
other senators who carried the primary roles.

On the railroads, Columbus legislators had made their opinions known. Though they managed to meet wartime demands
of the federal government and sustained the integrity of the
Union, they did so in an atmosphere of much acrimony. Rail-
road-building almost ceased during the war, with earnings
small or non-existent; but abuses multiplied. So the legislature
passed a futile law on discrimination and diversion and set up a
new tax system. This antipathy was not personal exactly; the
Union and Democratic parties put in the governor's chair three
successive railroad presidents, Dennison, Tod, and Brough.[70]

As far as John Sherman was concerned, his great interest lay
in proper financing of a transcontinental railroad. He favored
giving the United States first lien on the bonds advanced to the
Union Pacific and the Central Pacific. When this safeguard of
the 1862 law was abandoned in amendatory legislation of 1864,
he would withhold his vote. Disappointed in the failure of some

of his suggestions for protecting the federal investment, he did not abandon such efforts; and he took some consolation in government subsidy that permitted westward movement without waiting for paying freight.[71]

On homesteads, also, Columbus legislators and Ohio party leaders had shown interest, but more mildly. The local democratic organization had supported free homesteads, and their Douglas faction had not defended President Buchanan when he vetoed the bill sent him in 1860. That veto made northwestern Ohio particularly indignant. Canny Republicans picked up the cue and used it quite effectively among Germans of the Cincinnati area. To John Sherman the West was invitational, attracting him as a great asset for both the nation and the individual investor, a growth potential that never ceased to interest him.

On the land grant college act it was Wade, rather than Sherman, who introduced into the Senate the bill fashioned by Representative Morrill that finally got through. Both senators were aware that wartime action under it could not be really impressive, but Sherman lived to see Ohio State University originate, after much delay, from this measure enacted by the Congress, in which he justly took great pride.[72]

With satisfaction he wrote "W.T.": "On the whole the recent Congress may fairly appeal to their constituents for a favorable judgment. . . . The Union or rather Republican members made scarcely a single political speech in either House. They felt too constantly the pressure of practical matters demanding action." He had expected leisure for study and reflection as a senator. However, "although a *Junior* yet I had to carry the most important financial bills such as the Bank, Loan and Tax bills—subjects full of difficulty and detail. . . . I am truly thankful the session is over." [73]

Likewise, Finance Committee Chairman Fessenden in his fatigue found cause for gratulation, declaring the Thirty-seventh was "a most remarkable Congress," which had "discharged its great responsibility . . . with great vigor and devo-

tion. If the country is to be saved (and it is to be) Congress will
have saved it." This scarcely portrayed the President as a savior; and John Sherman was sure Lincoln was a national disaster—a belief that led to the most painful episode in his career,
one in which the politician (and not a wise one at that) took
precedence over the statesman, to the ultimate displeasure of
constituents and complete omission from the autobiography.[74]

VII

The northern reverses dominating the first two years of the
war had been exploited by a congressional cabal that became
determined to assume the functions of the Commander-
in-Chief. The cabal was organized around a joint committee
originally proposed in December of 1861 for investigation of
specific northern defeats of the previous months; but by that
time Senator Sherman was greatly exercised over misconduct of
the war, including misfortunes befalling Colonel Sherman,
and at his insistence the provenance of the committee was
broadened to include nothing less than "the conduct of the
present war." Thereon the committee did much useful work in
uncovering scandals and promoting efficiency.

But "Bluff Ben" Wade, the chairman of it, and most of its
seven-man personnel determined to weld it into an
antiadministration weapon to control the cabinet, to dictate
federal policy on the war, on Negroes, and on readmission of
seceded states. They proceeded to feed prejudices, foster rivalries in and out of the services, and generally operate as a Civil
War version of a McCarthy Committee. Wade, of Jefferson
County, was the only Ohio member; but at various times
committee objectives were facilitated to varying degrees by
Chase, Sherman, Garfield, Schenck, and other Ohioans. The
press eagerly took committee handouts. Result: Lincoln had to
fight two wars simultaneously, one with the South and one with

a relentless faction of Republicans who came to be called the Radicals, or the Jacobins.[75]

Sherman came to share much committee agitation, in part because Lincoln's treatment of his brother displeased John from the outset. Before Sumter he had taken his West Point–trained brother, then a civilian just up from Louisiana, to the White House to warn Lincoln of southern eagerness for war. Lincoln had dismissed the warning with "I guess we will manage to keep house." Thereafter the Shermans waited many weeks (partly through "W.T." 's hesitancy about accepting some astute counsel from John) before "W.T." received a much desired colonelcy in the regular army. That fall the choleric colonel suffered a brief nervous breakdown aggravated by ineptitude in Lincoln's secretary of war, Cameron, and in an adjutant-general; reporters blew this up with glee, for the colonel profanely denounced their habit of publishing information useful to the Confederacy and thus convinced them that he "would see them all in Hell before supplying a line of copy." [76]

Through two long years "W.T." 's rank in the regular army remained only that of a colonel, although he became in May, 1861, brigadier general, and one year later major general, of volunteers. During this period Lincoln placed over him for a time as superior officer John A. McClernand, an Illinois War Democrat who disliked West Pointers as heartily as they him. Worst of all, when Thomas W. Knox, reporter for the *New York Herald*, libeled Sherman as a coward before Vicksburg, and was convicted by a court-martial, Lincoln had proposed to let him off if Grant agreed. Grant did not agree.[77]

The indignant Senator assured his brother, "Lincoln's order that McClernand should supersede you was one of his petty weaknesses." "You will live to serve your country when 'Old Abe' is consigned to infamy as a fool and baboon." The latter "title" reflected the Senator's disgust at earthy jokes in which he could find no amusement. Also, the President's temperament as a whole was alien to the Senator's understanding; for example,

the fits of deep depression Sherman diagnosed as a weak surrender to monomania. He told other senators seeking to purge
Lincoln's cabinet of conservatives that since the President himself was the real difficulty, it would do no good just to oust
Seward.[78]

As the Thirty-seventh Congress drew toward its close, the
blame for military and political misfortunes was increasingly
laid on Lincoln. When Murat Halstead of the *Cincinnati Commercial* wrote Sherman, "If Lincoln was not a damned fool, we
could get along yet. He is an awful, woeful ass," he addressed a
like-minded recipient. Sherman's sense of proportion was under
terrific strain by reason of "W.T." He, agonized by reporters'
charges, by presidential interference, and by rivals' jealousies,
was threatening to resign. John warned him that this would be
"ungrateful" and "folly" in a man highly regarded by people
who counted. "Do you wish to humiliate me and not only me
but Halleck, Stanton (the Secy. of War who is truly your
friend) [and] Mr. Ewing?" This would be "a confession of
weakness that I would rather die than make. . . . Great God I
wish you had been libelled as much as I have been and got used
to it." The colonel, fortunately for John, Lincoln, and the
nation, did not resign.[79]

But gloom rested heavily on many in the nation when the
much touted "Fighting Joe" Hooker lost to Lee at Chancellorsville, May 1–5, 1863. Two days later, John wrote despairingly
to his brother of Lincoln's war management.

I was among the first of his political friends to acknowledge how
fearfully we were mistaken in him. He has not a single quality be-
fitting his place. I could name a thousand evidences of this but that
Knox affair is one. He is unstable as water. . . . I never shall cease
to regret the part I took in his election and am willing to pay a
heavy penance for this sin. . . . He is unfit to control events and it
is fearful to think what may come during his time. . . . He looked
upon Hooker as his 'last card.' I anticipate some sudden folly adopted
hastily without consultation and in such a way as to commit him and
excite his stubborness. . . . It may be better that the Democrats be

allowed to take the helm. They could not make Peace and then war would be more vigorous and united. I certainly would be glad to support a War Democrat—anybody rather than our monkey President. . . . How fervently I wish Lincoln was out of the way. Anybody would do better." [80]

Such "reasoning" under despair led the Senator to co-operate in a disastrous effort to find a better "anybody" to run on the Republican ticket come 1864. He could not realize the extent to which July 3 and 4 of 1863 (bringing northern victory at Gettysburg, and the fall of Vicksburg with opening of the Mississippi) had pleased the public. In so far as his brother, a brigadier general in the regular army from July 4, 1863, assisted in the western victories, he contributed to bolstering the popularity of that President whom John wished to see removed. Thus can politics and the military confute each other; and the General would do this to the Senator again, fourteen months later. John's blindness was due in part to political strains in Ohio.

As the northern victories of Gettysburg and Vicksburg in 1863 were followed by reverses elsewhere, Ohio's Peace Democrats aggressively capitalized on the calendar, which decreed that a governor should be elected that year. So Ohio had to continue to cope with political war within her own borders despite the fact that she had some 100,000 of her sons fighting on the Union battle lines against the Confederacy. Political opportunism fanned campaign feeling to white heat. The Peace Democrats were emboldened to choose as their candidate the rabid pro-southerner, Vallandigham, who in May of 1863 had been convicted as a traitor and exiled by Lincoln to behind the southern lines. Frightened Republicans and War Democrats, continuing the "Union" party of the previous year, chose as candidate a War Democrat, John Brough. With the Copperheads the Unionists exchanged the most bitter of denunciations, and were so unsure of the popular will that their gubernatorial candidate himself estimated his victory at only a plurality of 5,000 on the eve of his actual October majority of over 100,000.[81]

Despite this Union landslide, the Republican sector of the combination, including such leaders as John Sherman, was assailed by a worrisome feeling of party insecurity. Not only had they been compelled to unite again with War Democrats to achieve a Unionist victory, but they well remembered that a year earlier the Democrats had captured fourteen of the state's nineteen seats in their House of Representatives. Lincoln, some Republicans judged, had issued his pledge of an Emancipation Proclamation at a time when it had contributed to that 1862 defeat. In the state legislature they had had to postpone for a year the re-election of Senator Wade.

Wade had made it in 1863, but another national campaign confronted Ohio Republicans in 1864. Could they win with Lincoln? And, if Lincoln were re-elected and the North won the war, would he dictate a firm retribution upon the Rebels? The radically inclined faction of Republicans, including Chase, Sherman, and Representatives Garfield, Ashley, Eckley, Schenck, and Spalding (the corporal's guard remaining in Congress after Ohio's slaughter of the Republicans in 1862) had serious doubts. He had demonstrated, they thought, that he lacked both the vigor and wisdom needed to push the war to a successful conclusion, and thereafter to punish the Rebels as they deserved.[82]

Sharing the popular error that the taking of Richmond should have highest priority, Ohio critics of Lincoln, like other Radicals in New York, Pennsylvania, and elsewhere, resented the failure of six successive generals, all Lincoln appointees, to take the Confederate capital. The anti-Lincoln Republicans took inadequate solace from the federal penetration into the lower Mississippi Valley and the tightening blockade of the southern ports. They schemed further while the President they heartily distrusted and disliked won acclaim from Gettysburg and Vicksburg.

Lincoln himself expedited their organized attack upon him late in 1863. The day after Congress convened, December 7, he issued his Amnesty Proclamation promising concessions to properly repentant rebels. Radical Republicans were infuriated; the Executive should know that such a decision was the prerogative of Congress. Those arrogant rebel leaders through many years had blocked northerners' political and economic advancement, and had snubbed them socially to boot. Lincoln's Amnesty simply was too much for the Radicals to take. Two prongs of an attack on him—one outside Congress and one within legislative halls—were launched.

Outside Congress, December 8, a small group whose first central committee included two Ohio congressmen and an army paymaster and newspaperman, both from Ohio (out of a total membership of seven), formed a tentative organization to boom Chase for President. This prospect displeased neither Chase nor his ambitious daughter Kate. The central junta expanded its Senate and House membership, with Sherman and Garfield apparently becoming part of it, and neither Chase nor Lincoln was unaware of its objectives. Henry Cooke, at the head of the Washington branch of Jay Cooke and Company of Philadelphia, ardent friends of Chase, eased more funds in this direction than Jay realized at the moment.[83]

The Chase-Lincoln contest came to a head on indications that Lincoln's friends hoped to sew up his nomination by inducing state legislatures to endorse him before a national convention should meet. The *Dayton Daily Empire* of January 26 noted rumors that some 100,000 copies of a Chase magazine were soon to be circulated free. The pamphlet went into the mails from Washington ten days later, with the rousing title, "The Next Presidential Election."

Here was a document that did not mention the Secretary of the Treasury by name but had plenty to assert, in terms of contempt, about the President under whom Chase was serving. It argued that Lincoln sought to use patronage and party machinery to perpetuate his power, in violation of a "one-term principle" followed since 1836 and essential to preservation of true republicanism. Further, if the Democrats chose their candidate wisely, Lincoln would be "most unquestionably defeated," for his "weak and vascillating" policies had prolonged the war and bade fair to oppress the people with unbearable war debt.[84]

Pursuing their quarry, the cabal ten days later substantially repeated their arguments in a "Pomeroy Circular" (named for Senator Samuel C. Pomeroy of Kansas), although they used less abusive terminology toward Lincoln. They came to their point, with a strong endorsement of Chase's nomination. Both documents assumed a pretense of privacy while assuring wide circulation in and outside the press.

At once there was outcry, suggesting to wiser politicians that the cabal had overreached itself. In Sherman, as in others of the anti-Lincoln faction, fear and frustration had destroyed good judgment. He who eighteen months before had declaimed against the "claptrap" over subjugation now found Lincoln too conciliatory. Worse for him, he now became the prime target of Ohio supporters of Lincoln, for at home recipients of "The Next Presidential Election" could but note that it reached them free, bearing Sherman's frank; and the less abusive "Circular" served to underscore their reactions. Some approved. More waxed indignant at rank abuse of "Old Abe." His popularity and Sherman's unpopularity became emphatic in letters sent the Senator and the press. A Republican caucus of the Ohio legislature made it official, February 25, by endorsing Lincoln. By March 3 the beleaguered Senator was seeking weak refuge—denying that his frank was used with his knowledge. Two days later, a somewhat chastened Chase was tentatively suggesting "that no further consideration be given my name." [85]

However, the Chase candidacy enjoyed such strong support from the Radical minority in Washington that it could not be

abruptly halted by such demonstrations as the Ohio endorsement of Lincoln or by like action (in January) by the
Union League of Philadelphia. The Chase committee, chaired
by Senator Pomeroy, was able, through Henry Cooke of the
Washington branch of Jay Cooke and Company, to involve
that firm in some $20,000 of outlays; and the Cooke publicity
machine used magazine and newspaper editors, not forgetting
to plant Chase material in home-town papers conveniently
delivered to congressional desks. Treasury employees at their
various posts over the Union, many of them Ohioans, labored
in the vineyard.[86]

Somewhat belatedly, Jay Cooke concluded it was time to
withdraw himself and his firm from the Chase candidacy. It
proved impossible to recoup on all the candidacy loans, but it
was announced that brother Henry (who had been much involved) was in poor health from his labors on the 5–20 bonds,
and would spend the summer in Europe, arranging sale of
United States bonds abroad. June 7 witnessed a Baltimore
gathering of Republicans and War Democrats, assembled as a
"Union" convention, where Lincoln's tremendous popular support forced the Radicals to accept his nomination.[87]

His opponents, however, did not accept this verdict as final.
The first session of the Thirty-eighth Congress had not adjourned. Its Radical faction had in hand work designed to
forestall implementation of the mild reconstruction process
projected in Lincoln's Amnesty Proclamation, and in the pending application of Arkansas and Louisiana for readmission to the
Union. In this work Senator Sherman's services had been enlisted. Thus he was involved in the other prong of the attack on
Lincoln—the one more openly pushed—in the legislative proceedings of Congress.

This fight has to be reported in some detail here because it
shows the kind of experience a senator goes through during an
intraparty fight in times of crisis. Legislators reach their decisions
in an environment pervaded by confusion, tension, uncertainty,

intrigue, parliamentary manipulation, irrationality, contradictions, and murky objectives. John Sherman and his fellow
lawmakers were breathing that kind of polluted air in the
first session of the Thirty-eighth Congress.

The pollution was emanating from many sources, and Sherman had perhaps unwittingly contributed to it back in the
Thirty-seventh Congress. He then introduced a measure in the
Senate at the request of a personal friend, Henry Winter Davis,
ex-representative from Maryland, an ex-Know-Nothing subject
to ardent enthusiasms. Davis was one of those who abhorred
Lincoln's intention to admit ex-rebel states on the basis of a
proven oath-of-loyalty-taking population of but 10 per cent,
without wholesale disqualification of Confederate leaders. His
original measure conveyed the belief that this kind of forgiveness was dangerous. The Senate deposited the measure in
the Judiciary Committee.[88]

Lincoln's Amnesty Proclamation of December 7, 1863, galvanized Davis into vigorous countervailing action, which he
could take because he had been again elected to Congress. The
fact that he, like Wade and Chase, dreamed of the presidency
further stirred him to a demonstration of executive ability. He
and his closest Radical associates felt that the President purposed to exceed his authority, that punitive reconstruction
under strict congressional control was imperative. So, a week
after the Amnesty Proclamation, Davis secured establishment
of his own "Select Committee" on the "Rebellious States,"
empowered to report a bill "to guaranty a republican form of
government" in the reconstructed areas. Davis got his bill
authorization by a margin of only eleven votes, with Ohio's five
Republican members voting aye and her fourteen Democrats
voting nay. James M. Ashley, Republican from Toledo, was
made a committee member.[89]

Davis did not have an easy time getting his bill enacted. On
May 4, after a number of speech-making night sessions and the
use of appropriate parliamentary devices, the end came. A

Davis "substitute" was passed after a Davis explanation that it
stipulated a majority of the population must have taken the
loyalty oath, but that it softened the exclusion of Confederate
leaders. Oddly enough, at this point Ohio's solid phalanx of
support broke down. Garfield and Eckley did not participate in
the crucial vote on tabling the bill. Why? Did they dislike the
bill, yet hate to vote with Ohio Democrats? Six of that ilk also
avoided voting that Wednesday afternoon. At least, on Davis'
bill these eight representatives demonstrated again Ohio's
many-mindedness; and the next day, too, when two of these
dubious Democrats crawled back into the nay column.[90]

In the Senate Wade managed to get the bill up late on July
1, and a curious drama was acted out in the next twenty-four
hours. The members were perspiring under the giant skylight
over the Senate Chamber and wanted to go home. As Carlile of
West Virginia feelingly put it, "It is now growing late, and
sitting in this furnace beneath this heat I would prefer conclud-
ing what I intended to say upon this bill tomorrow or some
other day."

"Some other day" was precisely what Brown of Missouri
offered the Senate in the form of a substitute bill that avoided
the hot problem of politically-conditioned reconstruction by
stipulating simply that states would be admitted under legislation to be enacted in the future. This gentle substitute passed
the Senate three times, thanks to Senate rules, which are
peculiarly independent of Robert's *Rules of Order*, in hot
weather as well as cool. The successive votes tallied at 17–16
with 16 not voting, 20–13 with 16 not voting, and finally 26–3
with 20 not voting. Sherman stood stoutly with Wade in the
negative on the first two tallies; but both voted aye on the third,
though Sherman left unexplained the apparent contradiction
between his nays and his aye.[91]

The reason for the Sherman-Wade final aye on July 1 is
suggested by their success on July 2. Overnight they doubtless
conferred on the morrow's technique. So Davis advised the

House not to accept the Senate substitute but to seek "a conference." Meanwhile, Wade in a small Senate got a vote to recede from the Brown substitute, thus getting acceptance of the Davis bill. The ayes had it (18–14 with 17, including Brown, not voting) with the silent Sherman still faithful with pro-Wade votes. Thuswise, the "conference" committee never met—officially, that is—and the Wade-Davis bill went to the White House. Sherman watched while Lincoln gave the bill a pocket veto July 8, underscored with a public "Proclamation." Later, Sherman believed that the President regretted his decision and that acceptance of the bill would have forestalled more extreme legislation, which split the next Congress and Executive.[92]

Sherman tended to keep his ear closer to the ground, as intraparty strife raged through July and August. While he privately denounced Lincoln in letters to his brother, he does not seem to have participated actively in eastern schemes to substitute General Benjamin Butler and Wade for the Lincoln-Johnson ticket. Not Sherman but Garfield came to be accused of part authorship of the Wade-Davis "Manifesto," which on August 5 rent the air with an anti-Lincoln blast. Evidence accumulated that popular opinion in Ohio (and in the North generally) favored Lincoln; he got a boost when the Peace Democrats named the military failure, McClellan, to run against him on a defeatist platform nailed together by Ohio's prime pro-southerner, Vallandigham; "Gentleman George" Pendleton of Ohio for Vice-President.[93]

But it was the Senator's brother, now major general, who dashed any hopes that John may have retained for the election of any other Republican than Lincoln. "W.T." 's forces took Atlanta September 2. The public was overjoyed. So, the Middle West, in the person of Chandler of Michigan (hitherto a Radical par excellence), patched up relations between eastern Radicals and the administration. Before September was past, Wade, Davis, *et al.* were joining Sherman and Garfield on the stump for election of Lincoln. The General knew what he had done to

John, and John knew what the General thought of the political game.[94]

VIII

The statesman in Sherman preferred to play down the politician. As politician, he had temporarily besmirched the image of the statesman, and his constituents had rebuked him for it, denouncing his stance on "The Next Presidential Election." He would not like to remember it, and so, thirty years later, he gave scarce a whisper in his autobiography of his part in the anti-Lincoln fight. He merely mentioned in passing an "alleged rivalry" between Chase and Lincoln. This had a sounder basis than pride, although pride was in it. He had the sense to realize that—in the long run—constructive legislation has far more influence upon a nation than does political infighting. So, looking back from 1894, he stressed the first session of the Thirty-eighth Congress as "perhaps the busiest and most important one in the history of our government." [95]

In Sherman the interminably dragging war, which warped his political judgment, posed also another kind of challenge, one he better understood—the need to meet the continuing economic and military requirements of the nation. With the other members of the second of the two wartime Congresses, the Thirty-eighth, he had to face the fact that basic legislation of the Thirty-seventh Congress required reconsideration, and that newly emerging needs must be met. Such aspects of senatorial life were welcomed by the "practicing economist" as an opportunity to try the exercise of statesmanship. While recognizing that any legislation would continue to be handicapped by wartime pressures for hasty action, he nevertheless could strive for a long-range view.

Reference already has been made to some of his insistencies carried over from the Thirty-seventh Congress into the

Thirty-eighth. He continued to advocate that taxes be a strong
adjunct to loans in financing the war; that income taxes be
made a regular feature (although he opposed taxing the
wealthy at higher rates) ; that bond sales be adjusted to the
realities of their possible market, including purchase by the
ordinary citizen; that the primary objective of wartime tariffs
should be revenue; and that military manpower needs could be
met only by strict enforcement of a scientifically-designed
conscription plan.

Financing the war was a continual obligation and trial to a
senator desirous of economy and order in finance. He cut civil
expenses as far as he could within political realities and fought
appropriation riders to extraneous bills. Yet he had to press for
increases in revenue and loan totals that further heightened the
impact of the national government upon the individual citizen.
At least, the tax increases somewhat countered the rampant
inflation. The greenbacks worried Sherman, although the
public liked them and the bankers favored them over national
bank notes; he was glad of a greenback rider to the revenue bill
of 1864 that prohibited further issue of them.

Conservative financing tended to be his criteria for judging
other legislation also, such as the 1864 amendment of the
Union Pacific Railroad Act and the new Northern Pacific Railroad bill. He warned the Senate that he introduced the Union
Pacific bill "without committing myself at all either as to its
general principles or its details." He wanted to protect the
government's investment by tightening controls over stockholders, construction, branch-building, timber rights, and bond
issues. He spoke of "extreme reluctance" to vote for it; he is
listed as "absent" when the bill passed the Senate. The fact that
it made the first lien of the United States for bonds advanced to
the company subordinate to the liens of the company's bonds
sold in the market struck him as a "fatal error"; and he found
in the Northern Pacific act "scarcely any safeguards to protect
the government." [96]

He pointed out concessions also in the other principal amendatory act of the Thirty-eighth Congress—the 1864 bank act. In reporting the bill back to the Senate, he frankly admitted the pressure from the state banks and the small-bank lobby. He assured the members, "This bill says nothing about taxing the state banks." National banks, on the other hand, were made subject to federal taxes on their circulating notes, deposits, and capital stock, and were not freed from state and municipal taxation. Further, the bill set the minimum capital at $50,000 because a decided House vote favored the lower figure "with a view to help remote and thinly populated sections of the country and smaller towns." Sherman would "much prefer" a minimum of $100,000. "If I had my own way . . . I would have left out the small banks." But the "practicing economist" asked the Senate to accept the House figure, which they did. Furthermore, the bill lowered the permissible denomination of notes from $5.00 to $1.00.[97]

However, the 1864 law retained Sherman's original (unfortunate) limitation of national bank notes to $300,-000,000—a limitation rising from his fear of depreciated currency and inflation; it safeguarded the use of bonds, placed restraints on the use of notes, and eased the transition from state to national bank status, including permission to keep their favorite names. Altogether, this measure furnished a capital illustration of the techniques of the statesman-politician.

Those techniques were challenged by a new responsibility in the second session of the Thirty-eighth Congress (the last of the war period) because Sherman became chairman of the Committee on Finance. Five days before the first session adjourned, Secretary of the Treasury Chase, in a pique over patronage, tendered one of his periodic resignations. Lincoln, to the dismay of Chase, accepted this one with alacrity. The Cookes and some others hoped John would be offered the place and would accept it, but Lincoln finally chose Fessenden. Thus Sherman got the chairmanship with the honor, obligations, and worry of managing bills on appropriations (current and deficient), currency, loans, tariffs and taxes, and any other legislation primarily concerned with finance, for the Senate did not yet have a separate Committee on Appropriations. In loan aspects of this work the Cookes continued to proffer counsel.[98]

It was Secretary Fessenden who proceeded to help the new chairman to a cherished objective, which Senator Fessenden earlier had opposed: the Secretary now expressed support for a 10 per cent tax on state bank circulation. This prohibitive levy, inserted in the Revenue Act of 1865, effectively ended competition between state and national bank notes. It induced state banks to become national banks, a transformation in which Ohio had been setting an example poorly imitated elsewhere up to this point.[99]

Yet another rider testified to Sherman's continuing hope to lead government finance into more efficient and economical practice. Way back in his first Senate session, the Senator had obtained authorization for a commission to report on government salaries and "for other purposes," with a view to pruning and regularizing outlays. Wartime conditions had frustrated this hope, imposing on him instead three solid years of painful experience with what he defined as "a great deal of crude legislation." In 1864 he had tried again, putting through the Senate a joint resolution for a three-man commission to investigate means for raising more money by taxation. This estimable measure was killed in the House by a Democratic member victorious in Ohio's Republican holocaust of 1862, "Sunset" Cox of Columbus. But in 1865 Sherman managed to revive this project by fastening it to the revenue bill. He forestalled opposition by asserting, "In my deliberate judgment such a board of commissioners as this, organized one year ago, would have saved us more than a million dollars." It should be remembered that one hundred years ago a million dollars was a horrendous sum.[100]

A committee chairman in the last session of the wartime

Congress had to crowd all his duties into the short-time span of three months, contending with the clamor of other chairmen. The traffic jam was the greater because adoption of a thirteenth amendment to the Constitution ending slavery (which was not Sherman's primary responsibility) siphoned off much precious time. In the hectic last week preceding Lincoln's second inauguration John complained of the late date at which the House sent over the revenue bill; he had to "urge the Senate to pass judgment upon the numerous provisions of this bill rather than discuss them." His long-lasting memory of his arduous responsibilities was one of devastating fatigue. "During the entire session my labor was excessive, and when it closed my health and strength were greatly impaired." [101]

IX

Judgment upon wartime leadership after the fact has all the frailties of the "Monday morning quarterback." Only a partial, distorted picture can emerge from the inadequate records preserved and available for historical research. In judging the milieu of the past, historians must admit that they are handicapped also by their own milieu. What the people of Ohio and the exigencies of a civil war demanded of a senator we can but feebly estimate. We are helped by reflecting that very possibly political office-holding aggravates, rather than diminishes, one's experience with kindness and malice, hope and despair, certitude and uncertainty, honesty and falsehood.

So in John Sherman we find a leader who as statesman and politician was sometimes wise, sometimes foolish, sometimes blind, sometimes farseeing. Some clarity of vision could come to him at times, as it does to all of us. It came to him after Lincoln's assassination. Then he met the funeral train, at 4:20 A.M., at the border of the state and accompanied the body to

Columbus. Returning to Mansfield, he there delivered to his fellow-citizens a stirring eulogy on their dead President.

Few man have been more severely denounced, yet you will not find in any of his writings, or speeches, or conversations one word of reproach or unkindness to man, woman or child—white or black, enemy or friend. There was in his character no mixture of resentment. He was ardently attached to his personal friends, and sometimes adhered to them unwisely, and for his adversaries he had no bitterness, and met all friendly advances with heartiness and sincerity. . . . When the links of the great chain of events, through which we are passing, will no longer be obscured by temporary passions, mankind will perceive how wonderfully the character of Abraham Lincoln was moulded by early trials; by peculiar traits of head and heart; by a mixture of gentleness and tenacity, for the great part he was to play in our National Drama.[102]

1. Chase had won an 1849–55 term as U.S. Senator through a fusion of Democrats and Free-Soilers. He got the governorship as a Free-Soil, Independent Democrat in 1855, and as a Republican in 1857. Again as a Republican, he was elected senator in 1860 for the term beginning March 4, 1861; but he resigned March 6 to become Lincoln's first secretary of the treasury.

2. His span of 1861–97 was interrupted by his 1877–81 tenure as President Hayes's secretary of the treasury; and his senatorial career was cut short in 1897 by calamitous acceptance of the State Department post from yet another Ohioan, President McKinley. His two Republican colleagues were Wade and Foraker, at the extreme ends of his service; the four Democrats in between were Thurman, Pendleton, Payne, and Brice.

3. *Congressional Globe*, 37th Cong., 1st Sess. (hereafter cited as *C.G.* 37C.–1S.), pp. 1493–94, Mar. 23, 1861.

4. See George Porter, *Ohio Politics During the Civil War Period* (New York, 1911), pp. 70–71. Sherman's election had been so uncertain that Henry Cooke wrote his brother Jay March 24, 1861, "We achieved a glorious success in the election of John Sherman over a combination that, as against any other man, would have been invincible." Cooke MSS, Historical Society of Pennsylvania. Jay Cooke helped to cover outlays of this candidacy according to Ellis P. Oberholtzer, *Jay Cooke: Financier of the Civil War* (Philadelphia, 1907), I, 131.

5. Herman Reuss, Columbus, Mar. 21, 1861, to John Sherman. John Sherman MSS, Library of Congress (hereafter cited as J.S. MSS, L.C.).

6. As early as Jan. 7, 1861, Robert McCune of Columbus had urged candidacy on Sherman as one who would tend to unify the dissident elements of the party. J.S. MSS, L.C. Numerous correspondents thereafter stressed this point.

7. See George Porter, *op. cit.*, pp. 13–18.

8. In later life he always asserted that he would have been nominated if he had had a military career (every president nominated between 1868 and the end of the century, except for Blaine, had a military title). This was confirmed at Mansfield during September, 1937, by numerous surviving friends of the Senator in conferences with J. P. Nichols. The fact was that in 1880 it was Ohio's refusal to unite behind him, because of his insistence upon resumption of specie payments as requisite for national welfare, that prevented the national consensus that might have forced the hand of his Ohio enemies.

9. His surviving associates indicated to J. P. Nichols that he always showed a very warm friendliness toward children, and they reciprocated.

10. Banking interests in New York, who were indebted to him in the specie resumption matter, disappointed him in failing to contribute as much as he had hoped for toward his nomination in 1880. Sherman to Charles K. Graham, Washington, Apr. 29, J.S. MSS, L.C.; Sherman to Thurlow Weed, Washington, May 1, *ibid.;* W. L. Strong to Sherman, New York, May 4, 1880, *ibid.*

11. His distaste for storytelling was most unfortunate in his relations with Lincoln, encouraging him to underestimate the ability of the President, which he was likely to do anyway for other reasons. He was wont at this time to refer to Lincoln as lacking in dignity; later, he came to realize the service that humor rendered Lincoln, as shown in his *John Sherman's Recollections of Forty Years in the House, Senate, and Cabinet, an Autobiography* (Chicago, 1895), I, 337–38 (hereafter cited as *Recollections*). As a young lawyer, he had failed at flights of oratory before juries; deciding that plain talk was better than peroration, he customarily eschewed rhetoric ever after.

12. For example, his account of his first senatorial election in his *Recollections*, I, 232–33, wanders so far from accuracy and from selection of significant factors as to make it difficult to understand why he carefully preserved letters bearing on his candidacies in his large body of correspondence.

13. *Mansfield Herald,* Apr. 11, 1861. For four years Sherman's junior was Milton S. Latham, serving (March, 1860–March, 1863) the unexpired term of Senator D. C. Broderick of California.

14. His efforts at compromise included a House resolution declaring that neither Congress nor the people of the free states had a constitutional right to legislate upon, or interfere with, slavery in any other state. It passed the House February 11, 1861, 224–25 (*C.G.* 36C.–2S., p. 857) .

15. *Mansfield Herald,* May 1, 1861. A good description of the life shared by volunteer officers and their soldiers is found in T. Harry Williams, *Hayes of the Twenty Third: The Civil War Officer* (New York, 1965) , pp. 9–47.

16. S. S. Kelley, tailor at 822 Walnut Street, had made a coat of blue "French cloth" for $31.00, with pants and vest to match, for $12.00 and $6.00, finding a colonel's passants for $4.00; a neat total of $53.00 for this customer who always dressed in good stuff of the current conservative mode. Jay Cooke got John a $50–$60 outfit "at cost"—field officer's sabre, $20.00; silk sash, $10.50; and sabre belt, $3.50; total $34.00. Shortly, Cooke was informing Sherman that this firm could furnish carbines and other equipment for regimental use. Cooke to Sherman, Philadelphia, Oct. 2, 4, Nov. 21, 1861. J.S. MSS, L.C.; *Recollections,* p. 249.

17. In addition, "W.T." 's brother-in-law, Hugh Ewing, was in mid-August made a colonel.

18. He had refused all compensation, but he must have taken at least some satisfaction out of the public Thanksgiving that the Sherman Brigade had held November 27. *Mansfield Herald,* November 27, 1861.

19. "A Civil War Diary of William McKinley," ed. H. Wayne Morgan, *Ohio Historical Quarterly,* LXIX (1960) , 279; Hayes to Mrs. Hayes, July 6, 1861, *Diary and Letters of Rutherford Birchard Hayes,* ed. Charles R. Williams (Columbus, Ohio, 1922) , II, 37.

20. It was this uncertainty that, from 1864 up until 1924, gave Ohio five presidencies (Hayes, Garfield, McKinley, Taft, and Harding) ; and every major presidential contest, except that of 1872, had an Ohioan, or an Indianian, on one ticket or the other.

21. Loan bills became law on July 17 and August 5 (*C.G.* 37C.–1S., Appendix, pp. 24–25, 40–41) , and a tariff measure including numerous other tax features was enacted on August 5, 1861 (*C.G.* 37C.–1S., pp. 34–40) .

22. Outstanding illustrations include such Republicans as N. P. Banks, J. C. Frémont, and Franz Siegel; incompetence was a supreme attainment of Benjamin Franklin Butler, whose parapetetic course among a succession of parties makes it difficult to label him other than as a perpetual politician. John did not join Radical associates in the violent hostility of some of them toward West Pointers.

23. *C.G.* 37C.–1S., p. 393, Aug. 2, 1861. He received some Ohio peti-

tions urging validation; for example, one from Norwalk dated August 5. J.S. MSS, L.C.

24. Negotiations were pursued in debate on *S.69, S.70,* and *S.72. C.G.* 37C.–1S., p. 438 *passim,* Aug. 5–6, 1861.

25. The involutions and convolutions of his thinking on slavery are reflected in his *Recollections,* pp. 146 (Mar. 4, 1857), 182 (Apr. 22, 1860), 229, 310–13 (Apr. 10, 1862), 330 (Sept. 22, 1862), and 346 (June 7, 1864).

26. *C.G.* 37C.–1S., p. 262, July 25, 1861.

27. *7th Annual Report of the Commissioner of Statistics for Year 1863* (Columbus, Ohio, 1964). No alarm over the blacks kept Sherman's senior colleague, Wade, awake nights. His alarm was over Lincoln's moderation in all its forms; and before the session was many days old, he had become established as chairman of a special "Committee on the Conduct of the War." See note 75 and paragraphs pertaining thereto.

28. *Recollections,* pp. 310–12.

29. *C.G.* 37C.–2S., pp. 3322–23, July 14, 1862.

30. A Lincoln bill for compensated emancipation had been sent to Congress and referred to the Finance Committee July 14; Sherman protested, "I do not believe the President of the United States has any right to introduce a bill here." *C.G.* 37C.–2S., p. 3323, July 14, 1862. The maneuvering between Congress and Lincoln at this juncture over confiscation is summarized in J. G. Randall and David Donald, *The Civil War and Reconstruction* (2nd ed.; Boston, 1961), pp. 283–85.

31. Figures from *Tribune Almanac* for 1863, p. 18, and 1864, p. 24, comparing enrollment December 2, 1861, with that of December 7, 1863. The most rabid anti-Union Democrat was Vallandigham, who was defeated for election to Congress in 1862 but retained sufficient influence to be nominated for governor in 1863, when again he was defeated; yet he was given a part in writing the Democratic party's national platform in 1864. Because Congress had altered Congressional districts, Ohio's apportionment had been cut from 21 to 19 representatives; Unionists in the legislature gerrymandered the districts in the thought of enabling Unionists to obtain 16 of the 19 seats. They were hoist by their own petard because they created too many close districts with the result that they won only five. Being entirely human, they blamed it partly on the lack of a soldier vote, but the assembly itself had deferred action enabling the soldiers to vote. Porter, *op. cit.,* pp. 96, 107–8.

32. John to William Tecumseh Sherman (hereafter cited as "W.T."), Mansfield, Nov. 16, 1892, R. S. Thorndike, *Sherman Letters* (New York, 1894), pp. 167–68. Some Republicans blamed defeat on the fact that Ohio was not yet collecting a soldier tally. In the tally of the five states that did so in 1862—Colorado, Iowa, Missouri, Pennsylvania, and Wisconsin—the

Tribune Almanac for 1863 (p. 63) reported a soldier majority of approximately 80 per cent Unionist. Loss of the New York gubernatorial place was a further shock to the Republicans.

33. Francis Fessenden, *Life and Public Services of William Pitt Fessenden* (Boston, 1907), I, 231–45; and M. G. B. Land, "Old Backbone: Bluff Ben Wade" (unpublished Ph.D. dissertation, Western Reserve University, 1957), p. 380.

34. On dissensions between and within Ohio's Union party and the Peace Democracy see chapters II and III in Porter, *op. cit.*, pp. 75–126, 128–99. He notes that Ohio regiments sent home resolutions pleading that patriotism displace party spirit. *Ibid.*, p. 115.

35. On treasury efforts to meet Civil War needs within the Independent Treasury System, see Esther R. Taus, *Central Banking Functions of the United States Treasury 1789–1941* (New York, 1943), pp. 57–64.

36. The necessity for the legal tenders, the arguments over legislation to obtain them, and the historical prejudice against them are brilliantly presented in Bray Hammond, "The North's Empty Purse," *American Historical Review*, LXVII (1961), 1–18; see also the longer and slightly more tentative analysis in the chapter "Origins of the Greenbacks" in Robert P. Sharkey's *Money, Class and Party: An Economic Study of Civil War and Reconstruction* (Baltimore, 1959), pp. 15–55.

37. Alley had won success as a shoe manufacturer of Lynn, Hooper as a merchant of Boston, and Sherman as a lawyer trained in an office handling problems in middle-western bank paper. Sherman must have been familiar, also, with the persistent quarreling in the Ohio legislature over radical currency solutions, summarized in Eugene H. Roseboom, *The Civil War Era: 1850–1873* (Columbus, Ohio, 1944), pp. 124–46. His main speeches defending legal tenders included several statements February 12 and his major argument February 13, 1862, *C.G.* 37C.–2S., pp. 789–91.

38. *C.G.* 37C.–1S., p. 789, Feb. 13, 1862. One of his most telling assertions was that the important banks of New York, Boston, and Philadelphia had tied up their capital in buying up public securities and could not assist the government further without legal tenders. R. Buchanan to Sherman, Cincinnati, Feb. 11, 1862, J.S. MSS, L.C.

39. *Recollections,* pp. 269–82, 296. His speech of February 13, *C.G.* 37C.–2S., pp. 789–791 was designed particularly to rebut arguments of Fessenden and Collamer.

40. On the second legal tender issue see Theodore Burton, *Life of John Sherman* (Boston, 1906), p. 109. The Revenue Act of June 30, 1864, forbade further greenback issues. The next year, the premium on gold having increased, the Ohio legislature paid interest on its state bonds in greenbacks. (Roseboom, *op. cit.*, p. 146.) He voted against the second issue

but voted for the third after its total had been halved. *C.G.* 37C.–2S., pp. 3079, July 2, 1862; *C.G.* 37C.–3S., p. 945, Feb. 13, 1863.

41. *C.G.* 37C–2S., p. 790, Feb. 13, 1862.

42. The principal Civil War tariff, tax, loan, and legal tender measures were occasionally joined in one bill, as indicated in the table below.

Date	Tariff	Tax	Loan	Legal ... Tender
July 17, 1861	...	...	X	
August 5, 1861	X	X	X	...
December 24, 1861	X	...	...	...
February 25, 1862	...	...	...	...
February 28, 1862	...	...	X	X
July 1, 1862	...	X	...	...
July 11, 1862	...	...	...	...
July 14, 1862	X	...	...	X
March 3, 1863	...	...	X	...
June 30, 1864	X	X	X	X

43. Sherman's wartime observation that "all productive industries were active because of the enormous demand made by the army for supplies of all kinds, and everyone who was willing to work could find plenty of employment" indicates his insight as to the general economic effects of wartime spending (*C.G.* 38C.–1S., p. 2563, May 30, 1864). He theorized on the inflation resulting from military spending.

44. His initial endeavor came when he easily got passage of *S.48* "Providing a Commission to Examine and Report as to the Compensation of All Officers of the Government" (*C.G.* 37C.–1S., pp. 253, 275, 285, 288, 331, 382, 385, July 25, Aug. 1, 1861). Its members were Senators Sherman and Daniel Clark of New Hampshire, and Representatives Justin Morrill of Vermont, Abraham Olin of New York, and William Allen of Ohio. Early in January, 1862, he began introducing measures for economy on outlays by Congress, for printing and on the pay of naval officers. Thereafter, any Senate debate on appropriations was likely to hear him call for economy.

45. Chase repelled bankers by his insistence on sale of debt instruments at par rather than at the market price, on a low interest rate sometimes actually lower than Congress authorized, on uncertain terms of repayment, and on issuance of bonds at intermediate term rather than the long and short term which bankers found more convenient. The *Recollections* praise Chase's management; for example, see p. 302.

46. *C.G.* 37C.–2S., p. 2310, May 23, 1862. Other items he tried to protect from increased taxation at various times were whiskey, wool, and beer. He felt the public was co-operative, especially on income levies, declaring to the Senate, "There never was a time in the history of the country when an income tax could be paid so cheerfully as this year." *C.G.* 37C.–2S., p. 2513, May 27, 1864.

47. Roseboom, *op. cit.,* pp. 23, 37, 49, 108, 113, 386, 394, 420–21. See also *Annual Report of the Commissioner of Statistics to the Governor of the State of Ohio* (Columbus, Ohio, 1863), pp. 3, 4, 24, 26, 34–37; and in 1865, pp. 23, 41.

48. *Recollections,* p. 304. Business taxes and death taxes got their first American use in the Civil War; see William J. Schultz and C. Lowell Harriss, *American Public Finance* (Englewood Cliffs, N.J., 1959), pp. 292, 407. Tax administration improved with the 1864 Act. The wartime flow of funds into the treasury was about $305.5 millions from customs, $356.8 millions from taxes, and over $2.5 billions from loans; see Davis Dewey, *Financial History of the United States* (10th ed.; New York, 1928), p. 299.

49. Cooke's achievement is detailed in Henrietta M. Larson, *Jay Cooke: Private Banker* (Cambridge, Mass., 1936), pp. 119–75.

50. The Republican party got its 1860 victory in Ohio partly because conservatives who were repelled by the extreme abolitionist faction of the party were attracted by both the tariff plank and by Lincoln's cautious approach. Chase had scrapped his antitariff principles for endorsement of protectionism while he was competing with Lincoln for the presidential nomination, and as secretary of the treasury, he endorsed mild increases in some iron duties. Roseboom, *op. cit.,* pp. 20, 30–31, 360–64, 369–70. The Republican *Cincinnati Commercial* denied twice (Mar. 13, Aug. 22, 1860) that protection was a party principle.

51. *Recollections,* pp. 189–90.

52. *C.G.* 37C.–2S., p. 3175, July 8, 1862.

53. *C.G.* 38C.–1S., p. 3038, June 17, 1864.

54. *C.G.* 37C.–3S., p. 990, Feb. 16, 1863; John Sherman to "W.T.," Mansfield, March 20, 1863. W.T.S. MSS, L.C.

55. Chase demanded that the banks pay for government securities with gold rather than with their own bank notes, but asked the banks to honor treasury notes in payment of government bills. His treasury notes tended to narrow the market for bank notes. The gold reserves of both the treasury and the banks were strained. On the predicament of the treasury at this time, see Bray Hammond, *op. cit.,* pp. 1–10.

56. *C.G.* 37C.–2S., Appendix, pp. 25–26, Dec. 9, 1861.

57. The notebook survives in the J.S. MSS, L.C. See also *Recollections,* pp. 82–83; Burton, *op. cit.,* pp. 133–35.

58. John to his wife Cecelia, Burton, *op. cit.,* p. 135. *C.G.* 37C.–2S., p. 3079, July 2, 1862.

59. *C.G.* 37C.–3S., Appendix, p. 2, Dec. 1, 1862. John Sherman to "W.T.," Mansfield, Nov. 16, 1862, *The Sherman Letters,* ed. Rachel S. Thorndyke (New York, 1894), p. 168.

60. John to Cecelia, Burton, *op. cit.,* p. 135.

61. The correspondence on this bill was forthright and abundant; see J.S. MSS, L.C., and Chase MSS, L.C.

62. *C.G.* 37C.–3S., pp. 667, 703, 820–21. Feb. 2, 4, 9, 1863.

63. See note 99. Doubtless the opposition was responsible for the fact that the tax imposed by the revenue Act of March 3, 1865 was not to be made effective until July 1, 1866.

64. *C.G.* 37C.–3S., pp. 826, 840–46, Feb. 9–10, 1863.

65. *C.G.* 37C.–3S., pp. 846–52, Feb. 10, 1863.

66. *C.G.* 37C.–3S., p. 874, Feb. 11, 1863.

67. *C.G.* 37C.–3S., pp. 869–882, Feb. 11, 1863.

68. Clifford P. Reynolds, *Biographical Directory of the American Congress 1774–1961* (U.S. Government Printing Office, 1961), pp. 1006, 1082, 1084, 1383, 1829.

69. *C.G.* 37C.–3S., pp. 896–97, Feb. 12, 1863.

70. Roseboom, *op. cit.,* pp. 52, 111, 118–20, 350, 394, 426.

71. See note 96 and paragraph pertinent thereto; *Recollections,* p. 334–35.

72. There may have been a possibility that John could attend college—at Kenyon, to which he later gave $5,000—but he early decided that instead he would study law in the office of an older brother and uncle. In the process he must have read fairly widely, judging by the quality of his congressional diction, *Recollections,* pp. 32, 47–50.

73. J. Sherman to "W.T.," Mansfield, Mar. 20, 1863. W.T.S. MSS, L.C.

74. William P. Fessenden to F. H. Morse, Portland, Apr. 5, 1863, Morse MSS, Western Reserve Historical Society.

75. On Sherman's argument for broad jurisdiction see *C.G.* 37C.–2S., pp. 31–32, 110, Dec. 9, 17, 1861; it passed 33–3. Wade was the only Ohioan on it. The correspondence of Sherman, Garfield, and Chase (L.C.), abundantly documents their sympathy for anti-Lincoln aspects of the Committee's work.

76. Murat Halstead to John Sherman, Cincinnati, Jan. 23, 1863, J.S. MSS, L.C.; J. Sherman, *Recollections*, pp. 241–42; *Memoirs of General William T. Sherman by Himself* (New York, 1875), pp. 200–218; "W.T." to John, Feb. 18, 1863, J.S. MSS, L.C. On relations between the press and the military see J. G. Randall and David Donald, *op. cit.*, pp. 307–8, 494–97; J. G. Randall, "The Newspaper Problem during the Civil War," *American Historical Review*, XXIII (1918), 303–23.

77. "W.T." to John, Jan. 17, Feb. (date uncertain), Feb. 12, Apr. 3, 1863, J.S. MSS, L.C.

78. J. Sherman to "W.T.," Washington, Feb. 16, 1863, W.T.S. MSS, L.C.; T. Harry Williams, Lincoln and the Radicals (Madison, Wisc., 1941), p. 209.

79. Murat Halstead to J. Sherman, Cincinnati, Feb. 8, 1863, J.S. MSS, L.C.; J. Sherman to "W.T.," Washington, Feb. 26, 1863, W.T.S. MSS, L.C.

80. J. Sherman to "W.T.," Mansfield, May 7, 1863, W.T.S. MSS, L.C.

81. Political conditions in Ohio during 1863 are detailed by George H. Porter, *op. cit.*, pp. 110–21, 167–87. See also W. H. Fossan, "Clement L. Vallandigham," Ohio Archeological and Historical Quarterly, XXIII (1914), 256–67.

82. In the 1862 campaign Ohio audiences greeted praise of the Emancipation Proclamation "with coldness and silence," especially in the southern part of the state, *Recollections*, p. 330; Sherman urged Congress to check on Lincoln. "We are here independent of the President; it is our duty to examine critically the question of his powers and the effect of his acts. . . . We must remember that the Executive is but one branch of the Government. His powers are defined by the Constitution. They are simply executive. He can neither make nor suspend the operation of a law." C.G. 38C.–1S., p. 439, Feb. 2, 1864.

83. The most detailed analysis of the Radical fight against Lincoln is provided by T. Harry Williams in his volume organized around military issues, *Lincoln and the Radicals, passim.* On the Cookes' involvement see Oberholtzer, *op. cit.*, pp. 363, 365.

84. For a comparison of "The Next Presidential Election" and the "Pomeroy Circular," see Charles R. Wilson, "The Original Chase Organization Meeting and the Next Presidential Election," *Mississippi Valley Historical Review*, XXIII (1936), 61–79.

85. J. Sherman to *Cincinnati Daily Gazette*, published Mar. 3, 1864; Chase to James C. Hall of Toledo, Mar. 5, 1864, Jacob W. Schuckers, *The Life and Public Services of Salmon Portland Chase* (New York, 1874), p. 503. Although the Sherman letters contain much demonstrating Sherman's dislike of Lincoln, the precise degree of his participation in the cabal remains a matter of speculation.

86. Oberholtzer, *op. cit.*, I, 360–67.

87. On an anti-Lincoln convention at Cleveland, May 31, and the controlled Republican convention at Baltimore June 7, see Randall and Donald, *op. cit.*, pp. 467–69.

88. *Recollections*, pp. 359–60. An Ashley bill along Davis' lines had been reported from the House Committee on Territories in 1862, when it was laid on the table without discussion.

89. *C.G.* 38C.–1S., pp. 33–34, 37, 45, Dec. 15, 17, 1863.

90. *C.G.* 38C.–1S., pp. 1243, 2107–8, 2132, Mar. 22, May 4, 5, 1864.

91. *C.G.* 38C.–1S., pp. 3459, 3448–61, July 1, 1864.

92. *C.G.* 38C.–1S., pp. 3491, 3518, July 2, 1864; *Recollections*, pp. 359–61.

93. On the Wade-Davis contretemps see Williams, *Lincoln and the Radicals*, pp. 317–33.

94. From the time of his 1861 observation of Washington politics through the years thereafter, "W.T." wrote frequently and sometimes spoke, ill of politics and politicos. On Republican techniques for corraling votes see Harry J. Carman and Reinhard H. Luthin, *Lincoln and the Patronage* (Magnolia, Mass., 1943), pp. 287, 299.

95. *Recollections*, pp. 330–31.

96. *C.G.* 38C.–1S. (debate on *S.132*), pp. 786, 2358, 2399, 2401, 2419, 2421, 2424, Feb. 24, May 19, 21, 23, 1864; *S.132* passed the Senate 23–5, 21 absent. This bill was virtually accepted by the House, but House rules resulted in its being passed as *H.R.438*, with Sherman making sure of the few differences, *ibid.*, p. 3291, June 27, 1864. *Recollections*, pp. 334–35.

97. The bill can be followed through *S.224* and *H.R.395, C.G.* 38C.–1S., especially pages 1771, 1865–75, 2206–7, 2622, Apr. 21, 26, May 10, June 1, 1864. The $300,000,000 limit proved a crippling influence, especially as the treasury allotted too high a proportion of notes to the eastern banks. On this measure, as on so many others, conferences were numerous among Sherman, Chase, and the Cookes (Oberholtzer, *op. cit.*, I, 358).

98. Chase letters to Sherman, and others, abundantly show the Chase reluctance to lose official status. Cooke letters show their persistent hope that Sherman would become secretary of the treasury, first when Chase left in 1864 and secondly when Fessenden returned to the Senate, March 4, 1865 (Oberholtzer, *op. cit.* I, 466–68, 496).

99. The state bank tax emerged as Section 6 of the Revenue Act of March 3, 1865, *C.G.* 38C.–2S., Appendix p. 133. Nine of the first twenty-five organized national banks were in Ohio (Oberholtzer, *op. cit.*, p. 341). Thirty-eight of the first 134 were organized in Ohio (Roseboom, *op. cit.*, p. 143).

100. On the 1861 effort see note 44; on that of 1864, *C.G.* 38C.–1S., pp. 3536, 3544, July 4; on that of 1865, *C.G.* 38C.–2S., pp. 885–88, 1240–49, Feb. 18, Mar. 1. A frequent student of financial administration abroad, he mentioned that "such commissioners are provided in England and France."

101. *C.G.* 38C.–2S., p. 1137, Feb. 27, 1865; *Recollections,* p. 350.

102. *Mansfield Herald,* May 10, 1865.

NINE

Artemus Ward and Petroleum Nasby

HARVEY WISH

THE HUMOR OF ARTEMUS WARD

Lincoln enthusiasts eventually meet Artemus Ward through a revealing letter by Secretary of War Edwin M. Stanton on the cabinet discussion of September 22, 1862, when the President insisted on prefacing his momentous announcement of the Emancipation Proclamation by reading aloud from *Artemus Ward: His Book*. That day the virtually humorless Stanton had occasion to groan at the rustic levity of that exasperating man from Illinois. When Stanton walked into the cabinet meeting room, he noted that Lincoln was deeply absorbed and loudly amused by a little book that he continued to read to himself while the others waited impatiently. "Gentlemen," he finally said, "did you ever read anything from Artemus Ward? Let me read a chapter that is very funny." He went ahead without any encouragement from his captive audience. Not a member smiled, and Stanton fumed at what seemed to him to be crude buffoonery utterly irrelevant to the war crisis. Lincoln paused to laugh heartily and then tried another chapter from Ward, tempting Stanton to consider walking out altogether. Finally, Lincoln threw his book down and observed sadly, "Gentlemen, why don't you laugh? With the fearful strain that is upon me night and day, if I did not laugh I should die, and you need this medicine as much as I do."

Then, unexpectedly, he began to read a draft of the Emancipation Proclamation. Stanton, now visibly moved, rose impulsively to shake Lincoln's hand. "Mr. President," he said, "if reading chapters of Artemus Ward is a prelude to such a deed as this, the book should be filed among the archives of the nation and the author should be canonized." [1]

Artemus Ward—a pseudonym for Charles Farrar Browne—did not know of this episode; and if he had, he might have protested this proposed canonization as a little out of character. He was then entertaining millions of his harassed countrymen during a war surprisingly rich in humorous lecturers and witty newspapermen.

Lincoln apparently loved these humorists who eased the tensions of the war years—Artemus Ward, Petroleum V. Nasby, Josh Billings, and many more. At the *Cleveland Plain Dealer*, where "Artemus Ward" was invented, there was Browne's friend David Ross Locke, the "Petroleum V. Nasby" whose homely puns and philosophy titillated the President. Locke earned national applause through his character in *The Nasby Papers* (1864). Nasby was an illiterate, hypocritical, Copperhead preacher who in effect satirized southern rebels and racists everywhere in grossly misspelled words and puns after the style of Artemus Ward.[2] Another Lincoln favorite, well known to Artemus Ward, was "Josh Billings," a pseudonym for Henry Wheeler Shaw, of Massachusetts. Ward not only inspired him with his own formula for bucolic jest but helped him get a publisher for the bestseller *Josh Billings: His Sayings* (1865). Probably Lincoln liked the fact that all three humorists made the unlettered common man with all his conservative social prejudices their hero (if Nasby may be reckoned one).[3] Far transcending the crude rustic style of these men was another friend of Ward's, Sam Clemens of the Virginia City *Territorial Enterprise*, who had just taken the pseudonym of "Mark

Twain." Ward's triumphal tour in Virginia City probably gave Clemens the idea of seeking a similar path to success. Like Josh Billings, the as yet unknown Mark Twain was aided by the generous and influential Ward to find a publisher and thus to win national attention with the "Jumping Frog" tale. Before long, Rocky Mountain crowds were saying that Mark Twain was just as good as Artemus Ward.[4]

Browne, like Locke and Shaw, came of rural New England parents. He was born on April 26, 1834, on a farm near Waterford, Maine, the son of a Massachusetts newcomer who served as town clerk and state legislator. His mother, early widowed, warmly encouraged her son's talents, but could not prevent her thirteen-year-old boy from going to work at once in his brother's printing shop. While setting type in Boston, he found time to stare at theatrical folk and longed for a public career. Restlessly, he wandered with a carpetbag across New England and Ohio, stopping to take up various jobs as a compositor, and once even agreed to teach school on the Kentucky side of the Ohio River until someone discouraged him by relating the prowess of the local school toughs in licking every school teacher. He returned to his composing stick, first, in Tiffin, Ohio, and, later, on the *Toledo Commercial,* where he attracted attention occasionally for his lively paragraphs on the passing scene.[5] One of those who recognized his talent was Joseph W. Gray, a former New Hampshire teacher, who turned lawyer and then newspaperman and became the publisher of the *Cleveland Plain Dealer.* Gray, who had been a lifetime friend of Stephen A. Douglas, vigorously supported Douglas' Compromise of 1850 as well as the Kansas-Nebraska Act, attacked the near-abolitionism of Joseph Medill's *Cleveland Leader,* and fought Lincoln's election in 1860 because he feared this would provoke secession and war. In the fall of 1857, Gray hired Browne as a full-fledged journalist at the then respectable salary of twelve dollars a week to carry on the tasks of commercial editor and, occasionally, city editor.[6]

Hopeful of a literary career, Browne went beyond the routine of collecting local police reports and experimented with writing humorous, though utterly fictional, interviews with noted people, even poking fun at his own editor as well as at rival newspapermen. In those days, the youth—he was still in his early twenties—was a tall, thin, awkwardly clad rustic; but a perceptive friend saw much more: "It seemed as though bubbling in him was a lot of happiness which he made no effort to conceal or hold back." [7] Politically, the *Plain Dealer* (which circulated extensively throughout the Old Northwest), with its conservative Democratic line, proved congenial to him, as his loaded satires showed. After all, Browne's parents had been Democrats too. And Gray's admiration for his fellow New Englander, Douglas, had committed him to an antiabolitionist, though mildly antislavery, viewpoint. Like his conservative employer, Ward shared the newspaper's skeptical attitude toward the current belief that progress was inevitable; and he derided the radicalisms, including feminism, Mormonism, abolitionism, and prohibitionism. The pro-Negro, feminist, and equalitarian ideas of nearby Oberlin College seemed ludicrous to him. So did John Brown of Osawatomie fame, who later became the Western Reserve's hero during the Harpers Ferry episode. When the Cleveland Theater produced an abolitionist play, Browne hastened to lampoon both the performance and the audience without bothering to attend the theater.[8]

The first newspaper communication of Artemus Ward appeared in the *Plain Dealer* on January 30, 1858, shortly after his arrival in Cleveland. It purported to come from the proprietor of a sideshow and reflected inspiration of the greatest living showman, P. T. Barnum. Charles Farrar Browne took his pseudonym of Ward from a colonial Boston landowner well known to the Browne family, but apparently unrelated to General Artemas Ward, hero of the Revolution.[9] In these *Plain Dealer* articles, Browne used a rustic style expressed in quaint

spellings and puns, and professed to report the doings of his village. He must have known the sophisticated regional dialect style
affected a decade before by James Russell Lowell, author of the
satiric *Biglow Papers* (1848). Browne was not Lowell, but his
appeal went beyond mere mechanical tricks of spelling and
gross puns, as is obvious from his successful adaptation to the
platform as a really humorous speaker.

So fervently did Ward admire the popular dialect humorist
"John Phoenix" that he freely adopted some of Phoenix's stock
in trade: the "punch line" in an excruciating pun, the grossly
exaggerated understatement, the pseudo-serious irony, and the
acute political satiric comments on the passing show. Mark
Twain, too, owed something to this literary inspiration. Phoenix was the pseudonym (authors felt undressed without
pseudonyms) of George Horatio Derby (1823–61), a
Massachusetts-born journalist then resident in California, who
published the humorous *Phoenixiana* (1855), a collection of
articles, and *The Squibob Papers* (1859). A West Pointer,
Phoenix fought with distinction in the war with Mexico, adven-
tured as an army explorer in Minnesota Territory, and, after
1849, utilized an army assignment in California to win a national as well as statewide reputation by penning witty anti-
Whig satires for the *San Diego Herald.*[10]

On the eve of the Civil War, Browne quarreled with Editor
Gray and resigned after failing to convince him to permit the
syndication of his articles in *Vanity Fair.* One story holds that
Browne was so lazy a reporter that he faked an account of a
local function and quit after learning that the event had never
taken place. But he remained a hero to Petroleum V. Nasby
and to the *Plain Dealer.* According to Archer Shaw of the *Plain
Dealer,* Ward later considered the purchase of this newspaper
on the assumption that the days of profitable lecturing upon
which he had embarked would soon be over.[11]

In 1861 Browne became the managing editor of the shaky
Vanity Fair, a new illustrated journal that aspired to rival

London's *Punch*. He loved to meet the New York literati and the minstrel entertainers, and had several "narrer scapes" with women. He wrote to a friend, "My passion for females is alas! as strong as ever, and I fall in love with a rapidity that would be appalling if I wasn't so well acquainted with myself." [12] In 1862 he published the best of his articles from the *Plain Dealer* and *Vanity Fair* as *Artemus Ward: His Book,* illustrated by sketches that suggested Dickens' own caricaturists. The book soon sold at least forty thousand copies; and new editions appeared intermittently even at the end of the century.

Meanwhile, Browne was sensationally successful with lecture audiences. Like Barnum, he lectured on his exhibits—imaginary though they were—and chose tantalizing subjects that had nothing to do with his anecdotes and witticisms on the current scene. The lecture poster kept its New England village flavor: "Artemus Ward Will Speak a Piece." [13] His first lecture success was "The Babes in the Woods," which he delivered at New London, Connecticut, on November 26, 1861, and then repeated in various New England towns as well as in New York City itself. At the end of his lecture, he hastened to refer to his subject, "I suppose that you want to hear something about the children in the woods. They were good children, they were unfortunate and, as far as I have been able to ascertain, entirely respectable." Here was the dead-pan humorist at work.

By 1863 Browne began to think of a western tour, but decided to do it on his own terms. When a San Francisco lecture manager wired him, "What will you take for forty nights in California?", he replied innocently, "Brandy and water." He arrived in San Francisco on November 1, 1863, and earned fabulous receipts despite the impression in some quarters that he was a traveling showman exhibiting waxworks, snakes, and other such attractions.[14] The Civil War theme inevitably made up much of the stories he had to tell, including imaginary interviews with Lincoln, in which he thwarted Lincoln's efforts to tell a story; Jefferson Davis, of course, came off badly in another interview and so did Ward's alleged persecutors in Dixie. He was never bitter, and his ambivalent arguments could scarcely inspire army recruiting, sympathetic as he was for the war and the Union.

When he arrived in Virginia City and other mining towns in California and Nevada, he found kindred spirits such as Bret Harte and Samuel Clemens. Virginia City gave him an ovation and offered incessant examples of its own riotous brand of entertainment, although one newspaper sourly denounced him as a mercenary clown. In later years Mark Twain was to lecture on Artemus Ward eleven times, and pictured his idol in his usual exaggerated style:

> He looked like a glove-stretcher; his hair, red, and brushed well forward at the sides, reminded one of a divided flame. His nose rambled on aggressively before him with all the strength and determination of a cow-catcher, while his red mustache, to follow out the simile, seemed not unlike the unfortunate cow.[15]

But this description resembles too much one given by contemporaries to Twain himself to gain absolute historic credence. More believable was his high praise of the Clevelander's talent, although his comments suggested a feeling of rivalry; and he expressed contempt for the "inferior breed" of "Ward's numerous and perishable imitators." [16]

In Utah, where Browne's incongruous descriptions of Mormon life had preceded him embarrassingly, Brigham Young welcomed him kindly nevertheless. But, as an overprivileged guest, he took away many fictionalized accounts about the Mormons for future audiences. No theme was more absorbing to him, and apparently to the average American, than Mormon polygamy. These were green fields of incongruity awaiting exploitation. "The pretty girls in Utah," he wrote, "mostly marry Young." Mark Twain, too, exploited the gold mine of polygamy, for example, in his story of Brigham Young's army of children clamoring for the same noisy toys in *Roughing It*.

Browne's career culminated and ended with his British tour

of 1866, when the Britons even outdid Americans in their enthusiasm. They did not mind his ribbing the allegedly slow Englishman: "Mr. Artemus Ward will call on the citizens of London at their residences and explain any jokes in his narrative which they may not understand," read a standard announcement. *Punch* and its staff made a great to-do over Ward, displaying his name in large letters in front of its building and welcoming his lengthy humorous letters in its columns. These later appeared in a popular little book for Englishmen. The highest praise of *Punch* was, "Artemus Ward has brains!" The London *Spectator* called him an intellectual Hans of the old German stories, who confided his thoughts to the people.

But suddenly, the damp London weather took its toll of the skinny, overworked American. He gave up his lectures after appearing with a flushed face that revealed his deadly bout with tuberculosis. On March 6, 1867, he died in Southampton, beloved about equally by the people of England and the United States.[17]

One reason for Browne's popularity had been the way in which he identified himself with the simple villager and all his antimodern prejudices. Conservative middle-class audiences as well as rustics laughed heartily at his gibes at masculine women who demanded equality, the vogue for Bloomerism, sentimentality on the race issue, and the vagaries of reformers. Here is his bucolic view of "Woman's Rights."

WOMAN'S RIGHTS

I pitcht my tent in a small town in Injianny one day last seeson, and while I was standin at the dore takin money, a deppytashun of ladies came up and sed they wos members of the Bunkumville Female Reformin and Wimin's Rite's Associashun, and they axed me if they cood go in without payin.

"Not exactly," sez I, "but you can pay without goin in."

"Dew you know who we air?" said one of the wimin—a tall and feroshus lookin critter, with a blew kotton umbreller under her arm —"do you know who we air, Sir?"

"My impreshun is," sed I, "from a kersery view, that you air females."

"We air, Sur," said the feroshus woman—"we belong to a Society whitch beleeves wimin has rites—whitch beleeves in razin her to her proper speer—whitch beleeves she is indowed with as much intelleck as man is—whitch beleeves she is trampled on and aboozed—and who will resist henso4th and forever the incroachments of proud and domineering men."

Durin her discourse, the exsentric female grabed me by the coat-kollor and was swinging her umbreller wildly over my hed.

"I hope, marm," sez I, starting back, "that your intensions is honorable! I'm a lone man hear in a strange place. Besides, I've a wife to hum."

"Yes," cried the female, "and she's slave! Doth she never dream of freedom—doth she never think of throwin of the yoke of tyrrinny and thinkin and votin for herself?—Doth she never think of these here things?"

"Not bein a natral born fool," sed I, by this time a little riled, "I kin safely say that she dothunt."

"Oh whot—whot!" screamed the female, swingin her unbreller in the air. "O, what is the price that woman pays for her expeeriunce!" . . .

"My female friends," sed I, "be4 you leeve, I've a few remarks to remark; wa them well. The female woman is one of the greatest institooshuns of which this land can boste. Its onpossible to get along without her. Had there bin no female wimin in the world, I should scarcely be here with my unparaleld show on this occashun. She is good in sickness—good in wellness—good all the time. O woman, woman!" I cried, my feelins worked up to a hi poetick pitch, "you air a angle when you behave yourself; but when you take off your proper appairel and (mettyforically speaken)—get into panty-loons—when you desert your firesides, and with your heds full of wimin's rites noshuns go round like roarin lions, seekin whom you may devour someboddy—in short, when you undertake to play the man, you play the devil and air an emfatic noosance. My female friends," I continnered, as they were indignantly departin, "wa well what A. Ward has sed!" [18]

Of the Mormons he observed pontifically, "Thar religion is singular, but their wives are plural." To him, they were engaged exclusively in "heartburnings and hairpullings." He convulsed audiences by telling of the seventeen pretty young Mormon widows who collectively proposed to him. In his dignified rustic style, he asked the weeping girls, "Why is this thus?" and then, correcting himself, restated it more properly, "What is the cause of this thusness?" Naturally, he embroidered yarns based on his hectic trip to the Far West, telling of startling stagecoach battles and fierce wolves.

He fought the Civil War in his own mild way as befitted a disciple of the *Cleveland Plain Dealer* and its Stephen Douglas brand of Democratic politics, which remained dubious of the Negro's potentialities. Like that paper, he, too, was convinced that the war must be won and the Union preserved. In his own inimitable way he stated the issue, "Shall the star spangled banner be cut up into dishcloths?"

Unlike his friend, David Locke of the *Toledo Blade,* who created the bigoted character of Petroleum Nasby as the total negation of Locke's own equalitarian views, Charles Farrar Browne used Artemus Ward as a bucolic vehicle for his essentially orthodox beliefs regarding the Negro's inherent limitations, feminism as an expression of masculine women, and that the hasty decision of the South to secede was the main cause of the war. While Nasby in effect reduces racial prejudices to an absurdity by appearing to advocate them, Artemus Ward, for all his humorous eccentricities, expresses the prevailing "common sense" outlook of rural whites on the basic equalitarian and wartime issues. Contemporaries insist that Ward actually loved Negroes and was an honored guest at a Negro church in Cleveland, but modern readers at least would note that his account of this church and of the Negro people generally is always condescending and not far from the level of the minstrel stereotype. Ward affected to be nonpolitical in his amusing account of an interview with Lincoln: "I hiv no politics. Nary a one. I'm not in the bisniss."

Audiences apparently shared his prejudices that regarded the Negro as a simple person unknowing of his responsibility for the war and indifferent to the impending fate of his presumably beloved master. "The origernal cawz is our African Brother," he said of the war. He poked fun at Oberlin's progressive ideas and pictured the college's boarding house as devoted to the ideal of Negro superiority. One Oberlin professor allegedly asked him if his blood didn't boil at the thought of three and a half million Negroes clanking their chains in the South. To this he promptly replied, "Not a bile! Let 'em clank!" He satirized the reformers' "glowrious work" for the Negroes, and insisted that a collection was being taken up to buy overcoats with red horn buttons for Canadian Negroes. Much of this simply reflected the racial attitudes of many in the Old Northwest who were hostile to the penetration of New England abolitionism in their northern counties and sympathetic to the older southern influences from across the Ohio River. Ward and his family obviously did not belong to the radical wing of the New England migrants. His alleged conversation with Jefferson Davis is revealing of his belief that secession was the sole cause of the war:

At larst I got a interview with Jefferson Davis, the President of the Southern Conthieveracy. He was quite perlite, and axed me to sit down and state my case. I did it, when he larfed and said his gallunt men had been a little 2 enthoosiastic in confisticatin my show.

"Yes," sez I, "they confisticated me too muchly. I had sum hosses confisticated in the same way onct, but the confisticaters air now poundin stun in the States Prison in Injinnapylus."

"Wall, wall Mister Ward, you air at liberty to depart; you air friendly to the South, I know. Even now we hav many frens in the North, who sympathize with us, and won't mingle with this fight."

"J. Davis, there's your grate mistaik. Many was your sincere frends, and thought certin parties amung us was fussin about you and meddlin with your consarns intirely too much. But J. Davis, the minit you fire a gun at the piece of dry-goods called the Star-Spangled Banner, the North gits up and rises en massy, in defence of that banner. Not agin you as individooals,—not agin the South even—but to save the flag. We should indeed be weak in the knees, unsound in the heart, milk-white in the liver, and soft in the hed, if we stood quietly by, and saw this glorus Govyment smashed to pieces, either by a furrin or a intestine foe. The gentle-harted mother hates to take her naughty child across her knee, but she knows it is her dooty to do it. So we shall hate to whip the naughty South, but we must do it if you don't make back tracks at onct, and we shall wallup you out of your boots! J. Davis, it is my decided opinion that the Sonny South is makin a egrejus mutton-hed of herself!" [19]

Far better balanced were his judgments on human foibles during the war. He enjoyed lampooning the verbose local war meetings, the blowhards, the irresponsible newspapers, and the slow government action in attempting victory. He reported the alleged repetitive news, "Gov'ment is about to take vigorous measures to put down the rebellion." Of civilians who liked to talk belligerently rather than fight, he observed, "A war meetin', in fact, without gas, would be suthin' like the play of Hamlet with the part of Othello omitted." His sometimes equivocal antisecessionism was picturesquely expressed: "Let's have the Union restored as it was, if we can; but if we can't, I'm in favor of the Union as it wasn't." Cheerfully, he asserted that "there don't seem to be anything the matter with the Goddess of Liberty beyond a slite cold." Yet, at the outbreak of war, in his imaginary interview with Lincoln, he advised the President to go ahead "by pursooin' a patriotic, firm, and just course, and then if any State wants to secede, let 'em sesesh!" Evidently, wise political judgments were not his forte. He even disparaged some war sentiment by arguing, "Better be a coward than a corpse," and satirized the tearful vogue for mother songs, asking whether "it wasn't about time somebody cared for the old man." In his mild strictures on the Confederacy and its leaders, he said of Jefferson Davis: "It would have been ten dollars in Jeff's pocket if he had never been born." Gravely, he explained the Yankee flight at Bull Run as a consequence of a rumor that there were three customhouse vacancies in Washington. The office-seeker theme was very popular indeed among humorists, particularly with Robert H. Newell, a Washington journalist,

who wrote a comic commentary on the war in the Artemus
Ward style under a pseudonym that reflected his chief theme,
"Orpheus C. Kerr."

He hailed the end of the war with his usual grotesqueries
about the Confederate collapse:

R. LEE

Robert Lee is regarded as a noble feller.

He was opposed to the war at the fust, and draw'd his sword very
reluctant. In fact, he wouldn't hav' drawd his sword at all, only he
had a large stock of military clothes on hand, which he didn't want
to waste. He sez the colored man is right, and he will at once go to
New York and open a Sabbath School for negro minstrels.

THE CONFEDERATE ARMY

The surrender of R. Lee, J. Johnston and others leaves the Confedrit Army in a ruther shattered state. That army now consists of
Kirby Smith, four mules and a Bass drum, and is movin' rapidly
to'rds Texis.[20]

His final judgment upon the Civil War as primarily concerned
with secession is expressed in a fictional conversation with an
angry southerner who was reluctant to eat with a Yankee:

He got full at last, and his hart softened a little to'ards me.
"After all," he sed, "you hav sum people at the North who air not
wholly loathsum beasts?"

"Well, yes," I sed, "we hav' now and then a man among us who
isn't a cold-bluded scoundril. Young man," I mildly but gravely sed,
"this crooil war is over, and you're lickt! It's rather necessary for
sumbody to lick in a good square, lively fite, and in this 'ere case it
happens to be the United States of America. You fit splendid, but we
was too many for you. Then make the best of it, & let us all give in
and put the Republic on a firmer basis nor ever.

"I don't gloat over your misfortins, my young fren'. Fur from.
I'm a old man now, & my hart is softer nor it once was. You see my
spectacles is misten'd with suthin' very like tears. I'm thinkin' of
the sea of good rich Blud that has been spilt on both sides in this
dredful war! I'm thinkin' of our widders and orfuns North, and of
your'n in the South. I kin cry for both. B'leeve me, my young fren',
I kin place my old hands tenderly on the fair yung hed of the
Virginny maid whose lover was laid low in the battle dust by a
fed'ral bullet, and say, as fervently and piously as a vener'ble sinner
like me kin say anythin', God be good to you, my poor dear, my
poor dear."

I riz up to go, & takin' my young Southern fren', kindly by the
hand, I sed, "Yung man, adoo! You Southern fellers is probly my
brothers, tho' you've occasionally had a cussed queer way of showin'
it! It's over now. Let us all line in and make a country on this continent that shall giv' all Europe the cramp in the stummuck ev'ry
time they look at us! Adoo, adoo!"

And as I am through, I likewise say adoo to you, jentle reader,
merely remarkin' that the Star-Spangled Banner is wavin' round
loose agin, and that there don't seem to be anything the matter with
the Goddess of Liberty beyond a slite cold.[21]

After the death of Ward, biographers and editors kept his
memory green by more than a dozen books and innumerable
articles. All were enthusiastic, sometimes unduly so. Thus Albert Jay Nock, the noted essayist, claimed that Ward was the
first really great critic of American society, easily comparable to
Peter Finley Dunne, creator of Mr. Dooley. This is a highly
exaggerated estimate, for Charles Farrar Browne lacked the
acute political acumen and sound democratic ideas of Dunne.
Nock even explains away Ward's crude prejudices on slavery
and Negroes as "realistic," but he admits that the quality of his
work is uneven.[22] More perspicacious—though not altogether
convincing—is the judgment of the Canadian humorist and
scholar Stephen Leacock, expressed in his luminous article on
Browne in the *Dictionary of American Biography:*

But behind the comic superficiality of his written work, as behind
the "mask of melancholy" of the comic lecture, there was always the

fuller, deeper meaning of the true humorist, based on reality, in the contrasts, the incongruities, and the shortcomings of life itself.

Possibly the most perceptive and convincing of all estimates remains that of his friend Bret Harte, who did not wait for the opportunity of an obituary to evaluate Artemus Ward. In a column of December 27, 1863, in the *San Francisco Era,* he gave his personal impressions of the man he had only recently met, but whose book was familiar to him. Ward, he said, did not profess to be the greatest American humorist, but professed a kind of humor that had more of a national characteristic than the higher, more artistic standard. He went beyond the grotesque spelling, which was the whim of a printer, and expressed audacious exaggeration. His humor belonged to a nation of boundless prairies, limitless rivers, and stupendous cataracts. In this respect Bret Harte saw Ward as the American humorist par excellence, a retailer of vivid anecdotes about stage coaches, canals, flatboats, campfires, and barroom stoves.

Certainly, some of Ward's stories, such as "A High-handed Outrage at Utica," which tickled Lincoln so much, are apt to leave the modern reader as cold as that one did Secretary Stanton and the other cabinet members; but to those who enjoy Western humor, the folk quality of his work is easily appreciated. Britons, too, looked upon him as an authentic interpreter of nineteenth-century American humor with its tall stories, shrewd and colorful rural flavor, and keen Yankee insights. His gift for hilarious understatement appealed to the Englishman's own sense of humor. Besides, as their press indicated, Ward possessed certain universal qualities of attraction. He could never hope for the heights reached by Mark Twain, but he certainly outshone his other contemporaries, the funny men of his day: Josh Billings, John Phoenix, and Orpheus C. Kerr, if not Petroleum Vesuvius Nasby. But all of these men gave their share of literary enjoyment as well as serving as morale-builders in the tense atmosphere of the Civil War.

PETROLEUM VESUVIUS NASBY

Artemus Ward's closest rival among the Civil War humorists was David Ross Locke, who knew him back in Toledo and Cleveland newspaper days—both were employed by the *Cleveland Plain Dealer* at various times. Ward is said to have inspired Locke to create the rustic comic character of Petroleum V. Nasby; but as already noted, the two journalists differed considerably in their social beliefs, especially in regard to the Negro. Ward expressed the *Plain Dealer's* conservative Democratic views that assumed the inferiority of the Negro, looked down upon the feminist movement as contrary to nature, and supported the war effort almost exclusively as a struggle against secession; but Locke shared abolitionist ideas, linked up with the Radical Republicans after the war, and sympathized with the current antebellum reforms including antislavery, feminism, temperance, and universal education.

Both men were nationally popular as lyceum speakers as well as humorists, but their propaganda motif—especially pronounced for Locke—may have cost them the patronage of the twentieth century. Locke even insisted at times that he was a satirist rather than a humorist, an estimate that was partly true. Their younger and more gifted colleague, Mark Twain, usually avoided the error of sacrificing art to the pressing journalistic issues of the day, although he too was spending these years as a brash printer-reporter and newspaper correspondent alert to local struggles.

Locke's New England ancestors missed the "Mayflower" by a close margin, but the family's long American residence had not enriched them materially or distinguished them. One important inheritance, however, was his father's reformist antislavery ideas and affiliation with Whig-Republican causes, including temperance. Since he lived to be ninety-seven, he set a long-lasting and concrete example for his sons. David was born on September 20, 1833, in the village of Vestal, Broome County, New York, not far from Binghamton. His formal education was meager indeed, for his hard-pressed father, a shoemaker, apprenticed him at the age of twelve for seven years with the printers of the Cortland *Democrat*.

Then began the familiar life of an itinerant printer followed by so many noted journalists and writers, taking him South at one time where he observed the land of cotton at first hand. He worked for the Pittsburgh *Chronicle,* and joined a partner in founding the Plymouth (Ohio) *Advertiser.* In Plymouth, Locke was comparatively stationary for four years, enough time to marry a congenial girl and to begin raising a family of three sons. He even became a respected prop of the local church, although he held rationalist beliefs not unlike those of Lincoln. With the usual small capital then needed for a newspaper business, he was again able in 1855 to found a local paper, the Mansfield (Ohio) *Herald.* One of his partners later recalled his rollicking humorous articles, especially the Sniggs Papers that dealt in autobiographical fashion with the bucolic adventures of characters modeled after Locke's relatives, who did not appreciate the compliment. But the Sniggs Papers somehow disappeared, and Locke did not try to resurrect them although his partner afterward insisted that they were even better than the Nasby Letters.

At various times, Locke was associated with the Bucyrus (Ohio) *Journal* and the Bellefontaine *Republican,* but his most important venture to date was the Hancock *Jeffersonian,* published in Findlay. According to most accounts, though recently challenged by Harvey Ford, the first Nasby letter appeared in the *Jeffersonian* on March 21, 1861. Old Ohio residents later observed that Locke was then a strong antislavery man, active in the Republican county committee, and aiding fugitive slaves to escape via the Underground Railroad. This background would account for the pronounced antislavery views of Locke and the strong propagandism of the Nasby articles in his Republican paper, the Hancock County *Jeffersonian*.

The name Petroleum Vesuvius Nasby was apparently inspired by the current oil rush at Titusville, Pennsylvania, with a middle name thrown in for euphony, and a surname derived from the Battle of Naseby in England's civil war (1645). The character may have been suggested by Artemus Ward, and the humorous phonetic misspellings as well as the grotesque bucolic hero were part of the current style in antebellum and wartime humor. For Locke the misspellings and improvised adventures may have been facilitated by his frequent habit of setting up type for the Nasby articles without going to the trouble of using copy. As for the literary use of dialect, this had been given prestige not long before by James Russell Lowell's antislavery satire, the *Biglow Papers* (1848).[23]

The occasion for the first article was Locke's personal reaction to a local petition by a bigoted Findlay loafer, Levi Flenner. This man was circulating a demand to the legislature that Negroes be expelled from Ohio and that no more should be admitted. Such a request was all too familiar in the Old Northwest, where many southerners had settled, but Locke was struck by the contrast between the shiftless Flenner and the hard-working Findlay Negro families he despised. Thus the good-for-nothing Petroleum V. Nasby of Wingert's Corners was created. In visiting this village, Locke professed to have heard fifty citizens declare for the Confederacy shortly after South Carolina's secession. "South Carolina hez left the Union," wrote Nasby, "and Wingert's Corners, ez trooly Dimecratic ez any uv em, hez follered soot." There followed a parody of the Ordinance of Secession, reciting the various oppressions suffered by the village at the hands of Columbus. "Wingert's Corners hez too long submitted to the imperious dictates uv a tyranikle government. Our whole history hez ben wun uv aggreshun on the part uv the State, and uv meek and pashent

endoorence on ours. . . ." [24] The tremendous popularity of
these Nasby letters swept the country through the practice of
newspaper exchanges; and the editor of the *Toledo Blade,*
Locke's future newspaper, invited him to send in the Nasby
articles as a non-resident contributor.

It is not surprising that Locke was anxious to fight in the
Union army and that he raised a company of volunteers; but
Governor John Brough refused to grant a commission to the
creator of Nasby, stating that Locke was far more valuable as
an influential fighting newspaperman than as a single soldier
on the battlefield. This was no exaggeration. The public's demand for the Nasby war satires grew very rapidly, especially
after Locke became manager of the *Blade* in 1865 and created a
national family newspaper through the *Toledo Weekly Blade*
edition.[25] Under his leadership, the *Blade* reflected an ardent
Republicanism that rejected everything Nasby stood for. Union
soldiers looked forward to the latest absurdities of Nasby, his
grotesque expressions of Copperhead disloyalty, his draft eva-
sions, his readiness to trade principle for a postmastership, his
love for whisky, and his revealing hypocritical sermons. Nasby's
praise of the Democratic party, which he identified with slavery
and secession despite the substantial number of loyal War
Democrats, aided the Republicans while his extreme racist
prejudices—which he also attributed to the Democrats—helped
to advance the idea that the war had as much to do with human
freedom and dignity as it did with the preservation of the
Union.

Naturally, our hero was a confirmed draft evader. "I hev
lost," he said, "since Stanton's order to draft, the use uv wun
eye entirely, and hev nowe inflammashun in the other. . . ."
He went on to amuse the soldiers with the tale of his desertion
to the Confederate army—and then back again—not forgetting
to remind dissatisfied Federal soldiers that the Confederates
were starving and ragged. As a temporary Confederate with the
Louisiana Pelicans, he listened to one disgruntled Johnny Reb

tell him that he had once been a planter but his slaves had kept him poor, and, with the war, the Confederate government had confiscated his property. Nasby, in his usual reverse fashion, aided the Lincoln administration by his crude flattery and caricature of Congressman Clement Vallandigham, the Ohio leader of the Peace Democrats, known as the Copperheads. Nasby signed himself as a pastor of the Church of St. Vallandigham when he was not pastor of the Church of the Noo Dispensashun. When his Copperhead difficulties multiplied, Nasby moved to Saint's Rest, New Jersey, to find a congenial community among the Democrats.[26]

For many years Locke deeply admired Lincoln, an affection that was reciprocated during the War. It is true that the southern-born statesman from Illinois had been compelled in his local speeches to make more concessions to racism than Locke would ever do, but the Ohio editor was of course in a more advantageous position to preach social equality. Lincoln as a senatorial candidate in 1858 had indicated his support of a legislative bill forbidding intermarriage. Commenting upon this measure, Locke had frankly said, "I shall never marry a Negro (he was already married), but I have no objection to any one else doing so. If a white man wants to marry a Negro woman, let him do it—if the Negro woman can stand it." He was ready to satirize the motives of those who opposed the Emancipation Proclamation. Thus he had Nasby offer counter-resolutions on behalf of sovereign Wingert's Corners: "Resolved that the Ablishnists who oppose these resolushuns all want to marry a nigger. Resolved, That Dr. Petts, in rentin a part uv his bildin to niggers, hez struck a blow at the very foundashens uv sosiety." [27]

Locke's pro-Negro attitude was not too common in Ohio or the Old Northwest outside of the Western Reserve, and it was decidedly a contribution to race relations when Nasby unmasked the street-corner prejudices and rationalizations of those who hated minorities. When Pastor Nasby built a college

for his village bigots, he called for a ceremonial act of whipping
a Negro to death. Much of this attack on racism was to be
emphasized in his postwar writings. There was none of Artemus Ward's ambivalence about race relations at Oberlin when
Nasby spoke of the college "that reskoos niggers and sets at
defiance the beneficent laws for taken on em back to their kind
and hevenly-minded masters!" [28]

Locke parodied the proslavery preachers through the semi-
literate Pastor Nasby of the First Democratic Church of Ohio in
a prescribed exercise for his congregation: "Readin uv one uv
the follerin passages uv Skripter: 9th chapter uv Gennysis, wich
relates the cusen uv Canaan, provin that niggers is skriptoorally
slaves; and the chapters about Hayger and Onesimus, wich
proves the Fugitive-slave Law to be skriptooral. (The rest uv
the Bible we consider figgerative, and pay no attenshun to it
watever.) " [29] Nasby's catechism answered the question "Wat is
the first duty uv man?" "To beware uv Ablishn lies; to rally to
the poles; to vote early; and to bring in the aged, the inform,
and the ideotik." At one pastoral visit he heard a three-year-old
boy swing his hat crying "Hooraw for Jeff Davis." Nasby was
touched. "Patting the little patriot on the head, I instantly
borrowed five cents uv his father to present to him." [30]

As a pseudo-Copperhead, Pastor Nasby minimized Union
victories—a subject of great concern to the North; called for
the election of Vallandigham; praised the mobs that attacked
recruiting officers; and hailed the brutal New York draft riots
as evidence of Democracy's wrath when "the prowd Anglo-
Saxon riz in his mite and stoned the niggers!" [31] Among his sage
remarks was one that reflected Locke's opposition to peace
negotiations that left the race issue untouched: "Eternal viggi-
lance is the price uv liberty and a old Dimekrat who hez never
scratched a tikket, and who never spiles his likker by dilooshn,
kin work in these perilus times. I am engaged in organizin
societies on the basis uv the Union ez it wuz, the Constitution ez
it is, and the nigger wher he ought to be."

Nasby told of his interview with Lincoln to end the war in November, 1863—an incident that had some basis of truth in it, for Locke did meet the President in response to a personal invitation; but unlike Nasby, he refused to consider a political post. Nasby, speaking as a moderate Democrat to a "goriller, a feendish ape, a thirster after blud," demanded of Lincoln in the usual Copperhead vein, "Restore to us our habes corpusses, as good ez new. . . . Protect our dawters from nigger equality. Disarm yoor nigger solgers, and send back the niggers to their owners to conciliate them." Also, he added, Lincoln must "re-moonerate our Southern brethern for the losses they hev sustaned in this onnatrel war." The "goriller" listened intently to these words of wisdom and even promised to consider resigning, among other concessions requested by Pastor Nasby.[32]

Lincoln was so delighted with Petroleum V. Nasby that he kept these pamphlets (possibly the *Nasby Letters* of 1864) in his desk drawer ready to read to his next caller, willy-nilly. He sent a gracious letter of thanks to Nasby for his services to the war effort and told Charles Sumner, "For the genius to write such stuff as that I would gladly give up my office." Frank Carpenter, the artist best remembered for his painting of the signing of the Emancipation Proclamation, recalled Lincoln's frequent resort to the Nasby Letters during the painful pressure of events shortly before the capture of Richmond. "I am going to write to Petroleum to come down here," said the President, "and I intend to tell him if he will communicate his talent to me, I will swap places with him." [33] Senator Charles Sumner, the Radical Republican who found Locke's views congenial to his own, even wrote an informal introduction to the comprehensive 1872 edition of *The Struggles of Petroleum V. Nasby*. He too recalled Lincoln's fondness for reading Locke in his spare moments, even while a score of distinguished dignitaries waited in the anteroom, and watched the evidence of emotional relief from tension that the President enjoyed. Nasby had the greatest charm for Lincoln among the rival war humorists. Furthermore, Sumner credited this type of war humor as a major ally in the struggle against slavery and in advancing Radical reconstruction. George S. Boutwell, Grant's Radical Secretary of the Treasury, even told a Cooper Union audience in New York City, "Three forces—the army, the navy, and the Nasby Letters—caused the fall of the Confederacy." By a tragic coincidence, the letters of Petroleum V. Nasby were the last literature read by Lincoln the day of his assassination.

David Locke's greatest campaign for human freedom came with the struggle over reconstruction. Since he was temperamentally as well as politically a Radical Republican, he turned the heavy artillery of the increasingly famous *Toledo Blade* in its various editions upon the southern treatment of the freedman.[34] Naturally, he enlisted Pastor Nasby as a racially-bigoted Democrat ready to turn the clock back to antebellum slavery. When President Johnson's new southern legislatures invented Black Codes to control the freedman paternalistically, restricting his rights as a court witness against whites and his freedom of movement, Nasby hailed the new President as a hero; previously, he had distrusted the successor of Lincoln. This enthusiasm grew markedly as Johnson vetoed the Freedmen's Bureau bills and the Civil Rights bills, both earnestly desired by the Radicals.

Seriously, Locke, like most Radicals, was concerned over the consequences of the removal of the "three-fifths" clause of the Constitution, which credited southern representation in the House with that proportion of the number of slaves. The elimination of slavery without any compensating voting strength for the freedmen would entrench the unrepentant white South more strongly than in antebellum days. Cheerfully, Nasby told of his dream in which he witnessed the return of the planters to power. "The genooine Demokrasy uv the North hed elected enuff members to give the South control uv Congress," he noted happily. Aided by his new friend, Thomas Nast, the German-born reformer who was staff artist for *Harper's Weekly*

(1862–86) and the powerful foe of the Tweed Ring, Locke secured a genius who illustrated an imaginative conception of Nasby in the widely-circulated pamphlets, *Nasby's Life of Andy Johnson* and *Swingin Around the Cirkle.*[35]

Locke hit the conservative Democrats hard and made the race issue the central one. Nasby urged Democrats to insist that the Negro could never take care of himself and would become a public burden; that freedom would bring so many Negroes North as to throw the whites out of work; and that Negro equality would hurt Caucasian pride. Besides, "Ef 'twant for niggers, what wood the Democrasy do for sumbody to look down upon?" Nasby advised the Johnson-sponsored legislatures in the South to set up stringent Black Codes:

Then, immejitly, yoor legislachers must pass stringent laws agin a nigger leavin his respective county, and then pass another law not allowin any man to give able-bodied wuns to exceed $5 a month, This dun, I hev faith to blieve thousands uv em will beg to be agin enslaved, about mid winter. Ef they will persist in dyin in freedom, we kin, at least, pint to their bodies, and say in a sepulkral tone: Wen niggers wuz wuth $1500, they wuz not allowd to die thus— behold the froots of Ablishn philanthropy! [36]

Nasby did not fail to note that northern legislatures were not far behind these enlightened sentiments, for they were passing laws barring Negroes from settling among them.

Numerous letters from the Lait Paster uv the Church of the Noo Dispensashun expressed the contemporary bigot's idea of race differences, the menace of social equality, and the threat of racial amalgamation. He warned his associates to use the right arguments to avoid embarrassing themselves:

Why shood we say that the nigger shan't vote, on the score uv his not being fitted by educashen or intelligence, when the first and chiefest qualification uv a strate Dimekrat is his not knowin how to read? Why, today in my county, ef a Dimekrat kin rite his name without runnin his tongue out, we alluz refuse to elect him a delegate in the county convenshun. It exposes him to the suspishun uv knowin too much.[37]

When he entered the bitter national debate over Negro suffrage, Nasby helpfully offered these irrefutable arguments for his friends:

Do you want a buck nigger to march up to the poles with you to vote? Do you want their children mixt with yoors in schools? Do you want em on juries and holden offis in yoor township? My God, think uv it! Think uv yoor bein brot up on a charge uv petty larceny, sich ez steelin sheep or chickens, before a nigger justis uv the peace! Think uv yoor bein sued for a store bill that hed run for ten years, afore a nigger squire! In the towns and cities, think uv bein arrested for bein drunk, by a nigger policeman, and bein arraned in the mornin before a nigger mayor. Contemplate these picters without a shudder, ef yoo kin.[38]

Locke liked to satirize the illiterate Negro-hater who asked an educated Negro to read something for him and then asserted that Negroes were too ignorant to vote! "Wen yoo desire a Dimokrat to froth at the mouth," advised Nasby, "yoo will find that a black face will anser the purpose."

Locke, speaking through Nasby—who was writing from his familiar address, "Confedrit X Roads (wich is in the Stait uv Kentucky)"—rubbed salt into the wounds of opportunists, unreconstructed rebels, and prewar proslavery men. Nasby spoke in his usual straight-faced manner of the (hypocritically) loyal Kentuckians who had been neutral in rifling the bodies of both sides and now praised the Star Spangled Banner "under wich I hed whipped my niggers and sold their children." Besides, "Ef my niggers run off, who so prompt in their pursoot ez the Demokratic marshals, which alluz returned em to me ef it wuz possible?"[39]

Locke, Nasby, and the *Blade* were now in hot pursuit of Andrew Johnson, who had turned to conservative policies that left the race question largely to the southern white. They joined the other Republican newspapers in attributing the change partly to the President's alleged alcoholism, Nasby, as a pseudo-champion of Johnson, accompanied the President as a chaplain in the famous "swing around the circle" of 1866, in which Johnson toured the northern cities to justify his conservative policies and win votes for an anti-Radical Congress. Nasby, of course, did not overlook the potential humor of portraying Johnson as a drunkard, heckled by "nigger lovers," or altogether ignored by the crowds that showed admiration for Grant and Farragut on this trip. Foes of the President—as was true—alluded to Memphis and New Orleans, where white mobs had attacked Negro parades and homes. Chaplain Nasby reassured "His Majesty" (Johnson) at St. Louis, "The Knights uv the Golden Cirkle [the wartime Copperheads] wich I spect is the identical cirkle you've ben swingin around lately, love yoo and approach yoo confidently."

One wonders whether Locke would have broken with his revered Lincoln had the Great Emancipator lived, for the Johnson policies greatly resembled the reconstruction policies of his predecessor. But Lincoln was obviously free of Johnson's inflexible temperament and far more motivated by humanitarian impulses that could have led him to a sounder policy than that of the "swing around the circle." Locke, like the Radicals, looked upon Johnson as the reactionary leader of a southern counterrevolution for white supremacy that tore down Negro schools and churches, hanged or tarred and feathered carpetbaggers and school teachers sent by the Freedmen's Aid Societies, and brought back the planter ruling class. Believing that Johnson intended to enslave the freedman, Nasby's circle at Confedrit X Roads hastened to enslave their local Negroes in anticipation of Johnson's victory in 1866.

When Nasby's Institute set up an arithmetic textbook with its political calculations regarding southern chivalry, illiteracy, the prowess of Confederate soldiers, and the Democratic feats

of hard drinking, the pastor added some problems regarding
Johnson:

Ef two nips at Washington wuz suffishent to perdoose the speech at
the inaugerashun on the 4th of March, 1865 [when Johnson, it is
said, could not hold the liquor given for medicinal reasons], how
much must have bin slung into A.J. to perdoose the 22nd uv Feb-
rooary effort [his veto of the Freedmen's Bureau bill], and how many
must he hev taken between Washington and St. Louis [on the swing
around the circle]? [40]

He imitated the appeal of the wealthy South Carolina ex-
planter, Wade Hampton, who was reported then to be concili-
ating the Negro in return for his vote. Nasby's version of
Hampton's speeches praised the Negro's goodness of heart, insisted that the only difference between the races was one of
greater sunburn, and deplored the occasional lapses from virtue
by Wingert's Corners into lynching bees and whippings. However, the local Negroes merely laughed at Nasby's efforts, resisted his public embrace, and reminded him that he still owed
them money for sawing wood and other services. They wanted
cash in advance before they did "sich a disagreeable ting" as to
embrace Nasby.[41]

Sumner and Stevens fared well in the Nasby letters, but the
erstwhile Radical, William Seward, who was now Johnson's
Secretary of State, forfeited his earlier humanitarian reputation
by his association with Johnson. Hence Nasby enjoyed a free
rein in satirizing the purchase of Alaska as "Seward's folly."
The Senate was pictured as responding in the passage of the
treaty to the pressures of the Frank Blair circle of politicians
involving bribery and the free use of patronage. He reported
that one expert had told Seward, "Anywheres for six hundred
miles back uv the coast strawberries grow in the open air." A
naval officer reported enthusiastically, "There is seals there,
and walruses so tame that they come up uv their own akkord to
be ketched." Seward was charmed and said to Johnson, "Imag-

ine the delicacy of polar bear meat fattened on strawberries." [42]

The imprisonment of "our sainted cheef," as Nasby described Jefferson Davis, had angered the planters and embarrassed the administration, but Locke felt no twinge of conscience for the plight of the former head of the Rebellion. Therefore, Nasby's praises for "the grate man" revealed a snob, a war criminal who had allegedly abused Federal prisoners at notorious Libby Prison, and a bigot shocked at the current concessions to Negro rights. Nor did Locke forgive the old abolitionist, Horace Greeley, for signing Davis' bail. Nasby reported that the local Confederates cheered for "Jefferson Greeley and Horris Davis—one and inseparable, now and forever!" [43]

Nasby also had his characteristic version of Ohio's defeat of the Fourteenth Amendment, in effect bolstering Locke's philosophy of racial equality and Negro suffrage. The Pastor of Confedrit X Roads demanded to know whether "7000 degradid niggers was to grind 500,000 proud Caucashens into the dust." He reported that the aroused local virgins were parading with placards reading "White Husbans or Nun!" In Nasby's supposed Kentucky home a resolution of fraternal greetings was sent to Ohio "with thanks for their effectooal squelchin uv nigger superiority." The pastor announced certain additions to the Democratic revision of the Bible, such as "Suffer little white children to come unto me, for uv sich is the kingdom of Heaven." In reporting that a local effort to re-enslave the Negroes in a night attack had met with resistance, Nasby concluded with a phrase obviously borrowed from racial conservatives: "The result demonstrated to me the impossibility uv the two races living together in harmony. There is a natral antagonism between em wich must result inevitably in a war uv races, onless their status is fixed by law." [44]

The *Blade* and Nasby rejoiced in the impeachment of Johnson and were disappointed in the failure of conviction by a narrow margin. The Chief Executive, according to Nasby, was trying to keep a stiff upper lip while reading telegrams from friends (including the Pastor of Confedrit X Roads) who had quickly adjusted themselves to the prospect of his early retirement or wished to turn the situation for the benefit of Democratic politicians. Johnson was counting upon the armies of Confederates whom he had pardoned, together with the Ku Klux Klan, to support him now.

Wingert's Corners formally denounced the Carpetbaggers as the spawn of the North and resolved:

That while the citizens uv the Corners blieve in perfect freedom uv thot and speech, and desire it above all things, they nevertheless view with alarm the comin hither uv Northerners who are Republikins and we pledge ourselves to bust the heads uv sich.[45]

As one citizen put it, "We denounce men ez carpetbaggers and interlopers and sich, not becoz they are carpetbaggers and interlopers, but becoz they don't interlope accordin to our noshens. The Parson isn't objectionable to the Corners, becoz the Parson kin punish ez much sod corn whiskey ez any uv you, and votes the Democratic ticket with fearful regularity."

In the election of 1868, during which the Democrats dropped Johnson for Governor Horatio Seymour of New York, Locke supported Grant, whom he admired at first, and correspondingly berated Seymour. Petroleum V. Nasby offered this dedication for the New Yorker in his *Impendin Crisis uv the Democracy* (Toledo, 1868):

The troo Dimokrat, for whom my sole hez alluz gone out sense the riots in Noo York in 1863
In wich his frends demonstrated the sooperiority uv the Anglo-Saxon race by beaten out the branes uv all persons uv other races wich they cood reach.

Simultaneously, and again in 1872, the *Blade* campaigned for Grant's election and supported his Reconstruction policies. Locke published this pre-election editorial challenge to the South in 1868:

If the South would stop its blustering and bravado, would put an end to its Ku Klux Klan assassinations, would protect *all* its people in a peaceful enjoyment of their rights, would see to it that suffrage was unrestricted, if it would turn its attention to the development of its industries, to the cultivation of its lands, the improvement of its schools, it would begin to see the dawn of the new era and a prosperous one.[46]

While Nasby reported the politics of the day and the editor of the *Blade* expressed his Radical views without misspellings, Locke as a public speaker was lecturing to thousands on contemporary issues through the famous lyceum programs arranged by James Redpath's Bureau, of Boston. Redpath was a fiery abolitionist writer and currently a promoter of Negro schools and orphanages. In 1868 he opened his national lecture service and, ever a reformer, liked to thrust meliorist lecturers upon a community as part of a package deal in which he also permitted them to have their own preferences in addition to his. Each of his stars whom he sent out to staff an entire season's program for a city lectured for an average of 110 nights; these included such luminaries as Mark Twain, Henry Ward Beecher, Wendell Phillips, Josh Billings, Artemus Ward, as well as Petroleum V. Nasby. The decade of reconstruction coincided with the peak of the lyceum's popularity, and the crowds continued to prefer the humorists after they tired of the others.[47] Nasby and similar celebrities earned as much as $250 in fees when they spoke in the towns and up to $400 in the cities. Yet this was only one of the Toledoan's profitable activities. More important was the fact that the Redpath reformist policy enabled him to bring his plea for understanding to so many educated and often influential people.

Mark Twain observed Locke as a lecturer three years after the war, shortly after Redpath had organized his lyceum service. This was in the packed Hartford Opera House when the Ohio man spoke on "Cussed be Canaan!", a lecture that he repeated regularly several hundred times during these years—but without any effort at dialect rendition or the humorous formulas of Nasby. Twain wondered at times about the secret of Locke's success as a lecturer as he watched him tear his way through a lecture without changing expression, yet evoking continuous applause and laughter:

His lecture was a volleying and sustained discharge of bull's eye hits, with the slave power and its Northern apologists for target, and his success was due to his matter, not his manner, for his delivery was destitute of art unless a tremendous and inspiring earnestness and energy may be called by that name.[48]

And when Locke had finished, he simply walked off the stage, seemingly indifferent to the booming applause.

In appearance the man from Toledo was no Adonis, but a rather portly, lumbering person of average height. "He had the constitution of an ox and the strength and endurance of a prize fighter," recalled Twain. Little wonder that Twain was annoyed with critics who insisted that he looked like Locke. "I knew Nasby well and he was a good fellow," conceded the younger humorist, "but in my life I have not felt malignantly enough about any more than three persons to charge those persons with resembling Nasby." He cited a typical notice: "In form and feature he [Twain] bears some resemblance to the immortal Nasby; but whilst Petroleum is brunette to the core, Twain is a golden, amber-hued, melting blonde." [49] This could not have offended him too much! But the creator of Tom Sawyer and Huckleberry Finn came to sniff at the crude humorous techniques of Nasby, Artemus Ward, Josh Billings, and their like, for their heavy reliance upon phonetic misspelling, thus insuring themselves an early obsolescence.

The much-repeated lecture "Cussed be Canaan!" expressed rather soberly Locke's arguments for racial equality. "The Negro is a *man,* born in Africa, or descended from nations of that country; the Nigger is an idea which exists only in the imagination of persons of the haughty Caucasian race resident in the United States." [50] He revealed how thoroughly he was the liberal antithesis of the bigoted Petroleum V. Nasby as he praised the ideals of abolitionism and condemned the southern conservatives for trying to reduce the Negro to serfdom.

"Suppose we overhaul the laws of this country," he asked, "and strike out the word 'white' while leaving standing alone the all-sufficient word 'man.'" He suggested that the Declaration of Independence be incorporated into the Constitution. "I would tear down all bars to their [the Negroes'] advancement. . . . I demand for them full equality before the law." Thus he echoed the famous phrase of his friend Charles Sumner, who had used it in the noted Roberts school segregation case of 1849 and in the Senate fight for the civil rights section of the Fourteenth Amendment.

In another favorite lyceum lecture, "The Struggles of a Conservative with the Woman Question," he showed how far apart from Artemus Ward he was in regard to feminism. "I would give the ballot to woman for her own sake," he asserted, "for I would enlarge the borders of her mind." [51] Suffrage would also enable women to right their own wrongs and give them equality of opportunity. Yet, strangely enough, Locke did not use his *Toledo Blade* editorials as a forum for women's rights.

While Locke was lecturing on the lyceum circuit and fighting President Johnson, he was also advancing a prolific literary career. Many of his pamphlets and a huge travel book came from his articles in the *Blade;* but he also produced separately interesting plays and a didactic, sentimental novel in the Dickens tradition entitled *A Paper City* (1879), which told a story reminiscent of Mark Twain's *The Gilded Age* with its wild speculative spirit, its tinseled culture, and the fall of an over-promoted city. (The Twain and Charles D. Warner novel had appeared six years earlier.) Locke's persistent reformist spirit is clear even in his travel book *Nasby in Exile: Or Six Months of Travel* (Toledo, 1882). He did not see Europe in the mischievous spirit of Twain's *Innocents Abroad* (1869) but as a basically serious do-gooder who disliked British imperialism, the spectacle of the Irish evictions, the persistence of mass poverty and superstition, and other injustices. Those who sought scenic descriptions or the trivial foibles of the Old World would not find it in Locke's book. Though he was handicapped in formal education, he had read considerably, and his articles covered many facets of the changing world; now in his travels, he was an earnest observer (if not altogether an expert one) of the lands from which so many Americans had migrated.

His fortunes grew like the proverbial green bay tree and much if not everything that he touched turned to gold—shrewd real estate investments in Toledo's fast-growing downtown, more newspapers (one in New York), factories, and inventions (some of which, it is true, cost him too dearly and had to be written off as experience). Yet some of his contemporaries thought of him as financially reckless, a rather exaggerated estimate. Undeniably, the Locke family was a great success in every sense of the word. The *Toledo Weekly Blade* alone shone forth as a national beacon of responsible journalism. Its views were of course the same as those repudiated by Nasby, including city campaigns against segregation and drink. "Pulverize the Rum Power!" was a Locke slogan that would have delighted his temperance father. For decades, the *Blade* was known as "Nasby's paper," with all of its reform connotations.[52] But even if Petroleum Vesuvius Nasby became almost obsolete shortly after Locke's death on February 15, 1888, American literature has been loath to drop him from the college anthologies. Mark Twain was correct, of course, in noting the unfortunate dependence of Nasby, Ward, Billings, Kerr, and their generation upon frontier or bucolic misspellings. But Locke's unusual contributions to winning the Civil War and to advancing modern ideas concerning race relations were undeniable facts in the history of humanitarianism.

1. Quoted in Don C. Seitz, *Artemus Ward* (New York, 1919), pp. 113–15.

2. J. A. Estes, "David Ross Locke," *Dictionary of American Biography* (New York, 1928–58), XI, 336. Locke admitted that Browne suggested to him the image of Petroleum V. Nasby (*Cleveland Plain Dealer*, April 24, 1932). Don Seitz quotes an autobiographical statement of Locke's regarding Browne's significance in Cleveland (*Artemus Ward*, p. 27). Petroleum V. Nasby was created in a letter in the *Bucyrus Journal* for December 13, 1860, although the letter did not carry the Nasby signature; Willam H. Taft, "The Toledo Blade: Its First Hundred Years, 1835–1935" (Ph.D. dissertation, Western Reserve University, 1950), p. 275 *et passim*.

3. Jennette R. Tandy, *Crackerbox Philosophers in American Humor and Satire* (New York, 1925), pp. 123–24, 126–28.

4. Charles Neider (ed.), *The Autobiography of Mark Twain* (New York, 1961), pp. 166, 297.

5. *Letters of Artemus Ward to Charles E. Wilson, 1858–1861* (Cleveland: Rowfant Club, 1900); "Artemus Ward at Cleveland," *Scribner's Monthly* (October, 1878), pp. 785–90.

6. Archer H. Shaw, *The Plain Dealer* (New York, 1942), pp. 62–72, 135.

7. Seitz, *op. cit.*, p. 21; E. S. Nadal, *Essays at Home and Elsewhere* (London, 1882).

8. This discussion of Browne's ideas is largely based on *The Complete Works of Artemus Ward* (New York, 1898) and *Artemus Ward: His Travels* (New York, 1865). The original printed letters appear in "Artemus Ward Letters: I. Reprinted from the Plain Dealer" (scrapbook in the files of the Western Reserve Historical Society).

9. Edward P. Hingston, *The Genial Showman: Reminiscences of the Life of Artemus Ward* (London, 1881).

10. George R. Stewart, Jr., "George Horatio Derby," *Dictionary of American Biography*, V, 251–52; see Hingston, *op. cit.*, for the influence of Derby.

11. Shaw, *op. cit.*, pp. 62–72; William G. Vorpe, "Artemus Ward," in *Ohio Journalism Hall of Fame* (Columbus, O., 1932), pp. 9–17.

12. *Letters of Artemus Ward to Charles E. Wilson*, pp. 43, 61, 75, 81–86.

13. Hingston, *op. cit.*, p. 132.

14. Seitz, *op. cit.*, *passim*.

15. Quoted in Tandy, *op. cit.*, pp. 132–46; Mark Twain and others, *Practical Jokes with Artemus Ward* (London, 1872). Twain and Ward

took quickly to each other, became close comrades in Virginia City, and thereafter played practical jokes upon each other.

16. *Autobiography of Mark Twain*, p. 297. But Twain, as the Neider edition of the autobiography shows, was bitterly critical of Ward's admirer, Bret Harte.

17. H. R. Haweis, *American Humorists* (New York, 1882), *passim*.

18. *The Complete Works of Artemus Ward*, pp. 84–85.

19. *Ibid.*, p. 117.

20. *Ibid.*, p. 287.

21. *Ibid.*, pp. 288–89.

22. Albert Jay Nock, *Free Speech and Plain Language* (New York, 1937), pp. 92–94.

23. Most recently, James C. Austin has written *Petroleum V. Nasby* (New York, 1965). The chief biographic facts here are drawn from the *Toledo Blade*, February 15, 1888; the New York *Herald*, February 16, 1888; F. L. Dustman (Locke's editorial colleague), "David R. Locke," in *Ohio Journalism Hall of Fame* (Columbus, O., 1928), pp. 23–26; Cyril Clemens, *Petroleum V. Nasby* (Webster Groves, Mo., 1936); Jack C. Ransome, "David Ross Locke, Civil War Propagandist," *Northwest Ohio Quarterly*, XX (1948), 5–19; Roeliff Brinkerhoff, *Recollections of a Lifetime* (Cincinnati, O., 1900), pp. 95–98; H. P. Smith, *History of Broome County, New York* (Syracuse, N.Y., 1885), *passim;* Whitelaw Reid, *Ohio in the War*, II (Cincinnati, 1868), 383; Jacob A. Spaythe, *History of Hancock County, Ohio* (Toledo, 1903), p. 89; Jennette Tandy, *op. cit.*, pp. 103–4; and David Ross Locke, *Nasby: Divers Views, Opinions, and Prophecies* (Cincinnati, O., 1866), Introduction. Most recent is the Civil War Centennial booklet of Harvey S. Ford (ed.), *Civil War Letters of Petroleum V. Nasby* (Columbus, O., 1962), pp. 3–7.

24. David Ross Locke, *The Struggles (Social, Financial, and Political) of Petroleum V. Nasby* (Boston, 1888), pp. 39–40.

25. William Howard Taft, *op. cit.*, pp. 259–385.

26. *The Struggles of Petroleum V. Nasby*, pp. 81–82.

27. *Ibid.*, p. 42.

28. *Ibid.*, pp. 44–46.

29. *Ibid.*, p. 69.

30. *Ibid.*, pp. 70–71.

31. *Ibid.*, p. 79.

32. *Ibid.*, pp. 93–95.

33. Charles Sumner gives one version of Lincoln's praise in *ibid.*, Introduction; another statement is given by Twain's kinsman, Cyril Clemens, *op. cit.*, p. 31, and in Tandy, *op. cit.*, p. 124.

34. See Taft, *op. cit.*, pp. 259–385.

35. Albert B. Paine, *Thomas Nast, His Period and His Pictures* (New York, 1904), p. 114; Jack C. Ransome, "David Ross Locke: The Post-War Years," *Northwest Ohio Quarterly*, XX (1948), 144–58.

36. *The Struggles of Petroleum V. Nasby*, p. 187.

37. *Ibid.*, p. 204.

38. *Ibid.*, p. 210.

39. *Ibid.*, p. 233.

40. *Ibid.*, p. 398.

41. *Ibid.*, pp. 408–12.

42. *Ibid.*, pp. 417–21.

43. *Ibid.*, pp. 435–39.

44. *Ibid.*, p. 476.

45. *Ibid.*, p. 581.

46. *Toledo Blade*, Oct. 15, 1868.

47. Charles F. Horner, *James Redpath and the Development of the Lyceum* (New York, 1926), *passim*.

48. *The Autobiography of Mark Twain*, p. 184.

49. Quoted in *ibid.*, p. 300.

50. *The Struggles of Petroleum V. Nasby*, pp. 629–59.

51. *Ibid.*, pp. 660–86.

52. Taft, *op. cit.*, pp. 275–94, 313–53.

NOTES ON CONTRIBUTORS

★ ★

CONTRIBUTORS

CARL M. BECKER is an instructor in history at the Wright State University in Dayton, Ohio. His publications, dealing largely with the political and economic history of mid–nineteenth century Ohio, have appeared in such journals as *Civil War History, Ohio History,* the *Tennessee Historical Quarterly,* and the *Bulletin* of the Cincinnati Historical Society.

JAMES B. BELL is a research associate at Princeton University editing the papers of Thomas Jefferson.

DONALD W. CURL is associate professor of history at Florida Atlantic University, and is presently completing a biography of Murat Halstead.

ROBERT H. JONES is associate professor of history at Western Reserve University and the author of *The Civil War in the Northwest* and, with the late Fred A. Shannon, *The Centennial Years.*

FRANK L. KLEMENT is professor of history at Marquette University, Milwaukee. He is the author of more than thirty articles on various Civil War subjects and of two books, *Copperheads in the Middle West* (1960) and *Wisconsin and the Civil War* (1963).

477

MARY G. LAND is assistant professor of English at Washington State University, and has just completed a text on American intellectual history for University of California Extension at Berkeley.

JEANNETTE P. NICHOLS, research associate in economic history at the University of Pennsylvania, is the author of *Alaska, Twentieth Century America, James Styles and George Stuart,* and a contributor to *Alaska and Its History.* She is a co-author of *Growth of American Democracy* and the author of numerous journal articles on America's domestic and international monetary problems and the politicians who tried to deal with them.

ALLAN PESKIN is associate professor of history at Cleveland State University and is currently engaged in writing a full-scale biography of James A. Garfield. He is also the editor of *North into Freedom,* an autobiography of John Malvin, a free Negro who lived in Cleveland before the Civil War.

HARVEY WISH is E. J. Benton Distinguished Professor of history at Case Western Reserve University, Cleveland, Ohio, and is the author of numerous books, including *Society and Thought in America* and *The American Historian.*

KENNETH W. WHEELER is associate professor of history and acting dean of Metropolitan College at Boston University. He was the Historian Consultant to the Ohio Civil War Centennial Commission. His forthcoming book on early Texas cities covers the Civil War period.

INDEX

★ ★

INDEX